Final Cut Pro® 4
and the Art of Filmmaking

Jason Cranford Teague

David Teague

SYBEX® SAN FRANCISCO • LONDON

Associate Publisher: Dan Brodnitz

Acquisitions Editor: Mariann Barsolo

Developmental Editor: Willem Knibbe

Production Editor: Dennis Fitzgerald

Technical Editor: Diannah Morgan

Copyeditor: Cheryl Hauser

Compositor: Franz Baumhackl

DVD Coordinator: Dan Mummert

DVD Technician: Kevin Ly

Proofreaders: Laurie O'Connell, Nancy Riddiough

Indexer: Nancy Guenther

Cover Designer: John Nedwidek, Emdesign

Cover Photographers: John Nedwidek, Emdesign; Jason Cranford Teague, David Teague

Library of Congress Card Number: 2003115576

ISBN: 0-7821-4300-8

Manufactured in the United States of America

10 9 8 7 6 5 4 3 2 1

Acknowledgments

We'd first like to thank these people:

Uncle Johnny, whose ongoing support is always appreciated

Jay Garrigan and **Poprocket** for the use of their song "Bounce"

Neil Salkind and the good folks at Studio B for helping us get this gig

Joseph A. Linaschke and **Yvonne J Fulchiron** at Apple Computer

Kyle McCabe for his help with the first edition

Many filmmakers, editors, and production companies generously contributed to the "Real World Final Cut Pro" sidebars by sharing their time and experiences and by allowing us to reproduce their work. We'd like to thank all of the following:

Dave Macomber and **Mark Thomas** for *Duality*

Steven Gonzales, Erin Aldridge, Julie Fontaine for *George Washington*

Joseph Maidenberg for *Oxygen*

Dawn Bendick and **Giles Hendrix**, Trans / Chicago for *Multimedia Artist*

Steven Lippman of Flip Productions for the music films of Laurie Anderson and Sam Phillips

Lawrence and **Matthew Ferber** for *Cruise Control*

Mark Foster for *69 Minutes of Fame*

Susan Celia Swan and **Rob Sheridan** of Nothing Records for *And All That Could Have Been*

Rene Besson for *Boxes*

AJ Scnack and **Shirley Moyers** of Bonfire Films of America for *Gigantic*

Dorne Pentes for *Lullaby*

From David:

To everyone who put up with me while I was writing this book, especially Kyle, Jean, Caitlin, Cathryn, Justin, Linden, Nat, St. John, and Sean.

And to everyone who creates something of their own with film.

From Jason:

Tara, with all the love a mere mortal could have for a Sun Angel.

Jocelyn and Dashiel, my children

Pat and Red, my biggest fans

Judy, Boyd, Dr. G and The Teachers of America. Keep up the good work

Neil Gaiman, Douglas Adams, and Carl Sagan whose writings inspire me every day

The Cure, the The, Siouxsie and the Banshees, the Beatles, Shakespeare's Sister, Type-O Negative, Blur, Cracker, Danielle Dax, Nine Inch Nails, KMFDM, the Pogues, Ramones, New Model Army, Cocteau Twins, Cranes, the Sisters of Mercy, the Smiths, Bauhaus, Bad Religion, This Mortal Coil, Rancid, Monty Python, the Dead Milkmen, New Order, The Sex Pistols, Dead Can Dance, and ZBS Studios (for *Ruby*) whose noise helped keep me from going insane while writing this book.

For our parents, who made
this little collaboration possible.

Contents

PART I   GETTING STARTED

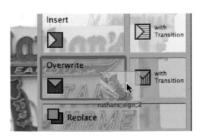

PART IV   FINISHING TOUCHES

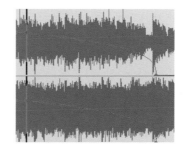

Introduction

Computers have been used for video editing for over 20 years (which seems like a lifetime to some people), yet until recently, the higher-end computers used were specially engineered systems that resembled mainframe computers, with controls that would make a space shuttle pilot nervous. These editing systems were prohibitively expensive for most people, and so video and film production was limited to larger production companies that could afford the cost.

Over the past decade, however, as computer memory, speed, and—most significantly—hard disk storage space have increased and their cost has decreased, desktop computers have become an increasingly popular alternative to complex and expensive editing stations. Since the early 1990s technologies such as Apple QuickTime, Adobe Premiere, and Adobe After Effects have increasingly simplified the process of editing and distributing video material. Yet they lacked a comprehensive and inexpensive video-editing program that produced professional films and video.

Final Cut Pro is revolutionizing the world of film and video editing. Just as programs like PageMaker and QuarkXPress rocked the publishing industry in the 1980s and 1990s by taking "desktop publishing" into the professional world, Final Cut Pro is changing the way people edit film and video by providing an affordable professional editing package that runs on relatively inexpensive hardware. Now, Apple Computer's powerful editing software provides a robust, easy-to-use, and inexpensive set of tools that anyone with a Macintosh can use.

Beyond providing a suite of tools for professionals, Final Cut Pro also opens the door to serious film creation for people who just a few years ago could only dream of making their own movies. But this means that many users may be approaching movie production with no or little formal training. This book will not only guide you through the use of Final Cut Pro, but also help you understand the skills needed to create compelling films.

What Is This Book About?

For decades professional video editing required a host of expensive equipment that took years to master. Final Cut Pro places all of these tools at your disposal in a single package that will run on a Mac, all for a fraction of the cost traditionally associated with video editing. However, getting started with such a complex program may seem daunting at first, especially for first-time video editors.

While preparing to write this book, however, we quickly recognized that using Final Cut Pro follows the 80/20 rule. That is, you will use about 20 percent of its features 80 percent of the time and the other 80 percent of the features no more than 20 percent of the time. The Final Cut Pro manual is thick—three volumes thick—and is helpful as a comprehensive reference tool. Yet, when you get right down to it, video editing should be a matter of instinct and craft, and it should not require constant referral to a manual.

Final Cut Pro 4 and the Art of Filmmaking is not a replacement to the manual but a guide to get your feet wet with video editing using step-by-step instructions and hundreds of illustrations to show you what you should be seeing while you are working. We want to show you the features you'll use every day that should, eventually, become second nature. We'll also look at many of the more advanced features and offer editing tips to help you use them effectively. It is crucial when learning a new system, especially one with as many options as Final Cut Pro, that you become well grounded in the basics first and then build on those skills as a foundation. That is what you will get out of this book: a thorough understanding of what it takes to get a film made with Final Cut Pro. Beyond that, this book is designed to help you explore Final Cut Pro and discover how to make it work best for you. No two editors will work the same way, and no editor works the same way on every project. Final Cut Pro is powerful because of its versatility, and as you use it, you will begin to tailor it to your own particular needs. We have included information to help you understand how to get the most out of the program without becoming overwhelmed with all of the possibilities.

How Is This Book Organized?

In this book, we will be covering everything you need to know to make effective use of Final Cut Pro. Although we have included a DVD with footage and exercises for you to practice with, this book is designed to help you edit your own film. To help organize the information, we have split the book into five main sections:

Part I: Getting Started　This introduces you to setting up your Mac and Final Cut Pro for optimum efficiency, offers tips for shooting your video footage with Final Cut Pro in mind, and shows how to log and capture your footage in preparation for editing.

Part II: Editing Your Movie　These chapters detail how to take the video footage and edit the clips together in the Timeline to create a sequence. Here you will learn all of the basics of editing two pieces of footage together and creating transitions between them.

Part III: Adding Effects　The chapters here concentrate on manipulating the footage using effects and filters for a variety of purposes, creating complex imagery using overlays, and motion with keyframes.

Part IV: Finishing Touches　These chapters teach you how to get the best quality audio as well as adding titles. The final chapter in this section reviews the entire process of putting your film together from placing down your edits, adding effects, and adding titles and sound.

Part V: After the Editing Is Done　This part concludes the book by showing what to do *after* you're finished editing: archiving with Final Cut Pro's newly revamped Media Manager tool, printing to videotape or burning to CD or DVD, and compressing for Internet distribution.

Each chapter in this book deals with a specific topic important to film editors. We have avoided making this book simply a laundry list of features (you can get that from the manual) and have instead concentrated on the real-world everyday tasks that video editors face. We show you how to use Final Cut Pro to full advantage for those tasks. Each chapter begins with an overview to help explain some of the reasoning and theory that the specific tasks in each section of the chapter covers.

Each section in a chapter provides step-by-step instructions for performing specific tasks. Nearly every step in these instructions also includes an illustration that shows what you should be seeing on the screen during the step. If you are using the tutorial provided on the DVD (see *Using the Companion DVD* on the inside back cover of the book) then these images should exactly reflect what you see on your own screen. However, even if you are using your own footage to edit with, the figure will help to visually explain what it is you are doing. In addition, many sections will include alternate instructions providing a different take on the same topic. The companion DVD at the back of this book also provides a host of files to assist you in completing the chapter tutorials.

Also, look for the *Real World* examples of how video editors are using Final Cut Pro on a wide variety of projects: everything from video art to feature filmmaking. These profiles not only help explain the equipment and processes these editors use; they can also provide inspiration for your own projects.

Who Is This Book For?

If the title of this book caught your eye, then you are probably familiar with Final Cut Pro and either already using it or thinking about learning to use it.

If you are already a working editor, this book offers you simple, straightforward instructions written to help you get started quickly using the features of Final Cut Pro that you will be using most of the time and bypassing features that may never make it into any of your work.

If you are new to DV editing, this book offers a clear visual guide to help you understand basic editing concepts and how they apply to Final Cut Pro. Rather than just dwelling on "how" the product works, we will present you with much of the "why" behind it.

What Tools Do You Need for This Book?

Obviously, for a book about Final Cut Pro, you are going to need a copy of Final Cut Pro—preferably version 4, although most of what we talk about in the book applies equally to version 3 (see the sidebar *Final Cut Pro 3 vs. Final Cut Pro 4*)—and a Macintosh computer capable of running Final Cut Pro and QuickTime Pro. In addition, Final Cut Pro 4 requires Mac OS 10.2.5.

The exact Mac system you use can vary widely, although video editing is what the faster dual-processor G5 Macs were designed to handle. You can also use a PowerBook, which is handy if you are editing on the road. To write this book, we primarily used G4 PowerBooks with 768MB of RAM.

In addition, you will also need some way to generate your own footage.

You may be getting footage from someone else, generating it using other computer software, or you may have your own camera and film crew. The exact source of the footage that you will eventually edit is not important in the scope of this book; you'll learn how to capture or import the raw media from all the commonly used digital or analog sources. In fact, even if you don't have your own footage, we have provided sample clips on the DVD to get you started (see *Using the Companion DVD*).

Other than that, we recommend equipment in Chapter 1 (especially an external reference monitor), but nothing that you absolutely must have to start using Final Cut Pro. We also recommend that you have at your disposal a word-processing program (such as WordPerfect or Word) and an image-editing program (such as Photoshop or GraphicConverter) to help create files that you will use with Final Cut Pro. Again, this software is not required to use Final Cut Pro, but it can significantly increase your productivity.

Installing Final Cut Pro

Before you can begin editing, of course, you'll need to install Final Cut Pro into your system from the installation DVD. The installation procedure is well documented in the Final Cut Pro manuals, so we won't duplicate that information here. Instead, we'll just offer a couple of quick tips:

- You'll also want to install the version of QuickTime Pro that comes on the installation DVD, and you should do that first, even before you install Final Cut Pro itself. A QuickTime Installer icon appears in the QuickTime folder on the DVD; just double-click it to begin. Once you've installed QuickTime Pro, you can double-click on the Install Final Cut Pro icon on the DVD.
- You'll have to accept the software licensing agreement and designate the hard drive you want to install Final Cut Pro to. As we explain in Chapter 2, it's best to keep the Final Cut Pro files on their own hard drive, away from other applications.

Now you're ready to dive into Chapter 1, which describes the tools you will need to work with Final Cut Pro, so you can set up your workspace into an effective editing suite.

TIP
Final Cut Pro 3 vs. Final Cut Pro 4

Although conceptually Final Cut Pro 4 is little different from Final Cut Pro 3, version 4 includes many changes that make it cumbersome to cover both programs in a single volume. Not only is the latest version only available for Mac OS X (version 3 was also available for OS 9 which limited its capabilities somewhat) but it has also undergone a significant overhaul in several key areas:

Interface Even though there were few complaints about the Final Cut Pro interface, Apple has changed some controls (especially in the Timeline) and greatly increased interface customization allowing you to add buttons for regularly used commands.

Unlimited Audio/Video Tracks You can now have as many video or audio tracks in a single sequence limited only by your computer's memory.

Keyboard Customization You can now specify keyboard shortcuts for any Final Cut Pro command allowing you to tailor the interface for your workflow.

Rendering Options Although often lamented, rendering is a fact of life in video editing. Final Cut Pro 4 now provides more exacting control over precisely what is rendered, cutting down on the time you spend waiting for a clip to render that you do not actually need.

RT Extreme Introduced in Final Cut Pro 3, Real-Time rendering has been greatly improved in version 4, allowing you to preview many effects without having to render as long as your computer is fast enough.

Auto Rendering You can now set Final Cut Pro to begin rendering effects automatically in the background while you are not using your computer. For example, if you are editing away, and the phone rings, after a few minutes of activity, Final Cut Pro can automatically begin rendering all effects until you return to work.

Audio Mixer Use a professional soundboard interface to mix your audio directly in Final Cut Pro.

Time Remapping Keyframes allow you to adjust effects over time. Time Remapping allows you to use keyframes to change the speed of a clip as it plays, allowing you to speed it up, slow it down or even freeze it while playing.

24fps Editing Final Cut Pro now supports editing in 24 fps directly in the Timeline for film and high-definition video. In addition, Cinema Tools is now included with the package.

Throughout this book, we will let you know when a feature is new to Final Cut Pro 4 not only in the text but you should look for the "4" icon: **④**

TIP
Beyond Final Cut Pro 4

In addition to the new features directly in the program, installed along with Final Cut Pro 4 are four stand-alone "helper" applications that can be used with Final Cut Pro to increase or improve its functionality. Although they are not an integral part of Final Cut Pro, you can easily use them as a part of your editing workflow or ignore them if not needed.

Soundtrack includes several gigabytes worth of sound loops you can use to compose musical scores for almost any purpose. For an overview of this program see the sidebar in Chapter 16.

Live Type provides editors with professional tools for creating animated titles. For an overview of this program see the sidebar in Chapter 17.

Compressor augments Final Cut Pro's export capabilities, to allow streamlined compression of Final Cut files for use on CD, DVD, and on the web. This application is detailed in Chapter 21.

Cinema Tools was previously sold separately from Final Cut Pro, but has been included in this release to allow editors who need to output their work in 24fps for film. For an overview of this program see the sidebar at the end of the bonus chapter provided on the DVD.

Part One:
Getting Started

Coney Island Memories

Editing is a creative process, and there is a lot to do before the cutting even starts: you've got to make sure your hardware and Final Cut Pro are set up properly, and that footage is in your computer and organized efficiently. These crucial first steps will save you hours of editing time. Part I first shows how to set up your system and configure your hardware, walks you through the Final Cut Pro interface, and shows how to prepare your footage for editing as you shoot. We'll then cover organizing your footage and bringing it from your source tapes into your computer for editing. By the end of this section, you'll be ready to unleash those creative juices and begin to cut your movie.

1 Setting Up Your Workstation

Setting up your workspace involves the first important creative decisions of editing. Every writer needs just the right desk, every painter needs just the right easel, and every editor needs just the right editing station to work efficiently and creatively. You have many choices to make when setting up your work area. These choices range from technical concerns such as how to hook up your speakers to making sure you're working in an area where you can think creatively without distraction. Installing Final Cut Pro is just the first step. You'll need to take a little time to hook up your equipment correctly and in such a way that you're not tripping over cords. It's important that everything you need is right in front of you and configured to meet your needs. In this chapter, we'll go over how to tailor your workstation for your special needs and how to set up your editing station for the two types of video capture: digital video (DV) and analog.

Overview

> *"It is important to have a good tool. But, even if it is the best possible, it is only a tool. No implement can ever take the place of the guiding intelligence that wields it. A very bad tool will ruin the work of the best craftsman; but a good tool in bad hands is no better."*
>
> Theodore Roosevelt
> *History as Literature*

While even the finest equipment cannot make up for a lack of skill, skilled professionals always seek out the best tools available to them. Final Cut Pro offers excellent capabilities bundled within an easy-to-use interface. However, although Final Cut Pro offers a multitude of features, it is only part of what you will need in order to create your video.

This chapter will help you set up your workstation for capturing and editing with Final Cut Pro. This chapter assumes that you have successfully installed Final Cut Pro, following the instructions provided by Apple. We will show you how to set up your machine to capture digital footage from an exterior video source such as a DV deck or analog sources like VHS and Beta-SP. We will also cover how to set up an exterior reference monitor and speakers. If you can afford adding these extra assets to your editing suite, we highly recommend it. The image you see on the computer monitor will not give you a true sense of the definition and color of the image, so a reference monitor is imperative if you're editing anything for professional use or broadcast. This chapter will help you understand how to set up your system for capture from either digital or analog source tape.

The Computer

Your computer is your tool. It is the device you will be using to create—to sculpt—your video. More than likely, you purchased this book because you already own a computer. If you are still in the market, check out the sidebar *Choosing the Right Mac*. However, you might not be sure whether your computer can handle Final Cut Pro 4, especially if you are upgrading from version 3. Not all computers sporting the Mac logo that ran older versions of Final Cut Pro will be able to run Final Cut Pro 4 so you'll need to make sure that your Macintosh has the following:

G4 or G5 processor (350MHz Minimum)   You will need a G4 processor running at 500MHz (or Dual 450MHz) for RT Extreme or Soundtrack. Obviously, the faster your processor, the faster you will be able to work. However, don't be afraid to use older machines if that's what you have. What counts are your skills.

OS X Jaguar (v.10.2.5) or higher   This is the standard Mac OS shipping with all new machines and is required for Final Cut Pro 4—the software will not run on versions under 10.2.5. If you are using OS 9 or older versions of OS X (10.0–10.1), you will need to upgrade to Mac OS 10.2 (Jaguar). In addition, if you have not upgraded from 10.2 to 10.2.5, you will need to do so, but this is a free upgrade. If you have an Internet connection, simply run the Software Update in your System Preferences. If you do not have a fast Internet connection, you can order the CD directly from Apple for $19.95 (www.store.apple.com).

384MB of RAM   This is the bare minimum you need for OS X and Final Cut Pro, but you will need at least 512MB to use RT Extreme and Soundtrack. It is especially true with digital filmmaking that the more memory you have, the faster you can edit. In addition, more memory will help prevent the problem of dropped frames. We recommend at least 768MB. Memory is relatively cheap these days so stock up.

1GB free hard-disk space This is the bare minimum needed to install Final Cut Pro, but you will obviously need more space while working. To install Soundtrack you will need an additional 5GB and another 4GB (9GB total) to install Live Type.

One or more FireWire ports These ports are used to capture and export video. (Although useful for downloading digital photographs, Universal Serial Bus (USB) ports are too slow for video.) Having one FireWire port is enough, as you can chain your hard drives and video deck, but having two or more is helpful if you are hooked up to other hardware that uses FireWire at the same time. One advantage that desktop Macs have over portables is that they include three FireWire ports (one FireWire 800 and two FireWire 400).

What Is FireWire?

FireWire is the trademarked name Apple Computer uses to refer to the input/output (I/O) industry standard known as *IEEE 1394*. Apple originally developed this standard to allow high-speed connections between peripherals (such as hard drives and DV cameras) and computers. There are two versions of FireWire IEEE (generally called FireWire 400) with data transfer rates of up to 400Mbps and the recently updated IEEE1394b (generally called FireWire 800) allowing transfer rates of up to 800Mbps. This speed is FireWire's most important advantage for video applications.

FireWire allows hot swapping. That is, you can plug in and unplug peripherals without having to turn your computer off, and the device will be immediately available to your computer with no further effort on your part. The Power Mac G5 desktop machine includes one FireWire 800 and two FireWire 400 ports.

Using FireWire you can connect as many as 63 independent devices to a single computer, where each device hooks into the previous device, and these devices can be seen by any other computer on your network. So, you can hook a hard drive to one computer, and use it over an office Ethernet with no difficulty.

Sony also uses the IEEE 1394a standard in most of its DV cameras; however, they call their product *i.LINK* instead of FireWire. Don't worry, though; whether you see FireWire, i.LINK, or IEEE 1394a, these names all refer to the same thing and will use similar (if not always identical) cables and plugs to allow various peripherals to talk to each other.

To find out more, visit the 1394 Trade Association (www.1394ta.org) or the Apple FireWire web site (www.apple.com/firewire).).

What Is USB?

Like FireWire, Universal Serial Bus (USB for those of us in a hurry) is an industry standard technology used to hook peripherals to computers. It is also hot-swappable, allowing you to hook and unhook peripherals without having to turn your computer off. There are currently two USB standards: USB 1 (allowing transfer rates of 1.5 to 12Mbps) and USB 2 (allowing transfer rates of up to 480Mbps). Although it is much slower than even FireWire 400 USB 1 has been more widely adopted and is used to hook up peripherals such as printers, keyboards, and mice. USB 2, while much faster than USB 1, still cannot

hold a candle to FireWire 800. However, it is fast enough for video transfer if there is no other option.

An analog-to-digital capture card can gain device control by hooking up a USB-to-serial adapter cable (such as the Keyspan Twin Serial Adapter) to your computer and your analog video deck. However, we strongly recommend the GeeThree Stealth Port over this option, as the Gee Three has proven much more reliable and is actually a cheaper buy. USB ports can be identified by the USB icon located near the port. To find out more, go to www.apple.com/usb.

DVD drive   Due to the increased size of Final Cut Pro 4, it now comes on DVDs rather than CDs for installation. This book also requires a DVD player to use the included project file and footage. In addition, if you want to create your own DVDs, you will need a DVD-R or DVD-RW drive.

QuickTime 6.1 or higher installed   You will need to install or upgrade to QuickTime Pro, but the software is included with Final Cut Pro 4 so you can upgrade from the provided disks. Again, you can use the OS X built in Software Update to ensure that you have the latest version or you can order QuickTime updates from the Apple Store (`www.store.apple.com`).

You can do several things to improve your Mac's performance, such as adding additional RAM. We suggest 384MB, but the more RAM, the happier your machine (and you) will be. Your cut, especially with more complicated edits with a lot of effects or composite imagery, will go much more smoothly if you don't have to wait around while the computer prepares or renders your footage.

TIP Choosing the Right Mac

Apple Computer offers several Mac models that either come out-of-the-box ready for video editing or can be tricked out to achieve the bare minimum. Generally speaking, all new Macs will be able to handle Final Cut Pro to varying degrees of proficiency. However, older models may not be able to handle the program:

iMac   Although thought of as a consumer-level machine, iMacs, even the older multicolored ones, are often used as basic video editing stations. Keep in mind that the newer flat-panel iMacs are at least as fast as the fastest Macs of just a few years ago. The major drawbacks of the iMac for video editing are lack of expandability, slower speed, and small screen size (on older iMacs).

eMac   Primarily intended for the education audience (which is where it gets that cute little e from), the eMac has the basics needed for Final Cut Pro, although you might need to add more RAM. The major drawbacks of the eMac for video editing are lack of speed and expandability.

iBook   Older (clamshell) iBooks will not work with Final Cut Pro because of their slow speed, small hard drives, and lack of FireWire support. However, newer iBooks have the bare minimum credentials for video editing. The major drawbacks of the iBook for video editing are small screen size (on smaller iBooks), lack of speed, and lack of expandability.

PowerBook   If you need to edit on the road, the PowerBook is your best bet. It provides most of the power of the desktop Power Mac and incredible portability. Final Cut Pro will work on later model "Bronze" PowerBooks (black casing) or with any of the newer "Titanium" Power-Books. The major drawback for video editing with PowerBooks is lack of expandability.

Power Mac   The powerhouse for video editing is the desktop Power Mac. Newer models include dual processors, which will speed any editing job. In addition, Power Macs are far more expandable than any other Mac model, enabling you to add or change graphic cards, use internal disks, or add other third-party expansion cards such as an analog-to-digital capture card. The major drawback of the Power Mac for video editing is lack of portability.

External and Internal Hard Drives

In addition to the computer, you will need a lot of hard drive space. A single minute of uncompressed (high quality) DV-format video requires 216MB. While the storage size of internal hard drives is going up—most Macs ship with hard drives between 40GB to 160GB—we recommend you get an extra hard drive to store footage and dedicate the built-in drive to running Final Cut Pro.

Remember if you are capturing analog using a capture card, you must capture to a SCSI drive over a SCSI PCI card, and not the ATA drive that comes with the standard G4s, unless you are using a media converter box. If you are using a RAID system, check with your documentation for the best connection type to use.

Digital video consumes massive amounts of disk space. Just 15 minutes of uncompressed video footage can eat 3GB of disk space. You will also need extra hard-disk space to store your raw media as you capture it from your digital videotapes. Although computers are coming with increasingly large hard disks, we strongly recommend that you use an external or separate internal hard disk to devote exclusively to media storage. Capturing media to your primary internal hard disk (the one that came with the machine) can cause problems, such as program crashes and corrupted video files if that disk is also being used to run programs (including Final Cut Pro).

Let's look deeper into why you want to separate the media files onto their own hard drive. Video editing requires precise timing, and a delay of even a few milliseconds can throw your video out of synch. If you are using the same hard drive both to run Final Cut Pro *and* store and access the video footage, the hard drive may be required to be, essentially, in two places at the same time. Playback may suffer, frames may get dropped, and the audio may stutter as the hard drive switches back and forth. Adding an internal or an external hard drive—using the FireWire connection—and placing all of your DV footage on this additional drive will alleviate this problem and improve the overall performance of Final Cut Pro.

An external hard drive is also a much better idea if you will be working on several different projects concurrently or if you are sharing a workstation with other editors. You can hook and unhook the hard drive to switch between projects and not have to worry about filling the fixed hard drive space.

You have two basic choices for adding hard disks:

Internal disk (Power Macs only.) This type of disk is installed in any empty media bay. The advantage is that internal disks take up less space than external disks and do not require an extra power socket. Internal disks tend to be cheaper, but you lose out on the portability factor of the external. Although it might seem daunting to pry open your precious computer to install a new internal hard disk, it is actually remarkably easy. Desktop Macs are designed to be easily opened, and additions can be simply snapped into place.

External FireWire disk (Requires FireWire.) This disk is installed by plugging it into any open FireWire port. The advantage of external disks is that they are hot-swappable, which means you can plug in and unplug the disks while the computer is running and you can link multiple disks together to create a chain of disks, cameras, or other devices all accessible at the same time. Remember that even though they are hot-swappable, you'll need to eject the disk by dragging it to the Trash before unplugging it.

FireWire hard disks are relatively cheap. You can now buy disks with storage in the range of 120GB for only a few hundred dollars. When you are deciding how much space you need, remember that 1GB can hold roughly 5 minutes of captured video.

Because digital video relies on timing, you need to consider several features of any hard disk you are using. These features are listed at the top of the next page.

- **Rotational Speed** 5400rpm minimum but 7200rpm or higher recommended. Hard-disk speed is measured in rpm (rounds per minute), just like a vinyl record. FireWire video runs at 4200 rpm, so you'll want to make sure the disk you buy is faster than that.
- **Buffer** 2MB minimum, but 6MB or higher recommended
- **Access Time** 8.9 milliseconds (ms)
- **Data Transfer Rate** 50MB

Although designed as a highly portable MP3 player, Apple's iPod includes a FireWire hookup that enables you to transfer any file type (even video), enabling it to double as a pocket-size hard disk. The iPod can store up to 20GB, which is plenty of space for a short film, even uncompressed.

Monitors

While Final Cut Pro can display your sequence in the Canvas window on the computer monitor, we highly recommend you have a reference NTSC or PAL monitor on which to view your edit because NTSC and PAL handle color differently than the way a computer monitor handles color. The Canvas window will certainly give you a usable image, but an external reference monitor will help you make important decisions about contrast, color, and brightness that the computer screen cannot. If you're going to be doing heavy image control effects or color correction, a reference monitor is crucial.

You can hook up Final Cut Pro to any external reference monitor, including most regular, consumer-grade TVs, as long as the TV input plugs are compatible with your system. You can also buy adapters if your monitor's inputs are not compatible. For professional use, you should get a reference monitor with S-Video or Component inputs so

that the image quality is at the highest grade. This is absolutely necessary if you are cutting anything for broadcast.

It is also helpful, but not necessary, to have a second computer monitor. Final Cut Pro uses four main windows to navigate the interface, and these windows can be cramped on one screen even at a high resolution. If you have a second computer monitor, you can open up your space and divide your palettes between the two screens, keeping your viewer in one and your controls and browser in the other. If you are using the Matrox converter card, note that its port for a second monitor is not compatible with the Apple flat-panel monitor. If you desire a second flat-panel, you must also purchase an additional Radeon PCI card.

The DV Deck or Camera

Most likely you will be using a digital video camera to shoot footage for use in Final Cut Pro. If the footage you are capturing was shot on a DV camera, you can use the DV camera as a DV deck system (basically a mini-VCR that plays and records DV tapes). While doing so is sometimes a financial necessity, we recommend that you purchase a separate professional DV deck, such as the Sony Mini-DV VCR Walkman or the Panasonic DV Compact Recorder/Player, if you are working on a lot of projects that require a hefty amount of capturing. The strain of capturing, especially batch capturing, is not good for a DV camera's internal transport mechanisms, and DV cameras can run slower than DV decks when cueing up clips for capture. Also, if you're using the camera as a capturing deck as well as for shooting, it can cause greater wear on the camera's head, which will inevitably lead to poorer video quality when recording.

Hooking Up to a DV Deck or Camera

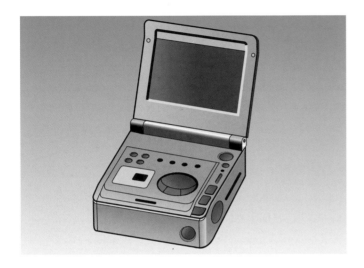

The most common setup for a Final Cut Pro station is with a *digital video deck*. As stated earlier, a DV deck is a like a mini-VCR that plays and records digital videotapes and can output that signal to your computer via a FireWire cable. It can also receive video through FireWire so that you can record your sequences onto DV tape. In this section, we'll go over the best ways to hook up your DV deck or camera to your computer. Make sure you've got all the necessary equipment in front of you. The bare

bones are your computer, a FireWire cable, and the DV deck. You may also have a reference monitor and external speakers. Hooking up your system with a FireWire connection to a DV deck ensures device control, which means you can control the VCR functions of the deck from within Final Cut Pro and also mark In and Out points on the raw footage to log your clips (see Chapter 4).

1. Plug in one end of the FireWire cable into the FireWire port on the deck. Plug in the other end into the FireWire port on your computer. If you are using a DV camera, make sure it is in VTR mode, not Camera mode. Use the smaller (4-pin) end of the cable to plug into your DV deck or camera. To plug into the computer, use a 6-pin connector if you are using FireWire 400 or a 9-pin connector if you are using FireWire 800.

Ⓐ FireWire to computer
Ⓑ FireWire to device

2. If you have an exterior reference monitor, first identify what kind of inputs your monitor can accept. These inputs could be Composite, S-Video, or another kind of video signal cable. Most DV decks and cameras have Composite and S-Video outputs. High-end professional DV decks, like the Sony DV Studio Player/Recorder, use Component Video outputs. Once connected with the appropriate cable, your monitor will now display whatever you play in your deck, and also what plays in the Timeline and Canvas within Final Cut Pro as long as the FireWire cable remains connected to the computer.

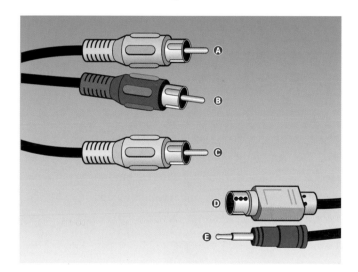

Ⓐ RCA Right Audio

Ⓑ RCA Left Audio

Ⓒ Composite Video

Ⓓ S-Video

Ⓔ Mini Plug

3. If you are hooking up external speakers, you have a number of options. If you are using a deck, find the Audio Out jacks, determine what type of cable they require, and route a cable between the deck and your speakers. If you are using a deck that does not have RCA audio output, plug a mini cable into the Headphones output of the deck and attach the other end to your speakers. You can, of course, just use actual headphones here if you prefer.

If you plug in your speakers through the camera or deck, your sound will be synched with the exterior monitor and not with the image on the computer monitor. There is a time delay of a few frames, so you should only hook up your speakers through the deck if you have an external reference monitor. Otherwise, use the internal computer sound via the headphone jack on your computer.

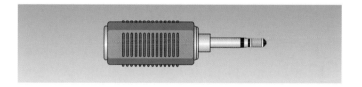

4. Now boot up Final Cut Pro. Make sure your DV camera or deck is on and the FireWire cable is plugged in or the program will not register the deck. If it's not, you can plug it in after you've booted the computer. If there is a problem, the program will alert you that there is no device hooked to the FireWire (see *Running Final Cut Pro for the First Time* in Chapter 2). Otherwise, you'll see the Final Cut Pro 4 splash screen, which means you are ready to start exploring the Final Cut Pro interface, which is the main focus of Chapter 2.

Hooking Up to a Media Converter Box

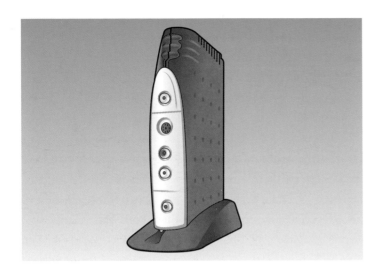

If you are capturing from an analog source (such as VHS, 1/4-inch tape, or Beta-SP) instead of mini-DV, you will need either a media converter or a special internal capture card. A media converter—such as the Matrox RTMac or the Hollywood DV-Bridge —is a device that converts an analog signal to digital and vice versa. It uses a FireWire cable to connect to a computer and S-Video and Composite analog video cables to connect to a video deck. This section will outline how to hook up your system so that you can successfully capture from

analog source material with a converter box. A converter box is a cheap way to translate your footage, but you should use a capture card if you want the more professional transfer via Component. Using a media converter can affect the color quality of the image and also degrade the audio. The biggest disadvantage is that the media converter box will not capture your footage with source timecode through FireWire, and therefore does not allow device control, logging, or batch-capturing.

1. Hook the FireWire cable into the FireWire port on your converter box. Attach the other end to the FireWire port on your computer. Remember that there are different kinds of FireWire plugs: 4-pin for the DV deck or camera and 6-pin or 9-pin for the computer.

Ⓐ FireWire to computer
Ⓑ FireWire to device

2. Determine what audio and video outputs are available on your analog deck. Most media converter boxes can accept S-Video, Composite, and RCA stereo cables. Hook a cable from the video output on your analog deck to the video input on the converter box. Do the same with the audio; hook the outputs on the deck to the input on the converter box.

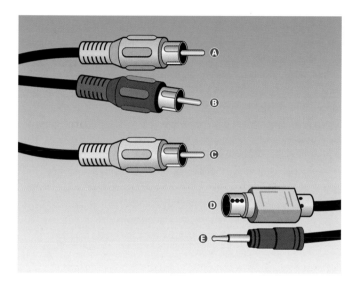

Ⓐ RCA Right Audio

Ⓑ RCA Left Audio

Ⓒ Composite Video

Ⓓ S-Video

Ⓔ Mini Plug

3. When you boot up Final Cut Pro, make sure the converter box is on so that the program will recognize the FireWire connection and can communicate with the converter box. Also make sure you configure the converter to import analog, as the signal you are inputting is analog and the signal you are bringing into your computer is digital. You'll want the Input source within Final Cut Pro to be set to DV.

This setup will allow you to capture from your analog source deck and convert the video and audio signals into digital files that will work with the DV codec (see the section on Installing an Analog-to-Digital Capture Card for a discussion of codecs) in Final Cut Pro. If you want to go the other way and export digital files onto the analog deck (for example, to make VHS dubs of your work), configure the converter to input digital. If necessary, change the cables between the analog deck and converter box so that the audio and video signals come from the output of the converter and go into the input plugs of the analog deck.

TIP

Editing Film, Digital Video, and Analog Video

analog *adj* (1948): of, relating to, or being a mechanism in which data is represented by continuously variable physical quantities.

digital *adj* (1656): of or relating to data in the form of numeric digits.

With all the talk about the digital revolution and the changing tides of video and film production to a digital world, let's look at what exactly is different about making and editing movies digitally. There are three main types of production media: film, analog video, and digital video.

Film is a strip of celluloid that records image through a chemical process based on exposure to light. Originally, editing was done entirely on film. Working prints of raw film footage were spliced together on an editing machine, which shuttled the footage back and forth on spools. When the editor was finished cutting and splicing, the original camera negative was cut to conform to the spliced working print, and a clean, unspliced print was made from this. Sound was added on a stripe along the side of the film, and voila, the film was ready for projection.

Both analog and digital video store their information on magnetic tape, by electrically charging the magnetic particles on the tape. The difference lies in the way the two methods represent information. With analog video-tape, images and sound are represented by continuous variations in the electrical properties of the magnetic particles. Digital video records the image by charging the magnetic particles into on/off voltages that can be read as ones and zeros. Digital video can therefore directly interface with your computer, and it does not lose quality as it is copied. Both advantages are significant.

With analog video technology, editing was done tape-to-tape. One tape held the raw, unedited footage, and the second tape held the assembled cuts in order; it was the final edited piece. Unfortunately, analog video degrades with every copy, as the signal from the magnetic particles on the tape becomes weaker with each dub. Analog editing therefore meant that the final version never had quite the image or sound quality of the original footage. This form of editing was called *linear editing* because shots were taped onto a master video one after the other, in a long "line" of video that could not be moved or shifted, only erased. If you wanted to make changes in shots you had already laid down, you had to go back and redo everything.

Because digital information can be stored and manipulated in computer memory, digital editing gives you the freedom to rearrange shots and shorten or lengthen them at will. This is called *nonlinear* editing because you are not trapped into a linear—one shot laid after the other—method of editing. What separates digital editing from editing on film is that the digital editing style is *nondestructive*, which means when you are cutting on your computer, you are not actually doing anything to the stored master media file. You are working with a representation of that file as a media clip, so no matter how many times you cut it or alter it, the clip stays intact as a file. All of your edited clips derive from that original media file, but they do not change it at all. With editing on film, every time you made a splice, you were actually cutting the film, so if you wanted to put a shot back together, you would have to re-splice it. Nonlinear digital editing saves you from having to keep track of all your snippets of stray film, because the media file stays intact no matter what you do editorially.

All of these formats can be converted to any of the other formats with various results. Digital video can be blown up to film, and footage shot on film can be transferred to DV and analog stocks and edited digitally. With each transfer, however, the footage will be affected by the characteristics of its current medium.

Installing an Analog-to-Digital Capture Card

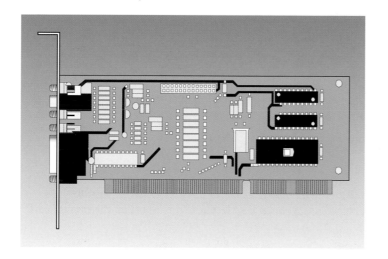

For a more professional way of working with analog source material in Final Cut Pro than using a media converter box, consider an analog-to-digital capture card. These cards maximize color quality by utilizing Component inputs and outputs. Like a converter box, a capture card converts the analog video into ones and zeros like the process in the converter boxes, but instead of using the DV codec, each capture card has its own proprietary codec. (*Codec* is an abbreviation for *compression/decompression* and refers to a type of extension software that allows QuickTime to communicate with Final Cut Pro so that it can capture, play back, and print to video. Codecs used by a capture card capture video without the degradation that DV converters perform on source material not originally shot on mini-DV.) Final Cut Pro supports these capture cards and their codecs: Digital Voodoo D1 Desktop, Aurora Igniter, AJA's Kona SD, and Pinnacle CinéWave.

This method alone, however, does not allow you to capture with *device control*. Device control is a technology that allows Final Cut Pro to control the deck and read the timecode on the source tape so you can shuttle through the footage and mark in and out points from the control panel in the program. With digital video, device control is already set up through the FireWire cable and timecodes are inserted automatically, but with analog, you will need a serial adapter. This section shows how to set up a video capture card and serial adapter.

TIP

Using a Serial Port with an Analog-to-DV Capture Card

If you are logging and capturing video with a high-end analog video deck (such as Beta SP, S-VHS, ¾ inch, or digital Beta), you will need a serial port added to your Macintosh to import timecodes from the video deck. Two serial port devices perform this function: the GeeThree Stealth Port (see www.geethree.com) and the Griffin Technology G-port (see www.griffintechnology.com/index.html/). Serial technologies are the only way to gain device control when capturing from an analog source.

In order to use the serial port, however, you must remove the internal 56K modem and install the serial port in its place. Instructions are provided in the accompanying products' manual—follow them closely as you perform the surgery. Neither of these two products comes with its own logging cable, so you must purchase this in addition to the port. This cable connects from the Time Code slot on the back of the analog video deck to the newly installed serial port on your Macintosh. While this device keeps a PCI slot open, it does prevent 56K dialup, leaving the only way for your computer to connect to the Internet through the Ethernet port (which is what DSL, cable, and T1 use).

Don't forget to change your Device Control tab in the Log/Capture window to the Serial Port when using this option!

1. Follow the manufacturer's instructions to install the capture card. This step generally requires opening your Mac and sliding the card into a particular PCI slot. Be careful when doing this, however, since the slightest static electricity may damage your computer. We recommend using a grounding strip when tinkering around with the inside of your computer. At the very least, touch a piece of grounded metal before you begin to discharge any static buildup.

2. Hook the audio and video cables into the output plugs on the back of your analog deck. These plugs should be clearly labeled. Most analog decks will have composite and RCA jacks. High-end professional decks like Beta-SP include Component jacks. You will need to make sure that the cable type accepted by the analog deck's output is compatible with the capture card's input plugs. See the *Video Cables* sidebar for information on the difference between the cables you can use.

3. Attach the other ends of the audio and video cables plugged into your analog deck into the inputs on the capture card you inserted in Step 1.

4. To allow device control over an analog capture card, you must install a serial port in place of the internal modem, attach a logging cable to your computer's freshly installed serial port, and connect the other end to the analog deck's timecode port. This will activate device control of the analog deck. See *Using a Serial Port with an Analog-to-DV Capture Card* for details.

5. If you are using an external reference monitor and speakers, you will need to connect them to the audio and video cables into the outputs of the analog deck as well as the capture card. There are usually two audio/video outputs on these analog decks. For the video signal, you should route signal 1 into the capture card on the computer, and route signal 2 into the external reference monitor to compare the color between what's being captured through signal 1 and what the source material looks like through signal 2. (Note: You can manipulate the color control levels in the Clips Settings tab of the Log and Capture window, which are grayed out when capturing DV.)

6. You will also need to connect the audio cables that come attached to the capture card into your deck's outputs. You must also change the Sound settings on your computer so that it knows to channel the sound through the capture card you have installed. Go into the Apple menu, scroll to Control Panels > Sound and, in the Input and Output tabs, select the appropriate source

(whichever analog capture card you have installed) in place of the default output. This will allow you to print to video and also to hear the sound from the computer itself as the video source is played on the deck.

7. When you boot up Final Cut Pro, make sure the analog deck is on, and if you are using an analog camcorder as a deck, make sure it is in VTR mode. If you are using device control, you will need to have the device control toggle on the analog deck set to Remote.

What Are the Different Video Cables Used with Analog?

There are three main types of video cables that you might use with Final Cut Pro when capturing from analog sources: Component, S-Video, and Composite.

Composite Composite cables provide the poorest quality of the three analog options, as they run all video information through a single RCA wire. Virtually all decks have composite RCA outputs, and this technology is useful for making tests.

S-Video Also known as Y/C, S-Video is a video input/output port that splits the video signal into four pins through one cord. It provides a signal that is better than Composite, but not as good as Component. Most higher-end decks have S-Video capabilities.

Component Component is the highest-end port. It splits the video signal into the three YUV signals or RGB signals, requiring three separate composite wires. These wires connect to the analog decks through BNC adapter ports. This is the standard for high-end professional projects, and gives the best quality transfer, with the least degradation to the color information of the original analog video. Many higher-end decks, such as a Beta-SP deck, will have Component jacks. Note that not all analog capture cards come with Component as part of the standard package. If Component is what you need, you may have to purchase an additional supplement to augment Component input and output for your capture card.

REAL WORLD

George Washington, Feature Film

George Washington was a media darling on the 2000 film festival circuit. After premiering at the Berlin Film Festival, the much-acclaimed feature went on to play numerous festivals including LA Independent, Newport, Edinburgh International, Toronto International, and the New York Film Festival. The film took several festival awards and was ultimately nominated for four Independent Spirit Awards, including Best Picture for 2001. Acquired for theatrical distribution in the United States by Cowboy Booking International, *George Washington* received much critical praise and made several top 10 lists for the year 2000, including *The New York Times* and Roger Ebert.

Directed by David Gordon Green, *George Washington* presents the complicated lives of a multiracial group of working-class kids living in a small Southern town. When accidental tragedy strikes, an innocent cover-up launches the kids on individual quests for redemption.

With such an original and unique perspective, it's not surprising to discover that the technology moving the image was also new: *George Washington* was the first feature film cut entirely on Final Cut Pro. Steven Gonzales, a co-editor of the picture, explained why he made the switch to the newly released editing software. "We started with Adobe Premiere, but it was just not working. Final Cut Pro came out, so we tried it, and we had success." Using 35mm film transferred to Beta-SP for the edits—which were captured over the Sony DV Media Converter and logged with the Griffin Technology G-port serial device—Gonzales describes the process of editing for film: "Film has code numbers created during manufacturing, which are located on every foot of 35mm." When the final edits were complete, he used FCP to export EDLs, and then imported them into Film Logic—a program that allows for accurate film-to-tape editing. He also used Film Logic to create cut lists for the negative cutter. "Film Logic keeps a database of the film edge codes, and relates them to the video timecode." This combination of Final Cut Pro and Film Logic allowed him to create 24 frame per second clips for frame-accurate editing of film.

An ambitious undertaking, both artistically and technically, *George Washington* was shot on 35mm, with a Moviecam, featuring anamorphic (super wide-angle) lenses from Joe Dutton. The film also used an Arri 35mm camera as the second-unit camera. All sets were shot on location in North Carolina.

Combined with the stunning cinematography of Tim Orr, the slow pacing of the film reflected the mood of the rural South. Gonzales further elaborates that "the languid pace was planned, and was shot in this way. Zene Baker (the other editor) and I worked closely with the director to cut the material in the most effective way." A teacher and student of the film techniques of V. I. Pudovkin, Gonzales discusses his philosophy of the process. "Editing is really a distillation process. For *George Washington*, the pacing really grew out of the raw material of the footage. We didn't approach the editing with a preconceived rhythm. We accepted the reality of our footage, and let it suggest its own rhythm."

Images Copyright Cowboy Booking International.

Nearly everyone on the *George Washington* production crew was affiliated with the North Carolina School of the Arts School of Filmmaking, where Gonzales is currently a faculty member. "We had all worked on dozens of

George Washington, Feature Film

films together, so our relations were established and we could relax into the process of filmmaking. The film was shot during the summer, so some of the crew who were still in film school could participate." *George Washington*, however, was not part of a thesis, but an independently financed film and— as is often the case with independent productions—choices of cast, crew, and technology were constrained by one thing. Gonzales, in using Final Cut Pro as his editing software of choice, tells it like it is: "Price was the main reason for our choice."

Gonzales has also edited the feature-length documentary *The Rough South of Larry Brown*, as well as the independent feature *Torn* for New York's Cynalex Productions.

George Washington is currently available on video, and a special feature DVD edition was released by the Criterion Collection. To learn more about this release or the film, visit the web site at www.criterionco.com.

Images Copyright Cowboy Booking International.

2 Getting to Know Final Cut Pro

If you've had any experience with digital nonlinear editing systems, Final Cut Pro will have a familiar a look and feel with only a few differences. If you're coming to the software with no editing experience, don't worry. With some practice and a little time, you'll be navigating comfortably in the environment. (And if you're a Macintosh buff, you'll be with it in no time!) One great benefit of the Final Cut Pro interface is that it offers multiple ways to work, so that you can use the program in a way that fits the way you think and edit. This chapter will help you get a general overview of the Final Cut Pro interface, and how you can structure the program to best work with your thought process. In it, you'll be introduced to the four basic pieces of the Final Cut Pro interface: the Browser, the Timeline, the Viewer, and the Canvas.

Overview

> *"Every film should have a beginning, a middle,*
> *and an end. But not necessarily in that order."*
>
> Jean-Luc Godard

This chapter will be a brief tour of the basic elements of Final Cut Pro. In subsequent chapters, we'll go into more depth about how these elements function, but a basic knowledge is required before we get very far. Here we'll cover the tools that let you interact with your footage. Final Cut Pro is divided into four task-oriented windows. These windows—the Browser, the Timeline, the Viewer, and the Canvas—have been created to interact together. Each window serves many different functions, and by using them all together, you'll be able to organize, edit, manipulate, and finalize your project.

Before touring the Final Cut Pro interface, we'll focus on setting your preferences. Because Final Cut Pro is highly adaptable to user needs, setting preferences can be quite complicated and can radi-cally affect your workflow, so it's important to know how to edit preferences. A lot of troubleshooting begins with checking and making changes to the editing preferences. We will also familiarize you with the program functions available to you as an editor.

Treat this chapter like a broad road map, with the four biggest sections of Final Cut Pro laid out in front of you. The Browser, the window where you organize your footage into bins, is like a giant filing cabinet for your clips. The Timeline, where you edit the footage together, is like a stack of film and audio reels all running together that you can manipulate and move into your final prod-uct. The Viewer, where you watch and make changes to individual clips, is like a little built-in VCR. The Canvas, where you can watch the results of your edits in the Timeline, is like a window onto your project as it evolves. We'll also look at the Tool Bench, a window that allows you access to the Video Scopes, previewing effects, and audio features. We'll also look at features new to Final Cut Pro 4 like the Keyboard Layout and the Button Manager. You'll probably find yourself referring back to this chapter as you read through the rest of the book, as it outlines the backbone of all your editing work with Final Cut Pro.

LESSONS

Running Final Cut Pro for the First Time

If you haven't already run Final Cut Pro for the first time before coming to this book (which is kind of like saying, "let's wait until after breakfast to open the Christmas presents"), then you may need some help with the initial settings.

1. The first time you run Final Cut Pro, after the registration information screen, you will be presented with the Choose Setup screen, where you can define several important options before you use the program. The Setup For drop-down list lets Final Cut Pro know which video file format your source material will use. Final Cut Pro 4 also includes options to capture footage with OfflineRT, which saves disk space by capturing low-quality footage for an offline edit (see *Using OfflineRT* in Chapter 5). If you are working with video in North America, you will probably want to stick with the default DV-NTSC setup.

In addition to indicating the source material type, you also have options to designate a Primary Scratch Disk and a User Mode. If you've added a hard disk (external or internal) for better performance as discussed in Chapter 1, you should designate the disk that will hold your video files (rather than your Final Cut Pro software) as the scratch disk. It's always advisable to have the operating system and all applications on a separate drive from your Final Cut Pro scratch disk.

The User Mode allows you to choose between the Standard interface and a more limited Cutting Station interface (see the sidebar *What Is the Cutting Station Mode For?*).

After you finish with the setup, click OK. This should be the only time you are presented with this screen at startup.

2. Every time you run Final Cut Pro (even after the first time) it will check to see if you have a deck or camera attached to the computer. If you do not, an alert appears, letting you know that it could not find anything. If you do have a device hooked up and still get this alert, make sure your cords are properly plugged in, the deck is turned on, and the camera is in VTR mode. Then click Check Again. The software will also look for your scratch disk—the drive where Final Cut Pro saves your media. If it can't find it (for example, the FireWire drive is not plugged in) it will prompt you to select a new scratch disk.

External A/V

Unable to locate the following external devices:

Apple FireWire NTSC (720 x 480)

Your system configuration may have changed, or your deck/camera may be disconnected or turned off.

Please check your connections and click "Check Again", or click "Continue" to set external device selection to None.

☐ Do not warn again

[Continue]   [Check Again]

3. If you do not have a camera or deck hooked up to your computer, click Continue. You may also want to check "Do not warn again" if you know that you will not be hooking up to a Deck. If you plug in the camera while Final Cut Pro is running, just

select Final Cut Pro > Easy Setup to run through Steps 1 and 2 again and mount the deck or camera.

4. Now you'll want to start a new project so that you can get to work. Once Final Cut Pro has loaded, select File > New Project (Shift+⌘+N). This will open a fresh new project. A project is the file in which you will add all of your clips, sequences, and effects to create your edit.

5. To save your new project, select File > Save Project As… When the save dialog box appears, choose where in your hard drive you want to save your project file and give it a name. A good rule of thumb is to save your project file on your main hard drive and not on an external drive where your media will be kept. This is a safeguard in case your media drive gets corrupted. If this tragedy were to occur, the project file would still be safe on your internal main hard drive.

Congratulations. You are now ready to use Final Cut Pro. The first thing you'll do is set your preferences for how the program should work.

FAQ
What Is the Cutting Station Mode For?

Cutting Station Mode is a special option that turns off many of the advanced operations in Final Cut Pro. This option lets you focus on basic cutting without a lot of the "bells and whistles" effects of the full Final Cut Pro software. This feature is useful if those effects and graphics are going to be added by someone else or if you are just getting comfortable with the Final Cut Pro interface and want to simplify the interface to the basic cutting tools. However, unless you really have a need for the Cutting Station Mode, it's best to work in the standard interface.

What Are NTSC and PAL?

NTSC stands for National Television Standards Committee, and is the standard video format used in the United States. Every VHS tape in North America, Japan, and several other countries is recorded in the NTSC format. NTSC runs at 29.97 frames per second and when digitized is roughly 720 × 480 pixels. PAL, which stands for Phase Alternating Line, is the format used in the United Kingdom and most of the rest of the world. It runs at 25 frames per second. The reason for the differences in the frame rate is based on voltage in various countries' electrical systems. North American systems, at 120 volts,

pulses at 60 pulses per second (60Hz). Most of the rest of the world runs on 220/240 volts, pulsing at 50 pulses per second (50Hz). Since one video frame is actually made up of two interlaced samples taken separately, a PAL video running at 25 frames per second gets a new sample with every pulse (if each frame has two interlaced samples, 25 frames will contain 50 samples, matching the 50 pulses of that country's electrical system).

You will want to make sure that you've set your presets so that they reflect the kind of video standard your source footage is coming from.

Setting Your User Preferences

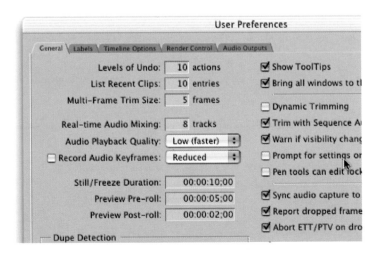

The Preferences window is a powerful tool that tailors your Final Cut Pro workstation to your individual needs. Here you will be able to set various aspects of how you want the program to work for you. You may need to use the User Preferences window only once in your career with Final Cut Pro, but it's important to know what is there so that you can tailor the software to work for you rather than the other way around.

1. To open the Preferences window, select Final Cut Pro > User Preferences (Option+Q). The Preferences window is divided into five tabs: General, Labels, Timeline Options, Render Control, and Audio Outputs. These tabs are your control center for customizing Final Cut Pro. This section will go over the most important and often-used preference settings they offer.

2. The first tab you will be greeted with after opening the Preferences window is the General tab. Here you will be able to set some of the basic functionality of Final Cut Pro.

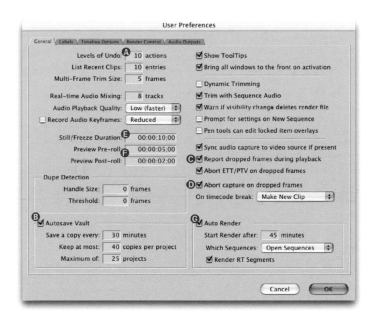

A **Levels of Undo:** Sets the default for the number of previous steps you can undo. The higher this number, the more memory used. We recommend 15 Undo levels, which allows for more elaborate experimentation without overloading the memory. You can, if you wish, set the undo levels up to 99.

B **Autosave Vault:** Controls how often the program auto-saves your work. You can also specify how many copies you want to keep for each project. You can also turn auto-save off by clearing the Autosave Vault check box. It's a good idea to auto-save about every 10 to 15 minutes. We recommend turning auto-save off when you are rendering a complicated series of effects, as auto-save can cause the program to freeze or crash.

C **Report Dropped Frames during Playback:** If this option is activated, a window will appear if your video drops frames during playback. This can occur in the Canvas, Viewer, or Timeline. Note that dropping frames during playback is not the same as Drop Frame timecoding. This refers to a method of recording timecode, while "dropping frames during playback" refers to actually losing frames of video. The terms are confusingly similar, but it's important to know the difference.

D **Abort Capture on Dropped Frames:** If this option is activated, the capture process will be aborted if a frame is dropped. This means that one or more frames were skipped over and not digitized during capture. Unless you aren't going to be using your project professionally, you should keep this option on.

E **Still/Freeze Frame Duration:** This sets the default for the length of a clip that is created for a single frame of a moving video clip.

F **Preview Pre-roll and Preview Post-roll:** This plays the video and audio around a frame designated by the location of the playhead. Set how much before and after this designated frame you want the Play Around Current function to start and stop. For example, if the Preview Pre-roll is set at 15 seconds, and the Preview Post-roll is set at 5 seconds, the Play Around Current will play a 20-second segment of the cut, with the designated frame 15 seconds into the segment.

G **Auto Render:** Lets Final Cut Pro start to render through a sequence when you leave the computer inactive for a designated number of minutes. See Chapter 9 for details.

3. Click the Labels tab. Here you can organize your clips by color to designate different type of clips. By clicking on a label, you can type in a name for it, such as "Bad Audio" or "B-Roll," so that you can quickly identify clips by sight.

4. Click the Timeline Options tab. In this tab you will be able to set preferences for the Timeline window.

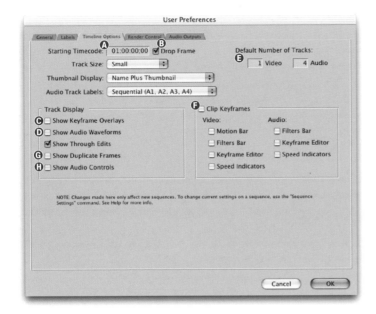

A **Starting Timecode:** By changing the timecode value in this window, you control what the timecode will be at the beginning of your sequence.

B **Drop Frame:** Toggles between Drop Frame and non-Drop Frame timecode in your sequence (see the sidebar *Should I Use Drop Frame or non-Drop Frame?*).

C **Show Keyframe Overlays:** If this option is checked, keyframe adjustments will be represented on the clip in the Timeline by colored bars. A black bar signifies adjustments in opacity (the transparency of a clip). A red bar signifies changes in audio levels. Unless you're doing very basic edits without keyframes, it's a good idea to have this turned on.

D **Show Audio Waveforms:** Changes the audio clips in the Timeline to show the waveform graphic within the clip. This takes a long time to load, so keep this off unless you need to see the waveform at a glance.

E **Default Number of Tracks:** Controls the number of tracks created in a newly created sequence. This number can range from 1 to 99. Additional tracks are used to layer clips on top of each other for composite shots, fades, and other effects.

F **Clip Keyframes:** Controls what types of effect keyframes will be shown in the clip in the Timeline.

G **Show Duplicate Frames:** Identifies when the same frame is used more than once in a sequence. This is especially helpful to keep you from accidentally reusing shots.

H **Show Audio Controls:** Opens up extra audio functions that let you isolate and mute tracks.

5. Click the Render Control tab. Here you can control what types of effects get rendered and what frame rate and resolution you render at. See Chapter 9 for an in-depth discussion of this option.

Click the Audio Outputs tab. Here you can select, edit, or create new (duplicate) an audio preset that determines how your audio will be outputted. The default preset will output your audio in stereo. To make a new preset, duplicate the default preset by clicking Duplicate and then change the settings in the Audio Outputs Preset Editor window that pops up.

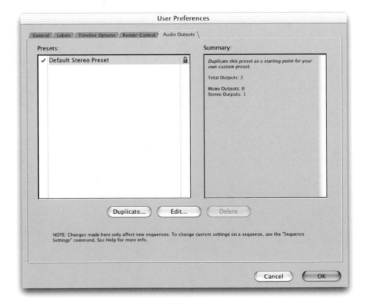

FAQ

Should I Use Drop Frame or Non-Drop Frame?

The terms *drop frame* and *non-drop frame* are defined by how the timecode references video frames. The last two digits of a timecode represent the frame number within the second. Thus, 00:07:30:14 identifies frame 14 at the 0 hours, 7 minutes, and 30 seconds time. This notation works smoothly in a video system where the frame rate is a whole number of frames per second, but it requires adjustment to work with a fractional rate of frames per second.

The PAL system, which runs at 25 frames per second, is non-drop frame: for every single frame of video, there is a timecode number to represent it, and this timecode increases without skipping any numbers with each video frame. You can divide each second into 25 frames, and easily represent these frames with the timecode numbering system. Things get tricky with the North American video standard, NTSC. The NTSC standard runs at 29.97 frames per second. When timecode is running with video at this rate, it can't represent every frame and keep its numbering system to whole numbers. Therefore, the timecode actually skips a frame number every now and then to keep itself in synch. Technically, the timecode must "drop" the 0 and 1 frame number on the first second of every minute, but there's an exception: if the minute can be divided by 10, the timecode doesn't drop its frames.

Through this convoluted system, the timecode can stay on track with a frame rate of 29.97 frames per second. Since the timecode must literally leave out frames numbers to keep up, this is called *Drop-Frame Timecode*. Check to see what rate the footage you are using was shot on and set your capture and sequence settings accordingly.

A timecode that is drop frame looks like this (note the semicolon instead of colon between the seconds and frames):

00:04:12;00

A timecode that is non–drop frame looks like this:

00:04:12:00

It's very important not to get these two types of timecodes (drop frame and non-drop frame) mixed up with the term *dropping frames*, which can occur as an error during playback or capture. The terminology is confusing; but these are the standard expressions, so we're stuck with them. To clarify, drop frame timecode is a normal process by which NTSC timecode keeps up with its 29.97 frame rate. *Dropping frames*, which can occur during playback or while capturing, is when random frames disappear and cause the image to stutter. This problem is usually caused by insufficient memory.

TIP

System Settings

The System Settings window lets you quickly review and customize your options for how Final Cut Pro 4 will operate on your computer. To access the System Settings window, select Final Cut Pro > Systems Settings (Shift+Q). The most important option within this window is the Scratch Disks tab,

which allows you to identify where the incoming media will be saved on your hard drive(s). See Chapter 5 for an in-depth look at how to use this window to define your scratch disks.

Audio/Video Settings

Besides the User Preferences window, the Final Cut Pro menu provides another tool for controlling how Final Cut Pro will operate: the Audio/Video Settings window deals with audio and video, and how they integrate with Final Cut Pro. This is also the window where you control the presets for your sequence, for capturing video and audio, and for device control. The presets allow you to specify and save different parameters for audio and video that you may need for different projects.

Why would you want to change the presets if you can select a ready-made setup (like the DV-NTSC setup) that already has default presets that will work? While these setups are good for general editing, you may be working on a project that requires you to alter these presets, or you may have personal preferences that aren't reflected in the given presets. For example, you may prefer to set longer pre- and post-roll times when capturing footage, so you would go into the Device Control preset and change this. Or you may be using footage that is anamorphic (shot with a special distorting lens so the image, when "un-distorted," is actually widescreen with a ratio of 16:9). If this were the case, you'd have to go into the Sequence preset and edit the preset so that the anamorphic option is turned on. You can also change the White Point settings, which toggles between White and Super-White. Choosing Super-White can brighten low-light footage, so you should make this change if you know the footage was shot in dim light. Once you're comfortable with presets, don't be afraid to go in and alter the presets to reflect your own needs and tastes as an editor. The setup defaults are helpful when you are starting out and for basic projects, but you'll often find yourself having to tailor these presets, so it's good to be familiar with your options.

1. Select Final Cut Pro > Audio/Video Settings (Option+⌘+Q) to open the Audio/Video Settings window.

2. The first thing you will see in the Audio/Video Settings window is the Summary tab. Here you will find a summary of the different preset tabs: Summary, Sequence Presets, Capture Presets, and Device Control Presets, as well as the options for A/V Devices. You can choose a different preset in any category from the drop-down menus. If you click one of the preset tabs, you'll be able to add or edit the presets as well as change the selection. In the Summary tab, you can quickly select the four different presets you want. If you are editing digital video that you are capturing through a FireWire cable, a common preset scheme is: Sequence Preset: DV NTSC 48kHz, Capture Preset: DV NTSC 48 kHz, Device Control Preset: FireWire NTSC. This is the preset default of the DV NTSC setup. If you are instead using footage shot on PAL, you can select that option here. The last option is A/V Devices and controls whether you will see your video on a monitor other than the Canvas window in Final Cut Pro. If you are using DV and want an external video option, select Apple FireWire NTSC (720 × 480). This outputs the video signal through your FireWire cable into your camera or deck. You can also route the audio either through your computer speaker or through the external FireWire hookup.

3. Click the Sequence Presets tab. In this tab, you can set the preset for your sequences. These presets should match the ones you set for your capture so that the footage will be compatible. (A *sequence* is a tab in the Timeline made up of tracks of audio and video where you have edited your clips together. You can have multiple sequences open in the Timeline, possibly with different presets, and they will be represented by different tabs.) The preset you select will set the default settings to be followed when a new sequence is created. In the left window is a list of saved presets. In the right window, you'll see the properties of the currently highlighted preset. To enable a preset, click next to the preset name so that a check mark appears. This preset is now active and the default.

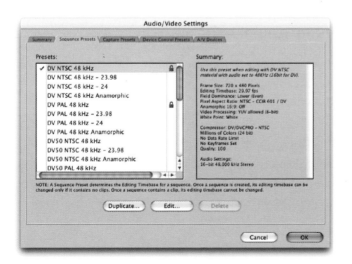

4. Click the Capture Presets tab. This tab lets you choose the preset you want to define how Final Cut Pro will capture your source footage and create online media files. The left window gives you a list of saved presets, and the right window gives you a list of the properties of the highlighted preset. If you are using an analog capture card such as Aurora or CinéWave, options for the installed card will appear. Again, the capture presets should match the sequence presets so that the captured footage will be compatible with the sequence. To enable a preset, click next to the preset name so that a check mark appears. This preset is now active and the default.

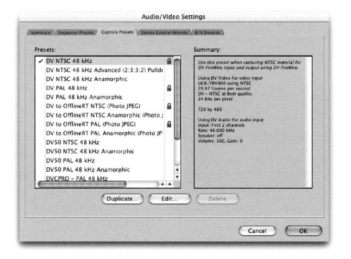

5. Click the Device Control Presets tab. This tab lets you choose a preset that controls the options for device control, which is the system that lets your computer communicate with your source deck. The left window gives you a list of saved presets, and the right window gives you a list of the properties of the highlighted preset.

To enable a preset, click to the far left of the preset name so that a check mark appears. If you are working with a PAL DV camera, you should select the PAL DV option. If you are working with an analog serial port like the GeeThree, it will appear as an option and you should select it. This preset is now active and the default. If your deck does not allow device control, you'll need to choose Non-Controllable Device.

mentioned in Step 2 in *Running Final Cut Pro* earlier in this chapter so that Final Cut Pro will go directly from the splash page to the program. This is useful after all the digitizing is done and you do not need to be connected to an external source. To do so, simply deselect the box reading "Do not show External A/V Device Warning when device not found on launch.")

6. Click the A/V Devices tab.

The Playback Output option allows you to set the default value for where to send an external video and audio signal. For example, many Final Cut Pro setups send out a video signal to a reference monitor through a FireWire cable (usually through a deck, camera, or capture card first). This way, the external NTSC or PAL monitor shows the video of whatever your playhead is currently playing. The Different Output for Edit to Tape/Print to Video option sets how the video footage is sent to be recorded to tape. You should only select this option if you want it to be different than where the video normally plays as set by the View During Playback option. (You can disable the alert

Defining Your Own Presets

The presets allow you to save your settings so that you can keep commonly used presets without having to change your settings every time. You may find that none of the presets offered in the window are exactly what you want, so you'll need to create and customize your own. In this section, we'll use as an example the task that you want to change the pre-roll and post-roll defaults. This is a Device Control preset and determines how many extra seconds the computer will pre-roll or then post-roll before and after it captures footage. This is especially helpful if you need to capture footage very close to a timecode break, so you would set the pre-roll to be a very short time so as not to cross the timecode break and confuse the computer.

To define a new preset, you'll take an existing preset, make a duplicate of it, and then edit the settings until they fit your needs. You can then save this preset under a new name and use it in your Final Cut Pro projects.

1. Select Final Cut Pro > Audio/Video Settings. This brings up the Audio/Video Settings window.

2. Select the preset tab you want to work with (in our example, choose Device Control Presets). In the window that appears, choose the preset that most resembles the preset you want to create (in our example, you can choose the FireWire NTSC preset). Highlight it by clicking the preset name once.

Click Duplicate at the bottom of the window. This will bring up the Preset Editor window and create a new, identical preset that you can edit without affecting the original preset.

3. The Preset Editor is where you will make all of your changes to the preset. Make all of the changes you want to make until the preset reflects your specific needs. (In our example, change the Pre-roll to 5 seconds and the Post-roll to 5 seconds.) Give the preset a new name, such as 5 Second Pre/Post Roll."

Once you've made the changes and renamed the preset, click on OK. This will save your preset to the list of presets in the Preset window.

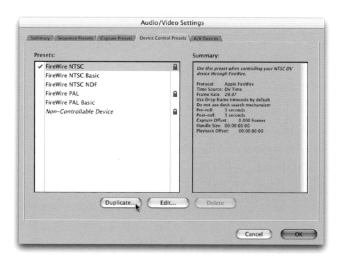

4. You can now activate your new preset by clicking to place a check mark next to its name in the list. When you enable your new preset, the computer will follow the guidelines set by your customized preset.

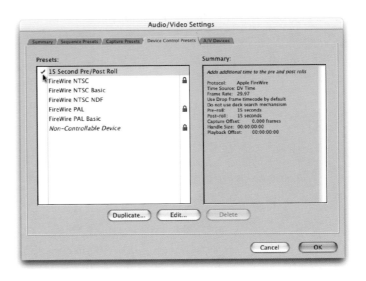

The Browser

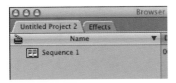

The Browser is like a filing cabinet for your footage in Final Cut Pro, or, for those of you coming from editing on film, it's the digital equivalent of your reels and trim bins. The Browser is an incredibly useful tool, and it does more than just store and organize all your media information about your clips. It also houses the Effects tab, which contains folders of all sorts of filters and effects. These are covered extensively in later chapters.

1. The Browser should automatically be open as soon as you enter Final Cut Pro. However, you can select Window > Browser (⌘+4) to (re)open or close this window.

2. The Browser creates a tab for each of your projects, and within each tab/project, the Browser allows you to add clips or create bins (just like the old trim bins where you'd let your film footage hang) to separate and organize your clips. You can create bins within bins, and the whole system is set up in the same way your Macintosh organizes the files on your hard disk in folders. Remember that the clips within the Browser are only representations of the actual files on your hard drive. You can delete them from the Browser without deleting them from your hard drive.

In addition, the Browser contains a variety of information about the sequences and clips, which you can view using the horizontal scroll bar. You can rearrange these columns by dragging the column title left and right.

Ⓐ Column Title: Identifies the column and also allows you to sort clips and bins in standard or reverse alphabetic or numeric order. You can sort by any column in the Browser, such as name or duration. For example, you might sort by In point if you're looking for a clip and you know where it is located in the sequence but not its name. To sort by a column, click on the heading name. Click on the green arrow to toggle between sorting in ascending or descending order. You can also drag the sides of the columns to make them wider or skinnier.

Ⓑ Project Tab: Each open project gets its own tab.

Ⓒ Effects Tab: A tab containing all of Final Cut Pro's built-in effects.

Ⓓ Bin: A "folder" used to store related clips, sequences, audio clips, graphics, etc.

Ⓔ Horizontal Scroll Bar: Use this to view additional information about the clips such as the shot/take, file size on the hard disk, or notes you've written about the clip.

Ⓕ Sequence: A string of clips, containing audio, video, and graphic clips that have been edited together. A sequence is viewed in the Timeline or in the Canvas. The sequence is where you will do the majority of your editing.

Ⓖ Clip: A representation of a media file, which can be loaded in the Viewer or added to a sequence in the Timeline. This is not the actual media file itself, and deleting a clip from the Browser will not permanently delete the media file from the hard drive.

Ⓗ Contextual Menu: Control+click in any clear area of the Browser to choose different options such as the view mode, create a new bin or sequence, import files, set the top level of the project as the Log Bin, and paste copied elements into this project.

3. To create a new project, select File **>** New Project (⌘+E). To close a project tab, you can use File **>** Close Project or hold down the Control key while clicking on the tab in the Browser and select Close Tab.

4. To create a new sequence or a new bin, select File **>** New **>** Sequence (⌘+N) or File **>** New **>** Bin (⌘+B). Once you've created a sequence or bin, you can type in a name by clicking on the text by the bin or sequence icon, the same way you can name folders or files in your Macintosh operating system. Bins are like folders and sequences act like files.

5. As in most Mac windows, you can also set how the clips show up in the window: as a list, as small icons, or as large icons. To change the view, select View **>** Browser Items and then select the view style that is best for you: List, Small Icons, Medium Icons, Large Icons. List is the recommended way to go as it saves space and displays the most information. Shift+H will cycle through the different Browser styles.

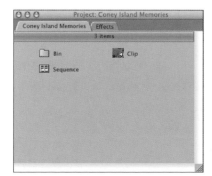

Small Icons

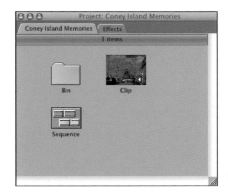

Medium Icons

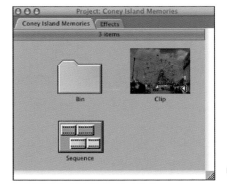

Large Icons

6. The clips in your Browser will either be online clips or offline clips. Online clips are clips whose video media has been captured and exists on the hard disk and are connected to the project. Offline clips have been logged but not yet captured, or the video media they represent is missing. (See the sidebar *Where Are the Video Files Really Stored…and Can I Move Them?*).

Offline clips are represented with a red slash through them. Clips are offline until they are captured to an accessible hard drive.

Don't get this term confused with doing "Offline edits," which means cutting footage that is not meant to be the final product.

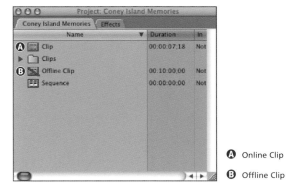

Ⓐ Online Clip

Ⓑ Offline Clip

7. Click the Effects tab to see the built-in video and audio effects offered by Final Cut Pro. The effects can also be found in Final Cut Pro's Effects menu, although the Browser's Effects bin is better organized and detailed.

The chapters in Parts III and IV of this book explore in detail the many effects that come with the software and how they can be used.

Why Do the Title Bars Look Different in Final Cut Pro?

One thing you might notice about the windows in Final Cut Pro is that their title bars (the bar across the top of all windows) look very different from standard Mac title bars in OS X. In order to save space in the interface, Apple decided to reduce the height of these bars and make them dark gray to be less distracting. Don't worry, though, they still work exactly the same: the Close button is first, the Minimize button is second, and the Maximize button is third.

Where Are the Video Files Really Stored…and Can I Move Them?

Remember that the Browser does not actually contain the media files, it contains clips that reference these files. As discussed in Chapter 1, Final Cut Pro is a nondestructive editing system, so no matter what you do to a clip in the Browser, it does not affect the file on your hard drive. You can trim your clip, make it black and white, or turn it upside down, but the original media that you captured from your source tape remains intact. All effects added to a clip are recorded separately in render files.

A word of warning: If you move the actual media files to a different folder or disk, clips that were once online may be listed as offline when you start Final Cut Pro again. This is because you have moved the clip from the location that Final Cut Pro knows about, and it can no longer locate the clip.

If this happens, Final Cut Pro will bring up a dialog box when you start the program, alerting you that clips are offline. To "reconnect" the media file to the representative clip within Final Cut Pro, click the Reconnect button. Then choose the type of files you want to reconnect (Offline, Online, or Render). Final Cut Pro will attempt to find the media files that match the name of the offline clip. If it cannot locate the files, the program may ask you to help it find the files, allowing you to search the hard disk for the missing media file. You can also do this manually within Final Cut Pro by choosing File > Reconnect Media. You can choose render files and/or movie files, and Final Cut will attempt to find the missing media files.

The Viewer

The Viewer is a multipurpose monitor that allows you to play through, prepare edits, and add special image or motion effects to a specific clip. The Viewer is in many ways similar in layout to the Canvas, although it serves a different function and can display any clip and its properties, not just what is seen in the Timeline. The Viewer is usually where you'll take your clip first to prepare it for the Timeline. A typical editing procedure begins with taking a clip from the Browser to the Viewer, trimming it there by setting In and Out points, and then bringing the trimmed clip into the Timeline. To open the Viewer, do one of the following:

1. Select Window **>** Viewer (⌘+1) to open or close the Viewer window.

2. You can bring any clip into the Viewer by dragging it from the Browser onto the Viewer or double-clicking the clip in the Browser. Once you've opened the clip in the Viewer, you can use the same VCR-like transport controls as in the Canvas.

Ⓐ **Video/Stereo/Filters/Motion Tabs**

Ⓑ **Duration:** The length of the current clip.

Ⓒ **Viewing Size:** Allows you to set the window size. Changing this from 100% may cause distortion in the Viewer but not in the final product. In addition, you can choose to view in square pixels (for computer monitors) or not (for video monitors).

Ⓓ **Viewing Options:** Allows you to change the way the image appears, including adding a title safe guide (see Chapter 17) and viewing the alpha channels (see Chapter 13).

Ⓔ **Current Time Code:** The current timecode under the Playhead.

Ⓕ **Timeline:** A linear representation of the entire clip loaded into the Viewer. You can use the mouse to "scrub" the playhead back and forth through the clip.

Ⓖ **Viewing Window:** Shows the current frame under the playhead.

Ⓗ **Frame Advance:** Allows you to move forward or backward one frame at a time.

Ⓘ **Previous Edit:** Sends the playhead to the previous edit.

Ⓙ **Play In to Out:** Plays only from the current In point to the current Out point.

Ⓚ **Play:** Plays the sequence from the current point.

Ⓛ **Play Around Current:** Plays a little before and a little after the current playhead position. Use the Preferences options Preview Pre-Roll and Preview Post-Roll to set the time before and after that will play.

Ⓜ **Next Edit:** Sends the playhead to the next edit point.

Ⓝ **Fast Forward/Rewind:** Shuttles the playhead forward or backward along the sequence.

Ⓞ **Mark In:** Sets an In point at the current playhead position.

Ⓟ **Mark Out:** Sets an Out point at the current playhead position.

Ⓠ **Add Marker:** Sets a marker at the current playhead position.

Ⓡ **Add Keyframe:** Sets a keyframe at the current playhead position.

Ⓢ **Mark Clip:** Sets the In and Out points at the current boundaries of a clip.

Ⓣ **Match Frame:** Moves the playhead in the Timeline to the same clip currently open in the Viewer, landing on the frame of the Timeline clip that matches the current frame in the Viewer.

Ⓤ **Recent Clips:** This brings up a list of clips recently opened in the Viewer that you can open instantly.

Ⓥ **Generator Pop-up Menu:** Brings up a list of generators and can open them in the Viewer. Generators are computer-created clips such as colored panels or titles (see Chapter 9).

3. You can also use the spacebar and J, K, and L keys on the keypad to move within the clip, just as in the Canvas (see the sidebar *Keyboard Shortcuts for the Canvas and Viewer*).

4. The Viewer works in conjunction with the Timeline, and you can drag clips from the Viewer into the Timeline (and vice versa), or you can bring up a clip into the Viewer by double-clicking on the clip in the Timeline (see Chapter 6 for more details).

5. One important aspect of the Viewer is that it allows you to view and edit the current clip's properties. You can adjust the audio, add special effects, and introduce motion control. To see how editing audio works, click the Stereo tab. This brings up the waveform image of the current clip's audio. Here you can adjust audio levels and the stereo spread. If the clip's audio consists of two channels linked as a stereo pair, you'll have the option to

select Channel 1 or Channel 2 of the audio, so that you can work on each channel separately. See Chapter 16 for more information.

6. Click the Filter tab. This is where you can view and edit any filters you've added to the clip. See Chapters 9–12 for details on the special effects you can add to clips.

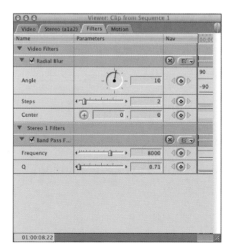

7. Click the Motion tab. This is where you can control the video image's size, borders, angle, opacity, and so on. See Chapter 14 for a detailed look at the motion controls.

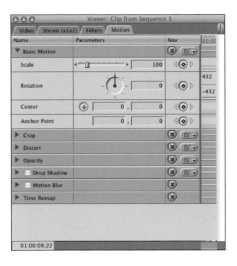

Keyboard Shortcuts for the Canvas and Viewer

You can also use the keypad shortcuts to move through your footage in the Canvas or Viewer depending on which window you have selected. Besides the stickers that come with the program, you can buy a special Final Cut Pro keyboard that contains all of the shortcuts listed on the keys. You can buy this keyboard at most stores that specialize in Mac products.

Spacebar: Toggles between playing and pausing the sequence.

Shift+spacebar: Plays the sequence backward.

J: The rewind key. The more you tap it, the faster the playhead will rewind.

L: The fast-forward key. Once again, tapping it a few times will increase the fast-forward speed.

K: The pause key. You can also hold down the K key along with the J or L key or use the left and right arrow keys to move forward or back one frame at a time.

I: Sets an In point at the current playhead location.

O: Sets an Out point at the current playhead location.

The Timeline

The Timeline is where all the action is. It's where the meat and potatoes of your cutting takes place. This is where you put clips side by side, add transitions, layer clips, position titles, and do most of your fine-tuning.

The Timeline displays a linear representation of your sequence, and gives you a visual picture of how your edited video looks, piece by piece.

1. Although the Timeline will generally be opened as soon as you enter Final Cut Pro, you can open and close it by selecting Window > Timeline (⌘+3). The Timeline consists of one or more tracks, containing both video and audio.

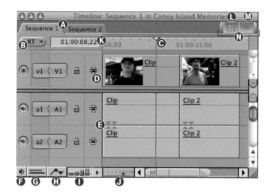

Ⓐ Sequence Tab: Allows you to select the sequence you want to work in. Each sequence added to the Timeline will have a separate tab. Switching the sequence here will cause the sequence to change in the Canvas as well.

Ⓑ Real Time: Allows you to choose the level of Real Time effects to use (Safe or Unlimited) as well as the playback quality, tape-recording quality, as well as whether to just playback without showing effects (base layer).

Ⓒ Playhead: Indicates where in the Timeline you currently are.

Ⓓ Video Tracks: Graphic representation of the length of the video track(s), where your video clips will be edited together. You can have up to 99 tracks of video in a sequence.

Ⓔ Audio Tracks: Graphic representation of the length of the audio track(s) where the audio clips will be edited together. You can have up to 99 tracks of audio.

Ⓕ Audio Controls: Allows you to control audio directly in the Timeline.

Ⓖ Clip Keyframes: Select this to create a space with color-coded bars under a clip. If a clip contains a filter, a green bar will appear. If a clip contains a motion effect, a blue bar will

appear. If keyframes are being used, the keyframes will appear at the top of the bar they are applied to. This feature also opens an area where you can keyframe various filter attributes and motion effects including Time Remapping.

Ⓗ Clip Overlays: Select this to turn on the display of overlays over your clips to show the opacity (transparency) of the clip and the audio levels of the clip.

Ⓘ Track Height: Sets the relative height tracks should appear. This can also be changed by Option-clicking and dragging the bottom of a track.

Ⓙ Track Size: The relative width all the tracks will appear. This is especially helpful when trying to "zoom in" on a specific part of the Timeline or "zoom out" to see the big picture.

Ⓚ Current Timecode: Shows the current Timecode under the playhead.

Ⓛ Toggle Linking: Turns on and off linking.

Ⓜ Toggle Snapping: Turns on and off snapping.

Ⓝ Button List: Includes Linking and Snapping as defaults; you can add buttons to this bar that will perform most actions in Final Cut Pro.

2. The video tracks are stacked in the top half of the Timeline, and the audio tracks are found in the lower half. On the left, you'll see the tracks numbered: V1 for video track 1, A1 for audio track 1, and so on. You can have up to 99 of either kind.

To the left of these track labels, you'll see a circular button that lights up green when you select it. This is the track visibility toggle. If the rectangle is lighted green, then the track will be picked up by the playhead during playback. If the track's visibility is off, the playhead will ignore that track and not play it. Final Cut Pro may lose its render files when you turn track visibility on or off, so do so carefully. Final Cut Pro will warn you before this happens.

To the right of the track label is a small padlock icon. By clicking the icon, you "lock" the track, so that nothing on the track can be altered. Clicking on the lock again unlocks the track.

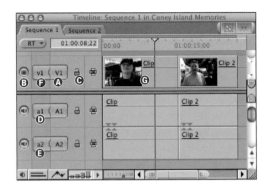

Ⓐ **Track Number:** Provides a numbered code for each track.

Ⓑ **Visibility:** Toggles clip on and off. When off, the clip will not appear (video) or be audible (audio) in the sequence.

Ⓒ **Lock:** When locked, clips in this track can not be altered.

Ⓓ **a1 Audio Target Track:** Designates this track as the target track for incoming audio. Used in conjunction with a2 Audio Target tracks if the incoming clip is in stereo.

Ⓔ **a2 Audio Target Track:** Designates this track as the target track for incoming audio that is the second part of a stereo pair.

Ⓕ **v1 Video Target Track:** Designates the target track for the incoming video clip.

Ⓖ **Clip Thumbnail:** A small image of the first frame in the clip.

3. The video tracks work in a hierarchy. Video clips on higher tracks take precedent over video clips on lower tracks. For example, if you have a clip on V2 and a clip directly under it on V1, you will only see V2 when you play the sequence. If you were to put a clip on V3, directly above both, you would then only see the clip on V3. Layering clips is useful when adding titles, or graphics, or when creating composite imagery.

What Is the "Playhead"?

The playhead is a graphic representation of where you are in a certain sequence or clip. The position of the playhead determines which frame is being currently shown. Represented by a small yellow triangle on top of a long vertical line, the playhead can only rest on one frame at a time. The playhead appears in many parts of Final Cut Pro. You'll see it most often in the Timeline, which plays the edited sequence you have constructed out of your clips.

A playhead also appears in the Viewer's scrub bar, for watching individual clips, and in the Canvas' scrub bar, where it parallels the Timeline's playhead location. Playheads work in conjunction with a scrub bar, the gray horizontal bar where the yellow triangle top sits, which acts as a mirrored version of the Timeline. You can move ("scrub") through a clip or sequence by dragging the playhead with the mouse forward and backward. You can also click anywhere on the scrub bar and the playhead will immediately position itself there, moving the playhead in the Timeline as well.

The Canvas

So the Timeline is where you do your editing. Fine, but how do you play your sequence? Enter the Canvas. The Canvas is a window that displays the video and audio from the Timeline. You can think of it as your "internal" monitor. The Canvas shows whatever frame your playhead is currently resting on in the Timeline. When you set the playhead in motion during playback, the Canvas becomes a monitor so that you can see the fruits of your work.

1. Although the Canvas should already be open when Final Cut Pro starts, you can open or close this window by selecting Window > Canvas (⌘+2).

2. The controls of the Canvas are like a VCR's remote control. Most of the window is taken up by the screen image, but at the bottom is a strip of buttons and controls. The round buttons in the middle control the playhead of the Timeline, and let you shuttle through your edited sequence.

A **Sequence Tabs:** Allow you to switch between different sequences in the current project. Switching the sequence here will cause the sequence to change in the Timeline as well.

B **Duration:** The length of the current sequence.

C **Viewing Size:** Allows you to set the window size. Changing this from 100% may cause distortion in the image in the Canvas but not in the final product. However, if you are using analog footage, it may not work at 100%, so try a smaller percentage. In addition, you can choose to view in square pixels (for computer monitors) or not (for video monitors).

D **Viewing Options:** Allows you to change the way the image appears, including adding a title safe guide (see Chapter 17), and viewing the alpha channels (see Chapter 13).

E **Current Time Code:** The current timecode under the playhead. If the playhead is playing the sequence back, it will roll ahead like a clock.

F **Viewing Window:** Shows the current frame under the playhead.

G **Timeline:** A linear representation of the entire sequence. You can use the mouse to scrub the playhead back and forth through the sequence.

H **Frame Advance:** Allows you to move forward or backward one frame at a time.

I **Previous Edit:** Sends the playhead to the previous edit.

J **Play In to Out:** Plays only from the current In point to the current Out point.

K **Play:** Plays the sequence from the current point.

L **Play Around Current:** Plays a little before and a little after the current playhead position. How far back and forward is played is set in your preferences.

M **Next Edit:** Sends the playhead to the next edit point.

N **Fast Forward/Rewind:** Shuttles the playhead forward or backward along the sequence.

O **Insert:** Performs an Insert edit with whatever is currently in the Viewer (see Chapter 6).

P **Overwrite:** Performs an Overwrite edit with whatever is currently in the Viewer (see Chapter 6).

Q **Replace:** Performs a Replace edit with whatever is currently in the Viewer (see Chapter 6).

R **Mark In:** Sets an In point at the current playhead position.

S **Mark Out:** Sets an Out point at the current playhead position.

T **Add Marker:** Sets a marker at the current playhead position.

U **Add Keyframe:** Sets a keyframe at the current playhead position (see Chapter 16).

V **Mark Clip:** Sets the In and Out points as the beginning and end of the clip in the target track where the playhead is currently resting.

W **Match Frame:** Will open in the Viewer a copy of the clip that is in the current target track where the playhead is resting. The playhead in the Viewer will be at the exact same frame on the clip as the playhead in the Timeline.

Customizing with the Keyboard Layout and Button List

(4) New to Final Cut Pro 4 users are two ways of cus-tomizing the interface: definable keyboard shortcuts and the button list. Final Cut Pro has always had key-board shortcuts, but they were fixed. You can now cus-tomize these keyboard shortcut keys to be whatever you like. In the Tools > Keyboard Layout window, you can assign any task (like setting an In point or placing a marker) to be any key you want. Also, in Final Cut 3, you had two small buttons in the Timeline that let you turn linking on and off and toggle snapping. Those but-tons are now part of a new bar where you can add buttons for many kinds of actions. For example, you can add a button to this bar that will add a transition by going to Tools > Button List and selecting this operation from the menu list.

1. Select Tools > Keyboard Layout > Customize (Option+H) to bring up the default keyboard layout.

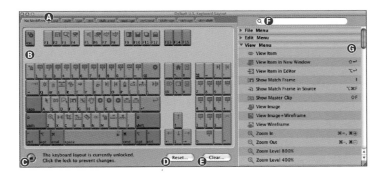

A **Modifier Keys:** Tabs to view the keyboard layout when using different modifier keys.

B **Keyboard:** Graphic representation of the keyboard with all of the tools and commands accessed by each key.

C **Lock:** Click to unlock the keyboard to allow customization.

D **Reset:** Click to reset the keyboard layout to defaults.

E **Clear:** Click to clear all shortcuts leaving a blank slate.

F **Search:** Enter search criteria to quickly find buttons.

G **Commands:** List of available commands with current keyboard shortcuts to the right.

2. Click the Lock button to unlock the layout.

3. Find the command you want to add in the list to the right—the commands are divided up into subcategories like View Menu and Modify Menu—click the command and do one of the following:

- Type the new shortcut you want to use.
- Drag the command to the key on the keyboard graphic that you want to define as the new shortcut key for that function. It will automatically be set for that new function.

The Button List offers a similar ability for shortcut commands, but uses graphic buttons on the Timeline instead of keyboard keys.

1. Choose Tools > Button List to bring up the Button List window.

2. Go through the list of menus to find the function you want to add (for example, you can add Batch Capture from the Capture menu. Drag the name or icon of the function to the Button List bar (right above the Timeline), and place it in the order you want it with the other buttons.

Now when you click on this button, Final Cut Pro will perform that action. To delete a button, click and drag it off the Button List bar. The button will disappear in a puff of smoke (literally).

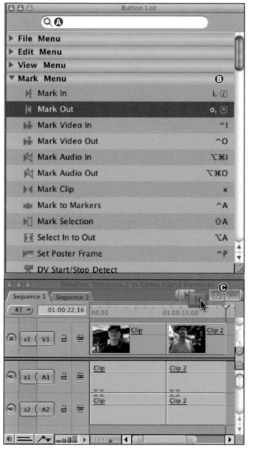

Ⓐ Search: Enter search criteria to quickly find buttons.

Ⓑ Commands: Click and drag command to add to its button to the button bar in the Timeline.

Ⓒ Button Bar: Add buttons from the button list for fast access to commands.

Using the Tools and the Audio Meter

The Tool Palette and the Audio Meter are two smaller windows worth a brief look. The Tool Palette will help you navigate through the Final Cut Pro environment, and the Audio Meter allows you to monitor your sound levels at a glance. The Tool Palette is a vertical bar where you can select tools to edit, group, cut, zoom, set keyframes, and crop. The Audio Meter acts a level meter, displaying the decibel level of the audio as your clips play.

1. Open or close the Tool Palette by selecting Window > Tools.

2. The toolbar allows you to select different virtual instruments for the variety of tasks you will perform while using Final Cut Pro. See Chapter 7 for a detailed description of these tools and the functions they can deliver.

Selection
Group Selection
Select Track
Edit
Item
Razor Blade
Zoom and Hand
Crop and Distort
Pen

3. In addition, each tool in the toolbar (except the selection tool) has sub-tools that you can access by clicking and holding the cursor on that tool for a few seconds. Each tool also has a simple single- or multiple-letter shortcut that you can press to access that tool instantly. All of these tools have "mirror" listings in the menu, but using the Tool Palette is the best and easiest way to access them.

Selection (A): The most used tool, this is a basic selection tool for clicking and dragging.

Edits Selection (G): Lets you select an edit point (the cut between clips) and opens the Trim Edit window for the selected edit point(s).

Group Selection (GG): Lets you select multiple clips at once.

Range Selections (GGG): Lets you select parts of clips not based on their In and Out points.

lect Track Forward (T): Selects everything on one track to the right of the cursor. An extremely useful tool.

Select Track Backward (TT): Selects everything on one track to the left of the cursor.

Select Track (TTT): Selects all clips on one track.

Select All Tracks Forward: Selects all clips on all tracks to the right of the cursor. Great for moving everything forward at an edit point to give yourself more room.

All Tracks Backward: Selects all clips on all tracks to the left of the cursor.

Roll Edit (R): Lets you perform a Roll edit (see Chapter 8).

Ripple Edit (RR): Lets you perform a Ripple edit (see Chapter 8).

Slip Item (S): Lets you perform a Slip edit (see Chapter 8).

Slide Item (SS): Lets you perform a Slide edit (see Chapter 8).

Time Remap (SSS): Let's you perform a change in the motion speed of the clip (see Chapter 15).

Razor Blade (B): Lets you cut a clip, creating two separate clips (see Chapter 8).

Razor Blade All (BB): Cuts everything in the Timeline at the spot of the cursor. Useful for making space for a new clip to be added in the middle of a sequence.

Zoom In (Z): Zooms in on the part of the Timeline you click on. Great for precise, frame-specific edits.

Zoom Out (ZZ): Zooms out of the part of the Timeline you click on, giving you a broader view of the sequence.

Hand (H): Used to move around in a magnified image in the Viewer or Canvas.

Scrub Video (HH): Lets you scrub through video in the Browser when the clips are in large icon view.

Crop (C): Lets you manually change the size of the video image in the Viewer or Canvas.

Distort (D): Lets you manually distort the video image.

Pen (P): Adds a keyframe (see Chapter 18).

Pen Delete (PP): Deletes a keyframe (see Chapter 18).

Pen Smooth (PPP): Smoothes a keyframe (see Chapter 18).

4. To open or close the Audio Meter, select Window > Audio Meter (Option+4). With the Audio Meter open, you can view the levels of whatever audio you play, with or without video. You should keep an eye on this meter to make sure that your audio is not distorted while editing. See Chapter 16 for information about working with audio.

FAQ Where Do I Put All of These Windows?

Dealing with the four main windows, plus the Tools window, the Audio Meter, and any other windows you may be working with can be an organizational nightmare. One solution, which we recommend highly, is to have a second monitor. If you don't have a second monitor, the following is a common and popular layout for all of this stuff: Set your Timeline to fill the entire bottom half to one-third of the screen. Set up your Viewer in the top-left third, the Canvas in the top-middle third, and the Browser in the top-right third of the screen.

Final Cut Pro comes with some preset window settings that can be accessed by selecting Window > Arrange. You can choose recommended setups based on whether you are doing more capturing, color correcting, or editing. You can then take these presets and tailor them to your own needs.

If you do have a second monitor, setting it up on a Mac is relatively simple. Most Macs have two monitor ports, and you can set the second monitor to either duplicate (where both monitors show the same image) or split

(where both monitors work together as one big monitor). To set your second monitor configuration, use the Monitors control panel. You can calibrate the monitors separately, which is useful if, for example, you are editing for television production. You can set one of the monitors to use the TV Gamma and preview your work there to get a better feeling for how it will look.

One recommended strategy with a second monitor is to use the split mode and keep your Browser in the second monitor so that you have a large space to view your many clips and bins. In your first monitor, have your Timeline take up the bottom half and split the top half between the Canvas and the Viewer, with the Viewer on the left and the Canvas on the right. This is especially useful if one monitor is smaller than the other—for instance, if you are using a PowerBook. Of course, you can set up the layout however you want, and you may want to try some different styles before settling on the one that is most comfortable.

The Tool Bench and QuickView

The Tool Bench holds different tabs: the QuickView tab; the Video Scopes tab; and the Audio Meter, Frame Viewer, and the Voice Over tab. The Video Scopes tab allows you to use color-correction tools such as the Waveform Monitor and the Vectorscope. The Voice Over tab allows you to record a voice-over directly into Final Cut Pro (see Chapter 16). The QuickView tab lets you quickly preview effects, especially complex effects such as densely composited video tracks or multilayered graphics, without having to wait to render them first. (This function does not render the clips, and you will eventually have to render them.) QuickView is simply a fast, efficient way of checking the look of your more complicated effects in motion. (As

discussed in Chapter 9, Final Cut Pro 4 now allows real-time display of many effects, such as Cross Dissolve, on sufficiently powerful G4 computers; use QuickView when you can't use these real-time effects.)

When you open the Tool Bench, you may not see all the tabs you want to use. To add tabs to the open Tool Bench, choose the tab you want from the Tools pull-down menu. In this example, we will be concentrating on the QuickView tab.

1. Select Tools > QuickView to bring up the Tool Bench with QuickView showing. Alternatively, you can select Windows > Tool Bench (Option+5) to open the Tool Bench, but the QuickView tab may not appear.

2. To use QuickView, simply click the Play button and whichever window is selected (Viewer or Canvas) will begin to play back for the number of seconds before and after the playhead as dictated by the range. You can change the resolution, view, or range

at anytime, and the clip will keep repeating over and over until you press the Play button again to stop it or close the window.

Ⓐ Resolution: This drop-down adjusts the resolution of the image you see in QuickView between Full (best Quality but slow playback), Half (medium quality), and Quarter (blocky but fast playback).

Ⓑ View: Selects which window QuickView displays the content of between None (blank), Auto (whichever window was last clicked on), Viewer, and Canvas.

Ⓒ Play: Starts and stops the clip playing.

Ⓓ Range: Sets the time in seconds around the selected window's playhead that QuickView will play back. For example, 4 secs will play the 4 seconds of footage immediately before and after the playhead, for a total of 8 seconds.

3. Examine the preview and then make changes in the Viewer or Timeline as needed. Changes you make are immediately reflected in QuickView. Once you are satisfied with your effects, you can close the QuickView window.

Remember that QuickView does not render effects in the clip. It is simply a viewing tool to help you make faster decisions about complex effects. You will eventually have to render the clips to be able to export them (see *Rendering Effects* in Chapter 8).

TIP The Audio Mixer

Final Cut Pro 4 users should be very happy that Apple has included a new, much needed feature in the latest version: the Audio Mixer. This window allows you to mix multiple tracks of audio at one time and also isolate or mute out certain tracks. To access the Audio Mixer, select Tools > Audio Mixer. For a more in depth look at this window and how you can use it to create a final mix for your soundtrack, see Chapter 16.

3 Creating Your Footage

Before you head to the editing room, you have a lot of important decisions to make that will save you time down the road. As many editors will tell you, how the footage is shot is a big factor in the edit; and if you think like an editor while planning your shoot, you'll end up with a much better, tighter final project and save yourself a lot of headaches! This chapter will address ways to organize footage *before* you bring it to Final Cut Pro, and how to think ahead when you are planning shots, labeling tapes, and keeping logs. If you are not involved in the shoot, you may want to discuss these issues with the director and production crew. It's best for the director to know any concerns you may have as an editor before shooting begins.

Overview

> *"The cinema is still very young and it would be completely ridiculous to not succeed in finding new things for it."*
>
> Orson Welles

Editing doesn't begin in the editing room. It begins long before the shoot itself, in preproduction. As locations for the shots are chosen and shots are storyboarded, the editor's task is being formed. When shooting begins, the raw material that will make up the editor's world is being created. However, in some situations, editors have no input on this stage of filmmaking, and their job begins when the raw footage is handed over. With this footage comes a set of camera logs and copious notes on how the footage should be put together. This chapter is mainly for people who will be shooting their own footage as well as editing it and will give helpful tips on how to shoot so that editing isn't an organizational nightmare. If you're not shooting the footage you'll be editing, you can learn what to communicate to the production crew to make sure you get what you need when it comes time to start cutting.

The decisions you make about the number of times you shoot a scene, from which angles you shoot, and how you record your audio will all deeply impact your editing in Final Cut Pro. Aside from technical concerns, it's important that you provide enough footage so that you won't be stuck in the editing room. It's a common practice to shoot a scene from multiple angles so that you can cut between different perspectives of continuous action. Also make sure that as you change angles, you keep the action relatively similar. This allows for *continuity*, which means that as you cut from one angle to another, the scene and action seem continuous. We've all noticed bad continuity in movies, where someone's cigarette keeps changing length or someone's wine glass becomes miraculously refilled when the angle changes. If you've got a big enough set, it's a good idea to have someone whose sole job is to make sure continuity is kept consistent. Taking Polaroid shots or digital photographs of the set can be a big help in remembering how things should be. Trying to cut around shots with poor continuity can be an editor's worst nightmare.

If you're shooting in North America, you'll most likely be shooting with the NTSC standard video, but you can choose to shoot with PAL, the standard in Europe and much of the rest of the world. As discussed in the Chapter 2 sidebar *What Are NTSC and PAL?,* the PAL system has the advantage of clearer definition, but this is helpful only if your final product is going to be on PAL or on a film blowup.

The most important thing is to be thinking ahead on set. If you can meet problems on the set instead of waiting until you're editing, you can save yourself a lot of time and headaches. Creating your footage with an editor's eye can make your project stand out and make the final result more impressive and professional.

LESSONS

Keeping a Camera Log

Although it's not completely necessary for editing footage, having a written or typed log of the shots taken on the set can be extremely helpful to the editor. This is especially true if you are working on a scripted narrative. Documentaries, especially those shot in a vérité style, will probably not have a shot-for-shot log, but more general notes.

Vérité is a French term for "truth" which has been co-opted into English filmmaking vernacular to mean non-fictional filmmaking, and implies a fly-on-the-wall, handheld camera aesthetic. It is similar to the American term "Direct Cinema" which was pioneered by documentarians like the Maysles Brothers in films like *Salesman* and *Grey Gardens*.

A log is a list of all shots contained in the unedited footage. Typically, a log is recorded by the second cameraperson and can include any number of notes about the shots. A log can be kept on paper, but it is becoming increasingly common on set to use a laptop, typing the information into a spreadsheet or word processing program. The completed log is then handed to the editor along with all of the tapes of footage. If the log is in a spreadsheet or word processing format, the editor can directly import the log into Final Cut Pro. The more precise and clear the log, the easier it will be for the editor to locate and access different shots. It's also helpful on the shoot to "slate" every take. A slate is a board, held in front of the camera before each take, that identifies the scene and take number, the name of the project, the director's name, and the cinematographer's name. By having a slate at the beginning of each shot, the editor can easily identify the footage on the screen, which helps keep things organized if there has been a mistake made in the camera log.

This section will show how to keep a log and will provide some samples of what one should look like. The most important elements to include in each log entry are the tape the footage is located on, the scene and take number of the shot, and a description of what happens. When you log and capture your footage, you can log individual takes to be separate clips in your bins. As we discussed in Chapter 2, the Browser maintains similar information about each clip as in the camera log. Your Browser offers many columns where you can record all sorts of information (see *Understanding the Browser* in Chapter 2). It's up to you which columns you want to use beyond the basics of reel number, timecode, and clip name. Once you are familiar with the kinds of information you can record in the Browser, you can easily transfer information from your camera log, and import or type in information (such as important comments) directly into your project's Browser in Final Cut Pro. In Chapter 4 we will begin logging clips into the program. Remember that if you are importing the log directly into Final Cut Pro, you will need to change the column names in your log to match the Browser columns exactly (Media Start, Media End, Shot/Take, Scene, etc.). Study the Browser columns and pick the ones you want to have filled in when you import the log.

To create a log sheet or file, you should create a form with a table layout. The following are suggested categories for the table's columns:

Tape or Reel #   This column will identify the tape or reel that is in the camera when the logged scene is being shot. You can devise whatever system you want for keeping your tapes organized as long as it is clear. Numbering is the simplest method, but you can also alphabetize or create a code that will help you keep the tapes straight. If dealing with footage you did not shoot, you will most likely be given tapes with precoded reel numbers, so use these as

these numbers will correspond to the camera log and be used for any later online editing sessions.

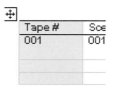

Scene   In this column, you will identify the scene that you are shooting. A scene is typically a single camera setup that will be taken a few times so that you have multiple versions of the same scene. If you are following a shooting script, most scenes will already be numbered in the script, and you should follow this numbering system. This way, the editor can follow the script and the scene numbers will match the numbers on the camera log. If you're shooting with multiple cameras, make sure you label the cameras to differentiate between them (for example, Camera A and Camera B).

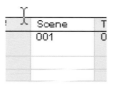

Take   This corresponds to the take number of a certain scene. A *take* is one uninterrupted recording of a scene. Typically, there will be many takes of the same scene so that the editor will have options of which to use, or will split up the best parts of different takes to create one scene for the final cut. Let's say you are shooting Scene 3. The first attempt at this scene is Take 1. The director may decide the light wasn't right or an actor's performance wasn't very good, so they will do the scene again. This would be Take 2.

This continues until the director is satisfied that the scene has been done correctly.

Take	TC
001	00

Media Start   Media Start records the *timecode* at the beginning of each take. The camera operator will relay this information to the person keeping the log at the beginning of each take. Timecode is kept is hours, minutes, seconds, and frames. A sample Media Start entry could be "00:23:14:04". This means that the take begins 23 minutes, 14 seconds, and 4 frames into the tape. If you are keeping a digital log, this information will imported into Final Cut Pro directly, and you won't have to search through the source tapes, as the clips are already delineated by their timecode.

TC Start	TC
00:00:00;00	00:

Media End   Media End is the timecode at the end of the take. Once again, the camera operator will communicate this information to the person keeping the log.

	TC End	Ap
00	00:00:00;00	f/16

Aperture   This area lets you note the measurement of how much light is being let into the camera. The more light let in, the brighter the image will be. The less light, the darker. The aperture measure-

ment on a DV camera is the same as movie cameras and still photography cameras and is measured in *f/stops*. The higher the f/stop, the less light is let in. A typical camera has an aperture range between f/2 and f/16. A camera operator may shoot different takes of the same scene at different f/stops so that it can be decided later which one looks the best. It is also helpful to record the f/stop in case the scene needs to be reshot. The camera operator will set the aperture on the camera and should communicate this information to the person keeping the log. To set the aperture correctly, use a reference monitor on the set to make sure the image is exactly as you want it. You can use the viewfinder on the camera to set the aperture, but using a monitor is always preferable. You can also use a light meter to get exact readings for a more sophisticated lighting design. Note that there is no column in the Browser for aperture, so if you are importing a log directly into Final Cut Pro, you'll want to leave this out.

	Aperture	De:
0	f/16	He
		mo

Description   This column should be used to describe the action in the scene. Unless something very different happens between different takes, you only need to write down a description once per scene.

e	Description	Co
	Hero approaches the motorcycle.	Ba

Comments   In this column, you can record any specific comments the director or the director of photography wants to record. Comments could be that the take had very good performances or that the boom mike was in the shot. These comments can help the editor determine that a particular take is unusable and should not be digitized at all, saving precious hard disk space, or the notes can help the editor sort through which takes to focus on when editing.

	Comments
	Bad angle.

Maintaining a Continuous Timecode

The most important job a camera operator has in making sure the footage is properly shot for use by an editor is to avoid any break in the timecode. On a DV tape, timecode is laid down as the tape records—it does not exist on the tape before shooting. On a tape that has been properly shot, the timecode should begin at 00:00:00:00 and progress until the end of the tape or until the tape is no longer being used. If the tape is shot all the way to the end, the final timecode should read about 01:05:00:00, meaning that one hour and five minutes of total footage has been shot (the average DV tape runs a little more than an hour). There should be no breaks at all if the tape is played from beginning to end. This is important because as the editor logs and captures the tape (see Chapter 4), the timecode needs to run straight without interruption or the process of batch capturing will not work smoothly.

How does timecode become broken? Broken timecode can occur when the seamless process of recording and pausing is interrupted. If the camera stops recording and is switched from Camera mode to VTR mode, the tape can be rewound or fast-forwarded. If the tape is fast-forwarded past the point where any image has been recorded and thus past the point where any timecode has been laid down, the tape will "break" the timecode; when it begins to record again, the timecode will default to 00:00:00:00 and progress from there.

To make sure that this does not occur, when you are preparing to record a shot, always check that there is readable timecode on the spot in the tape. If no timecode is available, rewind the tape until the camera can detect timecode on the tape. Some cameras provide an End Search button, which will automatically fast-forward to the end of the timecode.

You can also "black out" your tape first, which lays down a black image and timecode before you start shooting. Many decks will do this, and Final Cut Pro 4's Edit-to Tape function will also lay down black and timecode.

If you follow these tips and make sure that the timecode stays continuous, you will prevent a big hassle in the editing room as you try to log and capture your footage!

Shooting Video for Efficient Editing

Besides making sure that there are no time-code breaks, you have a number of other things to consider while shooting that will make the editing process go smoother. The following tips should come in handy and make the editor very grateful.

- If you're operating the camera, be sure to communicate all the pertinent information to the person who is logging: the time-code, the aperture, and any notes or comments that may help the editor in cutting the footage.

- Get familiar with your camera—find a good grip that is comfortable, practice zoom speeds and panning.

- Run the tape one to two minutes before shooting. This is called *prerolling*, and it makes sure that the tape stock being recorded on is top quality. Often, the stock at the very beginning and end of the tape is weaker because it has been handled to attach to the reels inside the tape. So it's always a good idea to roll off about a minute before you start shooting. In the same way, avoid shooting important material at the end of the tape. Remember that preroll will include timecode unless you fast-forward the tape instead of recording.

- Lay down Bars and Tone for the first minute of tape—many DV cameras have a built in Bars and Tone generator. This will also save you from recording footage on the first minute of tape, where there can be drop off, causing stuttering in the image.

- Make sure the boom (the pole that holds the microphone) and the boom shadow are out of frame! This can often ruin a great shot and keep an editor from using a great angle.

- Decide whether to shoot most DV tapes at SP or LP speed. SP will give you 60 minutes of tape and LP will give you 90 minutes of tape. Since the image is recorded digitally, either speed will have the same image quality, but you are more likely to experience a "digital hit" (a loss of information on the tape due to lost magnetic particles) in the LP mode.

- Leave padding at the beginning and end of every shot. When the director calls "cut" or an interview is over, don't immediately cut the camera off. Also make sure the director waits a moment before calling "cut," so you have room to really work with the scene. You can also often steal audio from the end of a scene if you're in a pinch. (See the sidebar *Recording and Using the Sound Tone*.) When the editor is logging and capturing the footage, it's very helpful to have at least a few seconds of padding to work with. Otherwise, heads and tails of scenes can get chopped off. Also, you can sometimes get good usable footage that the editor can use as a *cut-away* (a shot that isn't part of the main action but can be used as an accent or establishing shot) if you let the camera run a little after the scene is "over."

- Keep the aperture consistent. It's tempting to try to constantly readjust the aperture to find the best setting, but remember that the editor will be using all your takes, not just one, to construct the sequence. If you've shot a lot of footage at different apertures, it's going to be very difficult for the editor to make them match up when cross-cutting. If you're shooting with studio lights, establish exactly the setup you want before you start shooting. If you're shooting outdoors, try to keep the lighting as consistent as possible (i.e., wait for clouds to pass if you've been shooting in direct sunlight). You can also use reflectors to create a fill light if you're shooting in only natural light.

- After you've shot the main scene, shoot details, close-ups, and insert shots that could be used as cut-aways or B-Roll. (The main action of your scene is called *A-Roll*, and the other shots that can be cut into the A-Roll to make it more interesting or make it flow better are called *B-Roll*.) Often, an editor just needs a quick shot of something to make a transition or to smooth over the change between two angles that don't cut together well. If you provide an assortment of cut-away shots,

such as close-ups of hands, shots of the environment, or interesting abstract detail shots, the editor will have more options when trying to construct scenes.

TIP

Recording and Using Sound Tone

An editor often needs a piece of "silence" to blend two shots together or to fill in gaps in the audio created by piecing shots together. This ïthat is made up of the hums and murmurs when no intentional direct sound is being made. After you've shot in any location, whether it's a room with an air conditioner you can't turn off or a park with the wind rustling through the leaves, you should record at least one minute of this atmospheric audio. This is called *sound tone* or *room tone*, and will be used by the editor to keep the background noise in any given scene as consistent as possible. You should even record the sound tone in the camera log, so that it can be captured along with the rest of the clips. When you begin recording sound tone, have someone talk into the microphone, stating the beginning of tone, the length of tone, and the location.

Recording Audio on a Shoot

Audio is often the last thing people think about when they are preparing a shoot, but recording good audio is crucial to a successful video project. Your two main options are to record with the microphone on the camera (called *camera sound*) or use a more professional external microphone. If you are doing any type of professional shooting you will most likely want to use a microphone other than the internal one built into your camera. You can either plug an external microphone directly into your camera (see the *Using the Beechtek* sidebar if you only have mini audio inputs on your camera) or you can record sound separately using an audio recording device such as a DAT recorder. If you record sound separately, you will have to later synch up the sound since it is not recorded with the image on the DV tape.

Final Cut Pro offers a host of audio tools that you can use while editing. While it is always important to record the best audio you can on set, it's good to know what you can do in Final Cut Pro to fix problem audio. For example, if you're shooting an interview with someone and there is a hum from an air conditioner that you cannot shut off, you can use the graphic equalizer in the Audio Tools to remove as much of the hum as possible. Final Cut Pro can also remove a good deal of audio hiss, as well as microphone pops. Sets can be stressful places, and if there's nothing you can do about an audio problem while shooting, it's good to know that you can do something to help fix it when you get to the editing room. You'll learn more about working with Final Cut Pro's audio tools in Chapter 16.

TIP: Recording Separate Audio for Later Synching

Often, audio will be recorded on a separate format from the video like DAT (digital audio tape), and if you are shooting film, this will be a necessity. In this case, you'll have to bring in the audio separately from the video and then synch it up in Final Cut Pro. To prepare for synching, there are some things on set you should take into consideration.

Most importantly, you will need some kind of audio and visual mark to synch up picture and sound. The traditional slate or clapper is the best way to do this, although a handclap can be used in a pinch. This way, you can line up the visual of the slate clap with the sound of the slate on the audio.

It's a good idea to "back slate" shots too, which means you do a slate clap at the end of the take as well as the beginning.

On more professional shoots, you should get a slate that has a timecode display. This timecode will be played on the slate and will be visible in the shot. This method allows you to line up the timecode on the slate in your video image with the timecode recorded on the DAT. In this case, you'll need to make sure you can bring in the timecode from the DAT into Final Cut Pro—remember that using a media converter box like the Hollywood DV-Bridge won't read timecode so you'll need an analog capture card with device control.

You can also have the signal from the DAT fed into your DV camera with a mini or XLR cable. This will give you a good scratch track to cut with until you synch later with the clean DAT track.

Using an External Microphone

If you are shooting a project for broadcast or in any professional capacity, we recommend that you use external microphones. As stated above, you can either plug a microphone directly into your DV camera or record the sound completely independently with a device like a DAT recorder. Using an external microphone, you have much more control over what sound you are recording and where the microphone is placed. You can also get a very high quality external microphone that will be better than a less sophisticated internal camera mike. The two basic types of microphones are omnidirectional and unidirectional (also called a "shotgun" mike). Omnidirectional mikes pick up sound from all sides, so it's difficult to pick up the sound of a particular person over other noises or speech. Most internal camera microphones are omnidirectional. A unidirectional mike picks up sound only from the direction where the mike is pointed, so you can get clear audio from one person talking, even in a crowded, noisy room.

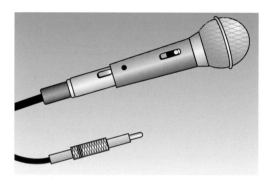

Using the Beechtek

A Beechtek sound device is a little black box that converts the professional-grade XLR microphone cable to a mini input, which is a standard input on most DV cameras. Most Beechteks have two XLR inputs, so you can plug in two microphones and use them to create a left and right stereo pair. The Beechtek has a ¼" screw head, similar to a tripod head, that screws into the bottom of the DV camera base. On the bottom of the Beechtek is a ¼" screw receptacle that will attach to most commercial tripods. Once you've attached the Beechtek to the bottom of the camera and plugged in the one or two XLR cables that connect your microphone, you need to plug it into the camera. The Beechtek will have a thin cord with a mini plug on the end that will plug directly into the audio input on your camera. You can set the audio input levels on the Beechtek itself by adjusting the volume knob on the back of the box, but you can also adjust levels normally in the camera. Consult your DV camera manual for information on how to set levels within the camera. Check levels over your headphones, and voila, your camera has been modified to accept professional-quality sound through XLR cables.

1. Plug the microphone into the camera. Most DV cameras have a mini input. While you can find microphones that plug into a mini input, most professional-grade microphones use the larger three-pronged XLR cord. To modify your DV camera for XLR input, you can use a Beechtek adapter, as described in the accompanying sidebar. Some high-end DV cameras (such as Sony's DSR-PD-150) have XLR inputs on the camera, so you can bypass the Beechtek and plug directly into the camera. This option will provide a better audio signal than using a Beechtek, as the sound does not have to downgrade. It will also allow you to shoot with mini-DVCAM, which, unlike regular mini-DV, keeps a link between the audio timecode and the video timecode.

2. DV cameras can record two separate tracks of audio as a stereo pair. You have the option to record one signal onto both tracks (mono) or record two different audio signals simultaneously. You can set this either with the Beechtek (see sidebar) or on the DV camera if your camera has XLR inputs. To record two different audio signals at the same time, you will need two microphones. If you are recording with only one microphone, you should record this one signal on both channels. Consult your camera or Beechtek manual to find out how to set the audio input to record one signal on both channels with your particular camera.

3. Once the microphone(s) are plugged in, check to make sure the signal is going through. Monitor the sound with headphones, and set the levels on your camera to a level that suits the loudness of the action you are recording. Consult your DV camera manual to adjust the levels. If you are recording two signals in stereo, you can adjust the levels of each signal individually. It is important to remember that in Final Cut Pro you will be able to separate the two stereo tracks, and you can adjust the levels separately then. You can also eliminate one of the stereo audio tracks in Final Cut Pro and double up the other audio track, so you are not locked into the stereo pair that you create while shooting. (See *Working with Stereo Pairs in Clips* in Chapter 7.)

4. Record a sample of the audio on tape and replay this section if you want to monitor how the sound will record on tape before you start shooting your footage.

Using the Camera Sound

If you don't have access to a microphone, or your shoot does not demand professional-quality sound input, you can use the camera sound, which is sound taken from the camera's built-in microphones. The quality of camera sound obviously depends on the model of camera you are using; the more high-end the camera, the better quality you will get. Most DV cameras record 16-bit sound, which should be quite good—except for the limitations inherent in mounting the microphone on a camera and being stuck with an omnidirectional microphone. With camera sound, you will pick up everything that is going on. With an external microphone, you can use a shotgun mike to capture sound from a single direction; but the camera sound cannot isolate a single direction. If you are using camera sound, have your subject stand directly in front of the camera and as close to the camera as possible. Also, try to eliminate as much background hum and noise as possible: close doors, turn off air conditioning, and so on.

1. Set the levels of the audio recording into the camera by consulting your camera's instruction manual. To set the levels accurately, have your subject talk at the same level you will be recording them and watch the levels on your camera. You want the levels to range from mid to high, but you don't want them to "peak," which occurs when the levels reach the highest point on their scale. This causes distortion in the sound.

2. Check the levels by plugging headphones into the headphone jack and monitor the sound. If your camera can display the levels, watch them to make sure they do not peak.

3. Record a sample scene and play back the tape to check and see if the audio is recording correctly.

69 Minutes of Fame, DIY Documentary Filmmaking

Punk rock has always been about getting up on a stage and playing music passionately about whatever you feel passionately about. Even if you can't actually play music. Even if what you feel passionately about is hockey and beer. Even if you're 38 and live in the suburbs. *69 Minutes of Fame,* a documentary shot on digital video and edited on Final Cut Pro, follows the punk rock band Two Man Advantage on a ten-day concert tour through the dingy bars and venues the band frequents and beyond.

© Copyright 2001 Mark Foster. Courtesy of Handyman Productions

According to the documentary's creator, Mark Foster, "the narrative for the film came really from the guys in the end. I wanted to let them tell their own story. I know a lot of people have strict ideas on what a true invisible documentarian is. I'm not one of them. I guess what that means is that from the day I went on tour with them for ten days crammed into a Ford van with eight guys and me and my camera, I knew there would be no filmmaking mysteries hidden from these guys. To them, me and my cameras were like the Coke bottle in *The Gods Must Be Crazy*. 'What's this button do? What if I touch this? How much would I owe you if I poured this right here...'—like that."

Foster used a Canon XL1, a Canon Elura, and a Sony PD100A to shoot with, but there was no lighting, and it was a one-man operation. Shooting on the road, under varied and often dark lighting conditions, presented a lot of problems when Mark got his footage back to his computer to edit. "If footage just looked crappy I'd make it look intentional by using Adobe After Effects and DigiEffects CineLook filters over it. A lot of the coloring was in-camera on the XL1 with its awesome white-balance features." But there was only so much that could be done in camera and with filters. "There was such a glaring difference in footage between the Sony and the Canon, I ended up using Final Cut Pro's color-balance stuff and brightness contrast to get them at least in the same neighborhood of each other."

Final Cut Pro proved to be more than just a sophisticated color-correction tool for the production of *69 Minutes of Fame*. "I had all 50 hours of footage digitized and available to me whenever I had an idea. I have just under 500 gigs of FireWire drives, SCSI drives, and internal ATA drives all full of punk rock and suburbia and it amazes me every time I turn it all on and the computer recognizes all the drives and Final Cut Pro finds all the media." But it was not all smooth sailing, "believe me I love the program but it was an absolute nightmare in the beginning."

For a documentary about a band, audio quality is obviously an imperative, and that's where Mark ran into a few problems: "Audio synching has been a constant thorn that never seems to go away, but I'm to a point where I'm less adventurous with experimenting in order to fix it because if I lose anything now it's the possibility of a lot of work to re-back up projects and media. I guess I'm a little superstitious that way."

And Foster's next project? "I'm working on a feature-length script which I'm not sure I'll shoot on DV or film yet. It depends on how the tone of the story develops. But I have no fears about cutting it in Final Cut Pro. A feature will use much less media than a documentary. Hell, a feature can fit in my backpack!"

69 Minutes of Fame premiered on September 22, 2001, at the Pioneer Theater in New York. It has also played at the IFP (Independent Feature Project) Market at the Angelika Film Center in New York. You can see a trailer for *69 Minutes of Fame* at www.twomanadvantage.com.

4 Logging Your Footage

Before you can start editing with Final Cut Pro, you have to gather your footage into the computer. This is a two-part process: logging and capturing. At some point (unless all your footage is generated on the computer, as in 3D animation), you will hook a camera or deck to your computer, specify information about particular clips (logging), and then digitize the logged clip(s) to a hard drive (capturing). However, this isn't just a simple process of transferring data like transferring a file from one computer to another. You have many variables and factors to consider to ensure you're capturing the footage in the best possible way. The logging and capturing process is also a great opportunity to start getting to know your footage. This chapter shows how to start the process by logging your footage, and Chapter 5 shows you how to capture it. If you are impatient to jump right in or are already familiar with the process, and don't mind missing out on the details for now, skip ahead to *A Quick Guide to Logging and Capturing* at the end of Chapter 5.

Overview

> *"My log saw something that night."*
>
> The Log Lady
> *Twin Peaks*

This chapter focuses on the techniques of logging your footage and preparing for the capture process (Chapter 5). It is important to make the best decisions about what footage to capture, how to organize it, and how to ensure it is captured to provide you with the greatest quality and flexibility for editing. The first step, if you have the ability to control your camera or deck from your computer (through device control), is logging your footage.

Alternatively, if your camera or deck does not have device control, as with analog cameras, you can still capture footage. However, you will only be able to capture one clip at a time and it will not have the camera's timecode reference. This will usually be the case if you are using consumer-grade VHS with a capture card or DV media converter. Without device control you will not need to log your footage, and you can skip ahead to *Capture Now: Capturing Clips on the Fly* in Chapter 5.

With digital video, Final Cut Pro has the built-in ability to log clips, allowing you to go through your tapes (the raw footage) and set In and Out points to define what footage will be captured from the tape(s) and which will be left behind. An alternative way to log your clips is to import the camera log (Chapter 3) as a batch capture list. You'll learn how to do that at the end of this chapter.

In Final Cut Pro logging is the process of going through your raw footage, and classifying and organizing that footage into separate clips that you will use to construct your final edit. While you are logging your clips, you will be assigning names to clips, identifying each one's reel number (the code for the original source tape it came from), making notes about the clips, designating the timecode for the In and Out points of each clip, and then placing the logged clip into a project or a bin (folder) within a project. You can also set markers while logging, covered in the Using Markers with Log and Capture section below.

This is the first time you'll really be working with your footage in the editing process, so take advantage of it. While logging, you'll start to become familiar with the footage that you have, so take the time to watch the footage as you log it. Start making notes about what shots look good, what visual ideas come to you, and what sort of editing structures might work well with the footage. Before and even after you've logged your footage, it's a good idea to go back and watch it a few times (depending on how much raw footage you have, of course; don't kill yourself) so that you know the footage inside out.

You'll find this to be extremely helpful later when you are editing and discover that you need a very particular shot. The more familiar with your footage you are, the less time you'll have to spend hunting for a shot or wondering if you have the shot at all.

You can also import a log list directly from a word processor or spreadsheet file. As mentioned in Chapter 3, more and more often on sets, an assistant cameraperson enters the camera log directly onto a laptop spreadsheet program or word processor.

This file can then be used by Final Cut Pro as the batch capture list, which will extensively shorten the logging process. See the section *Creating and Importing Batch Capture Lists* at the end of the chapter.

The only drawback to this method is that it *doesn't* require you to go through all the raw footage. That sounds paradoxical—how could such an obvious timesaver be a drawback? Well, it's still a good idea to go through the footage, even if all the clips are automatically logged. Often, you will find a shot or two worth grabbing that weren't part of a proper take that you would miss if you let the batch capture list do all the work. The most important thing is to get to know your footage!

Keep in mind that it's important to take the time to organize your project, bins, tapes, and camera logs before you start logging. Especially if you have a lot of footage, keeping things straight can become a nightmare; it's best if you have everything set up before you dive in. You should make sure you've got enough hard disk space on the designated drive and that you have a folder for your project where all the media clips and project files will go. When you've got everything in place, you're ready to start logging.

Getting to Know the Log and Capture Window

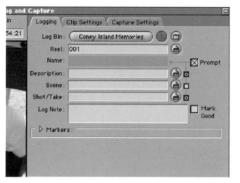

The Log and Capture window is a very powerful control console in Final Cut Pro. It is your control center for all logging and capturing functions. You can use it to log your footage quickly and then capture it to hard disk. Log and Capture plays media from your *source tape*, and this footage is not on your hard disk. Only the Canvas or the Viewer can play footage that is captured (i.e., on your hard disk). Let's open up the Log and Capture window and see what makes it tick.

1. To open the Log and Capture window, select File > Log and Capture (⌘+8).

2. The Log and Capture window is divided into two main areas. On the left are the monitor and playback controls that let you play the video on the source tape or deck. On the right are the controls, which are divided into three tabs: Logging, Clip Settings, and Capture Settings.

Ⓐ Monitor and Playback Controls: This is where you will view the footage from your source material and, with device control, play and shuttle through the footage.

Ⓑ Logging, Clip Settings, and Capture Settings Controls: This is where you set the parameters for logging and capturing, and control how you will capture your footage.

3. Like the Viewer and the Canvas windows (covered in Chapter 2), the Log and Capture monitor has VCR-like controls under its screen and the same timecode displays at top left and right. This is, of course, only useful if you have device control, and it cannot be used for analog capture unless you have a serial device.

Unlike the Viewer or Canvas windows, which play back a clip that is already a media file on the hard disk, the Log and Capture window plays back the source tape that is in the deck or camera hooked to the computer via FireWire.

Ⓐ Rewind: Shuttles the tape backward. You can also do this by hitting the J key.

Ⓑ Play In Point to Out Point: Plays a clip from the designated In point to the designated Out point. You can use this function to see exactly what will be digitized as a clip onto the hard disk.

Ⓒ Stop: Stops the tape from playing, fast-forwarding, or rewinding. You can use the K key to achieve the same effect.

Ⓓ Play: Plays the tape forward at normal speed. You can also do this by pressing the spacebar on the keypad.

Ⓔ Play around Current: Plays the footage starting before and ending after the current location on the tape. Use the Preferences options Preview Pre-roll and Preview Post-roll to set the time before and after that will play (see Chapter 2).

Ⓕ Fast Forward: Shuttles the tape forward. You can also do this by pressing the L key.

Ⓖ Shuttle Control: Allows you to use the mouse to play the footage backward or forward at various speeds.

Ⓗ Jog Control: Lets you move frame by frame forward or backward by clicking and dragging the slider.

4. If you do not have a camera or deck hooked up, or if your cables are loose, the controls will not appear in the window and you will see an error message—"Device Not Available"—in place of the controls. You will also see "No Communication" where you should see "VTR OK." If this happens when you should be getting device control (that is, when you are capturing over FireWire), check your connections and try to connect to the camera or deck again. You will need to close and reopen the Log and Capture window for it to register. If you are using a capture card with device control, make sure it is properly connected and restart the computer. If a tape is not loaded into the deck or camera, you will see "Not Threaded" to let you know.

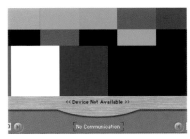

5. You can switch back and forth between different tabs by clicking the tab header. This will open that tab into the Log and Capture window.

Ⓐ Logging: Lets you enter information for each logged clip.

Ⓑ Clip Settings: Lets you change the settings that affect the clip being captured in Final Cut Pro, such as hue and saturation. As explained later in the chapter, these settings are manipulated as part of the capture process only with an analog capture card.

Ⓒ Capture Settings: Lets you control how and where the clip will be digitized.

FAQ How do I Set Timecode Values Using the Keyboard?

A crucial part of logging is setting the correct In and Out points. You do this by assigning timecode values that designate where the new clip should start and stop. As we've discussed, one method is to click the Mark In or Mark Out buttons or press the I or O keys to set the point at the currently displayed timecode value. You can also type the timecode in, and it doesn't matter if you're anywhere near that spot in your footage. For example, if you're at the beginning of a source tape you're logging, the current timecode will read 00:00:00:00. If you are using a paper camera log, and you know you want to log a shot that begins at 00:15:20:15 and ends at 00:15:40:12, you don't have to scrub to that part of the tape to set the In and Out points by clicking. You can simply type the values for the In and Out point within the In and Out timecode input boxes in the Log and Capture window. If you click in the input box, it highlights the timecode inside and you can type over this number to enter your new value. This option is helpful if you know an exact timecode you need to set (for example, from a camera log) or if you want to change a timecode setting by a few seconds or frames without manually rewinding or fast-forwarding the tape to that point.

You don't need to type the colons between the numbers, just type in the number as a string. For example, you would type in the timecode 00:15:20:15 as **00152015**.

To make things simpler, Final Cut Pro does not require that you type in the zeros that come before the first whole number. So, using this shortcut, you can type in the timecode 00:15:20:15 as **152015** and you'll achieve the same results. This method works with any timecode input.

FAQ Why Are the Video Settings Grayed Out in the Clip Settings Tab?

In the Log and Capture window's Clip Settings tab, the top half is devoted to "video settings." These settings let you alter the hue, saturation, or brightness of an analog clip as it is captured. This area will be grayed out if you are capturing over FireWire because FireWire is a straight transfer of digital information and will come into the computer correctly color balanced. Analog actually has to be converted to a digital signal, so the video may need to be calibrated to ensure accurate conversion. Remember that if you are capturing DV over FireWire you can later adjust hue, saturation, or brightness using Final Cut Pro filters after your footage has been captured.

TIP Keyboard Shortcuts in the Log and Capture Window

As in the Canvas and Viewer, you can also use keyboard shortcuts to move through your footage in the Log and Capture window (note that you won't move as quickly through this footage as you would with digitized footage):

Spacebar: Plays or pauses the clip.

Shift+Spacebar: Plays your sequence backward.

J: The rewind key. The more you tap it, the faster the playhead will rewind.

K: The pause key. You can also hold down the K key along with the J or L key, or use the left and right arrow keys, to move forward or back one frame at a time.

L: The fast-forward key. Once again, tapping it a few times will increase the fast-forward speed.

Using the Logging Tab

The Logging tab of the Log and Capture window lets you enter all the necessary information about an individual clip, including the name of the clip, a description, and other notes that help you make important decisions later about how to use this footage. You can review this information before you give the OK to log it into the computer. Before clicking the Log Clip button, which creates the actual clip in your project, you need to make sure you've defined an In and Out point and entered all the information you want recorded with the clip into the Logging tab.

1. The Log Bin field shows you which bin in your Browser (see Chapter 2) has been set as the logging bin. This bin is where all the clips you log will be filed. You can move your clips later to different bins in the Browser, but it is a good idea to go ahead and set your logging bin to the appropriate one to keep things organized. If you haven't made any sub-bins in the Browser, the clips will be placed in the top level bin of your project file. Remember that bins are folders in your project file that help you organize your clips.

The default logging bin is the top level of the project that is open or was last opened.

Ⓐ Log Bin Name: Opens the Log Bin in its own Browser window.

Ⓑ Up 1 Level: Moves the Log Bin up one level in the Browser.

Ⓒ Create New Bin: Creates a new Bin inside the current Log Bin and makes it the Log Bin (⌘+B).

2. You can also set the Log Bin in the Browser. Highlight the bin you want to set as the new Log Bin by clicking it once. Then select File **>** Set Logging Bin. A slate icon will appear beside the Log Bin. If you want to select the project itself to be the Log Bin, deselect all other bins and then set the logging bin. You can also CTRL-click the Browser and select "Set Log Bin".

Ⓐ Current Log Bin: Indicates that this bin is currently being used as the Log Bin.

3. The Reel input box is where you enter the number or name for the source tape from which you are pulling the clip. It is very important that you keep this naming system or code consistent, and make sure to change the Reel code if you switch tapes. This can prevent major problems later as you try to batch capture. The default is 001, but you can enter whatever you want or whatever reel naming system has been developed for your project for EDLs and later online sessions; it doesn't have to be a numerical value.

A **Increment Name:** Lets you increase, incrementally, the reel number or letter. For example, if the Reel is set at 001, clicking the slate button will change it to 002. If the Reel is 001a, the next increment will be 001b.

4. You can describe a particular clip several ways: Name, Description, Scene, and/or Shot/Take. Try to come up with something succinct, but descriptive. It's best with larger projects to come up with a coding system. For example, in our Coney Island documentary, we are logging Scene 1, Take 2 of our interview with Ivan, so we can name the clip "ivan_1_2." That name includes the Description, the Scene number, and the Take number.

Keep in mind that you'll probably want to organize your clips alphabetically or numerically, sorting by the first characters of the name you assign.

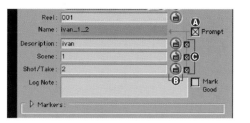

A **Prompt Box:** If this box is selected, you will be prompted when logging or capturing to enter a name for the clip.

B **Increment Buttons:** Lets you increase, incrementally, the numbers or letter used in the Description, Scene, and/or Shot/Take.

C **Use for Name:** When checked, the Description, Scene, and/or Shot/Take will be used to make the name automatically.

To save time typing, you can have Final Cut Pro construct the name for you automatically using the Description, Scene, and Shot/Take information you type in (separated by an underscore) by selecting the check box next to each. In fact, that's what we did to create the name "ivan_1_2."

5. In the Log Note input box you can add additional text, such as whether the clip is cut short or runs the full length, if the lighting was bad, if anything went wrong, if the take is very good, and so on. You can also use the Mark Good check box to indicate clips you intend to use.

A **Mark Good:** Use this to indicate that you liked this clip for whatever reason.

Logging Hints

Your style of logging depends on your own organizational needs and the type of footage you are bringing in. Here are some general guidelines to logging footage effectively.

- Make the decision whether you want to take in a lot of small and precise individual clips or whether you want to take in longer clips that you can comb through or subdivide later. On a documentary, it's often a good idea to take in B-roll clips individually with specific names as to what is happening in the shot. If you take in a long clip (or the entire tape in one clip), you can use the DV Start/Stop Detection function to mark each stop of the camera (see Chapter 5)

- Create bins to house specific types of footage. You can make bins in your project tab in the Browser to house footage that relates to a certain scene or that contains imagery of a particular place. For example, you may want to make separate bins for interviews, the B-roll, city skyline footage, etc. Press ⌘+B to create a new bin. You can type in any name you want after creating a bin.

- Make sure you always have entered the right reel number! This is crucial, as you may need to recapture the media at some point, and without the correct reel number logged, you won't know which tape to put in the deck.

Using Markers with Log and Capture

In addition to the other logging information, you can also set markers for a clip. Markers are helpful tools to make frame-specific marks and notes. This function in the Logging and Capturing window lets you mark parts within the clip to identify specific moments. For example, you may want to mark when a plane flies over and ruins the

sound, when a new actor enters the room, or when the camera zooms and changes the framing. You can, of course, add markers in the Viewer or the Timeline later when the footage is captured, but it is often helpful while logging to go ahead and mark the clips.

1. Set your footage at the frame you want to designate as the In point for your marker. Open the Markers window by clicking the arrow to the left of the Markers title.

Ⓐ **Open:** Click this to open the marker.

2. Click the Mark In button. This step puts a marker in your footage at the present location of the playhead.

Ⓐ Mark In Button

Ⓑ Mark Out Button

Ⓒ Marker Name

Ⓓ Marker List

3. Fast-forward through the footage to where you want the marked section to end and click the Set Marker Out button. You can now enter the name you want to identify this marker in the Marker text window. This name should indicate what you are marking, like "Bob enters room."

4. Now that you've set the In and Out points for the marker, and have given your marker a name, click Set Marker. Your markers, along with the timecode references of each marker's In and Out points, will appear as a list in the window below the marker controls.

5. If you want to change a marker in your list, click the marker, make the changes by typing in the new information, and click the Update button.

Adjusting Your Clip Settings

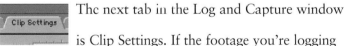

The next tab in the Log and Capture window is Clip Settings. If the footage you're logging is from an analog source, you can use these settings to make adjustments to the image that will affect how it is captured, as well as monitor and change the levels of the audio and calibrate the video image. The changes you make here will affect how the capture card converts the

audio/video signals to digital data. (Again, digital video transfers directly over the FireWire cable without conversion, so there is no need to make changes in the picture quality. As discussed in Chapter 11, Final Cut Pro provides a variety of tools for color correction and other image control tasks.) Capture cards usually have their own default settings for hue, saturation, brightness, and other values.

The top of this tab, which has the controls for hue, saturation, brightness, and contrast, should be used in conjunction with the Waveform Monitor and Vectorscope (accessible through the button at the bottom), which are standard tools for calibrating video signals. Relatively few Final Cut Pro users ever need to work with these tools, and Final Cut Pro 3 users will have access to sophisticated Video Scopes correction tools in the Tool Bench after capture.

1. Play through a representative section of the footage and watch the levels in the Clip Settings tab. Determine whether you need to increase or decrease the gain. The higher the gain, the louder the clip will be.

Ⓐ Audio Meters

Ⓑ Gain Scrub Bar

2. Adjust the gain by either dragging the scrub bar or typing in a new value in the box to the right of the scrub bar until you're satisfied with your levels. The higher the value in the gain window,

the louder the audio will be. You normally want the levels to peak around –12dB and not go above –3dB on the Audio Meter. Distortion can begin at around –3dB. If you want to monitor the audio with the built-in Audio Meter, choose Window > Audio Meters (Option+4). This will bring up the Audio Meter with a dB scale. It's best to leave the Gain at the 100 default unless you have real problems with the audio volume.

3. You can also set how you want to capture audio. In the Capture pop-up menu, you have the option of choosing Audio Only, Video Only, or Aud+Vid. You might choose the Video Only option if you are capturing footage transferred from film, which therefore doesn't have any audio on it. This method saves you the task of deleting a lot of empty audio clips.

When you are using a source such as a DAT tape—you can hook a DAT player's RCA outputs through an analog-to-digital media converter box (see Chapter 1)—or just want to capture the audio (such as a song) from your DV footage, you should use the Audio Only setting. If you are using a DAT tape captured through a capture card, remember that unlike DV audio, which is sampled at 48KHz, DAT audio can be recorded at different sampling rates, but 48KHz is recommended for editing in Final Cut Pro with DV footage. You'll need to change the Audio setting in your Sequence Settings to reflect this.

4. You can also choose how the different channels of audio will be brought in using the Audio Format pop-up window. Your options are:

Channel 1: Digitizes only the information contained in Channel 1 of your audio source.

Channel 2: Digitizes only the information contained in Channel 2 of your audio source.

Channel 1+2: Digitizes both Channel 1 and Channel 2, but it will not connect them as a stereo pair.

Stereo: Takes in both Channel 1 and Channel 2 as a stereo pair. We recommend this option for capturing DV footage. Remember that you can later break the stereo pairing if you want to separate the tracks.

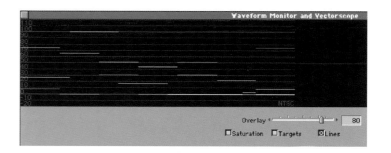

5. Finally, there are the Waveform Monitor and Vectorscope. These highly technical tools are only used when capturing analog video through a capture card. You can use the Waveform Monitor and Vectorscope to make sure that the digital file created in Final Cut Pro will best match the color and contrast signal of the original video.

Setting In and Out Points

A clip is defined by two timecode values: The *In point* and the *Out point*. You will define multiple clips on your source material, which you will later capture to use in Final Cut Pro to create your film. The Log and Capture window is designed to help you set In and Out points by providing additional timecode indicators and buttons tailored for the job. Note that to set In and Out points on source media from Final Cut Pro, the analog deck must be device-controllable (either through the FireWire cable or a GeeThree serial port), and device control must be enabled for the device in the Audio/Video Settings window as discussed in Chapter 2. You should also set preroll and postroll time values in Edit > Preferences > General. If you don't have device control, you'll need to skip this step and go directly to the *Capture Now* section of Chapter 5.

1. Set the tape to exactly the frame you want to designate as the In point using the Log and Play back controls.

This point will be the very beginning of the clip you want to digitize. Now, to set the In point, click the Mark In button (or press I).

The timecode value in the window will reflect the current position of the tape. Remember, this is the footage you'll have available when it comes time to make your final film, so it doesn't hurt to capture a little extra as long as there is room on your hard drive.

Ⓐ Go to In Point   Ⓑ Mark In   Ⓒ In Timecode

2. Now play through the tape until you get to the frame you want to be your Out point. This frame should be the last frame you want digitized onto the computer. Now, to set the Out point, click the Mark Out button in the Capture window (or press O).

The timecode value in the window will reflect the current position of the tape. Again, don't cut your Out point too close to the frame where you expect to end the scene.

Ⓐ Go to Out Point   Ⓑ Mark Out   Ⓒ Out Timecode

3. You have now set the In and Out points for this clip. This means you have given Final Cut Pro enough information to define the parameters of the clip and you can now log the clip into a Final Cut Pro project.

Logging Your Clip for Batch Capture

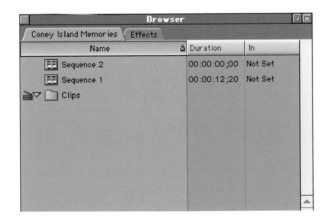

Once you have set your In and Out points and entered your reel number (along with any other information you want to include, such as the Name, Scene, and Take), you're ready to actually log the clip and create an offline media file in your project for batch capture later. If you just want to capture a single clip, you can skip ahead to Chapter 5.

1. Make sure you've got the proper In and Out points set by checking the In and Out timecode windows under the monitor. Check to make sure the Reel is entered correctly and that you've got the right tape in the deck.

Check that you've set a logging bin, and that it is the desired bin.

2. After you have entered all the information properly, click the Log Clip button (or press F2). It's that easy. If you want to just log and capture one clip very quickly, see *A Quick Guide to Logging and Capturing* in Chapter 5.

3. You should now have a new clip (offline) in the designated logging bin—designated offline by a red slash through the clip icon. You can repeat this process to log as many clips as you want and then batch-capture them later (see *Capture Batch: Capturing Multiple Clips* in Chapter 5).

It is important to remember that logging a clip does not digitize it, so it is not saved on your computer yet. (To remind you of this important difference, Final Cut Pro displays any offline clip with a slash through its icon.) What you have done is created a reference in the computer for a specific clip, and later, when you capture it, Final Cut Pro will use the information in the clip log to find the video on the source tape and then capture it (see Chapter 5).

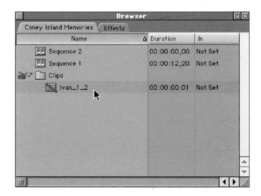

Creating and Importing Batch Capture Lists

Logging your footage in Final Cut Pro as we've just described is one commonly used method to prepare for capturing the clips you need for your edit, but it is not the only one. Another strategy is to create a *batch capture list* separately and import it into Final Cut Pro. In Chapter 3, we discussed keeping a camera log as you shoot to record information about each shot. If it is formatted correctly, this log can be imported directly into Final Cut Pro, automatically creating entries in the logging bin for the listed clips as shown here. You'll then be ready to capture your footage from the source tape.

Final Cut Pro can recognize a list written in most spreadsheets or word processors. It's most important that you pay close attention to the formatting, so that there is no problem importing the file into Final Cut Pro.

Specifically, you need to use tabs to separate each entry into your batch capture list. Final Cut Pro will be looking for properly formatted lists to create logged clips within your project.

1. Open a new document in a word processor, text editor, or spreadsheet. If you are using a word processor (or really any program that can create text files with tab-delimiters), create a table with the number of columns you will need to input all of your data. If your software can't create an actual table, use tabs to delineate the columns and the Return key to delineate rows. The first row needs to contain titles for all of the columns you want to include. These must exactly match the field entries available in the Browser, so you should take out any columns that don't have a Browser column (such as aperture listings) and change all column heads to read the same as the Browser's column heads (such as Media Start and Media End—which are the fields that should contain the timecode beginnings and endings of each shot).

Reel	Scene	Shot/Take	Media Start	Media End	Description	Comm
001	1	1	00:01:00;0	00:02:34;1	Woman walks across the street	Boom

BatchList.doc

2. Now enter your information in the table or spreadsheet data cells. Fill in the rows with all the information you have. If you have a laptop computer, you can do this directly on the set as the shots are taken; otherwise, you can copy it later from a handwritten camera log. Once your list is complete, save it (⌘+S). Give this file a name that will distinguish it from other batch capture lists, such as `ProjectA_CaptureList`.

3. In Final Cut Pro, create a new bin (see Chapter 2) and set it to be the logging bin. The logging bin will house the logged clips that you will import from the batch capture list. Open the bin by double-clicking it.

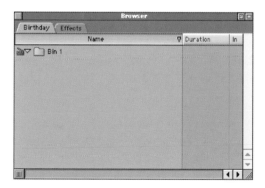

4. Now select File > Import > Batch List at 29.97fps (29.97fps refers to NTSC video's frame rate of 29.97 frames per second). This brings up the Import File dialog box.). Choose the file you saved from Step 2. You must have the Browser be the active window for this option to be available.

5. The logged clips, all offline, should appear in your bin. You can now capture these clips, either individually or in batches. We'll do that in Chapter 5.

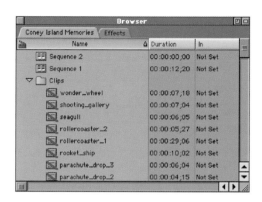

When Should I Use a Batch Capture List?

Batch capturing is especially helpful if you are on a tight deadline and do not have time to go through the footage shot by shot, logging each take individually. As an editor, keep in mind that if you do use a batch capture list, you'll lose out on watching the footage all the way through during the logging process, so you'll need to review once it is digitized. You can also watch the footage play while the computer is capturing the footage. We highly recommend you do this as problems can occur during capture (freezing, dropped frames, etc.) and also to make sure that the clips captured are the right ones—a typographical error in the logging process can cause the completely wrong footage to be digitized.

5 Capturing and Importing Your Footage

After logging your footage, you now need to capture it to your hard drive. *Capturing* is the process by which Final Cut Pro reads the footage from your source deck and transforms this video signal into a digital media file. After you have captured a clip, you're ready to use it in Final Cut Pro. Capturing is not simply a matter of letting the footage play while the computer reads it. You will need to set your capture settings for the particular footage you have filmed in order to make sure that it maintains the highest quality possible while being captured. This chapter will also look at how to import media that is already a file, like QuickTime movies and AIFF files.

Alternately, if you already have video files on your computer that you will be editing with, you can bring them into Final Cut Pro. For example, you may have existing video footage, sound files from CS, or even images generated in 3-D software or image editing software. These files can be imported into Final Cut Pro for use. Whether captured or imported, though, once the files are in Final Cut Pro, they will all behave the same way.

Overview

> *"In terms of other media such as the printed page, film has the power to store and convey a great deal of information. In an instant it presents a scene of landscape with figures that would require several pages of prose to describe. In the next instant it repeats, and can go on repeating, this detailed information."*
>
> Marshall McLuhan
> *Understanding Media*

We've reached the final step in bringing your footage from the source tape to your computer's hard disk. We started the process in Chapter 4 by carefully logging the footage: setting In and Out points, adding names and notes, and marking the pros and cons of particular clips. Now that the setup is done, we are ready to finish the procedure by capturing these clips.

As we did with logging, we will be using the Log and Capture window in this chapter as well (see *Getting to Know the Log and Capture Window* in Chapter 4). For capturing, however, we will focus on the three buttons in the lower-right corner of the screen. The clips you have logged are permanently saved as representative clips in your project tab in the Browser. The actual media files that your clip refers to will be saved on a hard drive in the location determined by your settings for the default scratch disk.

You have three ways to capture your footage from the source tape:

Capture Now　This option is typically used when a source deck does not allow device control (that is, you cannot run the deck from your computer; to play the source tape you must use the controls on the camera or deck). This is usually the case if you are capturing from a VHS player.

Without device control there is no readable timecode on the footage, so Final Cut Pro will create its own timecode starting with 00:00:00:00 at the beginning of the clip. If device control is available, you can use Capture Now to retain the source tape's timecode as a reference to the original timecode. This is helpful if you lose the media and have to recapture.

Capture Clip　This option will capture whatever clip you have just set In and Out points for in the source footage and is useful if you have to return to the source material to find a few clips to fill in the blanks of the current project.

Capture Batch　This is the most common way to capture clips. It takes multiple clips that have been logged and captures them to the hard disk. You can select as many clips to batch-capture as you want. If these clips are on different source tapes, Final Cut Pro will prompt you to enter the correct tape for each one by giving you the reel number or code. You can also import a batch capture log from a compatible spreadsheet or word processor. In Chapter 3, we discussed keeping a camera log, and in this chapter we'll show how to import this text log into Final Cut Pro so that it can use this information to batch-capture all the clips in your footage automatically.

We'll also look at using OfflineRT, a feature available to Final Cut Pro 4 users that allows you to capture footage at a much lower quality, saving precious disk space and generally speeding up the editing operations. This kind of editing is called "offline" because the final footage remains uncaptured, but it is very helpful if disk space is low or you are editing on the road.

Throughout the course of a project, you may use all of these methods for different reasons. You'll see the differences between them and learn which one will work best in a given situation as you review this chapter.

A video deck or camera connected via FireWire or capture card is not the only possible source of footage for Final Cut Pro. You may receive clips via CD or DVD, via your local network (where another FCP user may have already captured the footage), or via the Internet. The last section of the chapter shows how to import files that don't need to be captured.

To keep the difference between capturing and importing straight, think about it this way: You *capture* footage that exists on a piece of media stock (outside of the computer). This can be a Mini-DV tape, a VHS tape, a Beta-SP tape, or other sources. You need to capture it because it does not yet exist as a file on your computer. You *import* footage that is already a digital file, but isn't a part of your project file within Final Cut Pro. So you can import a JPEG image, a Photoshop file, or any QuickTime or Final Cut Pro media file. Importing simply adds that file as a clip into your Final Cut Pro project.

Creating Your Capture Settings

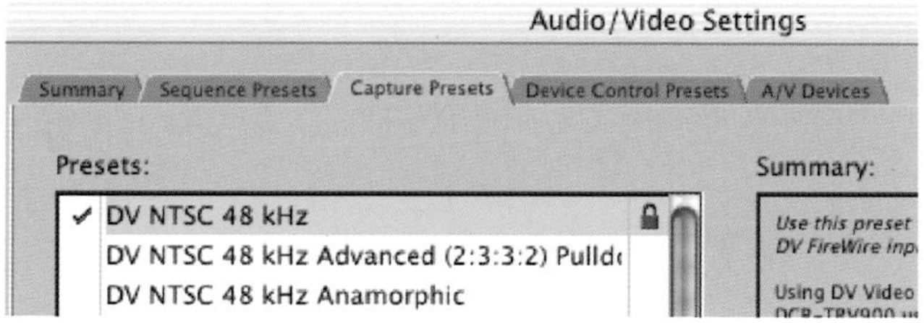

Audio/Video Settings

Summary | Sequence Presets | Capture Presets | Device Control Presets | A/V Devices

Presets: Summary:

✓ DV NTSC 48 kHz   Use this preset
  DV NTSC 48 kHz Advanced (2:3:3:2) Pulld   DV FireWire inp
  DV NTSC 48 kHz Anamorphic   Using DV Video
                                         DCR-TRV900 w

When capturing a clip, Final Cut Pro needs to know certain information about the frame size, audio settings, and video settings. One way to keep these settings consistent between clips is to create a Capture Settings preset, which is a list of all of the attributes that you have set up and saved. It's very important to make sure your preset is tailored to your hardware and software configuration, particularly the video hardware that your source media is coming from. You may need to set up several different presets if your clips will come from different hardware sources or to meet the needs of different projects.

1. To open the Audio/Video Settings window discussed in Chapter 2, select Final Cut Pro > Audio/Video Settings or press Option+⌘+Q. Click the tab for the Capture Presets window.

2. On the left of the tab is a list of all the saved presets that you can choose from. A check mark appears next to the preset that is currently active; this also appears in the Summary tab. A lock appears next to any presets that cannot be directly changed. (However, you can still copy one of these presets, make your changes to the duplicate, and save that under a different name.) The Capture Presets window lets you choose between the built-in capture presets, and also lets you edit them to customize a preset to your needs.

When you click on a preset in the Presets list, a detailed description of its settings will appear in the Summary window.

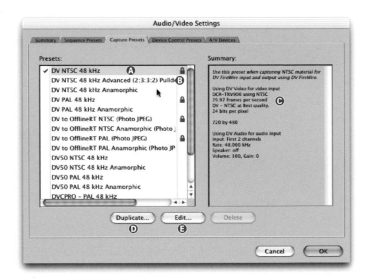

A **Presets List:** There are many built-in presets and a generic Capture Template you can use to build your own preset. Final Cut Pro 4 users can select OfflineRT here (see *Using OfflineRT* later in this chapter).

B **Preset Lock:** Presets can be locked to protect them from being inadvertently deleted or changed. If you try to change a locked preset, you will instead be asked to create a new preset that starts with all of the attributes of the locked preset but must be saved with a different name.

C **Summary:** Shows you the current attributes of the selected preset.

D **Duplicate:** Creates a copy of the currently selected preset.

E **Edit:** Allows you to change the attributes of the unlocked presets or creates a copy of a locked preset and allows you to edit it.

3. By double-clicking on a preset or selecting a preset and then clicking either Duplicate or Edit, you will bring up the Capture Preset Editor with a copy of the preset you selected. Here you can make changes to the various capture attributes. When you are finished making changes, click OK to save the changes and close this window.

A **Name** and **Description:** Use these fields to give the preset a name and description that will help you remember what it is.

B **Frame Size:** Sets the aspect ratio and frame size for the clips that will be captured. 720 × 480 is the standard DV-NTSC video setting. 720 × 486 CCIR 601 NTSC (40:27) is the standard for analog capture. The Anamorphic setting is for special footage shot to be viewed at a 16:9 ratio. If you aren't using this kind of footage, Anamorphic should be unchecked.

C **Digitizer:** Sets the interface over which you'll be capturing. If you're using a capture card, you can set this to reflect your installed card.

D **Input:** Select the input type of video you want to use. Many capture cards have different video inputs, like S-Video or Composite, so choose the one you are using.

E **Compressor:** If you are using FireWire and standard DV, choose DV-NTSC. If you are using an analog capture card, select the codec suggested for that card.

F **Quality:** Choose the quality you want the video to come in at if you are capturing footage other than DV over FireWire. Higher quality takes up more disk space.

G **FPS (frames per second):** If you are using NTSC, choose 29.97. If you are using PAL, choose 25.

H **QuickTime Audio Settings:** These settings contain information about the audio signal you are capturing from, such as the capture interface (e.g., DV Audio) and the sample rate (48.000 kHz is the DV standard sampling rate; 44kHz is the standard for analog and music CDs). In the Advanced settings, under the Sample menu, make sure Audio is set to Off While Recording or Off. Setting it to On can cause out-of-synch sound in analog and occasionally in DV captures.

4. To make a preset active, click to the left of the preset's name. This will put a check mark by that preset, designating it as active. To delete a preset, select the preset and click the Delete button. You cannot delete a locked preset or the default preset.

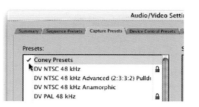

Adjusting Your Capture Settings

Before you capture your clips, you may need to review your capture settings. The easiest way to do this is from the Capture Settings tab in the Log and Capture window. This tab provides an at-a-glance summary of your current Device Control, Capture/Input, and Scratch Disk settings and allows you to switch between different presets.

1. If you do not already have it open, open the Log and Capture window (File > Log and Capture) and then select the Capture Settings tab.

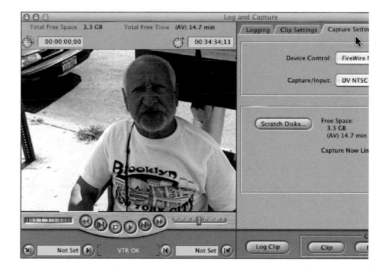

2. You can now make changes as desired to your capture settings. When you have everything just the way you like it, you are ready to capture your footage.

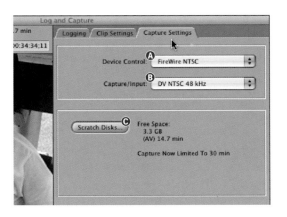

A Device Control: Here you can choose the type of device control, if any, you will be using for capture (i.e., FireWire NTSC). This tells Final Cut Pro what sort of connection it has to the source deck. If you set this for noncontrollable device, you can use Capture Now to capture footage from a deck that doesn't support device control.

B Capture/Input: Use this to select a preset that sets attributes to control how video is captured. See *Creating Your Capture Settings* earlier in this chapter. Final Cut Pro 4 users can select OfflineRT here (see *Using OfflineRT* later in this chapter).

C Scratch Disk: This button will open the Scratch Disk tab in the Preferences window (see *Setting Your User Preferences* in Chapter 2). Remember that you should select a disk other than the one containing the OS and FCP.

TIP
Capturing and the Preference Window

Before you capture your footage, it is a good idea to check three important preferences that directly affect the capture process. Two of these are set in Final Cut Pro's Preferences window, and the third is set in the Mac OS. To access the Preferences window, select Final Cut Pro > Preferences. The preferences that you should be aware of are on the General tab:

Abort Capture on Dropped Frames   If you have this option checked, Final Cut Pro will stop a capture session if it detects that a frame has been dropped coming through from the source tape. Dropped frames can cause synch problems, and other issues, so you should usually keep this checked. If you do experience dropped frames, it is probably because the hard disk is not transferring data quickly enough. Often, if you simply recapture, this problem will disappear. If it persists, it may be a fault with

your hard drive and you should check with the manufacturer. It also a good idea to "clean house" by periodically reformatting the drive.

Remember that experiencing dropped frames is different from *drop frame timecoding*. Dropping frames is a bad thing, as you are losing frames due to a problem. As discussed in Chapter 2, drop frame timecode is a normal type of timecode measurement that skips numbers to keep up with NTSC's 29.97 frame rate, but does not skip actual frames of video.

On Timecode Break   Here you can choose what will happen if there is a timecode break in the footage you are capturing. You can choose to have Final Cut Pro make a new clip at the point of the break, abort the capture, or to simply warn you of the break after capturing is complete. We recommend making a new clip as you will retain the footage already captured.

Capture Now: Capturing Clips on the Fly

Capturing Clip - NOW CAPTURING (press 'esc' to stop)
WARNING: Capture Now is limited to 30 min

Capture Now is most commonly used for non-DV clips that lack timecode and that come from source decks without the ability to use device control. Simply put, Capture Now will take whatever is being played in the Log and Capture window and create a clip out of it. It will start from the moment you press the Capture Now button (with a short delay) and end when you press the Esc key to stop capturing.

Without device control, you'll have to control the video deck manually, using its built-in controls.

With this capture method it is especially important to make sure you leave handles (extra footage) at the beginning and end of your clip since you aren't able to be frame-precise. The delay between clicking capture now and the actual capture process beginning can be as long as 15 seconds. This delay is based on the number of minutes you've limited Capture Now to in your Preferences Window. The key difference between this and the other capture options is that you cannot set the frame-specific In and Out points as shown in Chapter 4. Instead, In and Out points will be set when the computer begins and ends capturing. Another important difference is that the clip will be imported without timecode from the source tape.

1. If it is not already up, open the Log and Capture window by selecting File **>** Log and Capture. If the camera or deck you are using cannot be controlled by Final Cut Pro, make sure you've set the Device Control setting to Noncontrollable Device in the Capture Settings tab (see previous section). You will only be able to use the play controls on the deck or camera itself.

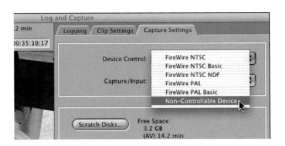

2. Enter in any logging information you want (Reel, Name, etc.) in the Logging Tab (see *Using the Logging Tab* in Chapter 4).

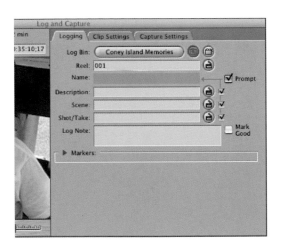

3. Start playing your footage. You will have to control the device from the deck itself, not through Final Cut Pro. You will probably want to play through the footage a few times to decide where to start and end the clip.

4. When you are near the section of video that you want to capture, click the Capture Now button (Shift+C). You typically want to do this about 10 seconds before the first frame you want to capture.

5. When you reach the end the footage you want to capture, wait a few seconds to give yourself some padding, then press Esc to stop the capture process and to create your clip. You can now stop your source tape.

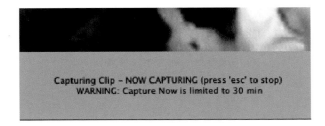

6. The clip will now appear in the logging bin in the Browser and will be saved to the scratch disk. Watch the clip to make sure you have all of the footage that you want.

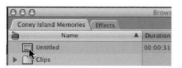

7. You've now successfully captured a clip from a source tape. Click on the name of the clip to rename it if you haven't already specified a name. If you were using a camera or deck without device control, Final Cut Pro will assign the clip a timecode that begins at 00:00:00:00 and runs through the length of the clip.

If you used device control, the timecode will be taken from the tape. You can now use the clip as you would any other, and start cutting with it in the Timeline.

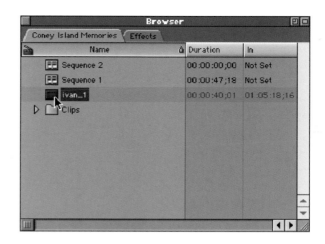

Capture Clip: Capturing One Clip

Capture Clip lets you capture one logged clip at a time. This is especially helpful if you just need to quickly capture one clip and don't want to bother batch capturing but want more precision in defining the clip than you can get using Capture Now. However, you must have a device-controllable source deck to use Capture Clip.

1. If it is not already up, open the Log and Capture window by selecting File **>** Log and Capture. On the Logging tab, enter the appropriate logging information (Reel, Name, etc.) in the Logging tab and mark the In and Out points for this single clip, as discussed in Chapter 4). Remember, you can quickly set In and Out points using the I and O keys.

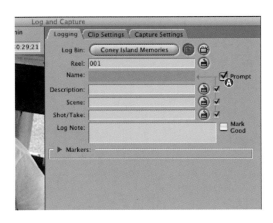

A **Prompt:** Check this if you want to be prompted for logging information while capturing a clip. This is the quick way to log and avoid filling out all the info, as it asks the bare essentials: Name, Description, and Mark Good.

2. Once you've entered all your logging information and set In and Out points for the clip you want to capture, click the Capture Clip button.

3. The Log Clip window will appear if you have selected the Prompt box in the Logging tab. Double-check the information in this window and click OK.

4. The tape will cue itself to a point right before the In point. Remember that you can set the number of seconds of preroll in the General tab of the Preference window. Then the tape will play through, and Final Cut Pro will begin capturing at the designated In point and stop at the designated Out point automatically.

5. Once this process is complete, you should now see your clip in the Browser with the name you gave it. You've now successfully captured a clip with the source tape timecode. You can use the clip in your project and start cutting with it in the Timeline.

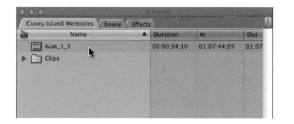

Batch Capture: Capturing Multiple Clips

In Chapter 4 we showed you how to log multiple clips for batch capturing. These clips contain all of the information you've entered about timecode, In and Out points, name, reel number, and so on, but they do not include the video itself yet.

If you click one of these clips to open it in the Viewer, a "Media Offline" message will appear, letting you know that these clips have yet to be captured, or that the video media cannot be found on the hard disk.

Batch capturing is the process of selecting a number of clips and having Final Cut Pro use the logged information to capture the video media and create usable clips for editing. Batch capturing is the most efficient and often-used method of capturing, as it allows you to capture a lot of clips at once, letting the computer find the clips on the source tape. If you are capturing clips that come from multiple source tapes, Final Cut Pro will prompt you to put in the correct tape by giving you the reel number that you assigned to the clip's tape when logging it (Chapter 4).

1. If it is not already up, open the Log and Capture window by selecting File **>** Log and Capture. Enter the appropriate logging information in the Logging Tab and mark the In and Out points for all of the clips you will be capturing (as discussed in Chapter 4).

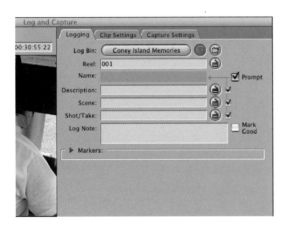

2. Now go back to the Browser (⌘+4), and you can see all of your offline clips. If you want to capture some but not all offline clips, you will need to select some or all of these clips to batch-capture. There are two ways to select:

Selecting clips with the mouse   You can select multiple clips or bins by Shift+clicking (to select a whole range of clips in the list or ⌘+clicking (to select multiple clips that are separated in the list).

Designate a logging bin   By designating a logging bin, you select all the clips in that bin (and any bins nested within it).

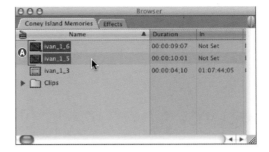

Ⓐ **Offline Clip Selected:** Three of the six offline clips have been selected for batch capturing.

3. Back in the Log and Capture window, select the Batch button or choose File **>** Batch Capture (⌘+H) to bring up the Batch Capture window. You can also Ctrl+click a selected clip to bring up the contextual menu and choose Batch Capture.

4. Look over this window to make sure all the settings are correct. The main option you need to be concerned with is Capture; this option determines which clips will be captured (Offline, All, or Selected).

Once you've made sure that all of these settings are correct for your batch capture session, click OK.

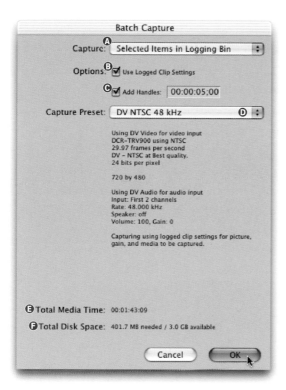

ⓓ Capture Preset: Here you can choose the capture preset that you want to use. The default listed here will be the same as the preset selected in the Audio/Video Settings window. See *Creating Your Capture Settings* for more information.

ⓔ Total Media Time: Shows you exactly how much media in total is being captured.

ⓕ Total Disk Space: Shows a ratio of how much space the footage will take once captured in relation to how much space is left on the scratch disk. If the space available seems wrong, check to make sure you've set the correct scratch disk.

5. You will be prompted to insert the reel that contains the clips. If you are capturing clips from multiple source tapes, you'll be given a list of all the reels needed, and you can select which one to capture from first by double-clicking the reel name or clicking Continue.

ⓐ Capture: Offers the following options:

Offline Items in Logging Bin: Selects all of the offline clips in the selected logging bin for batch capture. Offline clips are represented by a red slash through the clip icon.

All Items in Logging Bin: Sets all of the clips in the set logging bin for capture and will recapture clips that have already been captured overwriting the old clips.

Selected Items in Logging Bin: Captures only the clips that you have selected and highlighted that are in the logging bin.

ⓑ Use Logged Clip Settings: This option will make sure that each individual clip is captured according to the logging instruction unique to each clip. If this option is unchecked, all clips will be captured according to the Clip Preset tab.

ⓒ Add Handles: You can specify adding extra media at the beginning and end of every logged clip. Choose this option if you want to have a little more room to play with while cutting your footage.

6. Final Cut Pro will begin capturing each clip. The deck will cue itself to a point a few seconds before the first logged clip, and then progress through the tape until all the clips are captured. If you want to interrupt the batch capture process at any time, press the Esc key. Pressing Esc stops the capture session, and any remaining clips not yet captured will remain offline.

Ⓐ Clip Being Captured

Ⓑ Remaining Capture Time On Current Reel

7. Once Final Cut Pro has successfully captured all the clips on a reel, it will prompt you to select another reel. This will continue until all the reels have been selected, and all of the designated clips have been captured. When you are finished capturing clips from all of your reels, click Finished.

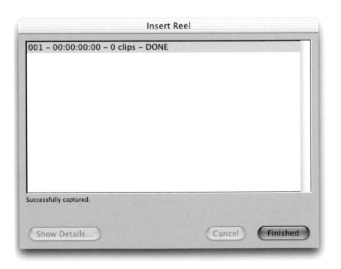

8. The red slash will be eliminated from all of your clips that were captured. This means that the media for these clips is now on your hard disk and the clips are now online. You can now start to use the clips in the Viewer and the Timeline as a part of your edit.

Now is a good time to sit and watch the clips while they are being captured. Go fix yourself a cup of coffee and take notes. This is a great chance to familiarize yourself with the footage without interruption. While watching the footage being captured, you're taking a step towards coming up with your editing strategy, visualizing a plan, and developing ideas for how all of this footage is going to come together.

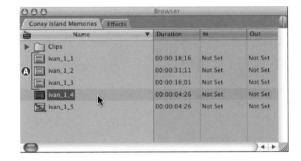

Ⓐ Three clips have been captured.

TIP

Capturing Analog Video

If you are capturing analog video over a capture card, you will need to adjust settings in the External Video tab in the Audio/Video Settings window. Select Final Cut Pro > Audio/Video Settings (or press Option+⌘+Q) to open the Audio/Video Settings window and select the External Video tab. Make sure that the "Mirror on Desktop" options for Playback and Recording are turned off. If you don't do this, FCP may drop frames during capture, and your video will stutter when it plays.

Understanding Final Cut Pro 4's DVCodec

Final Cut Pro 4 supports a number of DV codecs (codec is short for "compression-decompression" and is the way in which the video footage is digitally coded). The standard is DV-NTSC for DV video in North America, but Final Cut Pro 4 also offers default settings for a number of other codecs. If you are using footage shot on a Panasonic DVCPRO50, you can select this codec in your capture preferences. Final Cut Pro will now capture at this higher resolution codec.

Using OfflineRT

OfflineRT can be used to save an immense amount of footage on a limited amount of hard disk space by capturing the footage at a lower image quality. Since the footage is of lower quality, it takes up less disk space and is generally faster to load and work with, yet still includes the timecode for frame accuracy while making edits. Once you are satisfied with your edits and effects, the footage can then be recaptured at a higher quality, replacing the low-quality footage to create the final product, called an "online edit." See Chapter 19 for information on upgrading OfflineRT footage to online quality.

To configure your Final Cut Pro station for capturing with OfflineRT, you'll need to choose an offline setup.

1. Choose Final Cut Pro > Easy Setup (Ctrl+Q) to open the Easy Setup window, which allows you to change general settings.

2. In the Easy Setup window, choose OfflineRT NTSC or OfflineRT PAL, depending on the video system you are using, and then click Setup to configure your project for capture with OfflineRT.

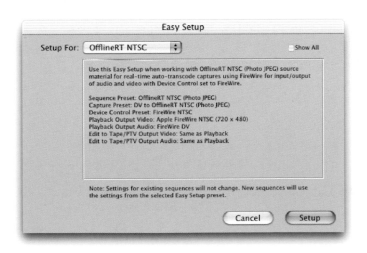

3. Now when you capture footage from a DV source or use an analog conversion method, the clips will be captured at "offline" quality. You are now ready to capture footage and edit.

4. After you have finalized your edits with the offline footage, you'll need to recapture your footage at a higher quality in order to create your final film.

FAQ How Does OfflineRT Work?

OfflineRT uses the QuickTime Photo-JPEG codec instead of the usual (and higher-quality) DV codec, allowing images to be massively compressed, although not nearly as crisp. Generally, you will be able to get 40 minutes of footage per 1GB of hard drive space compared with the usual 5 minutes per gig.

OfflineRT gets its name from the fact that the footage you will actually use to create the final film is still "offline." Using OfflineRT is extremely help-

ful if you are editing with a laptop on the road. You can edit the project offline with the typically small internal hard drive of the laptop and then recapture the footage later at higher quality when you have access to larger hard drives.

While you are editing with OfflineRT footage, you can still create high-quality graphics, import stills and titles, etc. When you upgrade the offline footage to online, your graphics and effects will remain the same.

Using DV Start/Stop Detection

Final Cut Pro offers a handy tool for logging your DV tapes called DV Start/Stop Detection. If you've shot on DV and are capturing via FireWire, you can take advantage of the DV Start/Stop Detection function to save you a lot of time by capturing an entire tape in one long clip. Final Cut Pro will then automatically split the clip up at every point the camera stopped and started while shooting, taking advantage of the digital cues embedded in the video.

If, for example, you are editing a narrative movie, the camera most likely was stopped and started only at

the beginning and end of individual takes, so these start/stop points provide an internal division that you can use to automatically create separate clips in Final Cut Pro. Using the DV Start/Stop Detection, you'll be able to instantly make clips based on when the camera started and stopped. To use DV Start/Stop Detection, follow these steps:

1. Capture the entire tape as one long clip using the Capture Now method. This saves you the time of going through and logging each clip one after the other.

2. Highlight the captured mega clip in your browser and select Mark > DV Start/Stop Detection. Markers will be automatically added at every point where the camera started and stopped.

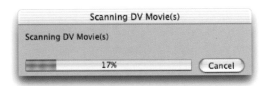

Be careful though, because inevitably some camera starts and stops are mistakes (quick flashes or when a forgetful cameraperson left the camera running or accidentally hit the record button). You'll need to make sure you weed out these unwanted bits from the marked selections you actually want to use! To do that, simply click on the subclip in the Browser and press the Delete key.

Importing Existing Media Files

Sometimes, you won't be pulling a clip from a video source at all. You may be taking a video file that has

been sent to you electronically, a QuickTime movie off the Web, a previously captured clip from another Final Cut Pro project, or importing a file that isn't technically a video file, like a still image JPEG file. In this case, you'll bypass logging and capturing altogether, and simply import the file into your project in Final Cut Pro. (This is how you will bring the footage that is included on the DVD with this book into a new project. See the book's *Introduction* for complete instructions.) Note that if the file you've imported is not a Final Cut Pro clip, you'll need to render it when you open it in the Timeline.

It's important to remember that importing a file completely eliminates the need for logging and capturing. *Logging and capturing* take a piece of source media (from a Mini-DV or VHS tape, for example) and transfer that media into a file on your hard disk. *Importing* is used for media that is already a file on your hard disk, like a Photoshop file or a QuickTime movie.

1. Move or copy the file you want to import to its target project folder *before* you import it. This isn't strictly necessary, but it is simply good organization to make sure all the media files pertaining to a project are housed in the same folder.

2. Double-click the bin you want to designate as the target bin so it opens as its own window. If you want the main project folder to be the target, select the project's tab.

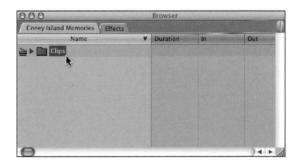

3. Select File **>** Import **>** Files (⌘+I) to open the Import dialog box.

4. Select the media file you want to import in the Import dialog box, and click Open.

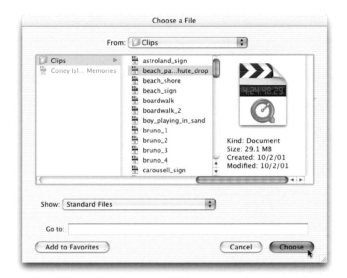

5. The file will appear as an online clip in your designated project and bin. However, this will not change the location of the file on your hard drive.

Importing Clips by Dragging Them into Final Cut Pro

A quick way to import clips is to simply drag them from your desktop into the Browser window. This will automatically create a clip of these files in the Browser bin you dragged them into. This is a great trick when you need to pull quick stills or CD tracks into your project file.

Alternative Steps: Importing a Folder of Files

You can also import an entire folder of material into your project rather than just a single media file. Someone may give you a disk with a folder of image files, or a few folders of video files organized by scene. In this case, you'll want to keep the files together when you bring them in as clips, and import them all at once instead of one at a time. Follow step 1 above and then do the following.

2. Select File > Import > Folder to let Final Cut Pro know you want to import an entire folder.

3. In the Import dialog box, select the folder of media files you want to import and click Select.

4. The folder will appear in the target project and bin. The folder will contain all of the clips readable by Final Cut Pro that were in the folder you imported.

Again, this will not move the clips into the project folder on the hard drive, so you may want to move or copy the folder there yourself before importing them.

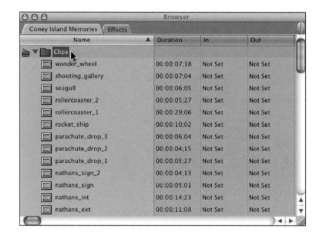

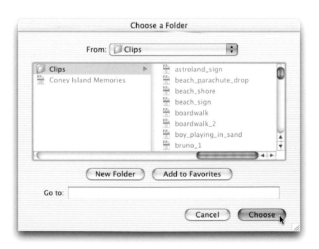

A Quick Guide to Logging and Capturing

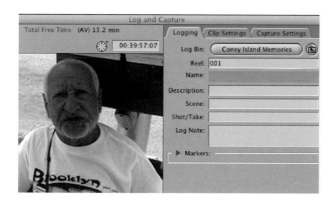

Chapter 4 and the first part of this chapter discussed several different logging and capturing scenarios in detail so that you will understand the process thoroughly. Most often, however, the process is much simpler than you've seen so far. In fact, if it really took this long to get a clip, we'd still be waiting for Hitchcock to finish his first movie. After you have reviewed these two chapters, you can use this quick guide to logging and capturing to help you go step-by-step through the process much more quickly.

1. Set your logging bin in the Browser.

2. Choose File **>** Log and Capture to bring up the Log and Capture window. Check the clip and capture settings tabs to make sure you've set the correct audio and video information, that you've selected the correct device control option, and that you've set the right scratch disk. Remember, if you're working with DV in NTSC format, the default settings are already configured for you in FCP in the DV-NTSC setup.

3. In the Logging tab, enter the name, description, scene, shot/take, and any notes, or click Prompt to have Final Cut Pro ask you for this information when a clip is logged or captured.

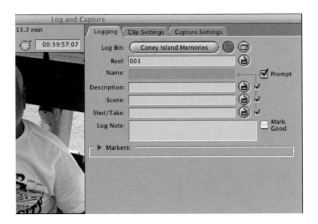

4. Using the play controls in the Log and Capture window, find the first frame of the footage you want to capture and click the Mark In button (or press **I**) to set this frame as your In point.

Now, play or fast-forward through the footage to the last frame of the footage you want to capture and click the Mark Out button (or press **O**) to set this frame as your Out point.

5. If you want to batch-capture multiple clips at the same time, click the Log Clip button (or press F2). Your clip will be logged (but not captured) and an offline clip icon (with a red slash through it) will appear in your Browser. To log additional clips, repeat Steps 3–5. Once you have logged all of the clips you want to capture, you are ready to batch-capture.

6. In the Capture box, click the Batch button and the Batch Capture window will appear. In the Batch Capture window, you can choose whether to capture all items in the logging bin (which will overwrite exiting captured clips), offline items (clips that aren't connected to any online media), or items you have selected. Check all of your settings and then click OK.

7. You'll see the Insert Reel window. Click the reel you want to capture first and insert that reel into your deck and click Continue.

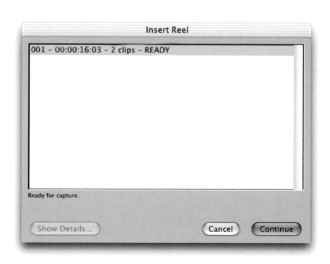

8. The Capture window will now appear, displaying the footage as it is being captured. Final Cut Pro automatically moves the tape to the In point and will capture the footage to the Out point. This will be repeated for each clip you have logged for capturing.

9. After all of the clips on a particular reel (tape) have been captured, you will either need to insert the next tape and continue capturing or click Finished.

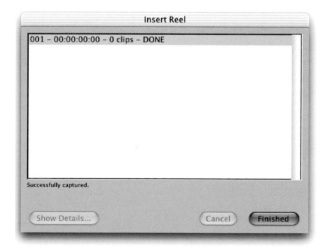

10. The captured clips will now appear in your Browser with the names you gave them. The red slashes indicating offline clips are gone, and you are ready to begin editing them (Chapter 6).

Alternative Steps: Using Capture Clip

Alternatively, you can just capture a single clip. Follow Steps 1–4 of *A Quick Guide to Logging and Capturing* and then pick up here.

5. To capture the clip you just set In and Out points for, click the Clip button in the Capture box.

6. If you set the Prompt option in Step 3, a window will appear, asking you to name the clip. Enter the name for this clip and a log note and click OK.

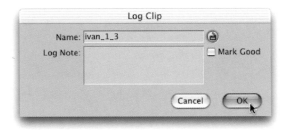

7. The Capture window will now appear, displaying the footage as it is being captured. Final Cut Pro automatically moves the tape to the In point and captures the footage to the Out point.

8. The captured clip will now appear in your Browser with the name you gave it, and you can use it to create your film.

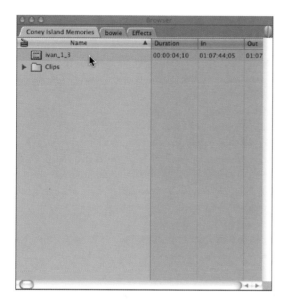

Alternative Steps: Using Capture Now

If you do not have device control, or just prefer to capture clips in a less structured manner, you can use the Capture Now option. Follow Steps 1–2 of *A Quick Guide to Logging and Capturing* and then pick up here.

3. Start playing your footage. A few seconds before the beginning of the footage you want to capture, click the Now button.

4. The Capture window will open and begin capturing whatever footage plays until you press the Esc key to stop it.

5. The clip you just captured will appear in the Browser's logging bin. Click on the name of the clip to rename it.

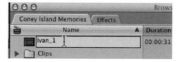

The Short Music Films of Laurie Anderson and Sam Phillips

New York-based director/editor Steven Lippman runs Flip Productions, which uses Final Cut Pro exclusively to create productions that range from television documentaries to short music films. Recently, Lippman completed two short music films for Laurie Anderson and Sam Phillips. Commissioned by Nonesuch Records, the director/editor produced two unique, distinctly different pieces to represent the varied artists.

"My directorial style is to stay emotionally true to the material. Laurie Anderson's music was sonically dense and would reveal many layers each time I listened. Sam Phillips' music is sonically very spare, though no less complex. Therefore, these aspects were reflected in the visual style of both pieces," says Lippman.

Image © Copyright 2003.
Courtesy of Nonesuch Records

Before production on the Anderson shoot, Lippman edited together a musical suite that was developed into a cohesive audio track—featuring interwoven segments of five songs from Anderson's new record. "The Laurie Anderson project was actually filmed quite simply. We spent one day shoot-ing Super 8mm with two cameras in various places in New York." The Super-8 footage—shot on the Nikon R-8 and Canon S14 XL-S—was then processed and transferred to mini-DV stock. All of the footage was then edited to the musical suite that Lippman had developed. Once completed, the cuts were taken to the second day of production in a studio, where they were projected against various canvases—including Laurie Anderson herself. This second day of production was shot on a Sony TRV900 mini-DV camera. The director, using Final Cut Pro, created densely composited and layered imagery to achieve what Lippman describes as "a dream essay."

Lippman created the Sam Phillips production on a similar schedule—one day in the studio, and one day shooting Super 8mm in the streets of New York—but with very different concepts. The piece mixed three of Phillips' songs into a single audio suite. Each song has its own visual style, and for the song *Incinerator*, the studio setup featured Phillips in a dark room standing in front of a globe of light—etching her in a starkly contrasted silhouette. Lippman describes the segment by saying, "I wanted her to resemble a post-modern Marlene Dietrich—funny and sexy in a very adult way." That song, which features Phillips singing to playback, was shot on a Canon Super 8mm camera hooked up to a crystal sync box—a device that assures precise 24 fps footage so that when edited in Final Cut Pro, the footage would stay in synch with the song. Another song, *Soul Eclipse*, featured the work of production designer Gabriella Simon, who designed a miniature labyrinth with original plastic figures.

For some of the shots in the film, Lippman resurrected some archaic, and stunning, in-camera techniques. "We used some prism and kaleidoscope 35mm lenses from the fifties that were fitted to the Super 8mm camera, just to experiment with effects in camera. It looked fantastic." By shooting on Super 8mm, Lippman achieves a unique aesthetic that other film and video stocks can't achieve. "Super 8mm is an extraordinarily expressive medium.

REAL WORLD

The Short Music Films of Laurie Anderson and Sam Phillips

I love all the dirt and grain. It feels alive. I also love the accidents, the danger of not quite getting the right exposure but still getting something beautiful. It feels incredibly voyeuristic too. It makes everything seem like you've discovered something hidden and secret."

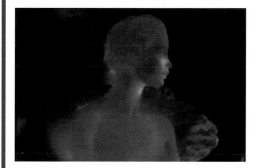

Image © Copyright 2003.
Courtesy of Nonesuch Records

When he started using Final Cut Pro, Lippmann changed his approach to production, gaining more artistic control and saving money. "Until Final Cut, I never physically edited my pieces myself. I directed the editor, so to speak. That has all changed now." Lippman continues, "Final Cut is the closest tool I have that acts as fast as my thoughts, so the tool helps me realize my work in its most pure form. I can finally enjoy the freedom of editing, and I think it's made my directing more adventurous." In constructing his work with Final Cut Pro, Lippman's editorial style is different than most music film editors. "I generally hate editing on the beat. The hidden rhythms are the thing. Really paying attention to all the details of every instrument and vocal inflection is key."

The use of effects differed greatly between the Anderson and Phillips projects. The Anderson video used a lot of post-production effects tools available in Final Cut Pro and DigiEffects CineLook. For the Phillips video, post-production effects were sparse. But in either case, the central focus was on the production itself. Lippman explains his approach. "In the biography of William Wyler, he says that if the set doesn't look right to the naked eye, then it's not going to look good on screen. That's very valuable advice for me, and one reason why I don't see myself working with blue screen and such. I like to keep everything fairly organic, and not rely on creating these effects in post. It's just not the same." To achieve the proper look, Lippman emphasizes the work of his production crew. "I work exclusively with collaborators from the film world and not the TV commercial/music video world. It's just what I gravitate towards in terms of aesthetics, and I need that shared sensibility."

Laurie Anderson's *Life on a String* and Sam Phillips' *Fan Dance* are both currently available from Nonesuch Records. The Laurie Anderson video has been featured at the White Columns gallery in New York and played in competition at the 2002 Berlin Film Festival.

Steven Lippman and Flip Productions can be contacted via e-mail at slippman55@aol.com. More information on both of these artists can be obtained through the web site www.nonesuch.com. Laurie Anderson's web site can be found at www.laurieanderson.com.

Part II
Editing Your Movie

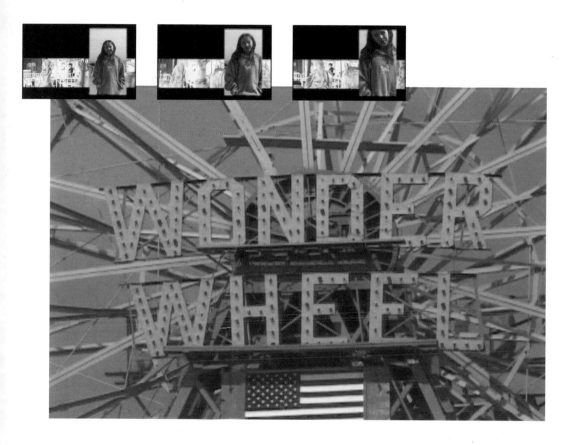

In Part I, you learned how to gather your footage from different sources. Now it's time to get your feet wet with some actual cutting. At first the raw footage in your hard drive—waiting to be shaped and formed into a finished project—may seem intimidating. Where to begin? How will you work with all of this footage? In the following chapters, we will explore the nuts and bolts of editing and using Final Cut Pro's trimming tools, using them to craft your raw footage into a well-edited final project.

6 Starting Your Edit

You've successfully loaded your footage into the computer. You've organized all of your shots into clearly labeled clips and bins. Now the fun begins. This chapter will cover the heart of the editing process, teaching you how to interact with Final Cut Pro to begin structuring your project. Final Cut Pro offers numerous ways to manipulate your footage. Some projects may require a mathematical approach, relying heavily on the keyboard and making edits based on calculations in the Timeline. For other projects a more intuitive approach may make sense, relying on the mouse to click and drag for a visual editing style. No strategy is ever *wrong*; you just need to find the best one for what you and your project need. In this chapter, you'll learn not just the tools Final Cut Pro offers to make edits, but also how best to choose which ones to use.

Overview

> *"To me the most fantastic part of constructing a film is taking many disparate elements and making some sense out of them, making them work together and inform each other."*
>
> Su Friedrich
> *filmmaker*

In this chapter, we'll look at the mechanics of creating a rough cut, that is, getting your clips into the Timeline in the general order you want them to appear in the final video. This process will help you see the project come together and how the structuring of clips affects the meaning and message of the piece. We will also be looking at how to bring clips into the Timeline from the Browser or Viewer, using Overwrite and Insert edits. In Chapter 8 we'll look at making finer cuts and specific trim techniques such as the Ripple, Roll, Slip, and Slide edits that you use once your footage is in the Timeline to tweak existing edits.

It's important to differentiate edits like Overwrite and Insert, which edit clips *into* the Timeline, from trim edits like Ripple and Roll, which fine-tune existing edits in the Timeline.

As you familiarize yourself with Final Cut Pro and begin to edit images and sound, it is a good idea to try out the different editing methods the software offers. Final Cut Pro provides you with the

---

FAQ What Is Three-Point Editing?

The three-point editing system follows a basic premise that goes back to linear video-to-video editing. To make an edit that inserts a clip from your source media into your destination track in the Timeline, you must set three points. The first two points define either the In and Out points of the clip *or* the In and Out points in the Timeline that the clip should fit into. The third point indicates either the In or Out point for the clip (if the other two points are in the Timeline) *or* the In or Out point in the Timeline (if the other two points are in the clip). This means there are four options, defined by what the third point represents:

In point in the Timeline: Two points define the In and Out points for the clip. The third point defines the *In point in the Timeline*. The In point for the clip will be matched to the In point for the Timeline.

Out point in the Timeline: Two points define the In and Out points of the clip. The third point defines the *Out point in the Timeline*. The Out point for the clip will be matched to the Out point for the Timeline.

In point for the clip: Two points define the In and Out points in the Timeline that the clip will be cut to fit within. The third point defines the

In point for the clip. The In point for the clip will be matched to the In point in the Timeline, and the end of the clip will be trimmed at the Timeline's Out point.

Out point for the clip: Two points define the In and Out points in the Timeline that the clip will be cut to fit within. The third point defines the *Out point for the clip*. The Out point for the clip will be matched to the Out point in the Timeline, and the beginning of the clip will be trimmed at the Timeline's In point.

Keep in mind that three-point editing determines what part of a clip will be used and where it will fall in the Timeline. It has nothing to do with whether that edit is an Overwrite or Insert edit. You'll learn about these essential types of edits later in this chapter; the important point here is that three-point editing can achieve either type.

You will use this method whenever you make an edit by dragging a clip into the Canvas Edit Overlay window. You may want to refer back to this sidebar as you review the section *Editing Clips into the Timeline through the Canvas* later in this chapter.

flexibility to work in several different ways and choose the best method for you. The basic editing functions have many different buttons and shortcuts. So try them all a few times before deciding which methodology you prefer. For example, a music video typically requires very strict edits worked out mathematically in advance to keep the image and music in synch, so you'll probably use the keyboard, typing values into input boxes, to make your cuts frame-exact. By contrast, if you are editing together a quick montage of images for a documentary, such as various street scenes, you may decide to edit by "feel," using the mouse to trim and juxtapose the images as you watch them to create a rhythm that you can see in real time. The way you interact with the program will affect your final outcome. Try as many methods as you can until you hit on the right combination for your project. This chapter will present many options for alternate ways to attain the same results.

Final Cut Pro uses the *three-point editing* system. As explained in the *What Is Three-Point Editing?* sidebar, whenever you edit a clip into a longer sequence, three points determine how the two clips will fit together. The points you specify may be the start and end points of the clip plus its start or end point in the sequence, or vice versa. This overarching concept should become second nature (if it is not already) and will help you visualize how Final Cut Pro

performs edits and how you can set up your cuts so they are properly prepared for editing. If you have edited on film or on a digital nonlinear/nondestructive editing system before, many of the concepts this chapter covers should be familiar. Now you need to learn how Final Cut Pro's interface allows you to prepare and perform edits and other functions such as linking or using the Clipboard.

The most important thing this chapter can provide is a sense of how to approach an editing task and choose the best solution for it. Every editor encounters new and unexpected problems every day, and the more you are able to "think differently" and are not bound by a single solution, the sooner you will solve any problem you may come across in the cutting room.

Chapter 6: A Blank Slate

In this chapter, you can begin using the clips included on the supplied DVD. The installation instructions are included in the *Introduction*. Once you have the files installed on your computer, open the Final Cut Pro project file labeled *Coney Island Memories*. After this file loads in Final Cut Pro, follow the instructions in *Creating a New Sequence* to create a new blank sequence for Chapter 6 and then use that sequence to practice adding clips to the Timeline and moving them around.

Creating a New Sequence

When you first start editing, you'll need at least one sequence to start cutting in. A Sequence is a tab in the Timeline where you can lay out clips in order and then view the edits. When you first open a project, an icon for a sequence named "Sequence 1" will automatically appear in the Browser. Double-clicking it opens up the Timeline. To rename this sequence, click on the name and type in a new one.

However, you often want to work with more than one sequence as you are cutting together a project, so you'll want to create a new sequence.

1. Select File > New > Sequence (⌘+N).

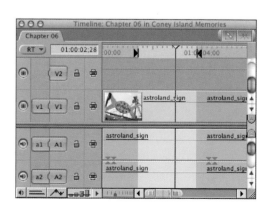

2. A new sequence will appear in the Browser numbered sequentially. Click the sequence name in the Browser to rename the sequence to suit your project. For this exercise, rename it "Chapter 6".

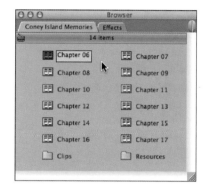

Opening and Closing a Sequence

While working in Final Cut Pro, you will use at least one and possibly multiple sequences within a single project:

- To open a sequence to start editing, double-click the sequence icon in the Browser and you will see it appear in the Timeline and the Canvas as a Tab.

- To move between different open sequences, click the desired sequence tab in the Timeline or Canvas.

menu. The sequence will still be available in the Project File's tab in the Browser: simply double-click it again to open.

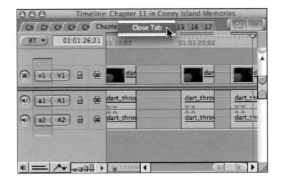

- To close a sequence (thus removing its tab from the Timeline and Canvas), choose File > Close Tab (Ctrl+W) or control-click the tab in either window and choose Close Tab from the contextual

Deleting a Sequence from a Project

Sometimes you may decide that you need to delete a sequence. To delete a sequence, select the sequence icon in the Browser and then press the Delete button on your keyboard. The sequence will be deleted from your project and will no longer be available. It will not, however, delete any of the clips that sequence used, which will still remain and be available in the Browser.

Working with Clips

Clips are the basic building blocks of your project. Think of them as the atoms that create your universe (which would make the individual frames subatomic particles). Much of the rest of this book deals with how to use and manipulate clips, but let's start by looking at a few clip basics: how to select them, organize them in bins, and set specific In and Out points.

Selecting Clips

Final Cut Pro uses selection as a common tool to specify on which clip or clips an action should be performed (move, delete, menu command, etc.).

- To select a single clip in the Timeline or Browser, click the clip icon. If the clip is in the Timeline, simply click in the middle of the clip. The clip will darken to show that it is selected.

- To select multiple sequential clips in the Timeline or Browser, click the first clip in the sequence of clips and then Shift+click the last clip in the sequence. Both of these clips and all clips in between them will be selected. You can also "lasso" the clips by dragging your mouse around the clips you want, drawing a square over the clips you want to select.

- To select multiple nonsequential clips in the Timeline or Browser, click the first clip and then ⌘+click the next clip. Only those two clips will be selected; however, you can ⌘+click additional clips to add them to the selection.

- To deselect selected clips, click on another clip or on an empty part of the Browser or Timeline: the clip(s) will become deselected.

Adding Bins to Organize Your Clips

As you edit, you will want to organize your footage as best you can. We've compared the Browser to a filing cabinet, and bins are the folders within this cabinet to help you separate clips into groups. Use these bins to categorize your clips to make them easier to find. For example, if you have several shots of an interview, you may want to collect all of those shots into a single bin so that you can quickly access them while piecing together the interview. To use bins, follow these steps:

1. Select File > New > Bin (⌘+B) or control-click an empty space in the Browser.

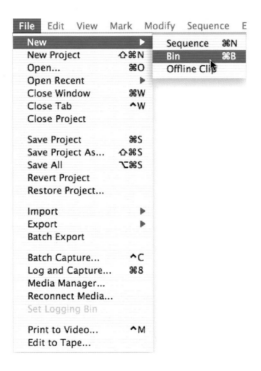

2. A new bin will appear in your Browser numbered sequentially. Click on the name to rename it to reflect the kind of clips it will be housing. For this exercise, call the new bin "Jean and Frank."

3. Drag clips into the bin by dragging and dropping them onto the folder icon. To select multiple clips, Shift+click each clip to be moved and then click and drag one of them (the others will follow). You can see the contents of a bin by double-clicking it or selecting the arrow to the left of the folder icon. For this exercise, practice dragging the clips named jean_frank from the Clips bin into your new bin.

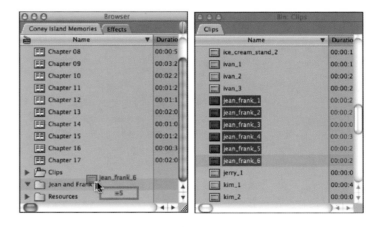

You can also put bins inside other bins for more detailed organization. Either drag an existing bin inside another or create a new bin when a bin is open in its own window (by double-clicking it). You can also Option-double click a bin to open it in its own tab in the Browser.

Setting a Clip's In and Out Points

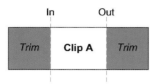

In order to set which part of a clip is to be shown during playback in the Timeline, you will probably need to *trim* footage from the full media file. The In and Out points specify where a clip begins and ends playing, thus trimming footage from the beginning and end of the full media. You already set absolute In and Out points (the beginning and end of the media) while logging your footage to be captured (see *Setting In and Out Points* in Chapter 4). Adding In and Out points to a clip is similar to that process but allows you to more closely refine your cuts to get the exact entry and exit points you desire.

However, just because you trim footage from your clip does not mean that the trimmed footage will disappear onto the cutting room floor. Instead, that footage remains a part of the media; it simply is not played in the Timeline. This is one of the biggest advantages of nondestructive digital editing over destructive editing.

The downside of this convenience is that making a decision about a cut is sometimes too easy. An editor may not spend enough time considering what would be the best edit, because it is so easy to change. When you're setting In and Out points, always carefully consider the decisions you are making, and don't rush through the edits.

1. To set the In and Out points for a clip globally (that is, to set where those points appear automatically in that clip when you pull it from the Browser), first locate the clip you want to work with in the Browser and double-click so that it displays in the Viewer window. You can also drag the clip into the Viewer with the mouse.

Alternatively, you can set the In and Out points for a particular clip in the Timeline by double-clicking it or dragging it from the Timeline into the Viewer. The In and Out points you set in the following steps will then affect only that one instance of the clip in the Timeline; the clip in the Browser will be unaffected.

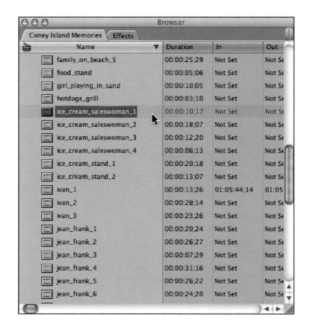

2. Play the clip in the Viewer. You can scroll through it by using the J, K, or L keys and the spacebar (see the *Keyboard Shortcuts for the Canvas and Viewer* sidebar in Chapter 2), by dragging the scrub head, or clicking the Play button on the Viewer control panel.

3. Determine the part of the clip you want to use in your sequence and then use the keyboard arrow keys (frame-by-frame keys) to move to the exact frame in the Timeline you want to be the first frame of your new editing clip—the In point.

Ⓐ Playhead

4. Set the In point here by either pressing the I key or clicking the Set In Point button on the Viewer window. You may have to spend some time going back and forth to find just the right spot, but remember that you can always come back later and reassign the In point.

Ⓐ Set In point

Ⓑ In point

5. Play through your clip to the point where you want it to stop—the Out point. When you are on the exact frame you want, press the O key or click the Set Out Point button in the Viewer window. Again, you should spend some time finding the right point, but if you change your mind later, you can always come back and change the Out point.

Set Out point

Ⓑ Out point

6. Your clip has now been trimmed to start and stop exactly where you want it. The following sections will discuss what to do with your clip now that you've established its length. Of course, you can change your In and Out points at any time by repeating these steps, so you aren't locked into these settings.

Ⓐ In point

Ⓑ Playhead

Ⓒ Out point

Adding Blank Tracks in the Timeline

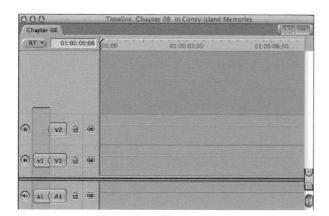

The Timeline is where the real cutting of your projects will take place. As we showed you in Chapter 2, the Timeline consists of separate tracks, and these tracks are where you will place your audio and video clips to create the edited product. When you add a new clip to the Timeline (as you will learn how to do later in this chapter), tracks can be automatically inserted into the

Timeline to accommodate the new clips. However, you may also want to manually add a track to the Timeline before you add the clip.

Adding tracks is helpful if you are not satisfied with a clip already in your sequence and want to quickly try out a different clip. If you drag a new clip and place it on an additional track directly over another clip, the new clip will "cover up" the old one. Track hierarchy in Final Cut Pro works so that clips on higher tracks play over clips on lower tracks. Now play your sequence, and the new clip plays instead of the old clip underneath it. You can immediately evaluate this new clip without touching or removing the old clip and the clips around it. You'll also use multiple tracks to create transitions and composite shots that mix the imagery of two clips stacked one on top of the other (see Chapters 10 and 13).

1. Select Sequence **>** Insert Tracks to bring up the Insert Tracks window.

2. In the Insert Tracks window, type in the number of video and/or audio tracks you want to add to your Timeline. You are given options for where you want those tracks to appear. They are:

Before Base Track: This inserts tracks under the first video track or above the first audio track and pushes the existing tracks to outer track numbers.

After Last Track: This option creates a new track after the very last track. If your last track is V7, this will create a V8.

3. After you select the option you want, click OK to create your new tracks, which will then show up in the Timeline.

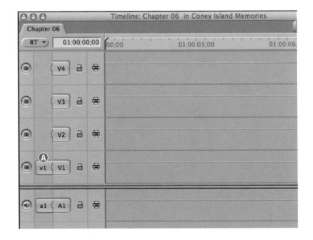

Ⓐ Target track

You can also quickly add or delete a single track by control-clicking in an empty area around a track number to open the contextual menu, then selecting Add Track (to add a track above the selected track) or Delete Track (to delete the selected track).

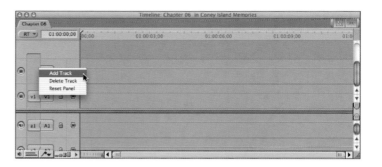

Deleting Blank Tracks in the Timeline

You can also easily delete tracks as they become unnecessary in your edit. To delete video and audio tracks, do the following:

1. Select Sequence > Delete Tracks to bring up the Delete Tracks window.

2. In the Delete Tracks window you are given several options for deleting audio and video tracks from the Timeline. They are:

All Empty Tracks This is a very useful tool. Often, you'll create tracks as you drag clips into the sequence, and they can pile up. This function removes any track that has no clip in it.

All Empty Tracks at End of Sequence This functions similarly to Empty All Tracks, except it only deletes tracks that are numbered higher (in the case of video) or lower (in the case of audio) than the last track with media on it.

3. After you select the option you want, click OK to delete the tracks. The selected tracks will then disappear from the Timeline.

Editing Clips into the Timeline

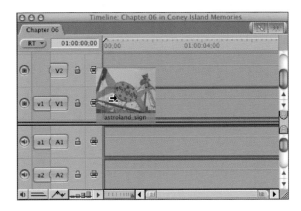

The fastest and most common way to start working with your clips in the Timeline is simply to drag and drop them. You can drag a clip from either the Browser or the Viewer, and drop it directly into the Timeline. We recommend setting the In and Out points for the clip first in the Viewer (see earlier section in this chapter). Once you've set the In and Out points on your clip, you can then drag it from either the Browser or the Viewer window into the Timeline.

1. In the Browser, find the clip you want to open and double-click the clip to open it in the Viewer window. In the Viewer, you can review the footage, create or check the In and Out points, and make any adjustments you might want.

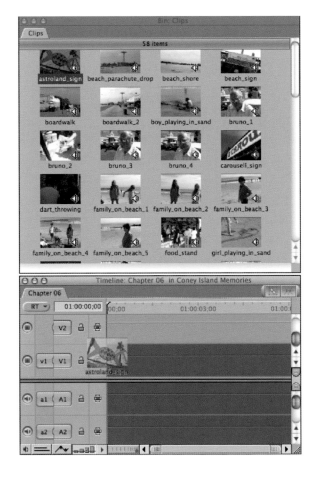

2. Drag the clip from the Viewer window to the Timeline by clicking the video image in the Viewer (make sure the Video tab is in front), holding down the mouse button, and dragging the clip into the Timeline. You can also drag a clip directly from the Browser without opening it in the Viewer. Click on the clip in the Browser, hold the mouse button down, and drag the clip to the Timeline.

3. When you drag the clip into the Timeline, you'll see a *ghost clip* that you can position with the mouse by holding down the mouse button. The ghost clip is a visual representation of the clip, constrained by the In and Out points you have set. It shows how long the clip is, relative to other clips in the Timeline, so that you can visually decide where to put it. It's a good idea to have scrolled the Timeline to the section where you want to drop the clip before you start, but you can also scroll the Timeline while dragging your clip. While still holding the mouse button, move your ghost clip in the direction you want to move along the Timeline, and it will automatically scroll.

While dragging the ghost clip, you can choose to make either an Overwrite or an Insert edit (see the sidebar *The Seven Methods of Editing* for more details). To make an Overwrite edit, drag the clip onto the bottom two-thirds of the destination track (the cursor will switch to a down arrow).

To make an Insert edit, drag the clip onto the top third of the destination track you want the clip in (the cursor will switch to a right pointing angle).

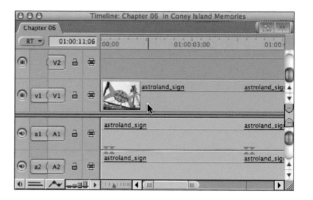

4. When you have positioned the ghost clip exactly where you want it in the Timeline, release the mouse button and the clip is placed there.

5. You've now brought a clip successfully into the Timeline, and you can view the clip in the Canvas window. Remember that the Canvas window is the monitor for what is in the Timeline, so once you put a clip in the Timeline, you will use the Canvas to view it. However, you can double-click any clip that is in the Timeline and open it in the Viewer to edit just that instance of the clip.

Alternate Steps:
Copying and Pasting into the Timeline

A "quick and dirty" way of moving clips around is simply to copy and paste them using the Clipboard in the same way you can move text in a word processor. Use the same keystrokes with the mouse selection to select multiple clips as you would in any other Mac application: Shift+click to select everything in a series, ⌘+click to select a number of individual clips, and so on.

1. Select the clip or clips you want to copy to the Clipboard from your sequence in the Timeline. You can select just one or as many clips as you want. Note that if you select a video clip that is linked to an audio clip, the audio clip will also be selected.

2. Use the standard Mac commands to copy or cut:

- Select Edit **>** Copy (⌘+C) to copy the clip into the Clipboard.
- Select Edit **>** Cut (⌘+X) to cut the clip from the sequence and into the Clipboard. This option will remove the clip completely from the Timeline, which is helpful if you want to move the clip to another point in the Timeline but not copy it.
- Ctrl+click one of the selected clips in the Browser and choose either Cut or Copy from the contextual menu.

The clip, or at least a stand-in for the clip, will now be in your computer's Clipboard memory. This is actually a little different from copying or cutting in most other applications, which literally record the text or graphic into the computer's memory. Final Cut Pro records only a reference to the clip, *not* the media itself. You do not have to worry that copying or cutting a clip will fill your computer's available memory.

3. In the Timeline, place the playhead at the point where you want to paste the clips into the sequence and then select Edit **>** Paste ((⌘)+V) or control-click in the Timeline and choose Paste from the contextual menu. The clip will enter the sequence as if you were making an Overwrite edit. If you have not set an In or Out point on the Timeline, the clip will paste into the sequence beginning at the current location of the Timeline's playhead.

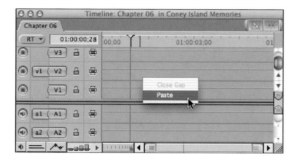

Setting Target Tracks

In Chapter 2, we reviewed target tracks in the Timeline. Let's review that here, and see how it affects the drag-and-drop method. When you drag a clip from the Browser or the Viewer, it will default to the tracks you have designated as target tracks. This means that when you drag the video clip into the Timeline, it will jump to the video track that has been set as the video target track. This also works for copying and pasting media clips into the Timeline. The audio will also appear on the designated audio track(s). Again, the interlocking icon beside the track number indicates the target track. Clicking another track's number will make it the target track.

1. Decide which track you want to place your clips on. If you are bringing a clip into an empty Timeline, it's probably best to have the first video track selected.

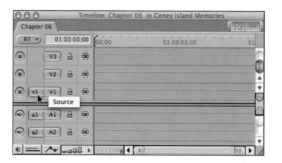

2. To set the target video track, click the video destination icon (uppercase "V": V1, V2, etc.) that you want to select in the Timeline. The target track icon will interlock with the track number, showing you that this is the target video track. You can only set one video target track at a time. Alternatively, you can drag the interlocking icon to the Video track you want to designate as target track.

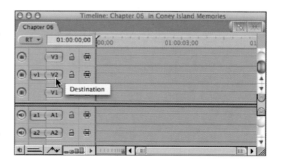

3. To have no target track set, click the video source icon (lowercase "v": v1, v2, v3, etc.) of the selected track. The interlocked icons will appear to separate, indicating that there is no selected track.

4. To set the audio target track, click the audio track number beside the destination audio track icon (uppercase "A": A1, A2, etc.).

With audio, you can select one or two tracks, and if the audio is in stereo, you can designate tracks for the left and right channels (represented by the two interlocking lowercase source audio track icons marked with a lowercase "a": a1 and a2). As with the video target track interlocking icon, you can drag the audio icons to whatever audio track you want. Click the interlocking icon to separate or link it to the track and to turn it on or off.

Even with a target track set, you can still place the clip on another track if you are using the drag-and-drop method to add clips. The target track sets the default track that the clip will initially jump to, but you can use the mouse to drag the clip to any other track and drop it wherever you want. It's important to note that if you don't have any audio tracks set as target tracks, no audio will appear with your video clip when you drag it to the Timeline, even if it has audio on it.

Editing Clips into the Timeline through the Canvas

Although editing clips directly into the Timeline is an easy way to see where a clip will fit, you also have the option of dragging clips from the Viewer or Browser directly into the Canvas to add them to your film at the point currently showing. This gives you additional editing options beyond the simple Overwrite and Insert methods available through the Timeline, allowing you to choose any of seven different methods to edit your clip into your film (see the sidebar *The Seven Methods of Editing*). But even though you are working through the Canvas, you are still adding the clip to the Timeline, so the end product is much the same as described in the previous section.

1. To prepare to edit a clip into the Canvas, set the In and Out points for the clip (as shown earlier in this chapter), set the playhead in the Timeline to the point you want to edit the clip into. Also make sure that you have set the target tracks into which you want the clip to be edited (see *Setting Target Tracks*).

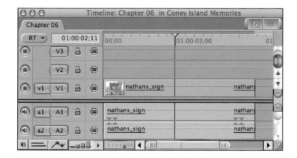

2. Drag the clip from the Viewer into the Canvas window. The Edit Overlay menu with its seven editing options will appear (see the sidebar *The Seven Methods of Editing* for a detailed discussion of each). For this example, drag the clip onto the Overwrite pane of the window, highlighting the frame, and release the mouse button. The clip will appear in the Timeline at the point and track you designated. The clip will replace whatever media was previously located in the Timeline.

Your clip has been successfully edited into the Timeline. Now you can continue to bring in other clips in the same way and begin to piece together a rough cut of your project. You should be careful when using Overwrite edits, as you can end up temporarily cutting out footage you want. It's not gone for good, but will take a few more steps to trim the footage forward again to regain the overwritten frames.

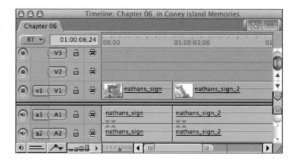

Alternate Steps: Using the Edit Buttons

Instead of using the drag-and-drop method, you can also use the edit buttons to add a clip to your film through the Canvas. For some people this will be a much faster and intuitive way of adding clips. After following Step 1 from the previous section to prepare your edit, pick up here:

2. Open the clip you want to edit in the Viewer. Do this by locating the clip in the Browser and double-clicking it.

3. Three buttons in the lower left corner of the Canvas control editing: Overwrite, Insert, and a toggle button that allows you to choose from the other five editing styles available. Click and hold to select the desired editing style. The last style you select will serve as the default used the next time you click this button.

Ⓐ Insert (F9)

Ⓑ Overwrite (F10)

Ⓒ Toggle currently showing Replace (F11)

Click the button for the edit type you want at the bottom left of the Canvas window, and the clip currently displayed in the Viewer will be edited into the film at the point shown in the Canvas. (You can also drag the clip from the Viewer onto the button.) For this example, click the red Overwrite button (F10). This immediately edits the clip into the Timeline. Repeat these steps to add more clips.

Ⓐ Replace (F11)

Ⓑ Superimpose (F12)

Ⓒ Fit to Fill (Shift+F11)

Ⓓ Insert with Transition (Shift+F9)

Ⓔ Overwrite with Transition (Shift+F10)

TIP The Seven Methods of Editing

The Edit Overlay window that pops up when you drag a clip into the Canvas and the edit buttons in the lower left corner both offer the same seven edit choices for your clip. Although the actions you take to use them are pretty much the same, the results for each edit style will be radically different. Most of these edits will use the three-point editing we described in the introduction of this chapter unless otherwise noted. The shortcut keys are listed in parentheses.

Insert Edit (F9)   This method of editing moves all the media in your sequence at the In point of the edit (underneath the playhead) forward to make room for the new clip. No media is lost, but clips at the In point of the edit will be split and pushed forward to provide room for the newly inserted clips.

Insert Edit with Transition (Shift+F9)   If you are editing a clip (we'll call it clip B) into a sequence, this allows you to perform an Insert edit but also adds a transition effect to the beginning of clip B if its In point rests on another clip (we'll call it clip A), thus creating a transition moving from clip A to clip B. The currently set default transition will be used automatically; this will be the Cross Dissolve unless you have changed it. See Chapter 10 for an explanation of transitions and how to set the default transition.

Overwrite Edit (F10)   This allows you to place a clip in the sequence without changing the timing of any of the other clips. However, if there is media under the point where the new clip is edited in, this media will be deleted and replaced by the new clip.

Overwrite with Transition (Shift+F10)   If you are editing a clip (we'll call it clip B) into a sequence, this allows you to perform an Overwrite edit but also adds a transition to the beginning of clip B if its In point rests on another clip (we'll call it clip A). Therefore, it creates a transition moving from clip A to clip B. The type of transition inserted is whatever has been set as the default, typically Cross Dissolve. The currently set default transition, the Cross Dissolve unless you have changed it, will be used automatically. See Chapter 10 for an explanation of transitions and how to set the default transition.

Replace Edit (F11)   This edit follows different rules than the rest. The Replace edit removes a whole clip in the Timeline and replaces it with a new clip from the Viewer, taking up the exact same amount of time as the old, replaced clip. Think of this edit as a special kind of Overwrite. A Replace edit ignores the In and Out points set in your Viewer; it only looks at where the playhead is in the Viewer, and uses the playhead's current frame as the In point. In the Timeline, a replace edit will either use the location of the playhead as its In point or, if In and Out points have been set, the Replace edit will attempt to fill the duration between those points. If there is not enough footage following the playhead in the Viewer to fill the gap in the Timeline left by the replaced clip, you'll get an "Insufficient content for edit" error.

Fit to Fill (Shift+F11)   The Fit to Fill edit works like a Replace edit but will actually change the speed of the source clip (clip B) to fit into the space of the clip currently under the playhead in the Timeline (clip A). If there is no clip currently under the playhead, it fits the clip into the blank area in the Timeline. If clip A is shorter than the clip B, then clip B will be sped up and shortened to fit. If clip A is longer, clip B will be slowed down and made longer to fit. A Fit to Fill edit is the only edit that uses *four* edit points instead of the usual three.

Superimpose (Shift+F12)   A Superimpose edit puts your source clip directly on top of your target track, superimposing it over the underlying image. Superimposing is a technique that shows two (or more) images at the same time, so that the two are blended together. Superimpose editing uses the three-point editing system. However, if In and Out points have not been set in the Timeline, the playhead is *not* used as the In point. Instead, the In point on the Timeline is set at the first frame of the clip that the playhead is resting on in the Timeline. This function is similar to Replace edit in that if the clip you are superimposing is shorter than the clip under it, you will see the error message "Insufficient content for edit."

Setting In and Out Points in the Timeline

While you can use In and Out points to trim a clip to show only a specific segment of footage (see *Setting a Clip's In and Out Points* in this chapter), you can also add In and Out points to the Timeline itself. Defining In and Out points in the Timeline is useful for designating where you want a clip to be edited into the Timeline as part of your three-point editing (explained earlier in the chapter). It's also useful for setting parameters for printing to video or exporting a part of a sequence, and for setting limits of a voice-over recording.

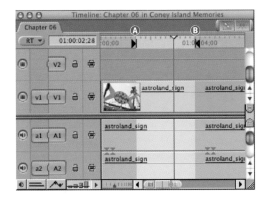

Ⓐ In point

Ⓑ Out point

In and Out points in the Timeline are also useful whenever you create an edit using the Canvas window's edit overlay options (see *Editing Clips into the Timeline through the Canvas*). The clip you insert will default to fit into the In and Out points set in the Timeline. However, the In/Out points will be automatically reset once the edit is made. If you have not set In and Out points, the clip will default to the position of the playhead and fill as much space as needed for the entire clip.

To set In and Out points in the Timeline, make sure the Timeline is the active window. Place the playhead where you want the In point to appear, and select Mark **>** Mark In (or press **I**). An In marker will be added in the ruler at the top of the Timeline. To add an Out point, place the playhead at the frame in the Timeline where you want the Out point to appear, and select Mark **>** Mark Out (or press **O**).

Other Timeline In/Out point options in the Mark menu include:

Mark Split   Sets In/Out points for audio and video separately.

Mark Clip (X)   Sets In /Out points around the clip or blank area currently under the playhead in the Timeline.

Mark to Markers (Ctrl+A)   Once you've set markers in the Timeline, this option sets In/Out points to the markers on either side of the playhead. If a marker has not been set on one side or the other, the default is the very beginning or very end of the footage in the Timeline. This also respects the markers in a highlighted clip in the target track of the Timeline.

Mark Selection (Shift+A)   Sets In/Out points around currently selected clips in conjunction with the autoselect track button.

Select In To Out (Option+A)   Selects all clips between the In and Out points.

Clear In To Out, In, Out, Split (Option+X, Option+I, Option+O)   Removes the In and/or Out points from the Timeline as indicated.

Tightening Your Cut with Ripple Delete, Lift Delete, and Close Gap

Once you have laid down the basic edits for your clips, you are ready to start refining by getting rid of unwanted clips and closing any unwanted gaps between clips. By selecting clips or the gaps in between them, you can speed up your edit process considerably by using Ripple Delete, Lift Delete, and Close Gap, which all function to remove either a clip or a gap between clips from your edit in the Timeline.

Performing a Ripple Delete

A Ripple Delete acts like a lift and tuck. Instead of just removing the clip, a Ripple Delete also closes the gap left by the vanishing clip. This edit adjusts the rest of the edit back to fill this gap.

1. Select the clip in the Timeline.

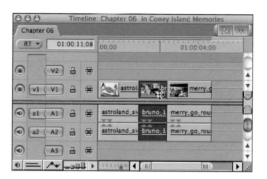

2. Choose Sequence > Ripple Delete (Delete key) to remove the clip and close the space it occupied.

The clip will disappear and the gap will be closed by the remaining footage to the right of the clip. If there is media in the way (i.e., an audio track that extends through the gap), a Ripple Delete cannot be performed.

Performing a Lift Delete

To lift a clip simply means to remove it from the Timeline without affecting the rest of the cut. This means you'll be leaving a hole or a gap behind when you lift the clip out of the edit.

1. Select the clip to be lifted (deleted) by clicking on the center of the clip in the Timeline.

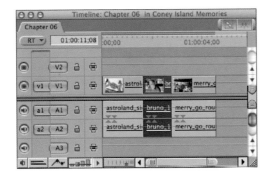

2. Choose Sequence ➤ Lift (Delete key) to lift the clip out of the sequence.

The clip will disappear and leave a gap in its place. Keep in mind that this does not delete the clip from the entire project. It will still reside in the Browser and can be added in as desired.

Closing a Gap

As you move clips around in the edit, you may be left with holes in your sequence that you want to collapse to keep the steady flow of images going. To close a gap, you'll need to make sure that the gap exists on all tracks of your sequence. If there is footage, either audio or video, on another track, you cannot close the gap.

1. Select a gap by placing the playhead within the empty area in the Timeline between two clips or between the beginning of the sequence and the first clip.

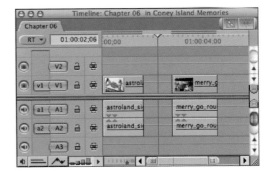

2. Choose Sequence **>** Close Gap (Option+G).

The gap will close and all of the following footage will move back to fill the gap.

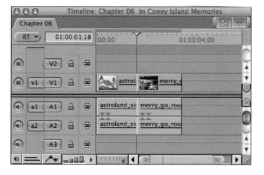

7
The Tools of Editing

Now that you understand how to set up sequences and work with your clips, we'll go to the next level: learning how to use your tools. Before you begin the real cutting of your piece, it's important to review some of the tools available to you, especially those new tools offered in Final Cut Pro 4. After you've become familiar with working with audio and using contextual menus to your advantage, you can really streamline your work as an editor.

This chapter pays special attention to audio, as dealing with links between audio and video tracks and stereo pairs can be confusing. Carefully review these exercises and most importantly, experiment on your own with how audio and video clips relate to one another.

Overview

> *"One must learn to understand that editing is in actual fact a compulsory and deliberate guidance of the thoughts and associations of the spectator."*
>
> V. I. Pudovkin

When you are cutting with Final Cut Pro, audio and video can be used together or separately to make edits. First, we're going to look at how audio functions in Final Cut Pro and how you can use linking and stereo pairs to cut with audio. Then we'll examine some of the new features in Final Cut Pro 4 that will help you cut more efficiently. These features include the updated contextual menu tools and new audio options in the Timeline.

Once we've reviewed these tools, you'll be ready to start using them in your own edit.

Options, Options Everywhere: Using Contextual Menus

Even seasoned computer veterans might be slightly intimidated by the Final Cut Pro interface. There is a lot going on and a lot of options. However, one often overlooked but extremely powerful feature of this application is the availability of contextual menus. These are little pop-up menus that appear when you hold down the Control key while clicking on an area with your mouse (referred to as control-clicking, or right-clicking if you have a two-button mouse).

Many windows and icons within the interface have contextual menus that enable you to access quickly the possible options for that object. For example, if you control-click in an empty area of

the Browser, you will be able to change the view for the window from a list to icons of various sizes, or vice versa.

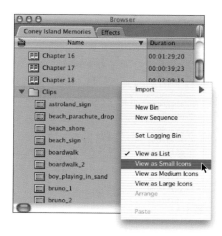

However, if you control-click on a video clip within that same window, you will see options for actions that you can perform on the clip, such as cutting, copying, or viewing it in the Viewer.

Although available in almost all applications, contextual menus are especially effective for Final Cut Pro. They can not only speed your workflow, but might even remind you of options that are otherwise buried deep within the menu bar. Since almost every element in the Final Cut Pro interface has a slightly different contextual menu—some with one option, some with over a dozen options— they are far too numerous to detail here. However, throughout this book, we highlight contextual menus with helpful shortcuts.

Locking Tracks to Prevent Editing Errors

Often in the heat of the edit you'll accidentally drag or trim a clip that you didn't mean to. Instead of constantly having to use the Undo command (⌘+Z), Final Cut Pro offers you the ability to lock tracks, rendering everything on that track temporarily static and unchangeable. Even if you click on a clip on a locked track, you can do nothing to move it without unlocking it first.

To lock a track that you want to temporarily prevent editing on, click the lock icon beside the track number. The icon will change to a locked icon and the entire track will appear with hatch marks.

Ⓐ Track is locked.

Ⓑ Track is unlocked.

Try to move a clip on the locked track—you can't. You're not even able to open a clip on a locked track in the Viewer. Now continue cutting without the worry that you will accidentally change anything on the locked track. You can lock as many tracks as desired. Once you are ready to begin working on a locked track again, simply click the filmstrip icon so that it is once again lit.

Making Tracks Invisible and Inaudible

The track visibility and audibility controls allow you to make invisible or inaudible a particular track. To make a single track invisible or inaudible, click the filmstrip (for video) or speaker (for audio)

icon next to the track number The icon will go dim and the track will be grayed out. You can click on as many video or audio tracks as desired to make them invisible or inaudible. To reactivate the track so it is visible or audible, simply click the icon speaker or filmstrip again so that it is glowing.

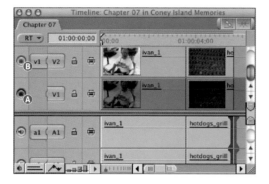

Ⓐ Track is hidden/inaudible.

Ⓑ Track is active.

Working with Markers

Markers do what they say: they mark a specific frame, area of a clip, or sequence so that you can make notes about that point, create a mark point to snap to, or just provide a reference for timing the clip's content.

Adding Markers

Markers can be added to either a clip or to the Timeline itself (so that they don't correspond to a particular clip) in order to add notes to specific points within the video. You can use a marker for a wide variety of purposes, limited only by your imagination. For example, in this book, we have used markers in the Chapters 5–10 sequences to mark where you should move in the Timeline to begin working on a specific exercise for that chapter.

To add a marker to the Timeline, make sure that the Timeline window is active and then put your playhead in the Timeline over the frame to which you want to add the marker. If you want to add the marker to a specific clip, select that clip in the Timeline. Otherwise, if you just want to add the clip to the Timeline itself, make sure no clips are selected. To add the marker at this point in the Timeline, do one of the following:

- Press **M**.
- Choose Mark **>** Markers **>** Add.
- Click the Add Marker button in the Canvas.

If you want to name the marker, add notes, or extend the marker over multiple frames, press the **M** key twice (**MM**) or double-click the Add Marker button when adding the marker. This opens the Edit Marker dialog box. In this dialog, you can specify the marker's name and duration to create a marker that spreads over several frames. Click the OK button when you finish.

Ⓐ Enter a name for the marker.

Ⓑ Enter any comments about this marker.

Ⓒ Enter a timecode for the beginning point of the marker.

Ⓓ Enter a timecode for how long the marker should last. If set, the marker will stretch across this duration.

Ⓔ Click to permanently remove this marker.

Ⓕ Press to add a note in the comments (see B) that this marker is to be used to delineate chapters in a DVD.

Ⓖ Press to add a note in the comments (see B) that this marker should be used to delineate compression changes when the video is being compressed.

Ⓗ Press to add a note in the comments (see B) that this marker should be used when adding the musical score to video.

A green marker appears in the Timeline's ruler. While the playhead is over the marker in the Timeline, you will also notice the name of the marker being displayed in the Canvas. If you've selected a clip, then the marker will appear on that clip and stay on

the clip unless you delete it. Now that your marker is placed, you can use it as a visual guide or as a reference point.

Using Markers Effectively

Markers have a wide range of uses, but here are a few tips for things you might want to use markers for:

- Marking a specific moment in the footage you know you want to use later, like a beautiful splash of light or a particular eye movement in a close-up shot

- A point in an interview where you will later want to cover with appropriate b-roll

- A part of a shot that is unusable—for instance if an actor flubs a line or the lighting isn't useable

- A sync point where you will later need to line up a video track—for example you can lay a marker down at the sound of a slate clap and since markers are snappable, use this to snap a video track into sync

Editing and Deleting Markers

After a marker has been set (whether it was initially edited or not), you can edit it anytime to change the name, comments, position, and duration. In addition, you can permanently delete markers when no longer needed. To edit or delete a marker in the Timeline, place the playhead on the marker (the marker's name should appear in the Canvas) and do one of the following:

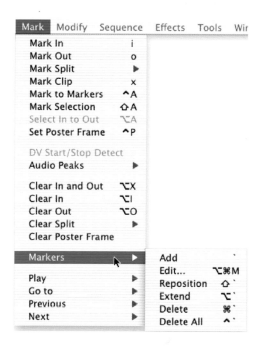

To edit the marker, choose Mark **>** Markers **>** Edit (press **M**) or click the Marker button in the Canvas. Type the information in the Edit Marker dialog box and click OK.

To move the marker, move the playhead to the right of the marker to the new desired position and choose Mark **>** Markers **>** Reposition (Shift+`). The marker to the immediate left of this

position will be repositioned here. You can, of course, also reposition the marker by using the Edit Marker dialog box.

To extend the duration of a marker, move the playhead in the Timeline to the right of the marker to the desired duration and choose Mark **>** Markers **>** Extend (Option+`). The marker to the immediate left of this position will now have its duration set to this point. You can, of course, also set the duration of the marker by using the Edit Marker dialog box.

To delete the marker, choose Mark **>** Markers **>** Delete (⌘+`) or open the Edit Marker dialog box and click the Delete button.

To delete all markers in the current sequence, choose Mark **>** Markers **>** Delete All (Ctrl+`).

Navigating Markers in the Timeline

After you start using markers in your work routine, you might not be able to stop. Markers can be indispensable for helping you keep large projects organized. But after you get more than two in a sequence, they can become hard to navigate directly by using the scrub bar in the Timeline.

To make navigation easier, you can use menu and keyboard shortcuts to move around the Timeline, jumping from marker to marker:

To move to the next marker in the Timeline, choose Mark **>** Next **>** Marker (Shift+Down Arrow). The playhead will move to the next marker.

To move to the previous marker in the Timeline, choose Mark **>** Previous **>** Marker (Shift+Up Arrow). The playhead will move to the previous marker.

To move to a specific marker in the Timeline, control-click in the ruler of the Timeline and choose from the list of markers in the current sequence located at the bottom of the contextual menu.

DVD Chapter 7: Three Edits

Open the Final Cut Pro project file labeled Coney Island Memories. After it loads in Final Cut Pro, double-click the Chapter 7 sequence in the Browser and it will open in the Timeline.

In this chapter you will begin by learning how to use contextual menus and markers to navigate the Timeline while working with linking and unlinking clips. Markers will not only be useful on your own projects, but also with the lessons provided on the DVD. Each chapter sequence has markers indicating the clips to be used with each lesson. Use the techniques we show you here to navigate to each lesson's marker in the Timeline starting with "Linking Audio and Video Clips," which is the first marker in the Chapter 7 sequence. Then, simply look for the marker in the Timeline with the appropriate section title to begin working.

Linking Audio and Video Clips

When you import a media clip into the Timeline, its audio and video tracks are "linked." This means that when you select such a clip, change its In and Out points, or manipulate it in any way, you do so to both the audio and the video simultaneously. That's usually what you want, but Final Cut Pro offers other options:

- You can turn linking temporarily off, which also allows you to work with audio and video separately but keeps the items linked in memory.

- You can unlink clips completely so that the video and audio are no longer linked, which allows you to work with audio and video as separate entities in the Timeline.

- You can link audio and video that were not originally together.

Turning Linking Off in the Timeline

Another option is to turn linking on and off within a sequence. This means that while the audio and video that are linked stay linked, you can disable the linking function and manipulate linked audio and video separately within that sequence. This is especially helpful when you need to adjust audio without affecting the video it is linked to. By turning linking off, you can have audio run longer or shorter than the linked video clip. This is called a "split edit" because it splits the In and Out points so that you have separate In and Out points for audio and video in the same clip. To toggle the Linking option on and off, do one of the following:

Click the Linking button on the top right of the Timeline in the Button List.

Select Sequence > Linked Selection. Press Shift+L.

Unlinking Video from Audio

Most DV clips enter Final Cut Pro with audio and video linked. If you want to work with audio and video separately, you'll need to unlink them. To unlink a clip:

1. Select the clip(s) you want to unlink in the Timeline. You should select both the video and audio tracks, which is automatically done unless you have turned linking off in the Timeline (see previous section).

2. Choose Modify > Link or press Shift+L to unlink the audio and video clips. The check mark will disappear from the Link command in the Modify menu.

3. With your audio and video unlinked, you can now move the audio and video as independent clips, and the two have no effect on each other. Note that the titles of the clips in the Timeline are no longer underlined indicating that they are not linked.

If you move either the audio or video clips, a timecode discrepancy will appear on the clip in the Timeline when you move video away from its source audio track. For example, if you move the video track 1 second and 3 frames away from the audio, the video clip will read +1.03 and the audio –1.03.

Creating a New Video/Audio Link

Linking an audio and video clip makes them run in synch, and as you move and manipulate the clips, they stay together in synch. To link a video and audio clip, first make sure that linking is turned off either for the entire Timeline or for the clips being linked and then follow these steps:

1. Select the video clip you want to link in the Timeline. Then select the audio clip you want to link to it by ⌘-clicking on the audio clip, making sure the video clip is still selected.

2. Choose Modify > Link or press ⌘+L to link the audio and video clips. A check mark will appear to the right of the Link command in the Modify menu.

3. With your audio and video linked, you can be sure that as you are editing and moving your footage around, the audio and video will stay synched together.

When clips are linked, they appear underlined in the Timeline. Clips that are not linked are not underlined. Notice that the time-code discrepancy shows up in the video track of the clip that has lost

its audio component. Also, note that if the audio has a different name than the video it will assume the video clips name once it's saved into the Browser and then brought back out onto the timeline.

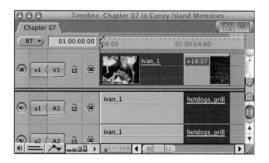

Working with Stereo Pairs

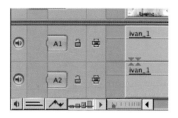

Audio files can be designated as *stereo pairs*, which means that one audio channel plays from the left speaker and the other plays from the right. These two audio tracks are linked together. When you capture footage, the audio comes in as you've specified in your Clip Settings. The default is to bring in two tracks (Ch1 and Ch2) mono but

you can change this to stereo in the Clip Settings tab of the Log and Capture window. In a stereo pair, when you select one channel, both are automatically selected. Linked stereo pair clips will show up in the Viewer as having two audio tabs: Channel 1 (track A1) and Channel 2 (track A2).

If a link doesn't already exist between two stereo pairs in a clip, you may decide to link two clips not previously associated with each other as a stereo pair. For example, you may want dialogue coming out of the left channel and environmental sounds coming out of the right. These tracks may have been recorded separately, but you can join them so they run as a stereo pair.

You can also dissolve the stereo link so that you can move or delete the two tracks separately. Why would you want to do this? Often, when you capture your footage from a DV source, the left and right audio channels contain sound that was recorded from two different microphones. You may decide to only use one of the channels and will therefore need to get rid of one. You can only do this if the audio is not linked as a stereo pair.

To toggle tracks as a stereo pair:

1. In the Timeline, select the audio channels you want to work with. The clips must each be on a different audio track in the Timeline (for example A1 and A2), and they should be lined up so that they play exactly in the synch you want them to. If they are already linked, you will see a series of triangles pointing at each other in the audio clips icon.

Ⓐ Triangles indicate that this is a stereo pair.

2. Choose Modify **>** Stereo Pair (Option+L). A check mark will appear to the right of the Stereo Pair option in the Modify pull-down menu.

If you have enabled Stereo Pairing, you can now move both stereo tracks in tandem by clicking and dragging on either of them. If you have disabled Stereo Pairing, then you can now move the channels independently. Notice that when you do, there will be a timecode discrepancy alert letting you know how far offset the two stereo tracks are.

TIP

Linking Clips with Modified Volume and Panning

Take note that if you have modified the volume and panning of two clips while the clips were not linked as a stereo pair then linking them will cause the settings in track one (Ch1) to be adopted by track two (Ch2).

Creating Subclips

Adding In and Out Points to a clip while editing allows you to specify which part of the clip shows in your video. You can also use these In and Out points to create "subclips," which, if you have a lot of trimmed footage, can be easier to work with than the full clip. Subclips appear in the Browser as their own icon (with ragged edges) but only include that part of the footage you set so that you can better organize and name specific sections of footage. This feature can also allow you to take a single long clip and create multiple subclips out of it. To create a subclip, follow these steps:

1. Open a clip in the Viewer by double-clicking it in the Browser, Canvas, or Timeline.

2. In the Viewer, set the In and Out points for the clip (see the *Working with Clips* section in Chapter 6) to determine the content of the new subclip you are creating.

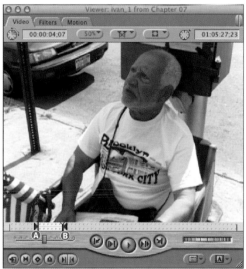

Ⓐ In point
Ⓑ Out point

3. Choose Modify **>** Make Subclip (⌘+U).

A new icon will appear in the Browser, with ragged edges. It will be named after the original clip with the addition of "Subclip" at the end. Additional subclips made from this clip will be numbered starting at 2. You can now use this clip like any other, including giving it its own In and Out points.

Ⓐ Subclip

Finding a Subclip's Source Material

"Matching" a clip allows you to backtrack in order to find the original source clip it was created from. To match a subclip, follow these steps:

1. Open the subclip in the Viewer by double-clicking it in the Browser, Canvas, or Timeline.

2. Place the playhead on a frame in the subclip that you want to be able to match to the original source clip.

3. Choose View > Match Frame >

- Master Clip (press **F**) to view the subclip's source clip in the Browser.
- Source File (Option+⌘+F) to view the subclip's original source file in the Finder.

Extending a Subclip

When you create a subclip, you necessarily set limits with In and Out points to create the smaller clip from a source clip. You may decide later that you were too stingy or too generous with your In and Out limits. If you want to change the In and Out points to a different limit on the original clip, you'll need to remove the subclip's limits and then reset them.

1. Open the subclip you want to extend in the Viewer by double-clicking it in the Browser, Canvas, or Timeline.

2. Select Modify > Remove Subclip Limits.

The In and Out points that limited the subclip will disappear and you'll have all of the original source media available to you.

Backbreakerneckbrace, Multimedia Artist Dawn Bendick

Ever since the first camera was pointed into its own television monitor creating a dangerous (but cool) feedback image, artists have tried to find ways to create art out of the pixilated screen, not only as a still image like all other media before it, but with moving images and with sound. The invention of film and video, still in artistic infancy compared to arts like painting and theatre, has presented new challenges to artists. Film and video artists have struggled to create work that directly addresses the properties of the media, expanding the boundaries of the screen, and providing a new and rich visual canvas. In the last decade, a new canvas—a digital one—has been embraced by artists as a fertile ground for work.

Multimedia artist Dawn Bendick has been using video as an artistic medium for 7 years. She studied at the Maryland Institute, College of Art, where she was exposed to experimental artists such as Granular Synthesis and Kristin Lucas as well as poets such as John Yau and Jeremy Sigler, whom Bendick attributes to her "writing ultra specific poems reflecting sculptural ideas."

She is currently working with Backbreakerneckbrace, an experimental audio and visual group, presenting work in audio/video festivals, galleries, clubs, and parties. Within this group her basic philosophy of visual action is that, "everything operates in reaction to everything else, in terms of motion, color and textures. The process is sculptural. Visual pieces are made up of elements such as molecular textures in motion, triggered by multiple line collisions, and supported by walls of vibrating color. All of these components are carefully layered upon one another."

However, even in video art, the artist is still an editor. For Bendick, editing is a concentrated process to find new and compelling ways to present audio and visuals. She comments that her editing is "very focused on collecting and researching various textures, movements, and images. Once we are finished with collecting we then begin to concentrate on how the two [audio and visual] will react to one another," and it is within this action and interaction Dawn finds her work.

With Backbreakerneckbrace, she works on imagery and collaborates with, Michael Haleta, who creates densely layered aural compositions "not just of clicks and pops, or dozens of drones, but of many audio variables to create an environment." These audio compositions then complement the visual works.

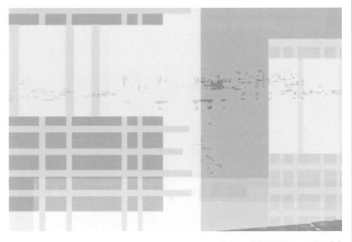

© Copyright 2003 Dawn Bendick
Images from "backbreakerneckbrace," courtesy of Dawn Bendick

As powerful as the tools in Final Cut Pro are, artists are always seeking new and expanded capabilities, so Dawn also integrates output from other software: "Final Cut Pro does not enable you to create animations or apply motion and shape tweens. Macromedia Flash has become an extremely important tool for us. Michael and I work on Flash animations, creating a library of motion designs to pull from. We then import the [Flash] files into Final Cut. Final Cut Pro's limitations are compensated for in its simple versatility."

One problem that Dawn encounters in her work is that she layers multiple clips, which, while a key element in her editing process, can consume a lot of hard drive space. To get around this, she exports her layered and rendered footage to digital video. "Once the edited material is exported to tape, I'm able to erase everything on my timeline, trash my render files and QuickTime captures, and then recapture what was already edited. This process creates space on the hard drive and saves rendering time."

For more on Bendick's work, visit www.backbreakerneckbrace.com.

8 Making Smart Edits

Now we're ready to dive into the real craft of editing. Trimming your clips to fine-tune your edit is in many ways the most exciting part of the editing process. Seeing how one image will cut to another, observing how sounds change the impact of your cuts, creating scenes that have a dramatic and emotional shape—this is where you will begin to shape and mold your work. However, as with all creative endeavors, you will need some basic skills to realize your vision. Final Cut Pro allows you to edit your clips in several unique ways, each with its own use in the editing process.

Overview

> *"Perfection is achieved, not when there is noth-ing more to add, but when there is nothing left to take away."*
>
> Antoine de Saint-Exupery

In previous chapters, we've shown you how to prepare and organize your clips for editing, and how to make a rough cut. All of that organization will now pay off as you navigate through your cut. This chapter will get you started making finer edits in Final Cut Pro. You'll learn how to move, rearrange, and trim your clips in the Timeline, and then view the result. You will practice the different editing methods Final Cut Pro offers, which include Ripple, Roll, Slip, and Slide editing. We will also show you how to perform editing and trimming directly to a clip with the mouse.

Once you've got your clips online in the Browser, you are ready to edit. Before trying out specific techniques, however, let's review some basic concepts.

What Is an Edit?

Simply stated, an edit is the point at which two clips meet each other in the Timeline. In that sense, you began editing when you created a rough cut of a Timeline sequence in Chapter 6. However, a "clip" in the Timeline is, in many ways, just the tip of the iceberg. The clip shown in the Timeline may be a small part of the total clip you added from the Browser. All you can see in the Timeline is the selected part of the clip between the In and the Out points that you've designated, but the whole media file is still at your finger-tips—you just have to change the In and Out points. So, to be more specific, an edit is the point at which the Out point of one clip meets the In point of the next clip. The rest of the clip is still on your computer's hard disk, as part of the *trim*, but does not show up in the Timeline as part of your sequence.

Remember that if you have not already set In and Out points, the beginning and end of the media file are absolute (that is, they do not have any trim); you don't have any room at the end and beginning to add frames if you are using the whole media file.

Editing Styles and Strategies

Most professional editors take one of three primary approaches to the editing process, often described as the *documentary, narrative,* and *music video* methods. All three are valid, and you can decide which way is best based on your individual preferences and thought processes, as well as the nature of the project.

The Documentary Approach   The first approach many editors take is to create a rough cut of the entire sequence by bringing in the clips and finding the basic order that the clips will fall in. That's what you did in Chapter 6. Then the editor will go back and fine-tune each cut, making each clip just the right length and tweaking the juxtapositions so that they flow with the desired effect. This "rough cut" approach is often best if you're working on a project that is less clearly mapped out from the beginning, as in a documentary. Much of the structure of a documentary is discovered in the editing room, so it's a good idea to play around with the whole structure before you make fine edits.

The Narrative Approach   The second approach is to make finer adjustments from the start, so that the sequence builds from one clip to the next, and a lot of time is spent adjusting each edit before moving on to the next one. To follow this approach, you'll need to use the Final Cut Pro editing tools that we'll explore in this chapter. This narrative approach is best when you've got a very specific outline of how the shots are going to be put together, as in a fictional film that has been storyboarded. (*Storyboarding* is the process of making drawings of the shots in order before filming.)

The Music Video Approach   This style combines the previous two, and is often used to create a music video that intercuts the musicians performing with other, non-synch footage. First, you'll place the performance down as you would in the narrative approach, making fine cuts and adjustments with each clip. Second, once you've laid down the performance footage, you can go back and start laying in the "B-roll" footage in between or even on top of the performance. The B-roll footage will often be used to set moods or convey information that does not require exact synching with the audio (for example, atmospheric shots of city streets). It's a good idea to use a second video track to lay in the B-roll. Here, you'll use more a documentary approach, laying in clips in a rough order, seeing how they work, repositioning, and so on, until you have a sequence that captures the mood and rhythm of the music.

It's up to you to decide how to work. Just find the strategy that is most comfortable for you. And remember, Final Cut Pro offers an extensive number of Undo steps (see *Setting Your Preferences* in Chapter 2), so use them! You can experiment with a cut and, if you're unhappy with the outcome, use the ⌘+Z shortcut key to undo back to your original edit. It's a good idea, however, to save your Timeline whenever you get to a point where you are satisfied with the cuts you've made so far. Then, if you become dissatisfied with the work after that, you can always restore to that last save. Another strategy is to save different versions of your work as you go along, giving each a unique filename so that you can compare different versions of the edits.

Chapter 8: Three Edits

Open the Final Cut Pro project file labeled Coney Island Memories. After it loads in Final Cut Pro, double-click the Chapter 8 sequence in the Browser and it will open in the Timeline.

In this chapter you will practice adding and adjusting edits in clips. Each lesson in this chapter has a set of clips marked with the name of that lesson in the Timeline. Simply control-click in the timecode ruler of the Timeline to view a list of all of the markers for this sequence and choose the one for the lesson you are working on. Each lesson includes practice clips, a 1-second gap, and then the same clips again showing the intended results of the exercise.

Remember that if you get to a point where you want to start over with the original clips, close the project (File > Close Project), click No when asked if you want to save changes, and then reopen the project. You should see the project name at the bottom of the File menu with other recently opened project files. Select this to reopen the project.

Trimming with the Mouse

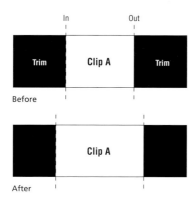

The least precise method of trimming, but sometimes the most intuitive, is to use the mouse. You can use the mouse to perform trim functions quickly by pulling or dragging the edge of a clip in the Timeline. Using the mouse to trim a clip can be helpful if you are looking at the Timeline and have a feel for where the clip needs to end or begin. (You may not know the exact number of frames, but you know that you need to drag it out to a certain point.) Remember, you can also drag the entire clip to different locations in the Timeline using the Selection tool. To do so, select the clip in the middle and drag it to wherever you want in the Timeline.

1. Choose the Select tool ⭦ (press **A**), and click the edge of the clip you want to edit. For this example, go to the clip marked "Trimming with the Mouse" in the Timeline.

If you need to get closer for more precise editing, see the sidebar *Using the Magnifying Glass*. Note how the cursor changes to a bar with a double-sided arrow when you approach the edge of a clip.

2. Drag the edge backward or forward. By doing this, you are automatically adding or subtracting frames, moving them to the clip from the trim, or vice versa.

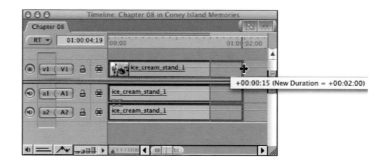

3. If snapping is on (see the sidebar *What Is Snapping?*), the clip will snap to the nearest clip In or Out point, marker, or the playhead, as you drag it. This method allows you to make quick edits, which you can then review by playing over them with the playhead. You may decide to start placing clips together this way,

and then turning to the more precise editing styles below to fine-tune your cut.

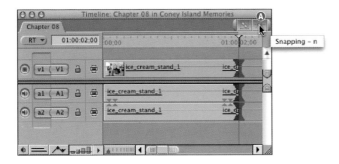

A Snapping is on

FAQ

What Is Snapping?

Snapping is a Timeline feature that helps you control how a clip is dragged or trimmed, and even how the playhead behaves. Snapping causes your cursor, when it's dragging something, to jump snugly to the nearest edit point. Why would you want to use this? If you are dragging a clip and want to make sure it is precisely lined up with the next clip, snapping is invaluable. It's also helpful when you are dragging the edge of a clip to extend it. If snapping is on, the clip's edge will leap to rest directly beside the next clip. To turn snapping on and off, choose View > Snapping (or press **N**), or choose the snapping control in the Timeline.

Alternate Method: Extending an Edit

Another quick way to trim the length of a clip, regardless of the clips that come after it or before it, is to use the Extend Edit command. This enables you to select an edit point, place your playhead, and then move that edit point to the playhead.

To use the Extend Edit command, follow these steps:

1. In the Timeline, select the edit point you want to trim. Place the playhead at the position where you want the selected edit point to be moved—this can be either before or after the current edit point.

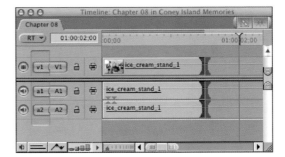

2. Choose Sequence > Extend Edit (press **E**). The edit point moves to the new position if there is enough footage available in the clip to allow it to extend to that point. If there is not enough footage, then nothing happens.

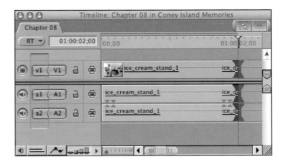

Extending an edit can be applied to either end of the clip and in either direction, making it a powerful tool for precise editing.

Using the Magnifying Glass

Often you'll need to change perspective on the Timeline. Sometimes it's necessary to see the entire project—"the big picture"—with all the clips visible at once. You'll find this technique most helpful when you want to see how long the piece is running or to quickly zip the playhead to any part of the sequence. However, you'll also find yourself needing to go in for a closer look, especially when you are dragging and trimming clips and need single-frame accuracy.

To quickly change the magnification of the Timeline, use the Magnifying Glass tool in the Tool Palette and click on your sequence. You can choose either a Zoom In tool ⊕ (press **Z**) or a Zoom Out tool ⊖ (press **ZZ**). The Timeline will zoom in or out so that the area of the Timeline you clicked on is centered. You can also use the Zoom control on the Timeline, sliding it back and forth to quickly pull your view of the Timeline in tight or out wide, with the playhead anchoring your center point.

Using the Razor Blade

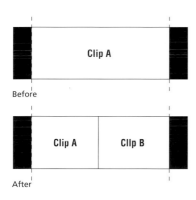

Before

After

The Razor Blade tool creates a cut in a selected spot in a clip in the Timeline, creating two separate clips that can be moved and manipulated individually. If the clip you cut with the Razor Blade is linked in an audio/video pair, both audio and video will be cut and divided (see

Linking Audio and Video Clips in Chapter 7). The Razor Blade tool is especially helpful if you want to quickly trim off an end of a clip, rearrange the footage in a clip, or apply an effect to a certain part of a clip.

1. Select the Razor Blade tool 🔪 (or press **B**) or the Razor Blade All tool 🔪 (or press **BB**) from the Tool Palette. If you need to zoom in for more precise editing, use the Magnifying Glass as described earlier. The single Razor Blade is used to cut a single clip in a particular layer in the Timeline, and the Razor Blade All tool is used to cut the clips in all of the layers in the Timeline at a particular spot.

2. Place the Razor Blade tool over the clip you want to cut in the Timeline. A line will appear over the clip at the frame where the cut will be made. You may want to use the playhead in the Timeline to view this frame before you make the cut.

3. Click the mouse, and a new edit point will be created at this spot. If you have selected the Double Razor Blade, a new edit point will appear on all clips above and below the current clip in the Timeline. The two new clips are now separate, and you can work with them independently

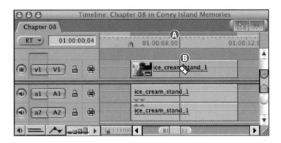

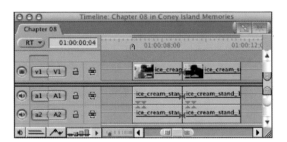

Ⓐ Playhead

Ⓑ Cut line

What Are Ripple, Roll, Slip, and Slide Edits?

Final Cut Pro provides tools for implementing four types of edits: Ripple, Roll, Slip, and Slide. Each edit will either add time to a particular clip or remove time from it, but each treats the clips before and after the edit in different ways. These tools, available via the Tool Palette and keyboard shortcuts, work with video, audio, and linked video and audio clips.

Roll The Roll edit adds frames to the end of a clip while subtracting the same number of frames from the clip beside it, maintaining the length of the sequence. This technique is useful when you are working with two clips that are in synch but need a different edit point between them.

Ripple The Ripple edit adds or subtracts frames from a clip without changing the duration or content of the surrounding clips. (Instead, it increases or decreases the length of the entire sequence.) This is most helpful when you want to extend or trim a clip without changing the surrounding clips.

Slip The Slip edit keeps the duration and position of a clip, but changes its content by shifting the In and Out points within the clip to show a different section of the original media file. The duration of the overall sequence is unchanged, as are the duration and content of the surrounding clips. This technique is helpful if you want to find a better part of a shot, particularly if it's a B-roll or accent shot.

Slide The Slide edit moves a clip left or right in the Timeline, maintaining the clip's duration and content, as well as the duration of the sequence. The surrounding clips will be extended or trimmed in the Timeline to fit the new location of the clip you are sliding. This can be helpful when you need to synch a clip with audio underneath it without disrupting the synchronization of the clips around it.

Making Roll Edits

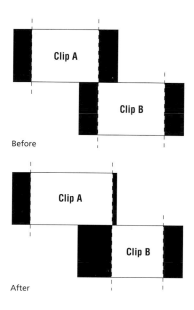

Before

After

A Roll edit keeps every clip at exactly the same position in the Timeline, but it adds or subtracts frames from the beginning of the incoming clip to accommodate the trimming of the outgoing clip. In the example shown here, if you add a few frames to the end of clip A, the first few frames of clip B on the same track in the Timeline will be subtracted to make room. Likewise, if you decided to take 10 frames off the end of clip A, clip B would start 10 frames earlier. In other words, you are moving the cut itself backward or forward. Compare this to the diagrams of other edit types you'll see later in this chapter.

The Roll edit is especially helpful in music videos or other projects where you have to keep precise synch with the audio.

1. After adding the clips that you want to edit to your Timeline (see Chapter 6) choose the Roll Edit tool ⚓ (press **R**) from the Tool Palette. Your cursor changes to the Roll tool and allows you to select an edit point to roll.

2. With the Roll Edit cursor, select the edit you want to trim by double-clicking between the two clips (which we will refer to as A and B). The Trim Edit window comes up with clip A (outgoing clip) on the left and clip B (incoming clip) on the right. (See the sidebar *Understanding the Trim Edit Window* for more details.)

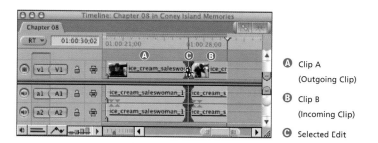

Ⓐ Clip A (Outgoing Clip)

Ⓑ Clip B (Incoming Clip)

Ⓒ Selected Edit

3. In the Trim Edit window, to "roll" the edit back and forth, click the Trim Back or Trim Forward buttons to add or subtract in increments of one or five frames at a time. For every frame increment that you add, clip A will increase and clip B will be cut by the same number of frames. As with other types of editing, however, this function depends on the frames clips A and B have available as trim. If you try to roll an edit past the beginning or end of the clip's original media file, Final Cut Pro will inform you that there is not enough media to perform this edit.

Ⓐ Trim Back

Ⓑ Trim Forward

Ⓒ Play Around Edit Loop

You can also specify an exact number of frames to add or subtract, by typing either the plus or minus key and then the number of frames followed by the Return key. For example, entering **+27** adds 27 frames to the selected clip at the point of the selected cut.

4. Now preview your revised edit by clicking the Play Around Edit Loop button (or pressing the spacebar). You can continue to adjust your edit by repeating Steps 3 and 4.

5. Once you've finished fine-tuning your edit, close the Trim Edit window either by clicking the Close button in the top-left corner of the window or by simply clicking in the Timeline. The clips in the Timeline will reflect the changes you've just made.

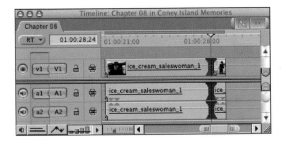

Alternate Steps: Roll Edits in the Timeline

The Trim Edit window gives you microscopic control over your Roll edits. However, you can also control Roll edits directly and

more quickly (although more roughly) in the Timeline. Starting after Step 1 of the *Making Roll Edits* procedure, do the following:

2. Select the edit between two clips you want to roll with the Roll cursor. This edit will become highlighted. You can zoom in for frame-by-frame editing with the Magnifying Glass.

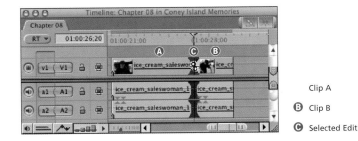

Ⓐ Clip A

Ⓑ Clip B

Ⓒ Selected Edit

3. Click and drag the clip to add or subtract frames from the two clips. This will change the In or Out Points of both clips. You can also click on the cut, type **+** or **–** followed by the number of frames you want to roll, and then press Return. Remember that the clip needs trimmed frames available at the edit point in order to be added using the roll. You also can't add frames past the Media Limit, which is the first or last frame you captured from the source tape.

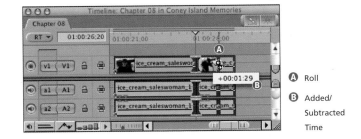

Ⓐ Roll

Ⓑ Added/ Subtracted Time

TIP
Understanding the Trim Edit Window

The Trim Edit window is useful for making precise editing decisions, letting you see the results of your cutting at a glance. This window shows you both clips simultaneously and lets you make your trims while keeping an eye on both clips at the same time. When it first appears after you double-click an edit to select it, the left side controls clip A (with the last frame of clip A currently showing), and the right side controls clip B (with the first frame of clip B currently showing). The clip that will gain or lose frames appears with a green highlight bar above it; you'll find this visual feedback from Final Cut Pro invaluable as you work.

Ⓐ Outgoing Clip: Displays the outgoing clip that you are editing.

Ⓑ Incoming Clip: Displays the incoming clip that you are editing.

Ⓒ Playback Controls for Incoming Clip: Standard VCR-style remote controls for viewing and cueing up your incoming clip.

Ⓓ Incoming Clip Duration: Shows the duration of the incoming clip.

Ⓔ Playback Controls for Outgoing Clip: Standard VCR-style remote controls for viewing and cueing up your outgoing clip.

Ⓕ Outgoing Clip Duration: Shows the duration of the outgoing clip.

Ⓖ Track Pop-up Menu: Lets you switch between multiple edits by track if you've selected more than one edit point. To select more than one edit point, hold the ⌘ key down to highlight multiple edits. Remember, you can't select more than one edit on the same track. The Track pop-up menu will let you choose any track number where you had a high-lighted edit.

Ⓗ Current Sequence Timecode: Shows what the timecode is in your sequence at the currently selected edit point.

Ⓘ Selected Clip: Indicates which kind of trimming function you are performing. A green bar on the left or right side means you are performing a Ripple edit. A green bar over both the left and right side means you are performing a Roll edit.

Ⓙ Trim Controls: Lets you add or subtract frames to your edit in increments of 1 and 5 frames. You can also customize these options, making them as large as 99 frames in the User Preferences window.

Ⓚ Previous Edit: Moves the edit immediately before the currently selected one.

Ⓛ Play In to Out: Plays from the current In point to the current Out point.

Ⓜ Play Around Edit Loop: This function plays the edit with a little pre-roll and post-roll.

Ⓝ Stop: Stops the playhead.

Ⓞ Next Edit: Moves the edit immediately after the currently selected edit.

Ⓟ Mark Out: Sets a new Out point for the outgoing clip. To do this, you must place the playhead in the Outgoing Clip window at the designated place, and then click the Out point. If you extend beyond the footage of the digitized media clip in the Browser, it will set the Out point at the Media Limit.

Ⓠ Mark In: Sets a new In point for the incoming clip. To do this, you must place the playhead in the Incoming Clip window at the designated place, and then click the In point. If you extend beyond the footage of the digitized media clip in the Browser, it will set the In point at the Media Limit.

Ⓡ Dynamic: By checking this box, you can use the J, K, and L keys to trim on-the-fly. Use the J key to rewind or the L key to play forward from the edit point. Pressing K lays down a new edit point, extending or shortening the clip.

Making Ripple Edits

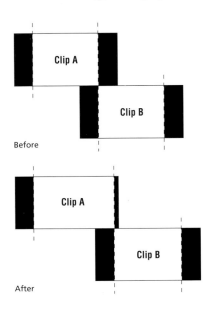

Before

After

A *Ripple* edit changes the length of one clip while adjusting the position of the subsequent clips in the Timeline to make room for or fill in the space left by the newly trimmed clip. In the example shown here, clip A is followed by clip B on the same track in the Timeline. When we use the Ripple edit to extend the length of clip A, clip B shifts down the Timeline to accommodate the added frames. Notice that the duration and content of clip B do not change, but the total length of the sequence increases.

1.   After adding the clips you want to edit to your Timeline (see Chapter 6), choose the Ripple Edit tool ⟨⟩ from the Tool Palette (or press **RR**). Your cursor changes to the Ripple tool, and you can now select either the left or right side of a clip (the In or Out points) to edit it.

2.   With the Ripple Edit cursor, select the edit you want to trim by double-clicking between the two clips (which we will refer to as A and B). The Trim Edit window comes up with clip A (outgoing clip) on the left and clip B (incoming clip) on the right. (See the sidebar *Understanding the Trim Edit Window* for more details.) This is a completely separate window that appears over the Canvas and Viewer, but does not replace them.

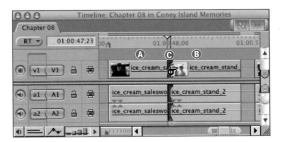

Ⓐ Clip A (Outgoing Clip)

Ⓑ Clip B (Incoming Clip)

Ⓒ Selected Edit

3. Click in the center of the left window to perform a Ripple edit on clip A. Click in the center of the right window to perform the edit on clip B. Notice the green highlight bar above the clip you have currently selected for the Roll edit. Clicking between the clips in the Trim Edit window will select both clips and allow you to perform a Roll edit, discussed in the previous section.

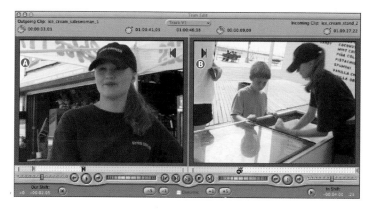

Ⓐ Clip A (Outgoing Clip) Ⓑ Clip B (Incoming Clip)

4. Click the Trim Back or Trim Forward buttons to add or subtract frames from the selected clip in increments of one or five frames at a time. This changes the In or Out point for the clip in the Timeline. You can also type in the number of frames you want to add or subtract by pressing the plus or minus key followed by the number of frames and the Return key. For example, entering +27 adds 27 frames to the selected clip at the point of the selected cut. If you are working with a clip that is linked to an audio clip (see *Understanding the Timeline* in Chapter 2), the edit will make these changes to both the video and the audio clips. If the clips are not linked, your changes will be made only to the video clip.

Notice that as you trim a clip, the Out Shift or In Shift will change to show you how much footage you have added or taken away from that clip.

Ⓐ Trim Back

Ⓑ Trim Forward

5. Now preview your revised edit by clicking the Play Around Edit Loop button (or by pressing the spacebar). You can continue to adjust your edit as desired by repeating Steps 3 and 4.

6. When you've fine-tuned your edit to the way you want it, close the Trim Edit window either by clicking its Close button in the top-left corner of the window or by simply clicking in the Timeline. The clips in the Timeline will reflect the changes you just made.

Alternate Steps: Ripple Edits in the Timeline

Although using the Trim Edit window will give you precise control over your edits, you can also perform Ripple edits directly in the Timeline. This technique is helpful if you want to make a quick edit, or if you want to take a more intuitive approach to the edit by making visual decisions about the relationship between your clips. Pick up after Step 1 of the *Making Ripple Edits* procedure.

2. Select the edge of the clip you want to ripple with the Ripple cursor. This edge will become highlighted. Notice how the cursor will switch to point the Ripple icon in the direction of the clip you want to ripple. If you need to zoom in for more precise editing, use the Magnifying Glass as described earlier.

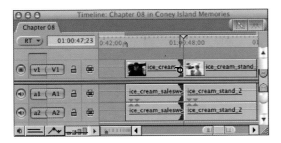

3. Click and drag the clip to add or subtract the number of frames you want (adding them to the trim for the clip). This will change that clip's In or Out point but not the In or Out point of the adjacent clip. Alternatively, type **+** or **–** followed by the number of frames you want to ripple (e.g., **+12**) and then press Return. Remember, though, that the clip needs to have extra frames available at the

edit point in the Timeline in order to be rippled. The clip will not add frames that do not exist in the original media file.

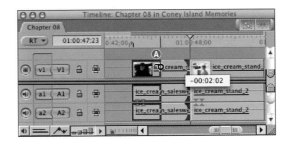

Ⓐ Ripple

Ⓑ Added/Subtracted Time

TIP

Locking Tracks

While you are editing, you'll want to make sure that you don't accidentally make changes to clips. A good safeguard is to use the *locking* mechanism, which freezes a track so that no changes or edits can occur. A locked track cannot receive media and will not respond to any edit or new footage.

To lock a track, click the little padlock icon to the right of the track number. The entire track will become crosshatched, symbolizing that it is now unavailable for editing. To unlock the track, click the padlock icon a second time, and all the clips on the track are available again for editing.

Shortcut keys for locking are:

- To lock a video track, press F4 and the track number (1–9).
- To lock an audio track, press F5 and the track number (1–9).
- To lock all video tracks, press Shift+F4.
- To lock all audio tracks, press Shift+F5.

Making Slip Edits

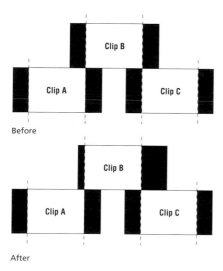

Before

After

Slip editing is a powerful function that lets you shift a clip's In and Out points (changing the content) without moving the clip's location in the Timeline. In the example shown here, clip B is between clips A and C on the same Timeline track. Using a Slip edit, we shift the In and Out points of clip B so that it starts and finishes with different footage than before the Slip edit. Clips A and C are not affected; nor is the total length of the sequence. The Slip edit basically allows you to change the footage within clip B to expose a different part of the master media file, while maintaining the duration and location in the Timeline.

1. Select the Slip Edit tool ⟷ (press S) from the Tool Palette. If you need to zoom in for more precise editing, use the Magnifying Glass as described earlier.

2. Select the clip you want to slip by clicking it and holding down the mouse button. Now drag the clip to the left or right to move the total clip within the In and Out points in the Timeline.

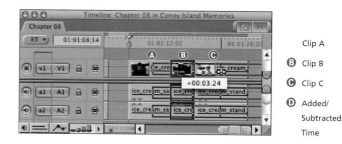

Clip A

B Clip B

C Clip C

D Added/
Subtracted
Time

3. Notice that when you drag the clip you are slipping, the Canvas window shows two screens. The left screen shows you the new In point of the clip and the right screen shows you the new Out point.

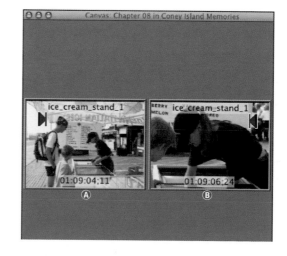

A New In Point

B New Out Point

4. Use the controls in the Canvas to play through your new edit and make sure it is the way you want it, or you can continue to Slip edit this clip further. If your audio and video aren't linked, a Slip edit will put the clip out of synch with audio. Both clips will now contain a window showing you how many frames apart they are.

Making Slide Edits

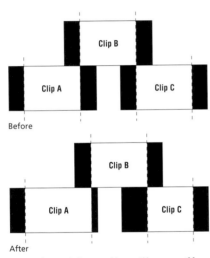

Before

After

Slide edits maintain a clip's duration and its In and Out points relative to the original media, but slide it back and forth over the other clips on the same track in the Timeline. This edit will not affect the position of any other clips, but it will affect the duration of the adjacent clips. In the example shown here, we are working with three clips on the same track in the Timeline. By sliding clip B forward, we increase the length of clip A and decrease the length of clip C. When you slide clip B forward, it leaves more room in the Timeline for clip A to play out, and trims away the beginning of clip C. The overall length of the sequence is unchanged, and clip B remains the same in content and in length.

1. Select the Slide Edit tool ⊕⊕ (press **SS**) from the Tool Palette. If you need to zoom in for more precise editing, use the Magnifying Glass as described earlier ⊕⊕.

2. Select the clip you want to slide by clicking it and holding down the mouse button. Now, to slide the clip, drag it left or right. A ghost clip will appear, showing you where your clip will land when you drop it.

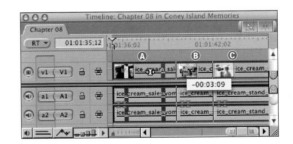

Ⓐ Clip A   Ⓑ Clip B   Ⓒ Clip C

3. Notice that when you slide the clip, two screens appear in the Canvas. The left screen shows you the Out point of the clip before the sliding clip and the right screen shows you the In point of the clip after the sliding clip. This way, you can see at a glance exactly which frames will be your new edit points.

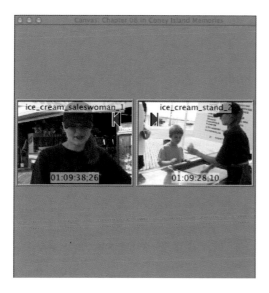

4. Play over your new edit in the Timeline and make sure it is right. If your audio and video aren't linked, a Slide edit will put the clip out of synch, and both clips will now contain a window showing you how many frames apart they are.

Can I Put One Sequence inside Another?

This is a common question, and the answer is *yes*, you can treat a sequence like a clip and edit it into another sequence. This creates what is called a *nested* sequence. The sequence responds like a clip in the Timeline; you can drag it from the Browser into the Timeline or the Edit Overlay window, move it within a sequence by dragging it, apply trims like Roll or Ripple, even add transitions like cross-dissolves (see Chapter 10). Double-clicking on a nested sequence causes this sequence to open as a separate tab in the Timeline. One great benefit of using nested sequences is that it reflects any changes you make to it within its own tab full of clips. You can also open the nested sequence in the Viewer by control-clicking it and selecting "Open in Viewer." The sequence will then open like a clip.

For example, suppose you have sequence A and sequence B. Sequence B is a short montage of images that you want to use as a part of your main movie in sequence A. So you drag sequence B from its bin in the Browser into sequence A and place it between the other clips there. Then you decide to switch the order of shots in the montage, so you open up Sequence B's tab and re-edit the clips. This re-editing will also occur in sequence A's nested sequence. If you shorten sequence B by editing it after you've also used it as a nested sequence, a gap will appear in sequence A after the end of sequence B. If you lengthen sequence B, however, it will not lengthen in sequence A, but that media is available if you drag out the end of the nested sequence B.

Using nested sequences is great on larger projects when you have many smaller individual scenes that make up the whole. You can create a separate sequence for each scene, and then drag the scenes as nested sequences into one behemoth final sequence. Then, it's easy to reorganize scenes without a lot of multiple highlighting, and your Timeline doesn't get as messy or disorganized.

You can also "unpack" a sequence into the Timeline by holding the ⌘ key down as you drag it. The contents of the dragged sequence will be edited into the current sequence.

Editing for Speed: Slow Motion, Fast Motion, and Reverse

Slow motion is a commonly used effect to create a romantic feel or to heighten a scene of extreme action. Hong Kong action filmmakers often use slow motion to zero in on the acrobatic moves of a film's characters. Slow motion can also easily look silly or hokey, so be wary of overdoing it. Final Cut Pro 4 also offers variable speed options with the Time Remapping function (see Chapter 15).

Fast motion is used less often but can be used effectively in slapstick comedies (think Benny Hill) or to create a time-lapse effect.

Reverse motion can be used to create an otherworldly effect—water falling up, people walking backward along the sidewalk, a broken glass coming back together into a whole. It can also be used to change the direction of a camera movement when it isn't evident that the footage is running backward.

To change the speed at which a clip plays, follow these steps:

1. Select a clip so that it is highlighted.

2. Choose Modify > Speed to bring up the Speed window (⌘+J).

3. Make sure the pull-down menu is set to Constant Speed. Now type in a new duration or a percentage to change the clip's speed. Typing in a percentage less than 100% will give you a slow motion effect (i.e., 50% is half speed) and typing in a number higher than 100% will give you fast motion (i.e., 200% is double speed). Notice that the speed of the clip is displayed next to the clip's name in the Timeline on the clip's thumbnail.

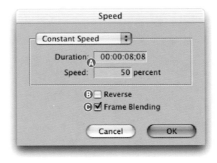

A To change the clip's speed, type a percentage value to indicate the change in speed. Typing a value less than 100% will slow down a clip. Typing a value greater than 100% will speed it up. You could also type a new duration for the clip, and the clip will speed up or slow down to fit this new duration. The clip will grow or shrink in the Timeline to accommodate the new length.

B To run the clip backward, click the Reverse check box to select it. This causes the clip to play from end to beginning. When you reverse a clip, Final Cut Pro literally takes the order of the clip's frames in reverse, so that it plays the last clip first. You can still alter the speed of the clip in reverse.

C To create a smoother transition between frames, select the Frame Blending check box. This will make the speed change less jerky.

4. Click OK and then render the clip to view in real time. Being able to type in an exact duration of time to make the altered clip allows you to create a clip of an exact length that might fill a hole or gap in your edit. It's not cheating to slow down a shot subtly to make it fit into a gap you have to fill to make your edit work. If you don't know the exact time you want, but just want to fill a gap quickly, you can also use the Fit to Fill edit function found in the Edit Overlay window of the Canvas.

Creating a Freeze-Frame

A *freeze-frame* is a single motionless image—like a photograph—that is taken from a single frame of moving video. Freeze-frames are used all the time as background for titles or elements in a montage. They can also be exported as a picture file (for example, a JPEG) so that you can use them in print publications or as stills on a web site.

To make a freeze-frame, follow these steps:

1. Place the playhead in the clip at the exact frame you want to use for the still image.

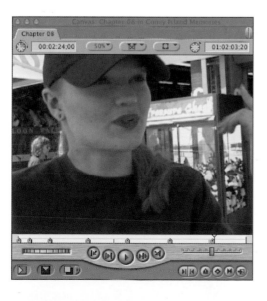

2. Choose Modify > Make Freeze Frame (Shift+N). A new freeze-frame clip appears in the Viewer window. The freeze-frame's name automatically incorporates the originating sequence's name and the timecode of the frame.

3. Set the In and Out points for the clip to set the duration of the freeze-frame.

You can now edit the freeze-frame clip directly into your video or drag it into the Browser to add it to your library of clips. Freeze-frames are real-time effect clips, which means that you can view them in real time in the Canvas, but you'll need to render your clip before output.

The default duration of a freeze-frame is 10 seconds as this gives you a good length to work with without the clip being unwieldy or too small. However, you can change the default in the Final Cut Pro > User Preferences window to suit your needs by typing in a new duration (i.e., 6 seconds instead of 10). You may decide that all freeze-frames need to be exactly 6 seconds, so this can save you time having to trim all the clips.

Part Three:
Adding Effects

Although films can be created directly from the original footage without any alteration other than editing the clips together, this is extremely rare. Even the most "natural" looking footage will require some augmentation, either to correct color and lighting problems or simply to add transitions between different scenes. The effects you add to your video footage can range from the extremely subtle to the extreme and bizarre. In the following chapter, we will show you the basics for adding a variety of effects including those located in the Effects tab and also image modes, motion, and using keyframes to change the effects as your footage plays.

9 Working with Effects: Real-Time and Rendering

Effects are used to change the visual and aural nature of your original footage. Although there are a finite number of effects (filters, transitions, generators, motion, and composite modes), the uses for them are limitless. In addition to common effects you have ways to play with the clip speed, opacity, and even animate the clips themselves. All of this power comes with one drawback: rendering. Every time you make a change that alters the clip, Final Cut Pro has to create a new clip that displays the changes in real time. However, advances in computer speed make it increasingly possible to preview effects without rendering them first. In this chapter we will look at how to apply an effect, how to set up Final Cut Pro to view effects in real time without rendering, and how to render effects for final output.

Overview

> *"Always design a thing by considering it in its next larger context—a chair in a room, a room in a house, a house in an environment, an environment in a city plan."*
>
> Eliel Saarinen

Any time you change the content of a clip, either to the video or audio, other than simply changing the edits, the clip will need to eventually be *rendered* before you can output your work. These changes will come in many forms:

Alpha Channels   Commands used to define the opacity of the clip.

Composite Mode   Commands used to define how the pixels in the clip of one track interact with the pixels of another track. By default, the clip in the upper track is opaque (no interaction); by setting the composite mode, the pixels in the two clips are combined.

Filters Effects   Effects used to change the appearance (video) or sound (audio) of the clip in a variety of ways.

Generators   Effects that make a new clip used to create specialized content such as titles, color slugs, and color bars and tone.

Motion   Controls that allow you to set the size, rotation, position, crop, distortion, opacity, drop shadow, motion blur, and advanced speed controls.

Speed   Controls that allow you to speed, slow, or reverse the clip.

Transitions   Effects used to create a smoother or flashier shift between the edits of clips.

Once changes are made to a clip, Final Cut pro will need to make changes to the actual appearance (or sound for audio) of the clip. Rendering is the process by which Final Cut Pro allows a change to the clip to be viewed in real time in the Canvas. For example, when you add any effects, such as Color Balance, you will need to render this effect before you can watch the clip in motion. Rendering actually creates a new file, called a render file, with the information needed for Final Cut Pro to play through the clip successfully.

Using Real-Time with Effects

Final Cut Pro 4 has many Real-Time effects—effects that can be previewed immediately without rendering. These effects use your computer's memory and speed so that you can watch them without creating a separate render file. However, even Real-Time effects will have to be rendered before the project is output for final viewing on the web, videotape, CD, or DVD.

Real-Time effects will appear in bold in your Browser's Effects tab, which lets you know that these effects are capable of playing back in real time as long as your processor is fast enough. The 3-Way Color Corrector and Desaturation are two types of common Real-Time effects. Note that Real-Time effects, while previewable, still need to be rendered before you can print to video.

Adding a Real-Time effect is the same as adding any other effect—you can drag an effect from the Browser's Effects tab into a clip or highlight a clip and select an effect from the Effects top pulldown menu. If you've added a Real-Time effect, a green bar will appear over the clip instead of the usual red bar (a red bar means you will have to manually render the clip).

The clip should have a green bar over it designating it a Real-Time effect and you should now be able to preview it. If the bar appears as red, your processor may not be able to handle the effect or you will need to change your Real-Time options (see below). Other color codes to designate types of render options and Real-Time Effects are discussed later in this chapter.

Setting Real-Time Options

Final Cut Pro 4 comes with settings to help you control your Real-Time effects. You can customize your Real-Time options to fit your project. For example, you may want to have all the effects play in real time, even if your computer isn't quite fast enough to handle them, so that you can watch a piece uninterrupted by "unrendered" screens. This option may cause you to drop frames, but it's worth it so you can evaluate the piece with all the effects in place.

To set the Real-Time options while you are working, open the RT effects popup menu located on the top left side of your Timeline. You can also access some of these options by selecting Final Cut Pro > System Settings and selecting the Playback Control tab to set them. Below are the important settings you can adjust in the dialog box.

RT: Unlimited   Plays all Real-Time effects in real time even if your computer is not fast enough to play perfectly. We don't recommend it, as it increases your chances of dropped frames during playback.

RT: Safe   Plays only the Real-Time effects your system can handle. We recommend this setting unless you are concerned about playback quality.

Play Base Layer Only (if render needed)   Plays through your clips, ignoring any effects that need to be rendered. If not selected, you'll get the familiar Unrendered screen when you try to play through them.

Video Quality   Lets you choose the level of quality you want to play your clips back at—the higher the quality, the more speed you'll need from your system for proper playback.

Record   Lets you decide whether you record at full quality or the customized playback settings when you print to video.

Setting Render Options

You can customize your computer's render settings to work best with your project. The Render Control tab is located in both the Sequence Settings window and the User Preferences window.

Open the Render Control tab by either selecting Final Cut Pro > User Preferences (Option+Q) or Sequence > Settings (⌘+0). In this tab, review your options:

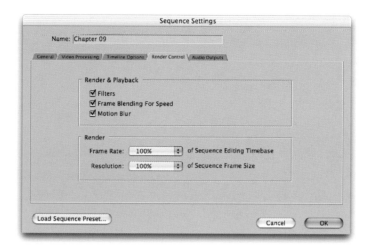

Filters Checking this box, Final Cut Pro acknowledges any filters on a clip. If the box is not checked, all filters will be ignored. You'll usually want this checked unless you want to preview your cut without filters.

Frame Blending For Speed Frame blending is a process that smoothes clips that have been slowed down. Unchecking this box will ignore Frame Blending.

Motion Blur Unchecking this box will make Final Cut Pro ignore any motion blur effects when rendering. Motion Blur creates a blurring between frames.

Frame Rate The lower the frame rate percentage, the faster rendering will occur, but at a proportional loss of image quality.

Resolution This percentage controls the quality of the resolution of the rendering. The lower the resolution, the faster a clip will render. Again, this setting will cause the rendered effect to look less sharp.

Setting Up Auto Rendering

Auto Rendering is a new feature of Final Cut Pro 4 that allows you to have the computer automatically render your clips if you step away from your computer. If there is no action at your computer for a period of time, Final Cut will just kick in and do the work for you.

This function is helpful if you are working on a big project that has a lot of rendered effects. Rendering can eat into your edit time, so by setting up Auto Rendering, you can have Final Cut Pro maximize your time away from the computer by churning through unrendered effects and preparing them for playback.

Select Final Cut Pro > User Preferences (Option+Q) and select the General Tab. Review the Auto Render box at the bottom right corner. The box should be checked to turn on Auto Rendering. Close the User Preferences to activate the Auto Render control.

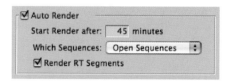

Start Render after *X* minutes This sets how many minutes of inaction it takes before the computer will start rendering.

Which Sequences Lets you choose which sequences should be automatically rendered: just the open sequences, the current (selected) sequence, or all open sequences *except* the current sequence.

Render RT segments Check this box if you want to have the Real-Time effects rendered with the Auto Render function.

Adding an Effect to a Clip

Before   After

Although there are many ways to alter a clip, the most common is the use of the effects located in the Browser's Effects tab. In Chapters 10, 11, and 12, we explore the implementation of the various effect types (transitions, filters, and generators) in greater detail. For now, we want to introduce the basic concepts involved with adding an effect to a clip so that we can then practice rendering the clip.

1. Select the clip you want to add an effect to in the Timeline by clicking it or placing the playhead within the clip. You can also Shift+click or ⌘+click multiple clips to have the effect applied to all of them, or double-click the clip to open it in the Viewer and apply the effect through that window.

2. In the Browser, click the Effects tab and open the effect type you want to apply. For this example, we will be using Video Filters > Stylize > Find Edges.

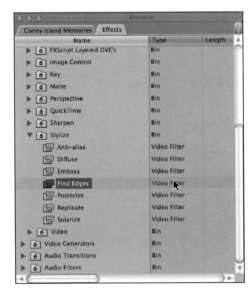

3. Once you have the effect you want to add, do one of the following:

- Drag the effect onto a clip in the Timeline. This will apply the effect only to that clip. If you have selected multiple clips and drag an effect onto one of them, then they will all be affected.
- Drag the effect to the clip showing in the Canvas. This will apply the effect to the clip underneath the playhead.
- Drag the effect to the clip showing in the Viewer.
- Shift+click multiple effects in the Browser to apply all of them simultaneously to one or more clips.

The effect is now added to the clip and can be manipulated in the Filters tab in Viewer. Notice in the Timeline that immediately above the Timeline ruler there is a colored rule. The color of the line will depend on the type of effect you applied, the processor speed of your computer, and your Real-Time settings. Red indicates that the effect must be rendered. For a full list of colors, see the *Rendering Clips* section.

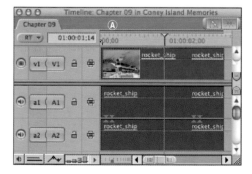

Ⓐ The render line indicates the part of the footage that has to be rendered. Different colors are used to indicate different render types.

Alternative Steps: Applying Effects Using Menus

Alternatively, effects can be added using the Effects menu.

1. In the Timeline, select the clip to which you want to add an effect by clicking it or placing the playhead within the clip. You can also Shift+click multiple clips to have the effect applied to all of them.

2. Choose Effects **>** Video Filters and then one of the filter types. For this example, use Effects **>** Video Filters **>** Stylize **>** Find Edges.

The effect will be immediately applied to the selected clip.

Rendering Clips

Final Cut Pro 4 has added many new types of rendering options and new divisions of Real-Time effects. They are explained in the sidebar below, *What Are Rendering Types?* The basic breakdown gives us Unrendered effects, Proxy effects, and Preview effects. Proxy and Preview are two types of Real-Time effects. Preview effects can be seen immediately without rendering, and Proxy effects show a close approximation of an effect (things like edge feathering may be left out to save memory).

No Effect Applied   *Does not need rendering.* No effects are applied to the clip.

Rendered   *Does not need rendering.* The clip has been rendered.

Needs Render   *Needs render for playback or export.* Rendering is needed to view the clip in real time or for export.

Rendered Proxy   *Needs render for export only.* Proxy effects (see below) that can be seen in real time.

Proxy   *Needs rendering for playback and export* Effect can be seen without rendering, but with only an approximation of the full effect (i.e., an edge feather or tint may be left out so the effect can play). The effect can be rendered as a proxy to view in real time.

Preview   *Needs rendering for export only.* A Real-Time effect that your computer can play back at a high quality preview without rendering.

Full   *Does not need rendering.* A Real-Time effect that can be previewed and outputted with full resolution without rendering.

Unlimited   *Needs rendering for export only.* Indicates clips with effects the computer may not be fast enough to play through without dropped frames.

Unsupported   *Needs rendering for export only.* Indicates that a Real-Time enabler file isn't supported, and frames may drop as a result.

Rendering a Single Clip

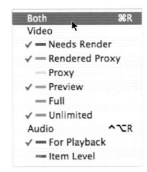

Rendering an effect is a simple process that creates a new render file and allows you to watch the effect and then print it to video. Rendering will be lost any time you change the clip—trim it or add a new effect.

1. In the Timeline, place the playhead within the clip you want to render. You can also Shift+click or ⌘+click multiple clips to have them all rendered at the same time. Remember to set the render quality when you set your render options as explained earlier in this chapter.

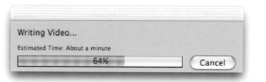

After the clip has been rendered, the render line at the top of the Timeline will change to a gray blue and the clip will play in the Canvas in real time. Your clips are now rendered and ready to be printed to video or exported for the Web or DVD.

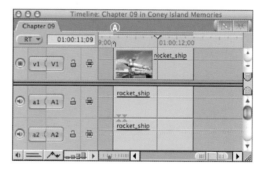

Ⓐ The render line is gray blue indicating that the clip has been rendered.

2. Select Sequence > Render > Both (⌘+R) to render both unrendered audio and video in the clip. You can also choose which types of clips are being rendered (see the *What Are Render Types?* sidebar). A Render dialog box will appear with a time bar and an approximate time for the rendering to occur. You can stop rendering at any time by clicking cancel without losing the render work that has already been done. The render time will depend on the size of the clip or clips and the number and complexity of effects applied.

What Are Render Types?

Although the basic process for rendering a clip is straightforward and prepares an clip for output, you can set several options to specify the types of renders being affected by your commands, whether you are rendering a single clip, a group of clips, or all clips in a sequence. Both the Render and Render All submenus list the different render types you perform by selecting them in the menu. The Render Only menu also presents the same list (with the addition of Mix Down), which when selected will render all effects of that type.

Rendering All Clips in a Sequence

You can also choose to render all the effects in a sequence at once.

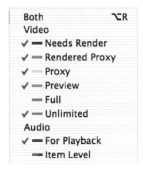

1. Open the sequence you wish to render in your Timeline.

2. Choose Sequence **>** Render All **>** Both (Option+R) to render both unrendered audio and video. If you want to have more control over the kinds of effects you are rendering, see the sidebar *What Are Render Types?*

A Render dialog box will appear with a time bar and an approximate time for the rendering to occur. You can stop rendering at anytime by clicking cancel without losing the render work that has already been done. Final Cut Pro will go through your sequence and render everything in order. Your clips are now rendered and ready to be printed to video or exported for the web or DVD.

Render Only Specific Clips in a Sequence

The Render Only option lets you render just specific types of unrendered clips. In this example, we'll only render Real-Time clips, leaving all the other edited clips alone.

1. Open the sequence that you want to work with or select a group of clips to isolate them for rendering.

2. Choose Sequence **>** Render Only and the render type you want. This option only renders clips in the sequence with the selected render type.

Your clips are now rendered and ready to be printed to video or exported for the web or DVD.

Managing Render Files

When you render a clip you are actually creating a new file, and these files can start to add up and consume hard disk space. While Final Cut Pro 4 will do a lot of work for you in deleting old files, you also have the option to delete them yourself. Of course, you can just go into the Render Files folders and trash them, but you can also delete files from within Final Cut Pro.

Select Tools **>** Render Manager to bring up the Render Manager window. You will see folders for all open and unopen projects. You can then go through and select specific projects or render files within project you want to delete.

To delete a render file or an entire folder of render files, put a check mark in the Remove column by that file or folder. Click okay and this will delete these files, clearing disk space.

Saving Your Favorite Effects

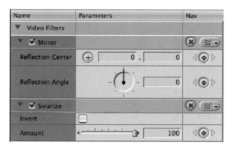

All filters can be copied from one clip to another or saved for quick access later in the editing process. This is extremely useful when you've modified a filter of group of filters to fit a specific look. Perhaps you have these filters on one clip and you want to apply exactly the same filters and settings to more clips, or maybe even all the clips in your sequence.

1. In the Canvas, Timeline, or Browser, double-click the clip that has the filter or filters you want to copy (the source clip) to open it in the Viewer.

2. Open the source clip's Filters tab in the Viewer window. Highlight the effect or effects you want to copy by clicking in the name of the effect. The clip's Name column will darken when it is highlighted. (To delete the effect from use in this clip, simply press the Delete key.)

3. Holding down the mouse button, drag the effect and drop it on a target clip in the Timeline. If you want multiple clips to contain this effect, highlight them all in the Timeline and drag the effect(s) from the Viewer to the highlighted clips in the Timeline.

Now you are ready to render the effects, as described earlier in this chapter.

Storing Favorite Effects

Once you have a filter customized the way you want it, you can store it as a *favorite* in the Browser. You can easily find your customized effect and apply it to any clip where it's needed.

1. Double-click the clip whose effect(s) you want to store in the Browser, Canvas, or Timeline so that it is open in the Viewer.

2. Open the Effects tab of the Browser and open the Favorites bin.

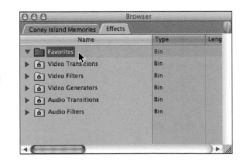

3. In the Viewer, open the clip's Filters tab and locate the effect you want to store as a Favorite. Drag this effect into the Favorites bin in the Effects tab of the Browser. This effect, with all the settings you have made intact, is now stored as a Favorite. You can rename the effect by clicking its name in the Browser's Favorite bin. You can also create a bin in the Favorites bin of your own to store a series of effects. You can then apply all of these at once by dragging the bin into a clip.

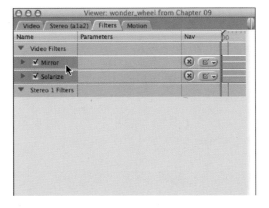

4. To copy a stored effect to a new clip, drag the effect from the Browser's Favorites bin and drop it in a clip in the Timeline or the Viewer.

Cruise Control, A Short Comedy

Charlie Chaplin said, "All I need to make a comedy is a park, a policeman and a pretty girl." While it's true that the situation of comedy may often be simple, it takes talent and a gift for unique observation to turn a simple situation into something that will make people laugh. *Cruise Control*, a satirical look into the phenomenon of what writer/director Lawrence Ferber calls "the cruising face" that many gay men make, does just that.

"During my years spent observing the people in gay bars, pride marches, Greenwich Village, hell, even a mirror, I noticed that when a queen sees someone he likes, he makes a 'cruising face'," says Ferber. "His lips might purse, his eyelids might squint or open wide, his eyes might drop. It can turn the sexiest guy into the silliest-looking freak. Straight guys can make cruising faces too, but rarely are they as bizarre, funny, or downright creepy."

Photograph courtesy of Lilliput Pictures

Cruise Control was shot using a Sony VX-1000 with Beechtek audio adapter on a tight time table, due to limited time at the location. So, the writer/director/editor team of brothers Lawrence and Matthew Ferber created a detailed storyboard and shot list, making sure to memorize these in advance of the shoot. According to Lawrence, "of course, by storyboarding and shot listing, a sense of editing came into play. I had ideas—some solid, some flexible—as to where cuts would be, and always made sure to have plenty of coverage. Matthew, who edits my films, always emphasizes its importance, and I've learned he's right numerous times. Nothing was left to chance on *Cruise Control* in that regard." Their careful planning paid off. Despite some complications—an unexpected party got scheduled at the club being used at the same time they were supposed to be filming—the shoot went off with out a hitch and they were ready to edit their comedy.

Matthew comments that "editing comedy is like anything else; you just follow the story and find the tone. Of course, you want the story to play as funny. In *Cruise Control*, the humor in the story came from the way characters saw each other and reacted." This interaction came in the form of exaggerated movement combined with stylistic post-production flourishes. "Essentially, we were stepping into the characters' minds and participating from their perceptions of the night's events. This is where digital filmmaking is exciting to me. If we had shot and were posting on film, we would have had to do expensive opticals to achieve some of the effects. Realistically, on a low budget, you would just have to live without these."

Matthew was impressed with the freedom that DV gave him. With film, "you need X number of frames on either end of a cut, so they can cut the negative, and if you don't like the camera speed you used, tough. Not with digital. No limitations. Once it's in the computer, I can do whatever I want. I can speed it up, slow it down, make it fit with a piece of music. I can do dissolves of any length (try sending an EDL to a film lab with a 17 frame dissolve then pull out your checkbook for another optical), as well as any host of other transition types, and I'm not counting them to see what it will cost."

In one scene where two guys with amorous intentions approach the main character, Matthew wanted to satirize the motion by slowing it down, "I wanted to exaggerate the very act of the approach, like it was something tremendous, exciting, and suspenseful. Of course, it isn't, so people laugh. Slow motion makes everything seem graceful and beautiful. The romance of that plays ironically." At the end of their dramatic approach, they run away in horror at the sight of the horrific cruising face.

Cruise Control premiered at the 2001 New Festival in New York. It has since played at various Gay & Lesbian film festivals across America, including Los Angeles' Outfest and Washington D.C.'s Reel Affirmations Film Festival.

10 Adding Transitions

There's more than one way to get from point A to point B (or clip A to clip B). *Transitions* provide a variety of ways to move from one image to another, beyond the straight cut that takes us immediately to the next clip. Transitions can be simple or fancy, and they control the way your viewer perceives what is shown on the screen. A transition can be a slow dissolve from the first image to the next, or it can make an image "wipe" across the previous one. A transition can suggest the passage of time, or it can create a visually stunning juxtaposition. While a straight cut provides a simple, no-nonsense way to move between images, sometimes the right transition can add a needed effect to your edit.

Overview

> *"Every thing teaches transition, transference, metamorphosis: therein is human power, in transference, not in creation; and therein is human destiny, not in longevity but in removal. We dive and reappear in new places."*
>
> Ralph Waldo Emerson

Final Cut Pro 4 offers a lot of built-in effects to move between shots. These transitions are found in the Effects tab in your Browser as well as in Final Cut Pro's Effects menu. In the Video Transitions folder you'll find a host of transitions that take you from one video clip to the next. In the Audio Transitions folder, you'll find effects that blend audio clips, a useful tool for smoothing out audio cuts. Deciding when and how to use transitions is an essential part of your editing process, and it can deeply affect the impact and style of your finished project.

The most common video transition is the dissolve (Final Cut offers several kinds of dissolves, the most common being a cross-dissolve). A dissolve fades in one image while fading out the previous. It's an effect that's used all the time, and it often creates a softer mood than a hard cut. That's why dissolves are particularly common in romantic or emotional scenes in movies. The dissolve can also signify the passage of time. For example, if you see a woman waiting in a doctor's office, and the scene dissolves to a different shot of her waiting in the office, you are meant to assume that some time has passed.

Dissolves are so commonly used, in fact, that some editors avoid them on principle, finding them to be "too easy" and too often used to mask a cut that wouldn't work as a straight cut. While the choice is obviously yours, we recommend that you don't overuse dissolves or use them indiscriminately. It's also important to remember that straight cuts and cross-dissolves are not interchangeable. They signify different things and have a different effect on an audience. Straight cuts are less noticeable, and generally insinuate a continuation of space and action. Dissolves typically insinuate a change in time or place, or connote a change in a character's perception of time and space (such as remembering an event seen in flashback).

Final Cut Pro also offers many other transitional effects, most of which are special effects that you would see in a commercial or a training video, such as wipes or irises. While these aren't as commonly used, it's a good idea to go through your Video Transitions folder in the Effects tab and see what is available to you. The sample clips included in the DVD tutorial give you three clips to practice adding transitions with. (Following these three clips are the same clips with cross-dissolves added.) After you've tried this chapter's lessons working with cross-dissolves, use the same original clips and see how the other types of transitions look with that footage. Do any of them seem to communicate more effectively? You'll see that some of Final Cut Pro's effects, like wipes and page peels, are not very useful simply because they are not very professional-looking, and many are just plain hokey. Unless the project demands it, it's best to stay away from these gimmicky transitions and stick to the basics.

The Audio Transitions folder contains two types of transitions, both of which fade one audio clip out while the next one fades in. This allows you to create seamless audio from disparate clips. You'll also notice how adding transitions in the audio affects the viewer's response to the video. Laying an audio transition between two clips will change the way the viewer responds to the cut itself.

Since transitions are effects (just like filters and generators), they can work with Real-Time but have to be rendered for final production as explained in Chapter 9. Audio transitions don't have to be rendered and will automatically take effect. The most important thing to remember is to use transitions wisely and with reason. Often, a straight cut will do the job, and doesn't need to be made "fancier." But when a transition is used well (think of the slow, dream-like dissolves between many of the images of *Apocalypse Now*), it can create a surprising impact on the viewer's response.

Chapter 10: Bridging the Gaps

Open the Final Cut Pro project file labeled Coney Island Memories. After it loads in Final Cut Pro, double-click the Chapter 10 sequence in the Browser and it will open in the Timeline.

In this chapter you will add transitions to audio and video clips. Four markers indicate which lesson the clips should be used with. The first set of clips is for you to practice with; the second set shows how it might look after performing the exercise in a section. Why "might" look? There are a lot of different variables for transitions. Although we show you one way, we want to encourage you to play around with the transitions and not follow what we say to the letter.

Adding Transitions

This section shows how to add any transition to your clips, using the most common transition, the cross-dissolve, as our example. A *dissolve* is a transition that fades out one clip while fading in the second clip. The cross-dissolve evenly blends the second image into the first one.

Before you can create a transition between two clips, you'll need to position them correctly. For all types of transitions, you have two ways to do this. Either have the clips on the same track, butted up against each other, or have them on two different tracks, one above the other, with an overlap. This overlap will determine the length of the dissolve. Once you've got your clips in one of these setups, you're ready to create a dissolve between them. You have multiple ways to add a dissolve to your clips. These choices include dragging the transition from the Effects tab in the Browser onto the edit point of the two clips or control-clicking on the edit point and selecting a default transition. You can also select the edit point and press ⌘ to add the default. Or, having selected the cut, go to the top menu, and choose Effects > Video Transitions > Cross Dissolve.

While this section covers cross-dissolves because they are the most common transitional effect, the techniques used to add cross-dissolves will work with any other transition available in Final Cut Pro. Once you've mastered adding a cross-dissolve, try experimenting with the host of other transitions available in Final Cut Pro. You'll find the technique for rendering transitions and other effects in Chapter 9.

1. Make sure your two clips are adjacent on the same track, or on two different tracks with an area of overlapping footage.

So What's Wrong with Straight Cuts?

Ever since the first filmmakers began experimenting with different ways to attach two shots together, creative transitions beyond the straight cut have been attempted. Final Cut Pro offers a number of transition types that reflect the major categories developed early in film history: transitions like the dissolve, the wipe, the iris, and the peel. Most of these transitions are now considered "cheesy" and are rarely used in a professional context, and this is generally a good attitude toward using them. As discussed earlier, cross-dissolves are the most common transition. You'll see a few in most Hollywood movies and more extensively in documentaries and music videos. Cross-dissolves create an interaction between two cuts that is different than a straight cut. They signal us that the cut is a transition in time or space, that we are now in a different world than before. Cross-dissolves are also sometimes used to create a sort of cubist perspective on one space or event, giving us different angles of the same scene, all smoothly pieced together with dissolving images.

Transitions like the wipe have artistic origins, but now are usually greeted with eye-rolling. A wipe has one image replace another as if a door were sliding away, or "wiping" across the outgoing image. Akira Kurosawa used a lot of wipes to add a theatrical element between scenes, as if adding a curtain-like effect to separate acts and scenes. *The Seven Samurai* frequently employs this device. George Lucas, a big Kurosawa fan, uses wipes in his *Star Wars* films in homage to Kurosawa, as a nod to the language of Kurosawa's old adventure tales. A wipe now is almost inherently self-referential, so it's very difficult to get away with unless you are trying to get an ironic laugh.

Irises also date back to the silent era and were a common form of transitioning. An iris closes out an image with a dwindling circular matte, and brings in a new image with an enlarging circular matte. Movies like *The Cabinet of Dr. Caligari* frequently used irises to transition between bizarre, dream-like places. Think also of the ending of Bugs Bunny cartoons, where the last scene ends with a black iris closing on the image. In the 1960s, French New Wave directors like Francois Truffaut and Jean-Luc Godard picked up on the iris technique and used it as a self-conscious cinematic trick that both brought attention itself and also was a knowing gesture to the early cinematic devices. Once again, the effect now is almost entirely referential, and used either to invoke silent cinema or as a jokey pun.

2. Click the Effects tab in the Browser to bring up the Effects menu. Open the Video Transitions folder and then the folder for the transition type you want to use (in this case, Dissolve).

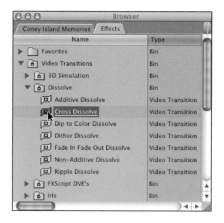

3. Drag the icon for the transition you want to use (Cross Dissolve) to the edit point between the two clips or, if they are on separate tracks, to the edge of one of the overlapping clips. Drop the transition on the edit point or edge. If you are dropping the transition on an edit point between two clips on the same track, you can choose to drop it before the edit point, centered on the edit point, or after the edit point. This placement will affect when the transition occurs and what footage is used in the dissolve.

- If you drop the transition to end on the edit point, the outgoing clip will disappear at the edit point.
- If you drop the transition to start on the edit point, the incoming clip will begin to appear there.
- If you drop the transition on the center of the edit point, the incoming and outgoing clip will be superimposed over each other exactly halfway through the dissolve at the edit point.

Remember that you must have extra media for the clips to have "room" to dissolve. A dissolve adds frames of media that it uses in the actual dissolve. You will need to make sure you have enough media and that the media doesn't cut away in the middle of the dissolve to another shot.

4. Now that the transition is in place in the Timeline, you can change its duration and location (see *Working with Transitions* later in this chapter).

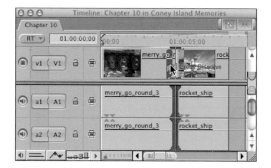

Alternate Steps:
Adding a Transition Using the Effects Menu

You can also add a transition by using the Effects menu.

1. Either click the edit point between the two clips you want to add the transition to, or place the playhead in the Timeline on the edit point.

2. From the main menu, select Effects **>** Video Transitions. Now select the submenu for the transition type you want (in this case, Dissolve) and then select your transition (Cross Dissolve). The transition will be added to the selected edit point.

3. Now that the transition is in place in the Timeline, you can change its duration and location. You'll learn how to do this in the next section.

Alternate Steps:
Adding a Transition Using Contextual Menus

You can add a default transition to an edit point directly in the Timeline using the mouse.

1. Control-click the edit point you want to add a transition to and choose Add Transition 'Cross Dissolve' from the popup menu. This will apply the default transition (which is initially set to Cross Dissolve) to this edit point. (See the sidebar *Changing the Default Transition* to learn how to change the transition available in this menu.)

2. Now that the transition is in place in the Timeline, you can change its duration and location, as explained in the next section.

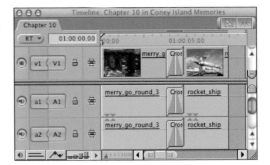

Changing a Transition's Duration

Once you've placed a transition between two cuts, you aren't locked into the placement or timing of the transition. You can easily edit these attributes until you've set the transition at the optimal place in the cut. The two main ways to edit a transition are dragging in the Timeline with the mouse, or typing exact values in the Transition Editor window.

Just as you can drag the edge of a clip to lengthen or shorten it, you can do the same with a transition to make it shorter or longer. You can also drag the transition without changing the duration so that it rests at different In and Out points in the two clips.

1. Choose the Selection tool ➤ from the Tool Palette (press **A**).

2. Drag the edge of the transition to the desired new length. When you drag a transition to change the duration, the following properties based on the transition's alignment will apply:

- If the transition ends on the edit point, you can only drag the left side of the transition.
- If the transition is centered on the edit point, you can drag both sides, and both sides will move together, meaning that if you shorten one side, both sides will shorten.
- If the transition begins on the edit point, you can only drag the right side of the transition.

Notice that the Canvas window will display the new In and Out frames of the transition as you make your edits.

Once you have made your changes, though, you will need to render (or re-render) the effect before you out put your finished work.

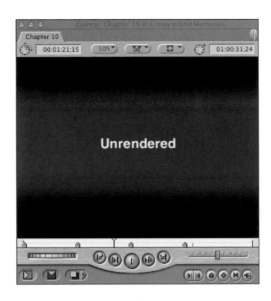

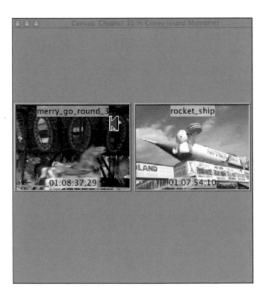

Alternate Steps: Changing Transition Duration Numerically

You can also change the duration of a transition more precisely using the Duration window.

1. Control-click the transition and choose Duration from the popup menu.

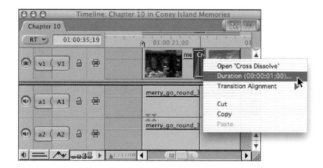

2. In the Duration window, type your desired duration in minutes, seconds, and frames, and click OK. If you enter a number that exceeds the available footage (that is, if you are at the very end of a clip and there is no more trimmed media to fill the transition), you'll hear a warning sound and be prompted to type in a new duration.

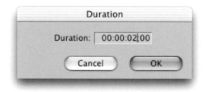

3. Depending on the speed of your machine, and your ability to take advantage of Real-Time effects, the transition will play as a blue screen with the word "unrendered" in the Canvas window. (See *Rendering Effects* in Chapter 9 for more details.)

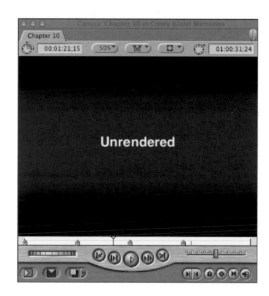

Working with Transitions

You can also view and edit the properties of a transition by bringing up the Transition Editor window. This window launches in the Viewer and gives you a graphic representation of the transition and the two clips (labeled Outgoing Clip and Incoming Clip) and a host of other controls for fine-tuning your transition. The Transition Editor window allows you to quickly alter the duration of your transition, change the alignment, and even trim the transitioning edit.

1. To open the Transition Editor window, double-click on the transition you want to edit. The Transition Editor will appear as a tab in the Viewer.

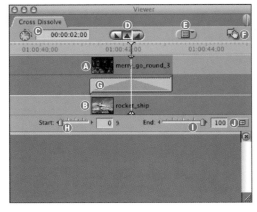

Ⓐ Outgoing Clip
Ⓑ Incoming Clip
Ⓒ Current Duration
Ⓓ Alignment
Ⓔ Recent Clips
Ⓕ Drag Hand
Ⓖ Graphic Transition
Ⓗ Start Opacity Slider
Ⓘ End Opacity Slider
Ⓙ Reverse Transition

2. To change the duration of the transition, you can use the mouse to drag the transition's start and finish points or simply type a new duration, as shown here. You can also drag the actual clips (as you would in the Timeline) to change the In and Out points. See the next section, *Trimming in the Transition Editor Window*.

3. To change the alignment of the transition, select one of these options, which determines where the transition begins and ends in the two clips: centered between the clips, ending on the edit point, or beginning on the edit point.

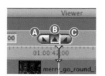

Ⓐ Begin on Edit

Ⓑ Center

Ⓒ End on Edit

4. To modify at what opacity (set in percentage) the transition will begin or end, use the Start and End sliders by sliding the scrub head left or right or type a percentage value in directly. For example, you could set a fade-in to start at 25% opacity and end at 75%. Most transitions have the outgoing clip go from 100% to 0% and the incoming clip go from 0% to 100%. The opacity sliders let you change this. This is rarely done, but it can be useful when you want a jarring effect.

5. To reverse the transition (for example, to change a left-to-right wipe to go from right to left instead), click the Reverses the Transition button.

6. To add the current transition you are working on to a different edit point in the Timeline, click the grab hand and hold the mouse button down to pick up the transition. Now drag the transition to the desired edit point in the Timeline and drop it. This transition will now

be used at that edit point. This copying is a great way to keep transitions consistent between clips.

7. When you are finished, simply click in the Timeline and the changes you made will be reflected in the transition. As with all changes to an effect (transition, filter, or generator), you will have to rerender them in order for the changes to show up in your film, unless you use Unlimited RT or the Matrox card for real-time viewing discussed in Chapter 9.

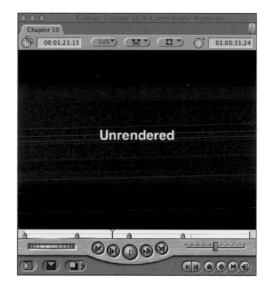

Trimming in the Transition Editor Window

You can perform a Roll or Ripple edit (see Chapter 8) directly in the Transition Editor window, keeping the transition between the two clips. A Roll edit will change the location of a transition, moving it forward or backward across the two clips. Begin with the Transition window open.

1. To perform a Roll edit, place the cursor in the graphic representation of the transition itself until it turns into the Roll Edit cursor, and drag the transition to the desired point (see *Making Roll Edits* in Chapter 8). Notice that the Canvas window displays thumbnails of the new In and Out points for your edits.

2. To perform a Ripple edit, place the cursor at either the end of the outgoing clip or the start of the incoming clip, depending on which clip you want to trim. The cursor turns into the Ripple edit cursor. Now drag the clip to the point where you want it (see *Making Ripple Edits* in Chapter 8). Notice that the Canvas Window shows you the new In or Out point for the clip being edited.

3. Depending on the speed of your computer, you will have to rerender in order for the changes to show up in your film (see Chapter 9 for more details on Real-Time Effects and rendering).

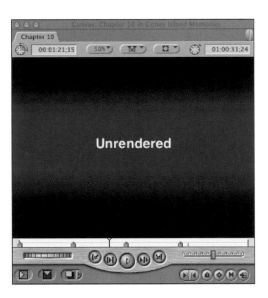

How Can I Create a Fade to Black?

We covered using transitions to link two clips with images, but how can you create a fade up or fade down to black? These effects are a common strategy in cinematic language to begin and end scenes, or to add a rhythmic, almost heartbeat-like feel to your montage. The easiest way to fade to black is to put a transition on a clip's In or Out point when it is not touching another clip. The transition will just hang off the edge of the clip, attached to nothing. If this clip has no other clips under it, so that it is above only the default black background, you have your fade! A fade from white or color can create a camera-flash effect, or it can insinuate a strange or unusual shift in time or place, as in David Lynch movies. To get this effect, you can use the Dip to Color fade which lets you choose a color to fade down to and up from.

Alternate Steps:
Changing Alignment in the Timeline

Although you can change alignment using the Transition window, it's often faster to change the alignment directly in the Timeline.

1. Control-click the transition you want to align in the Timeline, select Transition Alignment, and choose the desired alignment from the popup menu, either Start, Center, or End.

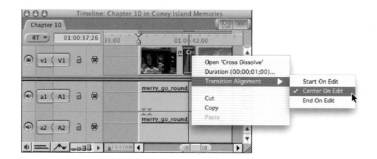

2. Alternatively you can use the following shortcut keys to set the alignment of a transition. First select the transition you want to align by clicking on it and then press:

Option+1: Start Transition on Edit Point

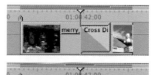

Option+2: Center Transition on Edit Point

Option+3: End Transition on Edit Point

Adding Audio Transitions

Besides adding transitions to the video, you can also add transitions to the audio portion of a clip. To add an audio transition, follow the same method you would for adding a video transition, but open the Audio Transitions folder instead. The two types of audio transitions are Cross Fade (0dB) and Cross Fade (+3dB). The difference is that the 0dB will have a dip in the levels of audio during the transition, while the +3dB will keep the levels constant during the cross fade. Typically you'll use a Cross Fade (+3dB) when you are cross-fading between two sounds and a Cross Fade (0 dB) when you are fading to silence.

1. Make sure your two audio clips are adjacent on the same track, or on two different tracks with an area of overlapping footage.

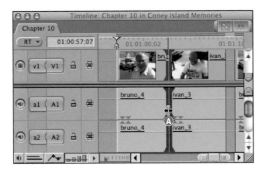

Ⓐ Edit between Audio Clips

Ⓐ Edit between Audio Clips

2. Click the Effects tab in the Browser to bring up the Effects menu, open the Audio Transitions folder, and select an audio transition. For this example, choose Cross Fade (+3dB).

3. Drag the audio transition you want to the edit point between the two clips or, if they are on separate tracks, to the edge of one of the overlapping clips in the audio tracks section of the Timeline.

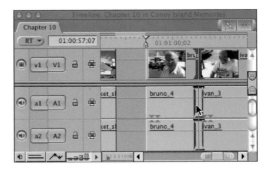

4. Drop the audio transition on the edit point or edge. If you are dropping the audio transition on an edit point between two clips on the same track, you can choose to drop it before the edit point, centered on the edit point, or after the edit point.

After adding an audio transition, its duration can be edited in much the same way as a video transition. You can click and grab its edges to edit it directly, or you can choose to edit it numerically by selecting duration from the contextual menu (control-click the transition). However, audio transitions do not use the Transitions editor in the Viewer. Instead, double-clicking the audio transition is an alternate way to open the numerical duration dialog.

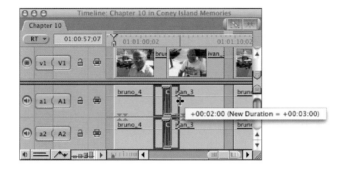

Alternate Steps: Adding an Audio Transition Using the Effects Menu

You can also add audio transitions using the Effects menu.

1. Select the edit point between the two clips where you want to add an audio transition.

2. Select Effects **>** Audio Transitions **>** Dissolve **>** Cross Fade (0dB) or Cross Fade (+3dB). A cross-fade will be added to the selected edit point.

Alternate Steps: Adding an Audio Transition Using Contextual Menus

A third way to add audio transitions is to do it directly in the Timeline.

1. Control-click the edit point where you want to add an audio transition and choose Add Transition 'Cross Fade (+3dB)' from the popup menu. This will apply the default transition (which is initially set to Cross Fade) to this edit point. As with video transitions, the default audio transition can be set in the Browser. (See the sidebar *Changing the Default Transition*.)

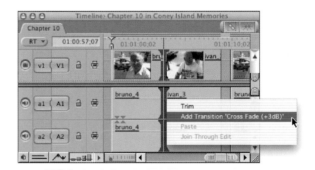

11 Using Filters for Color Correcting

It may be that your raw footage is exactly the way you want it: the colors are beautiful, the exposure is perfect, the saturation is lush. If that is true, then you are very lucky. More often than not, you'll want to do a little tweaking of the image to make it "pop," to correct for something that isn't quite right, or to make the image a little more stylized than the naturalistic raw stock. This chapter will introduce some of the controls in Final Cut Pro for changing the way your image looks.

Overview

> *"The Image is more than an idea. It is a vortex or cluster of fused ideas and is endowed with energy."*
>
> Ezra Pound

In this chapter, we'll look at specific tools available through the Browser's Effects tab (and the Effects menu) that let you control the video image in a host of ways. Many of these options were available to editors before digital nonlinear editing came along, but they were (and are) often extremely costly or difficult to implement. One of the advantages of using Final Cut Pro's effects is that they are easy to add, adjust, or take away. You'll also be able to see the new look of your video quickly with Final Cut Pro's Quick-View tab.

Just remember that actual rendering time (the process of preparing effects to play through) depends on a lot of factors, such as the speed of your processor, the amount of memory, and the complexity and number of effects. For more information on rendering, see Chapter 9. We'll start out with simple manipulations, like changing the brightness and contrast of the picture. If the cinematographer exposed the footage a little too dark, or if you need to match a darker shot with a lighter shot, you can often just take the brightness up a bit to make the shots work together. If this doesn't work, Final Cut Pro offers more advanced tools, such as the Color Corrector filter. Adjusting the gamma leaves the darkest and lightest parts of the image the same and affects only the midtones of an image. In these sections, we'll discuss how to make a decision about what effect to use, and how best to experiment with different "looks."

This chapter also pays close attention to color correction, which is the process of shifting and changing the color content of the video image to match a certain look or aesthetic. Final Cut Pro 4 users have access to some very powerful color correction tools that allow for very precise color manipulation. You may decide to drain the image of color (*desaturate* it), giving it a more bleak mood, or you may want to add a sunny yellow tint to the footage to give it a golden sheen. Consider two recent examples. Steven Soderbergh's *Traffic* and the Coen brothers' *O Brother, Where Art Thou?* both used color to create certain moods. *Traffic* switched between scenes in Mexico that were given a hot orange tone to evoke sweltering heat and scenes in Washington, DC, that were given a cool blue color to connote the isolated world of a government official. *O Brother, Where Art Thou?* had a sepia glow that reflected the film's setting in the hot, sun-baked South while simultaneously reinforcing a nostalgic feeling. You can see that color correction doesn't have to be just about making every image look the same or "naturalistic." You can use color correction to define a mood or affect the way an audience takes in the images they see. Final Cut Pro offers many color-correction methods, and they are all fairly quick to add and manipulate, so it's a good idea to try out a few different styles for your footage and then pick the one that works best with your project.

It's crucial here to have a reference monitor to evaluate your color corrections. The screen in the Viewer or Canvas cannot give you an accurate depiction of the colors as they will be seen on an NTSC monitor, so it's very important you have one as a reference point. While color correction and color manipulation are a big part of editing, they don't begin here—they begin on the set. Often, you'll be working with the director of photography (or his or her notes). On most films, it is the director of photography (DP) who has the final say on color correction, as it should reflect the vision the DP has for the film. If you're shooting your own stuff, think about how to shoot knowing what effects you will add later. For example, camera operators will sometimes intentionally slightly overexpose footage so that they can later darken the blacks, creating a crisper image with more contrast and more saturation.

Most likely, you will make general decisions about color before you begin cutting your project, since this decision may affect the overall visual tone of your film. However, it's difficult to edit and make changes to your cut when you are constantly rerendering your clips. Instead of applying your color corrections to the entire film while editing, it's often a good idea to experiment with color correction in your footage before you start cutting, so you'll know what options you'll eventually have. Take a few sample clips and play around with color correcting them. When you're satisfied that you've got something you like, save the effect style, turn off the effects in your clips, and cut your project as you would normally.

Then, once all of the edits have been fine-tuned, you can go back and add the image effects where needed.

Finally, be aware that in the following lessons you'll learn how to adjust the settings of various filters; and we assume throughout the chapter that you are making those changes to a filter *that has been loaded into a clip*. If you simply double-click a filter in the Browser's Effects tab, that will change the settings of the filter itself, and your new settings will stay as the default of the filter. This is not recommended unless you use a nondefault filter setting on a very regular basis.

Chapter 11: Filter Controls

Open the Final Cut Pro project file labeled Coney Island Memories. After it loads in Final Cut Pro, double-click the Chapter 11 sequence in the Browser and it will open in the Timeline.

In this chapter you will begin to learn how to use a very important feature of Final Cut Pro: filters. In this sequence, we have provided five sets of clips, one for each section in this chapter, for you to practice adding image control filters to. The first clip in a set is for you to use and the second shows one possible outcome. To see what we did to the second clip, open it in the Viewer by double-clicking it in the Timeline, and then check the Filters tab. Remember that all filters are types of effects, and all effects have to be rendered before they can be played back in the Canvas.

Adding a Filter

Before   After

A *filter* is a set of attributes that you add to a clip in order to change its appearance or, in the case of audio, to alter the sound. Most of these filters mimic the physical "filters" filmmakers might place on their camera lens, but now you can play around with them digitally while preserving your original footage. There are numerous filters that you can add to a clip in order to control its color, contrast, and other aspects of the clip's appearance. In Final Cut Pro, a filter is a type of effect (along with the transitions, slugs, and other effects described in Chapters 9 and 10) that changes an image by altering it based on the filter settings. For example, the Desaturate filter takes the color information of a clip and discards it, so that only grayscale information is left. You can add as many filters as you want to a single clip; this allows you the flexibility to produce a great diversity in your resulting clips. This section presents the basic method for adding a filter to a clip. The rest of this chapter will explore some of the more important filters you will use to control your images.

1. In the Canvas, Timeline, or Browser, double-click the clip to which you will add a filter; this opens it in the Viewer. It's normally best to choose your clip from the Timeline, so that only the specific clip in the Timeline will be affected, not the master clip kept in the project file in the Browser (nor the actual media file on your hard disk). Choosing the clip in the Browser will affect all instances of that clip in the Timeline.

2. With the clip open in the Viewer, go to the Browser to open up the Effects tab. Choose Video Filters and then select the filter type and filter you want to apply to a clip (for example, Blur > Zoom Blur), and then drag the icon for that filter onto the clip in the Viewer window. This will add controls for that filter type to the clip. You can also perform this function by selecting Effects > Video Filters > Blur > Zoom Blur.

3. If you opened the clip from the Timeline, you can, either in the Canvas or the Timeline, place the playhead over a representative frame in the clip. As you make changes to the clip in the Viewer, you will then be able to preview the changes in the Canvas, so it is important to pick a frame that will give you a good idea what the final product throughout the clip is going to look like.

Ⓐ Playhead

4. With your clip in the Viewer, open the Filters tab in the Viewer window by clicking the tab. Make changes to that particular clip using the controls provided, and preview the changes in the Canvas. As you'll see in the following sections, most of the filters you can apply are not simple on/off toggles; instead you'll control their application by using sliders, entering numeric values, and so on.

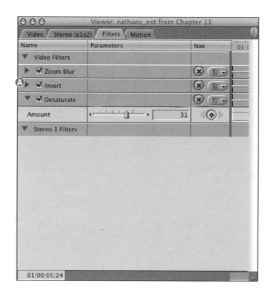

Ⓐ Filter Controls

Ⓑ Reset to Defaults

Ⓒ Filter On/Off

5. You can add multiple filters (even redundant filters) to a single clip. Each filter will appear in a collapsible list with the filters on the top appearing over top of filters underneath in the clip. It's extremely important to know that the order of the filters in the Filters tab will affect the look of the clip. If you place Desaturate before (above) a blue tint, the clip will still be tinted blue. If Desaturate comes after (below) the blue tint, the clip will be black and white. The effect hierarchy runs as if each effect were carried out in the order it is listed. You can change the order by clicking a filter's name in the Filters tab and dragging it to a different spot.

To turn a particular filter on or off, click its check box in the Name column of the effect listing. To delete a filter from a clip, select the filter by clicking its name, and then press Delete. Turning on and off a filter means you'll have to rerender the clip when you

turn the filter on again. And remember that you can click a filter's X button (in the Nav column) to restore the filter's default settings.

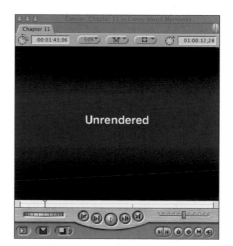

Ⓐ Collapse Filter Controls

If you step through the clip frame by frame, you will see the effect of the filter(s) on each individual frame. However, during playback, you will see the "Unrendered" message unless you have set your Timeline for Unlimited RT or rendered the effects to view them while they play (see Chapter 9).

Adjusting Brightness and Contrast

Before   After

Now that you've seen the general method for adding any filter to a clip, let's try some examples to explore the process in a little more detail and understand why particular filters are used. We'll start with Brightness And Contrast, one of the most commonly used filters used in Final Cut Pro. When you have two clips with different exposures, you can use this filter to adjust either or both of them so that they match seamlessly.

1. Add the Brightness And Contrast filter to the clip you want to work with (see *Adding a Filter* earlier in this chapter). The Brightness And Contrast filter is in the folder Video Filter **>** Image Controls, and can also be found in Final Cut Pro's pull-down menu.

2. Open the clip in the Viewer and bring up the Filters tab by clicking on the tab.

3. You should now see the Brightness And Contrast filter listed among the filters. To turn it on and off, you can click its check box.

This filter has two sliding scales: one for Brightness and one for Contrast. Notice that you can either drag the scale with the mouse or directly enter a value for each effect, ranging from –100 to 100. The image in the Canvas will update in real time to reflect these new attributes as long as the playhead in the Timeline is resting on the clip.

For Brightness, the higher the number entered, the more washed-out the image appears; and the smaller the number, the darker it will appear.

Increasing the Contrast setting will cause the image to appear harder, as the midtones separate into stronger blacks and whites.

Decreasing the contrast makes the image almost all midtones, with no strong blacks or whites.

Adjust the two effects (brightness and contrast) together until your image looks the way you want it to. Remember that you can click the X button in the Nav column to reset both Brightness and Contrast to their defaults, and you can delete this filter from the clip by highlighting its name and pressing the Delete key.

4. When you're done, view the clip in the QuickView tab to see if you've reached the effect you want.

Using the Brightness And Contrast Filter

Changing the Brightness And Contrast filter is often the first place an editor goes to correct or manipulate the image. Remember that you can use these tools not only to "fix" actual problems like exposure in the footage, but also to add a degree of stylization that gives the image a new and interesting look.

The Brightness and Contrast controls are often used in conjunction and so come within the same filter. Brightness is presented as a sliding scale that can increase the brightness of the image all the way to white or decrease it to black. Contrast controls the difference between the blackest and the whitest portion of your image. By increasing contrast, you are making the blacks "blacker" and the whites "whiter," giving your image fewer midtone colors and making the image appear sharper.

Decreasing contrast, on the other hand, increases the number of midtone colors, making the image more gray and washed-out in appearance. Like all other effects, Brightness And Contrast appears in the Filters tab of the Viewer when you've dragged it into the clip. It is here that you can do your manipulations of the clip currently being displayed in the Viewer.

Color Manipulation with Image Control Filters

Before   After

Color manipulation is not only an important part of taking your raw footage and making the colors flow naturally from clip to clip, it can also be used to apply a certain stylistic tone to your piece. Untreated video has a particular look that will affect how your audience perceives your work. If you want the option of creating some other effect, color correcting is a great way to give your project a unique feel. This section will look at using individual filters (like Tint and Color Balance) to correct and manipulate color information in your video. If you need to do color correction, that is, fixing problem footage, check out the next section.

Manipulating color can be a very tedious process and can take you down a lot of dead ends. There are so many variables to color balance and correction that you may feel overwhelmed by all the choices. A word of advice: Sometimes simple is best. Applying tons of color effects can often just muddy the image. When you catch yourself doing this, it's often a good idea to clear them all out and start again with a few basic effects.

1. Add a color-manipulation filter to a clip as shown earlier in this chapter (*Adding a Filter*). Some useful color-manipulation filters are in the folder Video Filters > Image Control. Within the Image Control folder are a number of filters you can use to color correct your footage, and you may use multiple effects in conjunction with each other. The main filters you will be using are Color Balance, Desaturate, and Tint. In addition,

you may want to use the Sepia filter to add specific tints to your clips.

Decide which of these three filters (or possibly all three) you want to use when color correcting your clip and drag those filters from the Browser onto your clip in the Viewer. Remember that you can use many other filters (such as Brightness And Contrast) in conjunction with the color filters, and each combination will have a different result depending on the order of the filters. Color correction is very much a process of trial and error, until you get it just right with all of the filters at your disposal.

2.   In the Viewer's Filters tab, adjust the filters to tailor the look of the clip to what you want. Listed below are the attributes of four Image Control filters you may want to use. Most color correction is minimal and simply tries to even out the footage so that it all looks consistent. Variations in lighting when the footage was shot can often give different parts of the footage different qualities. Some scenes may look overly blue; others may be too saturated

with bright colors. These are subjective decisions that an editor often makes with the director of photography. For more on color correction, see the section *Color Correcting Poor Footage*. As you adjust the settings, watch the changes that are made in the Canvas window. You can move the Timeline's playhead to other parts of the clip to see how the color changes affect other frames.

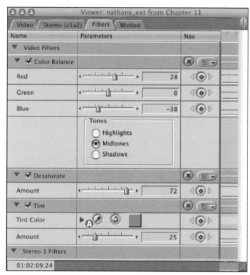

Ⓐ Color Sampler

Each clip has different color properties, so if you are working with multiple clips, you may find a group of settings work for one shot but not for another. You'll need to look at each clip individually and test settings for each (see *Copying and Storing Effects* in Chapter 9).

Color Balance   This filter lets you control the color values of the reds, greens, and blues in the video image independently. You can also choose whether this filter will affect the highlights, the midtones, or the shadows of the film. This tool is extremely helpful when an image is good but has, for example, too much blue and you want to take down the predominance of just that color. Each color has its own sliding scale (and input box to type in a numerical value). As the red, green, or blue scale moves to the right or the number increases up to 100, the color will become more dominant. Conversely, if you take that color down to as low as –100, its opposite color in the color wheel will become more dominant.

Desaturate   This filter lets you either increase or decrease the vividness of the color—that is, the *saturation*. The greater the numeric value (or the farther to the right you drag the slider) the less color information the clip will have (it will be desaturated). If you set the Desaturate value at 100, the clip will become completely black and white. Putting in a negative value (as low as –100) will increase the saturation of the clip, and the colors will become much more vivid. Be careful, because highly saturated colors, especially red, will often bleed on a video monitor.

Tint   This filter lets you add a specific color tint over the entire image. First choose the color either by clicking on the color swatch and selecting a color or using the eyedropper button to select a color from the Canvas window (you can move the playhead in the Timeline if you want to grab a color from a different clip in the Timeline). Once you've chosen your color for your tint, you can now choose how strong you want it to be, based on a percentage from 0 to 100. If you set the tint percentage at 100, the clip will become a monochromatic image of white and your color, discarding all other color information from the clip.

Sepia   Sepia is really nothing more than a tint whose color, an amberish orange, has already been selected. However, it is a very common tint used to give footage a historical or "old timey" feeling. You can also use the Highlight slider to brown

the whites, giving it a rustier feel. Use this one sparingly as it is often looked upon a clichéd effect. Sepia was a common tint used in silent films to provide a different chroma palette than just black and white, and was also a popular feature in African-American films of the 1930s and 1940s.

3.   Once you've massaged the color and saturation to reflect the look and feel that you want your clip to have, view the clip in the QuickView tab or render the effects (see *Rendering Effects* in Chapter 9) and watch the clip in motion. Often, a clip with color manipulation will look different in motion than as a still, so you may have to go back and tweak your settings a bit. Remember that you can click the X button in the Nav column to reset the color-correction filters to their defaults, and you can delete any filter from the clip by highlighting its name and pressing the Delete key.

Color Correcting Poor Footage

Color correction or color enhancement is a process of taking the raw video footage and adjusting the hue, saturation, and brightness of the image to correct for an improper shooting or to create a totally new look. In this section we'll look at how to use Final Cut Pro's Color Corrector 3-Way filter to fix exposure problems and footage that is incorrectly white balanced.

When you drag this filter into a clip from Effects > Video Filters > Color Correction, it creates a new tab in the Viewer, next to the Motion tab, and also appears as an effect in the Filters tab. The Color Corrector 3-Way tab contains three color wheels that allow you to adjust the color information of the clip by working with the blacks, midtones, and whites independently. A saturation slider bar underneath the three color wheels acts in the same way as the Desaturate filter, letting you drain color from the image or add saturation. The Limit Effect lets you single out a certain color in your image to apply color correction.

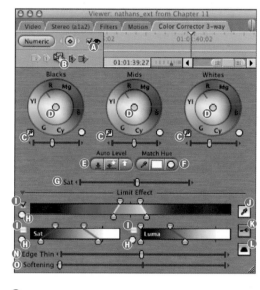

A **Hide Filter:** Click to turn the effects of the filter off without deleting it.

B **Drag Filter:** Drag this icon to another clip to add this filter with current attributes to it.

C **Select Auto-balance Color:** Use the eyedropper tool to select a color from the Canvas to set as the color balance for white, midtones, or blacks

D **Color Wheels:** Move the center dot to a color for color balance.

E **Auto Level (Black/White/Contrast):** Final Cut Pro sets best black level (left), best contrast (center), or best white level (right).

F **Match Hue:** Lets you match a color using the eyedropper or the color picker to alter the hue of your clip to match another adjacent clip.

G **Saturation Slider:** Increases/decreases image's color saturation.

H **Reset to Defaults:** Click to reset values to original.

I **Enable Limit:** Click to turn the effects of the limit off.

J **Select Color:** Selects a color for limit effect.

K **View Final/Matte/Source:** Toggles Canvas view between viewing the final effect, the matte, or the source (original).

L **Invert:** Inverts current Limit Effects attributes.

M **Numeric:** Switches to the Filters tab, with numeric input fields for controlling color correction.

N **Edge Thin:** Determines to what degree a limited effect expands out to the rest of the clip.

O **Softening:** Feathers the edges between parts of the image that are affected and parts that are not.

In the center of the tab are the Auto Black Level, Auto White Level, and Auto Contrast buttons, which operate in much the same way as similar effects do in Adobe Photoshop. Auto White Level sets the maximum level of white in the frame to be pure white, Auto Black Level sets the maximum black to be true black, and Auto Contrast Level combines those functions to create an image with both pure whites and true blacks. Using auto-contrast is usually a good idea, as it almost always makes an image much crisper.

Each color wheel has a slider underneath it that allows you to strengthen or weaken the levels of the blacks, midtones, or whites.

Each wheel in the Color Corrector 3-Way tab also has an eyedropper that you can use to designate the black, midtone, or white value in an image. For example, if a shot was white balanced incorrectly in the camera by a lazy videographer and the whites all look blue, you can use the Color Corrector 3-Way filter to fix this. Click the eyedropper for the Whites wheel and then, with the clip showing in the Canvas, click in the blue area that should be white. The Color Corrector 3-Way filter will then adjust the color information in the clip to whiten the areas that were blue. You can do the same with the Blacks eyedropper, clicking on the area of the image that you want to be true black.

As an alternative to working with sliders and eyedropper controls, you can use the Color Corrector 3-Way filter in the Filters tab, which allows you to make the same changes by entering numerical values. Some users find this a more effective way to work, particularly with the Limit Effects controls. The Numeric button in the Color Corrector 3-Way tab and a corresponding Visual button in the Filters tab allow you to switch between modes.

Brightening or Darkening the Image

Before   After

Even the best camera operator can accidentally over- or underexpose an image so that is too dark or too light. Or, the available light may be so poor that the director has no choice but to shoot footage that will look less than natural in the final video. There is a joke common on the film set that when something goes wrong, "We'll fix it in post"—meaning that the editor will do all of the work in the post-production phase. The Color Corrector 3-Way will help you brighten the image without washing it out or darken an image without losing contrast. To use the Color Corrector 3-Way, follow these steps:

1. Select the clip that is underexposed (either in the Browser, Timeline, or Canvas) and double-click it to open it in the Viewer.

2. Choose Effects > Video Filters > Color Correction > Color Corrector 3-Way or drag the Color Corrector 3-Way filter from the Browser's Effects bin and drop it onto the clip.

3. Click the special Color Corrector 3-Way tab of the clip in the Viewer and you should see the Color Corrector 3-Way graphic tool window. The bottom half of the window contains sliders for controlling the brightness and contrast of the image. You can control the brightness of the blacks, whites, and midtones separately, giving you maximum control over the image.

4. Now do one of the following:

- If the footage is overexposed (too light), drag the Mids slider to the left to bring down the brightness of the clip's midtones. This will darken the image without greatly affecting the blackest and whitest parts of the image. It should bring some more detail to the image by hardening the blacks in the image.

- If the footage is underexposed (too dark), first click the auto-contrast button to give the image strong contrast—that is increasing the difference between the blacks and whites. Now use the Mids (midtones) slider to bring up the brightness of the clip's midtones by dragging it to the right. This will lighten the image without greatly affecting the blackest and whitest parts of the image. Doing this may wash out the image's blacks a bit, so you may want to bring up the blacks with the Blacks slider by dragging it to the right.

5. You can click the check box next to the eye icon to hide the filter and go back and forth between a before and after view of the corrected clip. In this example, the clip is too dark and needs to have the contrast adjusted as well as the midtones. Once you have finished, you will need to render the filter as explained in Chapter 9 ($\mathcal{H}$+R) to view the finished piece in real time in the Canvas.

Alternate Steps: Fixing Poor White Balance

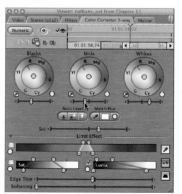

Before   After

White balancing allows you to set your camera so that it adjusts for the "color temperature" of the current lighting condition, correcting for too much blue (too cool) or too much orange (too warm). Most DV cameras have default settings for two types of light: daylight and tungsten. Daylight, of course, is outdoor light with the sun as its main source and will result in slightly bluer footage, while tungsten is used for most indoor lighting conditions (except for fluorescent lights) and will result in an orange tinge to your footage.

You may encounter two clips that were shot in the same place with the same lighting, but the white balance was accidentally changed between takes so that one clip is more orange than the other. Or you may get footage that was shot all outdoors but was incorrectly white balanced for tungsten, so that everything looks blue.

You will need to use your knowledge of daylight and tungsten to try to correct or change. You can use the color-corrector filter to correct for these mistakes. It can also be helpful to desaturate the images a little to make the color differences less pronounced if you are trying to match shots. No matter what you do, it will take some trial and error, but keeping in mind how color temperature works with scenes lit by daylight and tungsten can be helpful when correcting your image.

1. Add the Color Corrector 3-Way filter to a clip as described in Steps 1-3 of the previous section and open the filter controls in the Viewer

2. Choose the Whites eyedropper tool by clicking it and moving it to the Canvas window.

You should have the playhead in the Timeline over the clip you are working with so you can see its image in the Canvas monitor.

3. Now find a part of the image that you know should be white, but is either orange or blue because of the improper white balancing, and click it with the eyedropper tool. This can be a cloud, a white wall, a T-shirt, anything that you know should be white. Click the part of the image that should be white. Clicking this area will cause the clip to be re–color balanced based on that color being white instead of its original color. The colors in the image should now appear much closer to the correct colors of the real-life objects they were taken from. To reset the color balance to its default setting, click the small button at the bottom right of the Color Balance wheel.

If this does not look right, select the eyedropper tool again and click another area. Click the check box next to the eye to turn the filter on and off and see before and after views of the corrected clip until you are happy with it.

Once you are satisfied with the white balance correction, select and render your clips in the Timeline (see Chapter 9) so that you can view the results in real time in the Canvas (⌘+R).

Daylight or Tungsten While Filming?

Daylight has a much bluer color temperature, while tungsten (most indoor lights excluding fluorescent) has an orange color temperature. Setting the white balance on the DV camera corrects for these differences. Setting the white balance for daylight (usually a sun icon) makes the blue light of daylight seem a pure white on the video image, and setting the white balance for tungsten (usually a light bulb icon) makes the orange light of light bulbs seem white.

Color Adjustments with Gamma Levels and Proc Amp

Before   After

Gamma and Proc Amp are often confused with the Brightness and Contrast settings. They are a little more complicated and allow for more precise control of the image. Gamma, named after the mathematical term for a type of curve, is a filter that lets you adjust the midtones of an image, leaving the lightest and darkest parts of the image the same. Imagine Gamma as a curve stretching over a line that represents the gradation of black to white, with pure black on one end and pure white on the other. The highest and strongest part of the curve is in the middle, at the mid or gray tones, and the weakest at the ends, at the pure black and pure white.

With the Proc Amp effect, on the other hand, you can simultaneously adjust black levels, white levels, chroma (color level), and hue (a type of color perception, also known as phase). Proc Amp is named after an actual device used for video and film to video transfer called a Processing Amplifier.

1.   Add the Gamma or Proc Amp filters to your clip as shown earlier in this chapter. You will find both the Gamma and the Proc Amp filters in the Video Filters **>** Image Control folder or in the pull-down Effects menu under Video Filters **>** Image Control. The Gamma filter adds controls to allow you to darken or lighten the midtones, while the Proc Amp lets you go in and use separate sliders that control black levels, white levels, color levels, and hue.

Drag one or both of these effects into your clip in the Viewer window, depending on which you want to use.

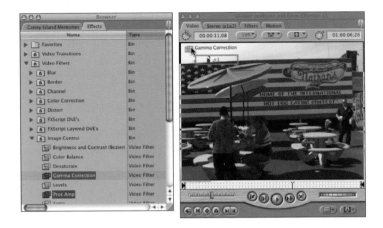

2. In the Viewer's Filter tab, use the Gamma or Proc Amp controls to make adjustments and tailor the look of the clip.

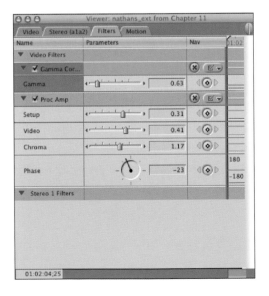

Gamma Correction   The Gamma Correction filter controls the midtones of a clip. Adjusting the Gamma is especially helpful if your footage is over- or underexposed. You can change the Gamma value by dragging the slider or entering a numeric value. If you have underexposed footage (too dark), you can decrease the Gamma to lighten the image without washing it out. If your footage is overexposed (too light) you can increase the Gamma and make some of the lost details more crisp. Some cinematographers will intentionally overexpose by half a stop when shooting and then increase the gamma later to create a saturated, crisper look. You can also increase the Gamma to give the image a stronger presence, increasing the detail of the blacks. The range extends from .01 to 4. The default is 1.

Proc Amp   This filter is more involved, and it's often a more effective way of correcting poor exposure. The Setup slider lets you separately control the black level of the clip, adjusting how dark the blacks will be. The range of this goes from –1 to 1, with 0 the default. The higher the number, the less black; the lower, the stronger the black. The Video slider lets you separately control how light the whites will be. The range of this goes from –1 to 1, with 0 being the default. The higher the number, the brighter the whites; the lower, the darker the whites. The Chroma slider lets you increase or decrease the level of color (think of this as the strength of the color information). The range of this goes from 0 to 2, with 1 being the default. The higher the number, the more vibrant the image. The lower, the more desaturated. The Phase control lets you adjust the hue of the clip. Hue lets you control color attributes as divided into red, yellow, green, and blue. This ranges from –180 to 180, with 0 as the default.

Watch the changes that are made in the Canvas window. You can move the Timeline's playhead to other parts of the clip to see how your changes affect other frames. Color correction is not an exact science, but rather a skill you will need to practice and develop.

3. Once you have the look you want with the clip, preview it in the QuickView tab or render the filters (see *Rendering Effects* in Chapter 9) and watch the clip in motion.

4. Often, a clip with Gamma or Proc Amp manipulation will look different in motion than as a still. You may have to go back and tweak your settings a bit by repeating Steps 2 and 3. Again, you can click the X button in the Nav column to reset these filters to their defaults, and you can delete any filter from a clip by highlighting its name and pressing the Delete key.

Using the Flicker and Broadcast Safe Filters

The Flicker and Broadcast Safe filters can be used to make sure your work looks its best when output to video.

The Flicker Filter   Many titles and other still images, especially those with small letters, appear to flicker when played on a TV screen. The Flicker filter, found in the Video folder of the Video Filters bin in the Browser's Effects tab, helps reduce the common "flickering" effect, a problem caused by the interlacing within still frames. You can set the filter to "minimal," "medium," or "max," depending on how soft you want the final image to appear. You can also change some of the Flicker filter's power in the De-Interlace filter, which has three levels of Flicker filter within.

The Broadcast Safe Filter   The Broadcast Safe filter, in the Color Correction folder in the Video Effects bin of the Browser's Effects tab, is a great way to make sure your colors will fall within TV broadcast standards. You may find that your luminance or chroma levels are not within acceptable broadcast limits; this problem is especially common with bright bleeding reds. By applying this filter, you can apply broadcast limits to your footage, making sure that the color and brightness will not exceed the standards of NTSC or PAL regulations. By turning on the View > Range Check, you can also see if your frame is in broadcast range.

Nine Inch Nails, *And All That Could Have Been*

Rock concerts are dark, noisy, crowded affairs. You are constantly being bumped, pushed, and pulled. And yet a really good concert can begin to feel transcendental. It's as if you are not just a part of the crowd, but you are the crowd. There is a loss of the sense of self and you are everywhere, seeing the events from every angle. Trying to capture this feeling within the confines of a television screen is not an easy task, but Trent Reznor—Nine Inch Nail's founder and mastermind throughout the band's 13-year history—does this in his concert film *And All That Could Have Been*, drawing you into the experience with the help of editor Rob Sheridan and Final Cut Pro.

Rob Sheridan ©2000 Nothing, All Rights Reserved, from the Fragility v2.0 Concert Tour.

The project began while the group was on tour in the United States. Sheridan had been traveling with the group, filming and photographing the show for the Nine Inch Nails web site. On the road, Sheridan had started using a G3 laptop to put rough cuts together. "We'd edit together little clips of fans or live footage from the shows and post them on our web site the next day. I still can't believe how well FCP will run on a laptop."

But Reznor wanted more: "Trent and I got to talking, and he was really proud of the way the live show had evolved and wanted to see it captured in some way." However, unlike other live concert videos, they didn't want to limit themselves to a single concert or one or two nights. Instead they started shooting every show and planned to create a concert DVD that would incorporate the unique multiple-angles feature of DVDs.

Eventually plans for the project expanded to include VHS and CD versions, but it was the idea of creating a DVD that really inspired Reznor and Sheridan, "From a video perspective the same edits were used on the DVD and the VHS; although for the DVD, considerations were made for a section with multiple camera angles." In addition, special considerations had to be made for the CD: "Some songs have been shortened slightly to save room, and certain sound effects from the video (keyboards smashing, mic thumps, etc.) were removed because they didn't make sense in an audio-only environment."

They shot using five Canon XL1 cameras and two Sony TRV900 cameras. "In general we'd have two or three people with handheld cameras, and the remaining cameras we'd mount throughout the venue—on the sides of the stage, behind the band, at the mix position, up in the bleachers, above the stage, etc." But often the venue dictated the camera angle: "One arena had catwalks running above the stage, so we made sure to film from up there."

By the end of the tour they had over twenty 60-gig hard drives crammed with over 200 hours of raw footage, and they had a dual G4 500Mhz desktop with 800 megs of RAM. Sheridan readily admits that video editing had been more of a hobby for him, and that this was the largest project that he had taken on, but Reznor gave him the opportunity to edit the DVD project using Final Cut Pro. "We went into the editing process thinking that if it came to a point where we were in over our heads creatively and/or technically, we'd turn the whole thing over to a professional editor. Thankfully, that point never came."

Nine Inch Nails, *And All That Could Have Been*

Instead of just focusing on the band with cut-aways to the audience, Reznor and Sheridan start the video with wide shots of the stage and the band from a distance and then slowly get closer as the show progresses. However, this led to a problem with the first song, *Terrible Lie*, which would have set a tone where the viewer thought the whole show was going to be seen from the back of the hall. "We actually fought with that song the most, because the balance of distant and mysterious yet still exciting was very hard to achieve. But once we were comfortable with the feel of *Terrible Lie*, slowly moving inward through the rest of the set came very naturally; and by the time you get to *Head Like a Hole* you're up close to Trent, you're in the crowd, you're behind the drummer—there's footage from all over the place, and hopefully it still feels fresh even an hour into the show."

Assembling footage from dozens of clips presented another challenge. Sheridan spent a lot of time with the members of the band getting the synch of the audio just right, "making sure, for example, that all the drum hits were right on and that what you see the guitar player doing actually fits with what you're hearing in the audio. Those types of things become major concerns since what you're seeing is almost never even from the same city as the audio you're hearing, but we have to create the illusion that it is."

He credits their success to Final Cut Pro, which allowed them to edit so many diverse clips, "because working on our own system we had the freedom to spend months digging through hundreds of hours of footage and trying out different things."

But then they ran into a snag: "Everything FCP rendered had a washed-out look to it, with no reasonable explanation as to why. We reinstalled FCP, QuickTime, the OS software, tried everything we could, but it didn't change." As with many computer problems, the problem was obscure yet highly annoying, "It turned out that a RadDV Codec extension was to blame, and removing that instantly fixed the problem."

Sheridan says that they used minimal effects in the video. "The only FCP effects we used were minor color adjustments and occasionally zooming in a bit or flipping a shot. Nothing very major was done at all, simply because

we didn't need it." Adding filters to dress up the final product seemed to be counterproductive: "A Nine Inch Nails concert isn't swooping camera cranes and gentle cross-fades. It's jerky and it's raw and it's an overload of information at all times; and I think the way we've put this together really captures that."

Rob Sheridan ©2000 Nothing, All Rights Reserved, from the Fragility v2.0 Concert Tour.

Nine Inch Nails Live: And All That Could Have Been is available on DVD, VHS, and CD formats from Nothing Records. Nine Inch Nails is online at www.nin.com.

12 Manipulating the Image with Filters

Sometimes your project may call for effects that go well beyond the usual color and exposure correction. This is especially true with projects that aren't narrative, such as experimental videos, music videos, or commercials. You may want to alter the image to create special effects that distort or heavily stylize the image. This chapter will cover these kinds of techniques, and we will suggest situations where you might want to use them.

Overview

> *"Anyone who has a little patience and who is fortunate enough to find in the attic an old-fashioned dress of chiffon or fine net, such as great-grandma used to wear, can make his own lens diffuser."*
>
> John Alton, *Painting with Light,* 1949

Parts of Final Cut Pro may seem more akin to graphics programs like Adobe Photoshop than a video-editing suite. Like Photoshop, Final Cut Pro has an extended list of filters for effects; but instead of applying to a single still image, they affect the moving image. Many of the filters in Final Cut Pro mimic special effects that were created optically for films edited on film as opposed to digitally, and many of the names of the Final Cut Pro filters reflect the optical process. For example, Final Cut Pro offers a Diffuse filter that gives the image a softer look, adding a textured blur. In the days before digital manipulation, cinematographers would often stretch a piece of thin gauze or sheer fabric over the lens of the camera to diffuse the light exposing the film. (You've probably seen this effect in many movies of the 1940s and 1950s when the camera cuts to an emotional close-up of the heroine.) This process is still used, and often the in-camera effects look better, but they are also permanent (since they are on the film or original video). Thus, Final Cut Pro has kept the term Diffuse for its digital version of the same technique.

What can you use the filters for? The list is endless, but you can use these effects to create funky title sequences, bizarre dream sequences, or even just abstract patterns that you might use as a backdrop for images in a promotional or industrial piece or in a multimedia installation. These effects can take something like an industrial video, whose purpose is informational, and make it more engaging and attractive.

The filters we'll be looking at in this chapter include the Gaussian Blur, along with some Distortion and Stylize filters. These include Fisheye, named for a type of lens that heavily distorts the image to look like it is bulging outward; and Solarize, named after a darkroom technique that flashes the developing photograph with light, dimming the midtones and maximizing the highlights and shadows.

Finally, we'll look at the Perspective filters, which can flop or mirror the image, giving you greater control over your compositions. You can create strange kaleidoscope effects, once again useful to create interesting moving backgrounds or a strange effect in a music video.

In Chapter 11, we showed you the general method for applying a filter to a clip, and we will use the same method to apply the filters in this chapter. Final Cut Pro comes with a long list of image-manipulation filters beyond those covered in these two chapters.

You can also purchase exterior software that interfaces with Final Cut Pro. Adobe After Effects, which complements Final Cut Pro, is a powerful program that most professional editing suites use for their effects and graphic creation. CineLook is another product that works in conjunction with Final Cut Pro, with the main purpose of simulating a film look with video stock. It allows you to select from a long list of actual film stocks (from Kodak's Vision 500T 35mm stock to Tri-X black and white Super-8). These effects mimic that grain and color of film, but they don't match the depth and image quality of something actually shot on film.

In this chapter, we cover the most commonly used filters in Final Cut Pro for image manipulation, but any other filter will be applied in the same way as described here. It's a good idea to comb through the Video Filters folders. Get to know how the filters are grouped and what they do. Once you've gone over this chapter, go back into the Effects bin and apply other filters using the same methods described in the chapter to become familiar with what all these effects can do. Experimentation is the name of the game, and every clip will react to these filters differently. Play around, try mixing and matching different filters, and let your creativity guide you.

DVD Chapter 12: More Fun with Filters

Open the Final Cut Pro project file labeled Coney Island Memories. After it loads in Final Cut Pro, double-click the Chapter 12 sequence in the Browser and it will open in the Timeline.

In the last chapter you learned how to add and manipulate filters. In this chapter we will look at some interesting but less common filters that you can add for a variety of effects. We have provided six clip sets for your use, one for each section in this chapter. The first clip in a set is for you to practice with, while the second clip shows the effect the filter being spotlighted would have on the clip. Remember that most filters have to be rendered before they can be viewed in the Canvas (see *Working with Effects: Real-Time and Rendering* in Chapter 9).

Blurring the Image

Before   After

The most common reasons to blur an image is to create an out-of-focus shot from an original in-focus shot or to soften a scene that is a little too hard-edged. The latter reason is used especially when working with facial close-ups. Final Cut Pro offers several types of blurs you can use to simulate motion or soft focus in various ways, but the most common, Gaussian Blur, is used to help quickly "touch-up" your footage. Often a close-up will accentuate pores and lines on the face, and a very minimal Gaussian Blur will smooth these out. (If you're curious about the name, it comes from the 19th century German mathematician Johann Gauss, who defined the distribution curve that the software uses in creating this filter.)

1. In the Canvas, Timeline, or Browser, double-click the clip to which you want to apply the blur filter to open it in the Viewer.

2. Add the Gaussian Blur filter to the clip you want to blur (see *Adding a Filter* in Chapter 11). The Gaussian Blur filter is in the Video Filters **>** Blur folder in either the Browser's Effects tab or the Effects pull-down menu.

3. In the Viewer window, open the clip's Filters tab. You should now see the Gaussian Blur effect listed. To turn the effect on and off, click its check box.

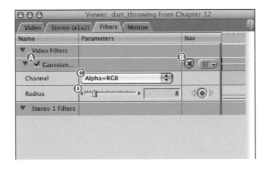

Ⓐ Filter On/Off

Ⓑ Reset filter to default values.

Ⓒ Choose the channels (color and/or alpha) to be blurred.

Ⓓ Use the slider or enter a value (0 to 100) for the amount of blur. No blur is 0, and maximum blur is 100.

The effect has a Radius sliding scale, ranging from 0 to 100, that allows you to choose how blurry the image will become. (Don't be confused by the name *Radius*; it refers to the underlying math for calculating the blurriness and not to any visible radius.) As the numerical value increases, the image becomes blurrier. Notice that, as with other variable effects, you can either drag the scale with the mouse or enter a numeric value. Slide the scale right or type in a higher number. The image in the Canvas becomes blurry.

You can also isolate a channel in the video image to blur (see Chapter 13 for information about alpha channels). Go to the popup menu to choose which channel(s) you want blur:

- Alpha+RGB to blur the entire image
- Just the Alpha (transparent) channel

- The individual Red, Green, or Blue colors
- Blur based on Luminance so that the brighter (more white) a color is, the more blur is applied to it

When you're done, preview the clip in the QuickView tab or render the clip in the Timeline and view it in motion in the Canvas window. You'll see that a small amount of Gaussian Blur is barely noticeable by itself, but it does change your emotional response to the image as it softens. But adding a lot of blur makes the images a mass of unrecognizable forms. With Gaussian Blur, you can take any piece of footage and make it into an abstract plane of color and movement. If you are creating an abstract image, such as for a title background, you will often use Gaussian Blur (a Real-Time Effect) in conjunction with other filters and color effects. Remember, you can add as many effects and filters to a single clip as you want. If you need to add a lot of effects to a single clip, we recommend increasing the memory allocation in the Final Cut Pro information panel.

Distorting the Image

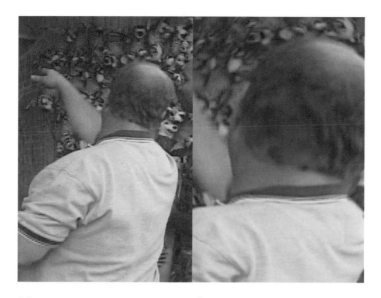

Before   After

The Distort folder contains filters that allow you to manipulate your footage in some fairly complex ways. In this section, we'll focus on the Fisheye filter. Fisheye is a Distort effect that mimics the fisheye lens of a camera, which bulges the center of an image outward. Fisheye lenses are most commonly used in shots showing the point of view of someone looking through a peephole in

a door. Remember that actual fisheye lenses are still used, and it is always a good idea to achieve an effect "in-camera" if you can. Optical effects generally look better and sharper than digital effects created in Final Cut Pro; but if using a fisheye lens isn't possible, you can create a similar effect with this filter. Fisheye, like many of these distortion filters, can look really cheesy or cheap, so use it sparingly or with a specific purpose. The most effective (and classy) way to use the Fisheye filter is with an abstract image. This further abstracts the image, adding interesting contours to the shape. It's best used to create such abstract backgrounds for titles or as imagery to project behind a performer in a music video. If you use the fisheye filter on an intelligible image, such as a person or landscape, it's hard to keep it from looking silly.

1. In the Canvas, Timeline, or Browser, double-click the clip you want to work with to open it in the Viewer.

2. Add the Fisheye filter to the clip you want to distort (see *Adding a Filter* in Chapter 11). This filter is in the Video Filters > Distort folder or in Final Cut Pro's pull-down menu.

3. Open the clip's Filters tab in the Viewer window. You should now see the Fisheye filter listed. To turn the effect on and off, click its check box.

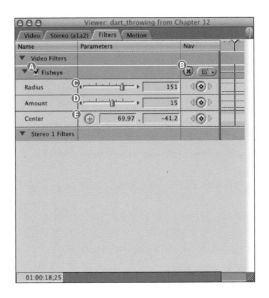

Ⓐ Filter On/Off

Ⓑ Reset filter to default values.

Ⓒ Use the slider or enter values (0–200) for the radius (center to edge) for the fisheye circle.

Ⓓ Use the slider or enter values (–100 to 100) for the amount of distortion. Negative values will appear to pucker in while positive values pucker out.

Ⓔ Click the crosshair and then click in the Canvas to set the center point for the bulge. You can also enter X, Y values directly.

You can use the slider controls to adjust the bulbousness of the bulge by the Amount slider and the radius of the bulge by the Radius slider as it appears on the image. You can also adjust the center of the bulge by using the Select Center tool and clicking a new center point in the Canvas (not in the Viewer) or by typing in new coordinates. The Radius controls go from 0 to 200, while the Amount goes from –100 to 100.

You can preview your changes in the Viewer.

4. Once you've gotten the fisheye to look as you want it, watch it in the QuickView tab or render the clip and play it back in the Timeline. See how the distortion changes as the image changes and moves. If you are unsatisfied with the results, simply open the clip in the Viewer again, play around with your settings, and then rerender the clip.

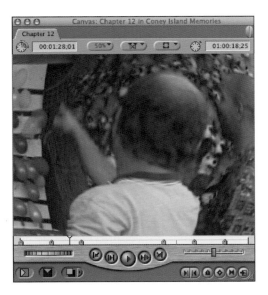

Changing the Perspective

Before   After

plex special effects that you can use to jazz up a promotional or educational video or use to create imagery for an experimental video. These controls are best used with *keyframes* to define where the effects begin and end and the degree to which you apply them. Keyframes allow for animated motion in a clip, and you should see Chapter 15 for a discussion of using keyframes with Perspective filters to create movement. You can, however, use all of the Perspective effects without keyframes to change the orientation of the image. The other perspective filters—Basic 3D, Flop, Mirror, and Rotate—are very helpful in changing the placement of a shot or flipping the image to reverse the composition. All these filters except for Curl are Real-Time effects.

4 The Perspective folder contains a number of filters that change the apparent spatial position of the clip. The folder offers a number of perspective-shifting effects that can aid you when the raw footage is not in the right spot or you want to create an unusual special effect. Changing the perspective, especially if you are using the Basic 3D and Curl filters discussed below, can create fairly com-

1. In the Canvas, Timeline, or Browser, double-click the clip you want to work with to open it in the Viewer.

2. Add a perspective filter to your clip (see *Adding a Filter* in Chapter 11). You will find the following filters in the Video Filters **>** Perspective folder: Basic 3D, Curl, Flop, Mirror, and Rotate.

In this example, we'll use Mirror, which creates a reflected split image of one side of your clip. Drag the Mirror filter into your clip in the Viewer window.

3. Open the Filters tab for your clip in the Viewer window. You should now see the Mirror filter that you dragged into the clip. To turn an effect on and off, click its check box.

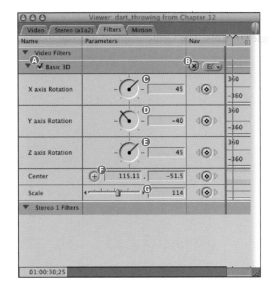

A Filter On/Off

B Reset Filter to Default Values

C Use the dial or enter values (–360 to 360) to set the rotation of the image around its X axis.

D Use the dial or enter values (–360 to 360) to set the rotation of the image around its Y axis.

E Use the dial or enter values (–360 to 360) to set the rotation of the image around its Z axis.

F Click the crosshair and then click in the Canvas to select the center point used for the image axis. You can also enter the X, Y values directly.

G Use the slider or enter a value (0 to 200) to scale the image. Values below 100 reduce the image size while values above 100 will enlarge the image.

Basic 3D Makes the image appear to be a flat surface floating in a simulated 3D space, so you can control it and rotate it along three different axes (X, Y, and Z). Remember that on a 3D array, X represents the horizontal axis, Y represents the vertical axis, and Z is the third dimension of depth. With Basic 3D, the Z axis turns the image clockwise and counterclockwise. Each of these is manipulated with a Radius tool that moves from 0 to 360. Adjust the clip's position along these axes by adjusting the angle controls. The Center control lets you locate the center point either by typing in coordinates numerically, or by dragging the crosshair to the Canvas. To reduce or enlarge the image, use the Scale slider control. Scale goes from –100 to 100. Remember that any clip on a video track under this clip will be seen behind the 3D clip.

Peel check box. Once again, any image on the lower video tracks will show under the curled clip.

Curl   Makes the clip bend and curl at the edges. Think of the video image as a flat photograph that you can curl up. Use the controls to change the direction, radius, and degree of curl. The Direction setting changes the direction in which the peel moves, on a radius of –720 to 720. Radius and Amount move in conjunction with each other. Amount signifies how much of the image you want the curl to cover (0 to 100%). Radius signifies how tight you want the curl to roll (1 is the smallest, and 100 the most). You can add another clip to appear as the back of the first clip (a two-sided image), by using the Clip control. You just need to drag another clip into the filmstrip icon. You can also toggle between two kinds of curls, Roll and Peel, by clicking the

Flop   Reverses the image along either a vertical or horizontal axis, or both. This is helpful if you wanted to switch a shot upside down (for example, if you were making a POV shot from someone on the floor) or to have greater control over creating pattern imagery for background and abstract forms.

Mirror

Acts like putting a mirror along a line on your clip. You control the orientation of this line by adjusting the center with the Reflection crosshair and coordinates, either by placing the crosshair in the chosen spot in the Canvas or by inserting numerical X, Y coordinates. Use the reflection angle to change the angle of the mirror with values from 0 to 360. You can add multiple mirror effects with different settings to create a kaleidoscope effect.

Rotate   This feature simply rotates the clip either 90 or 180 degrees clockwise or counterclockwise.

4.   When you're done, preview the clip in the QuickView tab or render the clip in the Timeline and view it in motion in the Canvas window. If you are unsatisfied with the results, simply open the clip in the Viewer again, play around with your settings, and then rerender the clip.

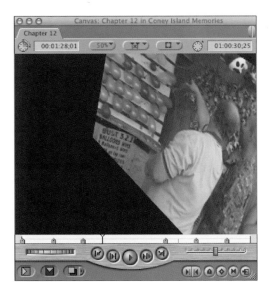

Adding a Border

Before   After

The Border filter allows you to create either a beveled or basic border of a solid color around the entire clip. This technique can be helpful if you are using the Scale control in the Motion tab to shrink the image and want it to stand out or highlight it as a window (see Chapter 14). In this example, we'll use the Bevel Border, which creates a border that is given a sense of dimension by the illusion that light is shining on it from an angle.

1. In the Canvas, Timeline, or Browser, double-click on the clip to which you want to add a bevel border to open it in the Viewer.

2. Add the Bevel Border filter to your clip (see *Adding a Filter* in Chapter 11). This filter is in the Video Filters **>** Border folder or in the Effects pull-down menu. You can also choose a basic border, which is made of simple lines.

3. Open the clip's Filters tab in the Viewer window. You should now see the Bevel Border filter listed. To turn the effect on and off, click its check box.

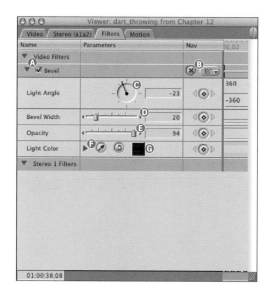

Ⓐ Filter On/Off

Ⓑ Reset filter to default values.

Ⓒ Use the dial or enter values (–360 to 360) to set the angle for the simulated light used to create the bevel.

Ⓓ Use the slider or enter a value (0 to 100) to scale the width of the border.

Ⓔ Use the slider or enter a value (0 to 100) to set opacity of border. As values approach 0, they will become more transparent.

Ⓕ Choose the basic color of the border using one of the color selection methods (see the *How Do I Pick a Color?* sidebar in Chapter 13).

Ⓖ Current Color

You can use the slider control to adjust the width of the border (with either Basic Border or Bevel), from 0 to 100. You can also change the color of the border by double-clicking the color swatch or using the eyedropper to sample a color from the Canvas window's image (with Bevel, you control the color of the light shining on the border). With Bevel, you can also use the Light Angle control to adjust the perceived angle (0–360) of light shining on the border; and the Opacity slider lets you control the bevel's prominence on the border, by making the light seem stronger.

You can preview your changes in the Viewer or the Canvas if your playhead in the Timeline is over the clip.

4. Once you've set your border, watch the clip in the Quick-View tab or render the clip and play it back in the Timeline. If you

don't like the results, simply open the clip in the Viewer again, play around with your settings, and then check the clip again.

Creating a Negative Image Using Invert

Before   After

Channel effects let you control and manipulate the color and alpha channels of a clip. One of the most common channel filters, which we'll use here as an example, is Invert. This technique creates a perfect negative image of the images in the clip (like a photographic negative). You can even choose which channels to invert. Invert can be used either for abstracting video imagery to create striking shapes and tones for title sequences or backdrops, or to create a flash negative image often used to highlight a photograph being taken. Negative imagery is also often used in dream or traumatic flashback sequences because it can insinuate the "opposite" or reverse of what we see, suggesting a dark or hidden side.

1. In the Canvas, Timeline, or Browser, double-click on the clip you want to work with to open it in the Viewer.

2. Add the Invert filter to the clip you want to invert (see *Adding a Filter* in Chapter 11). This filter is in the Video Filters/Channel folder or in the Effects pull-down menu.

3. In the Viewer window for your clip, open the Filters tab. You should now see the Invert filter listed. To turn the effect on or off, click its check box.

Ⓐ Filter On/Off

Ⓑ Reset filter to default values.

Ⓒ Choose the channels (color and/or alpha) to be blurred.

Ⓓ Use the slider or enter a value (0 to 100) for the amount of inversion. No inversion is 0, and maximum inversion is 100.

You can use the Channel popup menu to select which channels you want to invert. You can then use the slider to determine how much inversion you want to apply to the clip. A full inversion will create a pure negative image. You can also invert just a particular color (for example, inverting just reds will turn the red values green) or the alpha channel of the image (see Chapter 13 for more details) and also mimic ultraviolet light (UV). The Amount slider moves from 0 to 100. The 0 setting will apply no percentage to the effects. From 1 up to 50, the color manipulation affects midtones until becoming completely gray at 50. From 50 to 100, the color begins to invert from midtones to full tones by 100.

You can preview your changes in the Viewer or in the Canvas if your playhead in the Timeline is over the clip.

4. Once you've set your inversion the way you want it, preview the clip in the QuickView tab or render the clip and play it back in the Timeline. If you don't like the results, simply open the clip in the Viewer again, play around with your settings, and then check the clip again.

Stylizing Your Clip

Before   After

The Stylize folder provides another group of filters you can use to manipulate images. The example we will use from this set of filters is Solarize, which takes its name from a photographic process done in the darkroom that involves flashing a print with light while it is developing. The effect dulls the midtones and extremely heightens the shadows and highlights. (The photographer Man Ray is famous for his solarized prints.) This filter can create beautiful and strange imagery, especially if you are working with black-and-white footage.

1. In the Canvas, Timeline, or Browser, double-click on the clip you want to work with to open it in the Viewer.

2. Add the Solarize filter to the clip you want to solarize (see *Adding a Filter* in Chapter 11). This filter is in the Video Filters/Stylize folder, or you can choose it from the Effects pull-down menu.

3. In the Viewer window for your clip, open the Filters tab. You should now see the Solarize filter listed. To turn the effect on and off, click its check box.

You can use the Amount slider control to vary the degree to which the image is solarized. This ranges from 0 to 100, with 0 applying no effect, and 100 applying full effect. You can also check the Invert box to invert the image immediately, creating a negative of the solarized image (which may look a lot like the original image) and inverting everything except the whites.

You can preview your changes in the Viewer or in the Canvas if your playhead in the Timeline is over the clip.

4. Now preview the clip in the QuickView tab or render the clip and play it back in the Timeline. If you don't like the results, simply open the clip in the Viewer again, play around with your settings, and then check the clip again.

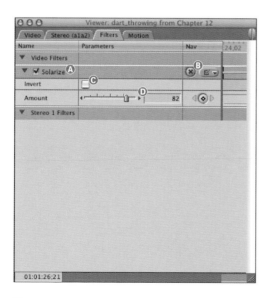

Ⓐ Filter On/Off

Ⓑ Reset filter to default values.

Ⓒ Check to invert solarization.

Ⓓ Use the slider or enter a value (0 to 100) for the amount of solarization. No solarization is 0, and maximum solarization is 100.

13

Compositing Images

Compositing is a process by which two or more layers of video are superimposed over each other so that images from multiple clips are seen at the same time.

Compositing in Final Cut Pro can create all sorts of special effects, including double or multiple exposures. This chapter will look at how to create composite imagery, and how using alpha channels (the layer in the clip that determines what is transparent and how transparent it is) can aid you in creating layered effects.

Overview

Compositing images in Final Cut Pro is the process of laying video clips—one on top of the other—on multiple video tracks in the Timeline. Basically, you are stacking clips and then adjusting the dimensions and opacity of these layered clips in order to expose the content of images underneath. When we discussed Cross Dissolve transitions in Chapter 10, we were using a form of composited imagery, as the two shots dissolve from the outgoing to the incoming and briefly overlap. Video tracks in the Timeline have a top-down hierarchy. That is, the video clip on the top track in the Timeline will completely cover any track below it until some part of that top track is made transparent. Only then will you see lower tracks. Once you've layered your clips, you can use a number of effects to create composite imagery.

Opacity

Opacity is used to make an entire clip more transparent. Think of lowering the opacity as turning the image from a photographic print, which you cannot see through, into an overhead projector transparency, which retains the color and shape of the image, but allows you to see any other images that lie beneath. By stacking clips and adjusting the opacity of higher-level clips so that they become more transparent, you can see all of the clips in the stack playing at once.

The imagery will mix together into one image, and you can change the opacity as a function of time in order to fade smoothly between clips. You can also change the compositing mode, which affects the way clips superimpose when you lower the opacity, allowing colors to interact with each other in a variety of ways.

Using Alpha Channels

An *alpha channel* tells you the variable opacity of an image. Normally a clip will be set to display the RGB (red, green, blue) channels that make up the full image. The alpha channel is a graphic map of the opacity values of the clip across its surface. However, you can view a video clip's alpha channel by selecting Alpha in the View popup menu in the Viewer or Canvas window.

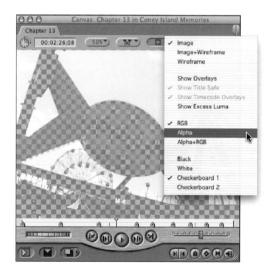

With the Alpha channel visible, the image you see is a grayscale depiction of transparency. Solid areas are seen as pure white, while completely transparent areas are completely black. Parts of the image where you've applied intermediate degrees of transparency appear as gray areas.

Alpha channels are often used when you import a graphic into Final Cut Pro from another program. For example, let's say you create a graphic title in Photoshop and import it into Final Cut Pro (see Chapter 17). Photoshop also uses alpha channels, and all of its alpha channel information will be recognized in Final Cut Pro. If you've created a title graphic containing text and a picture, with a transparent background, the imported clip will keep the information about the transparent background. If you drag this imported clip into the Timeline and place it on a track directly above another clip, it will automatically layer the text and graphic over the lower video clip, as in a text clip generated in Final Cut Pro.

Understanding how alpha channels work is very helpful when you are designing graphics or titles in a separate program for import into Final Cut Pro. In Photoshop, for example, you can set up the parts of the graphic or title you want to be solid, transparent, or translucent by adjusting the alpha channels. Then, when you import it into Final Cut Pro, the graphic clip is all ready to go and you just have to lay it into the Timeline. FCP will reproduce the transparency and opacity settings you applied in Photoshop. They are not static,

and you can change them in Final Cut Pro. As discussed in the next section, you'll need to make sure you've got the alpha channels set for the same mode you set in Photoshop.

Keying

Keying allows you to work directly with the alpha channel of a clip to change the opacity of different parts of the image. The changes will be based on parameters you set for attributes like color, brightness, or difference between two clips. The basic idea behind keying is to change the alpha channel to make certain parts of the image completely or partially transparent, allowing images from lower video tracks to show through. The kind of key filter you use (along with properties of the image itself) determines which parts of the image will become transparent (or translucent). When we hide part of an image based on one of these properties, we are said to be *keying out* that property.

Keying is a filter, just like Brightness/Contrast (see *Adding a Filter* in Chapter 11), that you add to the clip from the Browser's Effects tab. Final Cut Pro has three main kinds of key effects: Luma key, color, and difference.

Luma Key   The Luma Key filter can be set to make different areas of an image transparent, depending on their brightness or darkness. So, if you set the Luma Key filter to key out darker areas, the clip's darkest parts will become transparent. If you set the Luma Key to key out the brighter areas, the bright whites will become transparent. Wherever the Luma Key filter creates areas of transparency, the clip(s) or slug you've placed underneath will show through the keyed-out areas. You can use this effect to create unusual superimpositions, so that instead of mixing the two images equally, you might, for example, have a lower image appearing only in the shadows of the top image. This gives you greater control over which parts of the image are keyed out, so you can fashion more intricate and detailed special effects. While changing the general opacity in the Motion tab brings two images together in what still appears to be a flat image, keying provides a sense of depth and complex layering between the two composited images.

Color   Color keying is performed with either of two filters: the Color Key or the Blue and Green Screen. The effect is similar to Luma Key, except that instead of keying out the darker or brighter areas of the image, the filter keys out a color you specify. You can use this effect to remove a backdrop color from an image and, by putting a tinted slug on a video track under the clip, change the color of the backdrop. The Blue and Green Screen filter is used for effects that were shot with a special blue or green screen backdrop behind the objects being filmed. (There is a standard "Blue Screen" shade of blue, and at specialty photo and video stores you can buy backdrops that are this color.) To use the Blue and Green Screen filter most effectively, you should have footage that was shot with this special backdrop. While most people use Blue screen, if the subject for some reason needs to have blue on it, a Green screen can be used.

Difference   The Difference Matte filter keys out just the differences between two similar but slightly different clips (see *What Are Mattes?*). For example, suppose you have a shot of a person coming out of a house. The house you've shot, however, is not what you want to appear in the final video. So you want to isolate the image of just the person, without the background of the house, and superimpose that image over a drawing of a house created to match the perspective and shape of the house in the original footage. To do this with the Difference Matte, you'll need a second shot, showing just the house, with no person walking through the scene. Then, you can stack these two images over each other in the Timeline and apply the Difference Matte on the top clip (the clip with the person walking). The video image of the house will be keyed out but the person walking will remain, as the person is the only thing that is "different" between the

two images. This is often done in commercials where a real person is walking though a sketch or line drawing.

Keying can become a complicated endeavor, but it can also create some very sophisticated special effects. You can also use the Luma Key simply to let more black or white into the image, creating imagery that has more contrast and density. This is a common way of giving your footage a more "intense" look and also makes the footage look less like raw out-of-the-camera video. All of the key filters give you precise control over how much is keyed out of the image based on the key factor (such as darkness), and so there are a million looks and composite images that you can achieve. It's best to start with a general idea of what you want and then play around with the different settings. You may discover something you like even better than your original conception.

Also keep in mind that keying to create special effects often starts on the set. You can set up the shot and composition knowing that you will be keying it later, so you may want to make certain parts of the frame darker or lighter knowing this. We often underexpose the footage by a half a stop, knowing that we will be keying out the darker later to provide true black in the darker region.

DVD

Chapter 13: Visual Interaction between Clips

Open the Final Cut Pro project file labeled Coney Island Memories. After it loads in Final Cut Pro, double-click the Chapter 13 sequence in the Browser and it will open in the Timeline.

In this chapter you will experiment with having two clips, stacked on top of each other in the Timeline, visually interact with each other. We have added nine pairs of clips in the Timeline, one for each section in this chapter and three for sidebars in this chapter. You should use the first clip in a pair to practice with and the second to see what the possible outcome might look like.

Changing the Opacity of a Clip

Before   After

Compositing clips allows you to blend one or more clips by stacking them on top of each other in the Timeline and setting each layer's opacity. This technique is often used to create backgrounds for title or presentational sequences, to create moody transitions in a narrative, or to create interesting imagery for a music or experimental video. Compositing can create some intriguing effects and allow you to create striking images that convey a lot of feeling.

These techniques are not new, and can be found in early experimental films like Dziga Vertov's 1928 Soviet film *Man with a Movie Camera*, which used extensive overlapping of black-and-white imagery to play with form, content, and the way images function to represent life.

When experimenting with composite imagery, be careful in your selection of clips. If your clips don't blend well together, you might just end up with a lot of noise on the screen.

Also, remember that you don't need to adjust the opacity of the bottom clip, just the upper clip(s). If you adjust the opacity of the bottom clips from 100, that clip's imagery will simply fade closer to default black.

1.   Pick two or more clips you want to work with from the Browser and stack them on multiple tracks in the Timeline (see Chapter 6), making sure that the clips are directly over each other. For this example, we'll assume you are using two clips.

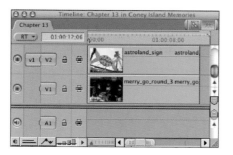

Place the playhead in the Timeline within your stack of clips. Notice that only the top track is visible in the Canvas.

Remember that Final Cut Pro uses a top-down track hierarchy—the top clip in the Timeline is seen first, then the next one down, and so on. If you need to work with one track and ignore those above it, turn off the higher tracks' visibility by clicking the green button by the track number (see *The Timeline* in Chapter 2).

2. Once you have the desired clip topmost in the Timeline, double-click it to open it in the Viewer, and then open the Motion tab. (Chapter 14 covers the rest of the controls in this tab.)

3. Scroll down the Motion tab to find the Opacity field. Initially, this field may be collapsed, and you will need to click on the arrow to open it.

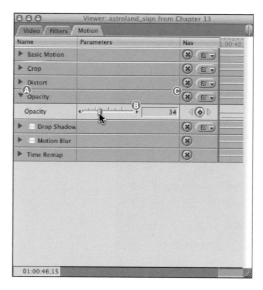

Ⓐ Open Control

Ⓑ Reset to Defaults

Ⓒ Use the slider or enter a value (0 to 100) for the opacity of the selected clip. Completely transparent is 0, while 100 is completely opaque.

You can set the Opacity of your clip by dragging the slider or typing in a percentage on the scale from 0 to 100. Setting the clip at 0 will make it completely transparent, while 100 will make the image completely solid. The image in the Canvas reflects your work; examine it closely. You want to make sure that the two or more superimposing images play well together, so check out multiple frames by moving the Timeline's playhead, or go ahead and render the effect and watch the composited clips. Use the Slip edit tool (Chapter 6) to make quick adjustments in the content of the clip if you don't like the timing of the two images together.

Notice how typing in a percentage lower than 100 lets in some of the image from the clip on the video track immediately beneath the top clip. If you have a stack of more than two clips and you want them all superimposed together, you will have to follow Steps 2 and 3 for each clip except the bottom clip.

Once you've set the opacity of your stacked clips to create the composited effect you want, you'll have to render the effect before you can view it in motion (see *Rendering Effects* in Chapter 9). In Chapter 15, we'll look at how to change the opacity at different points in the clip using Keyframes.

TIP

Moving Clips between Video Tracks

Suppose you have a clip in the Timeline that you want to move to a different video track but keep in exactly the same spot in the Timeline; that is, you only want to move it vertically. To drag the clip with precision, just hold down the Shift key while dragging. This will allow you to move the clip up or down, while freezing its horizontal position. This technique is especially useful when you're moving unlinked clips that should stay in synch or you need to clear a space below a clip without changing its location in the Timeline.

Alternate Steps: Changing Opacity in the Timeline

Another way to change a clip's opacity is to turn on the Clip Overlay control and graphically adjust the opacity in the Timeline. Select Sequence **>** Settings **>** Timeline Options, and make sure the Show Keyframe Overlays box is checked. Then pick up after Step 1 above.

2.   Click the Clip Overlay button at the bottom left of the Timeline. This will place a line over each clip, and you can use these lines to control each clip's opacity directly in the Timeline.

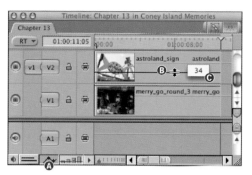

A **Clip Overlay:** Click to turn on opacity control in Timeline.

B **Opacity Control:** Click and move up or down to control clip's opacity.

C **Current Clip Opacity**

3. As you change the opacity in the Timeline, you can see a preview of what it will look like in the Viewer, as long as your playhead rests over the affected clip.

You will have to render your clips before you can view them in real time (see *Rendering Effects* in Chapter 9) or preview a section in the QuickView tab. Once they are rendered, view your work in the Canvas window.

FAQ

What Are Mattes?

A *matte* (sometimes called a *mask*) is basically an overlay that blocks out part of the image on a clip. Mattes are often used to obscure parts of the frame or to create a "wide-screen" look on footage that was shot at a 3:4 ratio. If you want to add a wide-screen matte to your video footage, you can add a Widescreen filter from the Effects > Video Effects > Matte bin in the Browser by dragging it into the clip you want to make wide-screen. You can choose standard film aspect ratios such as 1:1.66 or 1:1.85 to give your video a letterbox. When you add a matte, make sure you don't block off important action or pictures at the top and bottom. Mattes can also be used more generally to vignette the image or block out something, like a boom mike or light. You can use the Image Mask in the Effects > Video Effects > Matte bin to create rectangular, oval, and many other kinds of mattes to lay over your image.

Working with Composite Modes

Before   After

Composite modes are settings that control how the layers of your video will interact with each other. The Normal default setting applies your Opacity percentage setting uniformly across the whole image. Other settings control which parts of an image become transparent based on factors such as color and light. Composite modes are set within a clip, and they affect only the clip's interaction with other clips *below* it in the Timeline, not the clips above it.

1.   Select the clip whose composite mode you want to control, in either the Timeline. If you select a clip from the Timeline, it will affect only that one copy of the clip. In addition, if there are

clips above this one in the Timeline whose opacities are 100 percent, then this clip may not be visible.

2.   Control+click on the clip in the Timeline and choose from the Composite Mode submenu in the contextual menu. (You can also select a clip in the Timeline and then choose Modify > Composite Mode and choose a composite mode from the submenu.) These modes alter the way the clips look together by merging the color of pixels in the upper clip(s) with those below. Final Cut Pro offers the following composite modes:

Normal   The default setting, which applies the selected clip's Opacity setting uniformly.

Ⓐ Track V2 (top)

Ⓑ Track V1 (bottom)

Add   Adds the color values of the selected clip and the clip(s) beneath it. This will generally increase the color values, creating a lighter image.

Difference   Subtracts the color values of the lower clip(s) from the selected clip; this can create the impression of a color photographic negative.

Subtract   Subtracts the color values of the selected clip from the clip beneath it. The image will appear darker as it interacts with the clips(s) beneath by decreasing color values toward black.

Multiply   Multiplies each pixel's color values in the selected clip with those of the clip(s) beneath it. This will darken lighter images and is helpful to make white parts of the image, such as a bright sky or paper, completely transparent.

Screen   Multiplies the inverse of each pixel's color value in the selected clip with the clip beneath it. This lightens darker images and is useful in making transparent the dark black parts of an image, such as harsh shadows or a black backdrop. A common use of this is to make the dark area of the upper image transparent so that the lower image shows through.

Overlay   Calculates the color value of the pixels of the selected clip and applies either Screen or Multiply. If the color value is greater than 128, Screen mode is used. If the value is less than 128, Multiply mode is used. This will darken the lighter parts of the image and lighten the darker parts.

Hard Light

Adds an effect to mimic the effect of shining a hard light on the clip; this will generally add contrast on the selected clip.

Soft Light   Adds an effect to mimic a soft diffused light, generally reducing contrast on the selected clip and also adds transparency to the clip below.

Darken Compares each pixel of the selected clip and the clip beneath it, and shows only the darker pixel.

Lighten Compares each pixel of the selected clip and the clip beneath it, and shows only the lighter one.

Travel Matte (Alpha, Luma) Composites the selected clip with a lower clip that follows the form of a matte placed between them. There must be a matte placed between the two clips (see the sidebar *What Are Mattes?* for more information).

A single clip in the Timeline can only have one composite mode at a time, but you can overlap clips with different composite modes on different video tracks.

You will see the results of your selection in the Viewer. In the example shown here, the Difference mode was selected. As usual, you will have to render your clips before you can view the new effect in real time (see *Rendering Effects* in Chapter 9) or preview a section in the QuickView tab.

What Are Color Values?

The color of every pixel (the small dots used to create an image on the computer's screen) is defined by three values that specify the amount of red, green, and blue used to make up that particular color. These values can be specified in a number of ways, including:

RGB   A series of three percentage values (red, green, and blue): 0% (no color) up to 100% (maximum color).

Hex   A series of three values (red, green, blue) in hexadecimal notation: 00 (no color) to FF (maximum color). Hex notation is most often associated with Web or computer interface designs but will work fine in video.

HLS, HSB, and HSV   Specify values for hue angle, saturation, and either lightness (HLS), brightness (HSB), or value (HSV).

CMYK   A series of percentages that define the amount of cyan, magenta, yellow, and black in a color. Although you can specify colors this way for video, it is primarily intended for print publications and the color values are translated into RGB for other uses. This is subtractive color, while video uses additive color.

How Do I Pick a Color?

Final Cut Pro offers two basic methods for picking a color. One method is to enter values directly, and we recommend this method if you need to use an exact color. Another is to use the eyedropper tool to select a color from the screen. The values for this color are then automatically entered for you.

In Final Cut Pro, you can pick a color using the built in eyedropper tool, using the built-in HSB controls, or by clicking on the current color chip to bring up the Mac Color Picker.

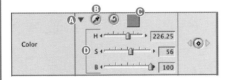

Ⓐ Hide/show HSB sliders.

Ⓑ Click this tool and then click anywhere in the canvas to choose a color.

Ⓒ Specifies current color. Click to use the Mac color selector.

Ⓓ Use sliders or enter values to set the Hue (0 to 359.9), Saturation (0 to 100), and Brightness (0 to 100).

The Mac Color Picker offers you a variety of ways to specify a color, but we recommend sticking with the HSV Picker, which allows you to select colors from a color wheel, or the RGB picker, which allows you to adjust relative levels of red, green, and blue.

You can also select a color using the magnifying glass tool in the upper left corner and then clicking on any color on the screen. Unlike the eyedropper tool included with Final Cut Pro—which is limited to selecting colors from the Canvas—the Mac Color Picker magnifying glass allows you to select a color from any part of the screen, even from other programs.

Changing Alpha Channel Properties

Before   After

In Final Cut Pro you may often work with graphics or clips from other sources that use alpha channels. For example, you may get title graphics created by a graphics studio that you will import into your project. However, there are different kinds of alpha channels. These different types affect the way the alpha channel is read, and therefore how your composited clips will interact with each other to create a composite image. So

when you import these clips, it's important to make sure they have the correct alpha channel set, or you won't get the intended effect and the image will not look right.

When Final Cut Pro imports a clip, it looks for an alpha channel and tries to identify what type it is. Final Cut Pro can work with three kinds of alpha channels: Straight, Black, and White (described below); and it can recognize that a clip has no alpha channel (None/Ignore).

You should communicate with the shop that supplies your graphics or video clips so that you know what kind of alpha channels you are receiving. You should also check after importing to see if Final Cut Pro correctly identified the alpha channel, as it can misidentify them. Black alpha types are typical with Photoshop files, and straight alpha types are often used with 3D animation. Take the following steps if you need to correct the alpha type.

1. In the Browser or Timeline, select the clip whose alpha channel you need to change and select Modify **>** Alpha Type.

2. You can change the clip's type of alpha channel by clicking the Alpha Type popup menu. You can select a new type here:

Straight This kind of alpha channel has no background information at all, and just records the pixels of the visible image. Images with a straight alpha channel will cleanly overlay over other clips.

Black This kind of alpha channel is a "premultiplied" or pre-composited image that includes a pure black background. This is typical of graphics created in Photoshop.

White This kind of alpha channel is a premultiplied or pre-composited image that includes a pure white background.

None/Ignore Instructs Final Cut Pro to ignore the alpha channel of a clip.

Reverse Alpha This is a check box that inverts the alpha channel information; that is, whatever was transparent becomes opaque, and vice versa.

3. After changing the Alpha channel type, render your clip and view it. If the clip still does not look right, check to make sure the correct alpha channel type was communicated. One common sign is a black fringe around the edge of the image. If you encounter this, you have probably mislabeled a Black alpha channel as a Straight alpha channel. Go into the clip and change the type to Black, and this should remove the fringe. And vice versa, a Straight alpha channel mislabeled as Black can cause a white fringe to appear.

Copying, Pasting, and Stripping Attributes from a Clip

When you control+click any clip in the Timeline, you have the option of copying from that clip or pasting copied attributes into the clip. Attributes include filters; composite modes motion controls opacity speed capture settings for video; and levels, pan, filters and speed for audio.

- To copy the clip (including its attributes) simply choose Copy from the clip's contextual menu.
- To just paste the attributes (and not the media) into another clip, choose Paste Attributes... from the clip's contextual menu, then

check off the attributes that you want copied into the clip and click OK.

- To strip particular attributes from a clip, choose Remove Attributes... from the clip's contextual menu and then check off the attributes to be removed. For filters, you may want to consider simply turning the filter off in the Filters tab in the Viewer. This has the same apparent effect, but if you change your mind later, you can turn the filter back on.

Keying Out Luminosity

Before   After

As its name suggests, the Luma Key filter uses luminosity values to select parts of an image to key out. It modifies the alpha channel of the clip it's applied to, making lighter or darker areas transparent based on your settings. Besides choosing between darkness and brightness to key out, you can specify how dark or bright an area must be for the filter to affect it; and you can apply the filter based on differences between luminosity values.

The Luma Key filter keys out parts of an image based on how light or dark they are. This filter can be set to a number of different modes that change the way it keys out imagery, and whether it keys out based on low or high luminance. See the sidebar after this section for tips on using the Luma Key.

1. Open the clip you want to work with in the Viewer by double-clicking it in the Browser, Timeline, or Canvas. You can also drag it into the Viewer from any of those windows.

A Playhead

B Selected Clip

2. Open the Browser's Effects tab and find the Luma Key filter. It is located in the Video Filters > Key folder. Drag this filter into the Viewer (see *Adding a Filter* in Chapter 11 for more details). From the Viewer, you can choose Effects > Video Filters > Key > Luma Key.

3. Open the Filters tab in the Viewer and you will see the Luma Key filter listed. A popup menu for Key Mode lets you choose to key out any of the following:

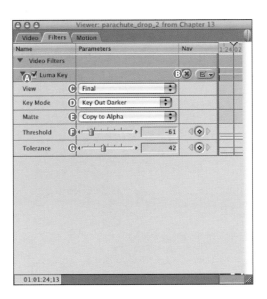

Ⓐ Filter On/Off

Ⓑ Reset to Defaults

Ⓒ Choose whether to view the source clip, the matte being used, the final results, or all three in a heads-up display.

Ⓓ Choose whether to key out Brighter colors, Darker colors, similar colors, or Dissimilar colors.

Ⓔ Choose whether to key out the alpha (transparency) or RGB channels.

Ⓕ Use the slider or enter a value (–100 to 100) for how far the matte should expand. Negative values shrink the matte while positive values grow the matte.

Ⓖ Use the slider or enter a value (0 to 100) for the softness of the edge of the matte. A hard edge is 0, while higher values create softer edges.

Brighter Keys out the parts of the image that are brighter than the tolerance you set.

Darker Keys out the parts of the image that are darker than the tolerance you set.

Similar   Keys out the parts of the image that have similar luminance.

Dissimilar   Keys out the parts of the image that have dissimilar luminance.

We'll try Key Out Darker as an example here, and note that you apply the other modes in the same way, by adjusting the Threshold and Tolerance sliders.

4.   Luma Key has two sliders—Tolerance and Threshold. The Tolerance slider ranges from 0 to 100 and controls the degree to which the keying occurs. With darkness, for example, it determines how dark an area must be before it will be keyed out. At the 0 setting it makes virtually the entire image transparent; at 100 only the true blacks will be transparent. When keying out the darker, try sliding the slider to the right and see how much less of the image is keyed out. The Threshold ranges from −100 to 100 and controls the sharpness of the edge between the part of the image keyed out and the part that remains (sort of like feathering the alpha channel). By sliding the Threshold slider to the left, decreasing the threshold, you will sharpen the edges, often creating a more digital effect.

Adjust the Tolerance and Threshold sliders together to achieve the look you want. You can either place a clip under your Luma Keyed clip and let it show through the darker parts of your top image, or you can use this filter to let in the default black background, giving the image the weight of true blacks.

5.   Render the results or view the effect in the QuickView tab and check out your work in motion. Repeat these steps if you want to make any changes.

There is also a Matte popup menu in the Luma Key filter. This allows you to create alpha channel information for the affected clip, and also to create a high contrast matte that can give an interesting black-and-white neon effect.

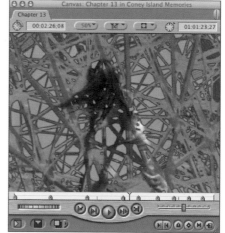

Using the Brightness Setting with the Luma Key Filter

If you are using the Luma Key with the Key Out Brighter setting, you may want to use the effect to make the lighter parts of your image a pure white. This gives the image a ghostly, washed-out look that can be very effective. Less subjectively, it can also be helpful in lightening up and bringing out the details in a very dark shot while keeping the blacks dark. If you apply a Luma Key with the brightness keyed out and no clip beneath the one you are keying, you'll see the default black background come through, creating a strange inverse effect on the image, which you probably don't want. A trick to using the "key out brighter" Luma Key filter to whiten the bright parts of your image is to place a white slug under the effected clip.

1. Make room on the track directly under your affected clip and drag a slug from the Video Generators folder in the Effects tab onto this track (see Chapter 6). This slug by default will be black.

2. Add a Brightness And Contrast filter to the slug and turn the brightness all the way up (see *Adjusting Brightness and Contrast* in Chapter 11 for a full description) so that the slug becomes pure white. You can also add the Invert filter in the Effects > Video Filters > Channel bin.

3. Drag the slug's edges in the Timeline to make it exactly the same duration as the Luma Keyed clip. With the white slug underneath the keyed clip, you will achieve a brightness effect that replaces the brighter area of your image with a pure white. This can be very beautiful, and can be used to create dream-like, washed-out imagery.

Remember, you can tint the slug any color you want, changing the effect of the Luma Key to apply a color to the brightest parts of the image for a more surreal effect.

Before   After

Making Video Look More Like Film

A common goal of image manipulation in Final Cut Pro when you are using DV or analog video source footage is to make the result look less like "video" and more like film. Video often has a lack of apparent depth in the image, and colors may be so saturated that they bleed. You can treat these and similar problems using the Luma Key. We've found that adding a slight Luma Key filter that keys out the darker (with the black default background under the clip) and adding a slight Desaturation filter (see Chapter 11) to a clip of DV footage creates a subtle deepening of the image, giving it more of the dimension and feel of film. Check out the clip with the marker "Making Video Look More Like Film" in the Chapter 13 sequence to see how this looks.

Before   After

Keying Out Color

Before   After

Keying out color follows the same basic pattern as keying based on luminosity, but you instead choose a specific color value to "hide" from your image, leaving transparent holes called the matte. This is good for taking out a background color you want to change to something else, or to remove a colored area so that another can play under it. You can use the Color Key, which we'll use in this example, or the Blue and Green Screen filter, which is used for special shoots that were shot with a blue or green screen background.

1. Open the clip you want to work with in the Viewer by double-clicking on it in the Browser, Timeline, or Canvas. You can also drag it into the Viewer from any of those windows.

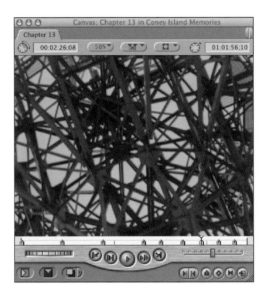

2. Open the Browser's Effects tab and find the Color Key filter. It is located in the Video Filters **>** Key folder. Drag this effect into the clip in the Viewer.

3. Open the Filters tab in the Viewer to see the Color Key filter listed. To select the color you want to key out, you can either double-click the color swatch or use one of the color selection methods described earlier in this chapter (see the *How Do I Select a Color?* sidebar). For this example, we selected the blue of the sky and made adjustments so that only the latticework design remains, but the girl on the beach shows through.

What Is Blue Screening?

Blue screening is a technique that has been around since long before digital effects. A famous example is in Akira Kurosawa's *Dreams*, where there is a scene of people walking through a field that is a giant Picasso painting. Essentially, you shoot a figure in front of a blue, evenly lit background. The blue is then masked out, leaving just the figure. Another shot, often a background scene that would have been prohibitively expensive to build life-size, is placed behind the figure so that the figure appears to be in the same space as the background image. (Blue is chosen because it is not a color found on the human body, and so is easy to remove without taking out any part of the person in the shot. Sometimes green is used, but blue is the most common.)

Final Cut Pro offers a built-in filter that removes the blue background from a shot; you'll find it in Effects > Key > Blue and Green Screen. To use this tool you will, of course, have to prepare your shots beforehand, shooting against the blue background (for best results, get an actual blue-screen backdrop at a professional photo store) and shooting a backdrop separately. Once both clips are in your Final Cut Pro project, you'll place the blue screen clip directly over your background clip. Apply the Blue and Green Screen Filter to the top clip. Make sure you select the proper color, blue or green.

Often there will be a bit of blue left in a halo around the figure. While you can adjust the settings in the Blue and Green Screen filter, first you should try using a Spill Suppressor, which comes in Blue or Green filters. This Spill Suppressor is also located in the Key bin with Luma Key and Blue and Green Screen. Drag the Spill Suppressor into the clip (make sure it is listed *after* the Color or Blue and Green Screen Key. If it isn't, you'll need to drag the filter in the Viewer's Filters tab down below the Key filter). It will eliminate the edge problem by desaturating the fringe. This method works best with footage shot on film or analog video, as digital video has more ragged, pixelated edges, although you can still use it to get an acceptable effect.

Generally, you will key out a specific color from the clip, so it is best to have the clip showing in the Canvas and select the color you want removed using the eyedropper tool. Then play around with the tolerance and feathering until the entire area of color you want keyed out is included.

Render the results or view the effects in the QuickView tab and check out your work in motion. Often keying can look a little weird or fakey in motion, so watch carefully. Repeat these steps if you want to make any changes.

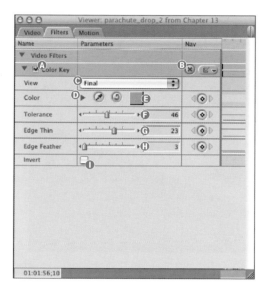

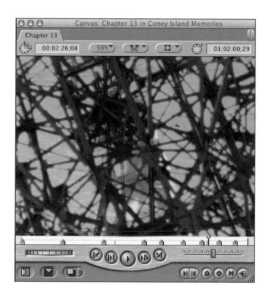

Ⓐ Filter On/Off

Ⓑ Reset to Defaults

Ⓒ Choose whether to view the source clip, the matte being used, the final results, or all three in a heads-up display.

Ⓓ Choose the basic color to be masked (see the *How Do I Pick a Color?* sidebar earlier in this chapter).

Ⓔ Current Color

Ⓕ Use the slider or enter a value (0 to 100) for how close colors in the image need to be to the selected color to be part of the matte. An exact match 0.

Ⓖ Use the slider or enter a value (–100 to 100) for how far the matte should expand. Negative values shrink the matte while positive values grow the matte.

Ⓗ Use the slider or enter a value (0 to 100) for the softness of the edge of the matte. A hard edge is 0 while higher values create softer edges.

Ⓘ Check to invert the area of the matte.

Replacing a Color

If you want to replace the keyed-out color with a different color or image, you should place a clip or slug containing that color or image on the video track directly below a keyed clip.

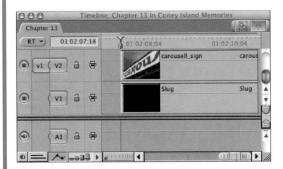

For example, you may decide to change the color of the curtain behind someone during a talking-head interview. To key out that color, you can sample it directly from the image in the Canvas window using the eyedropper tool. Once you've done that, go to the track below your keyed clip and place either a shot of fabric that's the color you want or a Final Cut Pro–generated slug you have tinted to that color. Make sure the slug clip has exactly the same duration as the top clip. The new color should now show through where the old color was. In the Chapter 13 Sequence marked "Replacing Color," the red letters have been keyed out and a white slug placed below giving the letters a ghostly blue-white pallor.

Before   After

Setting Up Your Shot for Difference Matte

Difference Matte can take some practice, but it is a very powerful tool and can create some really spectacular effects. It is another tool that requires planning and special shooting arrangements on the set. If you are going to be using the Difference Matte, you will have to shoot two shots with the camera in the exact same location and with the same framing. You will need to make sure that the light is basically identical in both shots, so if you are shooting outside, watch to see if the light is the same. Don't shoot one scene in sunlight and the other when a cloud is passing overhead. You may want to shoot several versions of the static shot if the light is not completely fixed, to have a few options.

Keying Out Difference

Before   After

Using the Difference Matte keys out the similar elements of two clips. The most effective use of this is to remove a static background, isolating just the moving figures. For example, if you have two people dancing in a ballroom and use a static image of the empty ballroom as a clip under the first one (shot from exactly the same angle, and using a tripod, so that they match), the Difference Matte will remove the ballroom, leaving the two figures dancing in a void. By placing another image or tinted slug under these two clips, the dancers will seem to dance on top of this new image. This is useful when you

are shooting someone in a specific three-dimensional space that you want them moving through and which you will replace with another image that matches the forms of the replaced space, so a blue screen wouldn't do. This key works by creating a matte that blocks out the similar part of the image.

1. You'll apply the Difference Matte to the clip that contains what you want to keep. Open this clip in the Viewer by double-clicking it in the Browser, Timeline, or Canvas. You can also drag it into the Viewer from any of those windows. Make sure that in the Timeline, the video track directly below this clip contains your second clip.

2. Open the Browser's Effects tab and locate the Difference Matte filter in the Video Filters > Key folder. Drag this effect into the clip in the Viewer.

3. Open the Filters tab in the Viewer to see the Difference Matte filter listed. A popup menu lets you view either the clip source (the original image), the matte that has been created, the new final image, or a four-way view of the source, difference layer, matte, and final image. You can use the Clip control to choose another clip for comparison. There are also Threshold and Tolerance sliders, which work in the same way as for the Luma Key described earlier. The Tolerance controls how much of

the image will be keyed out, from 0 to 100. This basically increases or decreases the areas around the "different" pixels that will be keyed out. The Threshold controls the sharpness of the edge between what is keyed out and what part of the image remains (sort of like feathering the alpha channel) and goes from –100 to 100.

You can also invert the matte, which keys out the different pixels and leaves the rest.

Render the results or view the effects in the QuickView tab and check out your work in motion. Remember, you can add a third clip under the two you are comparing to give a new background to the isolated part of the top clip. Repeat these steps if you want to make any changes.

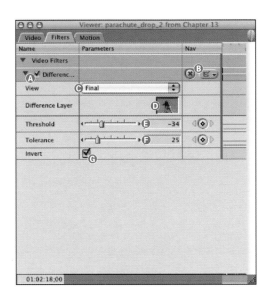

Ⓐ Filter On/Off

Ⓑ Reset to Defaults

Ⓒ Choose whether to view the source clip, the difference between the two clips, the matte being used, the final results, or all four in a heads-up display.

Ⓓ Drag image here to use as Difference channel.

Ⓔ Use the slider or enter a value (–100 to 100) for how far the matte should expand. Negative values shrink the matte while positive values grow the matte.

Ⓕ Use the slider or enter a value (0 to 100) for how close differences in the image need to be in order to be part of the matte. Exact is 0.

Ⓖ Check to invert the area of the matte.

Lullaby, Independent Film

Filmmaker Dorne Pentes began writing *Lullaby* in 1994, in response to a news story he read about a woman who had killed her abusive husband after he attempted to hurt her newborn baby. Although an emotional subject, Dorne wanted to explore how women struggle to define themselves in the male-dominated southern culture. *Lullaby* tells the story of Rane and Diesel, who love dirt track racing, partying, and each other. However, this idyllic life is upended when Rane gets pregnant and resists the stifling life that Diesel dictates for her and her child.

© Copyright 2002 Crescent Pictures, Inc

As with most independent films, Dorne ran into two problems: time ("We shot in 18 days—too fast") and money ("There was never enough"). Dorne got around the problem of money by begging, borrowing, and stealing, but couldn't add more hours to the day. "We just worked through it, but it was incredibly difficult and very trying. I had never been so wiped out by a schedule before." In these situations, your best asset is a good crew: "You must have a dedicated crew to get you through each day, and you must be incredibly nice and patient with them—let them do their jobs and try not to run everything or do everything yourself…especially if they're not being paid well."

Regardless of how hectic the shooting schedule, Dorne recommends taking a break between shooting and editing: "You need time away from a project—at least a day or so—before trying to decipher the footage."

Once the editing starts, Dorne works best through intuition. "I get a rough cut based on the script, but after that, I chop everything up to make the story work." One effect important to Dorne was to create the feeling of a late afternoon southern glow throughout the film regardless of the time of actual filming. To get this look, Dorne used a number of effects and filters, mostly dealing with contrast and color manipulation. However, filters did not come without their drawbacks. "The filters were very helpful, but difficult to apply, because they're not really tweakable on the spot—you've got to wait for a render."

© Copyright 2002 Crescent Pictures, Inc

To learn more about *Lullaby* and the films of Dorne Pentes, visit his website at www.wildwildsouth.com.

14 Using Motion Controls

The image you get when you bring captured footage over FireWire into Final Cut Pro fills the screen, centered in the middle. Initially the footage is completely opaque, with no transparency. However, you have the power to change all of this. Every clip, even if it is a computer-generated clip like text or 3D animation, has a Motion tab that allows you to make changes in its orientation and dimensions. In this chapter we'll look at the tools within the Motion tab and how you can use them to change the look of your clips.

Overview

> *"Never confuse movement with action."*
>
> Ernest Hemingway,
> quoted by Marlene Dietrich in *Papa Hemingway*

Video is about motion. Typically that motion is created "live" at the time of filming, but using the Motion tab, you can also add motion effects in your clip while editing. Unlike the effects we've explored in previous chapters—such as transitions, filters, and text generators—motion effects are all applied from within a clip, so you will not be adding effects as you would with a filter. Instead, the motion effects are found inside the Motion tab, which you can access by opening a clip in the Viewer window. The name of this tab is a little confusing at first, because while you can use keyframes to create actual motion with your clips, most of these settings don't "animate" or immediately create motion paths. They do, however, move, crop, and distort the physical properties of the clip. To learn how to use these effects in combination with keyframes to create actual movement, see Chapter 15.

The different control groups within the Motion tab are Basic Motion, Crop, Distort, Opacity, Drop Shadow, and Motion Blur. This chapter covers Basic Motion, Crop, Distort, and Drop Shadow. For a discussion of Time Remapping, which is included in the Motion Tab, see Chapter 15. This chapter shows how to use the controls within the Viewer's Motion tab, which allow a lot of flexibility in shifting and cropping the image. We began working with the Motion tab in Chapter 13 when we talked about changing opacity. Creating these effects on film is very expensive and requires optically printing the image to a different size or shape.

With Final Cut Pro you can re-create these effects from the Motion tab and quickly view the alterations to your clip; this frees you to spend more time concentrating on getting the right appearance rather than just making the effect.

What are motion controls good for? The list is endless, but the more common (and tasteful) uses involve creating graphically interesting sequences for something like a commercial or a promotional video. By adjusting the sizes and shapes of images in the Motion tab and stacking clips in different video tracks in the Timeline, you can create multiple smaller "windows" of video, all playing simultaneously. You'll need to set up the size and placement correctly so that you'll be able to see the different clips all playing at the same time. Remember that track hierarchy in the Timeline is top-down, so if two clips overlap, the clip that is higher in the Timeline will cover the lower clip. You can use this layering to your advantage, to create overlapping windows that will give the image a three-dimensional effect.

You can also use motion controls to shift an image if you don't like the composition or if there is something distracting at the edge of the frame. A common problem is a shot with the boom mike poking into the frame. You can use motion controls to shift the image, cutting the boom mike out of the frame. This is especially effective when using a wide-screen matte that will be applied in post-production. If you are staying full-frame, you may want to use this tool in conjunction with the Scale tool, which you can use to enlarge the image just barely so that it fills the screen and doesn't show the edge of the clip.

Ultimately, the limit of motion control use is up to you, your imagination, and how much time you have. You can use combinations of motion control effects to create all sorts of effects and compositions to make your video more visually interesting, from titles in commercials to graphics for experimental videos.

Changing Size and Orientation

Before   After

At the top of the Motion tab is the Basic Motion control. You can use the controls to alter the size and orientation of your clip, as we've done here. Basic Motion functions do not alter the content or aspect ratio of an image; they only resize the image or move its position.

1. From the Canvas, Browser, or Timeline, open your clip in the Viewer by double-clicking it or dragging it.

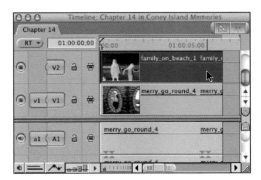

Chapter 14: Moving Clips Around

Open the Final Cut Pro project file labeled Coney Island Memories. After it loads in Final Cut Pro, double-click the Chapter 14 sequence in the Browser and it will open in the Timeline.

In this chapter you will be moving, bending, and cropping clips. We have provided five pairs of clips (one for each section and a fifth for the sidebar *Creating a Drop Glow*). The first clip in each pair is for you to use in applying motion controls, while the second clip shows one possible outcome.

Although you will primarily be working with the top clip (the one with two girls playing on the beach), we stacked this on top of another clip (the merry-go-round) so that you can see how multiple stacked clips can play and show at the same time. You can see how we changed the second clip by opening it in the Viewer and then checking the Motion tab.

2. Open the clip's Motion tab in the Viewer. If the Basic Motion control is not open, click its drop-down arrow to open the window. Play around with the controls until the clip is the size and orientation you desire. You can see the changes in the Canvas if the playhead in the Timeline is over the clip being changed.

Ⓐ Open Control

Ⓑ Reset to Defaults

Ⓒ Rotation Controls

Ⓓ Centering Control

Scale   Use to increase or decrease the size of the image. The clip will keep the same dimensions. The default setting is 100 percent, the size at which the clip was captured or imported. Typing a lower number in the input field or dragging the slider control to the left will shrink or enlarge the image to that percentage value. Typing in a higher number or dragging the slider to the right will blow up the image to that percentage. Keep in

mind that as you increase the size of the image, your clip will become less sharp and more pixelated.

Rotation   Lets you spin the clip. Click the dial to rotate the clip or type in a value in degrees into the input field. You can enter in a degree value from 0 to 360 to set a new angle, or, if you are using keyframes (see Chapter 15) to create a spinning image, you can exceed 360 and have the image rotate multiple times in either direction. The Rotation dial's small red hand shows you how many times the clip has been given a full rotation forward or backward. The red hand allows for eight 360-degree turns.

Center   Places the center of the clip at a specific coordinate location on the Canvas in pixels. You can think of the Canvas as a giant grid with X and Y axes whose origin (0,0) is at the center. Therefore, you can divide the screen's dimensions by 2 to find the edge position (+ or −). For example, if the screen width is 720 pixels, then the far right edge would be at 360 pixels and the far left edge would be at −360 pixels. You can position an object off the screen by exceeding these values. There are two ways to specify a center point. If you are doing precise movements with your clip, it's best to type exact coordinates into the input fields—do the math and get your clip exactly where you want it. If you can be looser with the placement, you can place the clip visually. Select the centering control and then click on the point in the Canvas (not the Viewer) you want to be the new center point.

Ⓐ Origin (0,0)

Anchor Point   Defines the point of the clip that is considered its center point (which will be lined up with the exterior center point you set in the Canvas with the Center control), and defines the center of the clip's axis for rotation. The default is 0,0 and is the true center of the clip. You can change it to any other point on the clip by typing in new X and Y coordinates. This is most helpful for changing how the clip will be rotated or spun when movement is added with keyframes, basically changing the point of the clip's own axes that it rotates on. You will only notice a change in the clip when you rotate it, as the anchor point doesn't change the clip's placement in the frame, only its internal rotation point.

You can play around with these settings, previewing your changes in the Canvas (as long as the playhead is over the clip being altered) until you've got the effect you want. Once finished, render the clip to view the effect in real time (see Chapter 9).

Cropping the Image

Before   After

the image with the Scale control by a small percentage until the image is big enough to fill the screen again. However, this technique has a tendency to degrade the image, adding unwanted visual artifacts.

Cropping an image cuts off the image at any of its four sides. Using the Crop control you can create thin strips of video or wide-screen effects, and you can use the effect to shave off video noise or borders that may be on the very perimeter of your clips. Cropping can also be used in conjunction with the Scale setting. If you need to shave off the top of an image because, for example, the boom mike is in the shot, you can crop the top off with the Crop control. However, you'll have a black bar at the top of the screen. To get rid of it, increase the size of

1. Starting from the Canvas, Browser, or Timeline, open your clip in the Viewer by double-clicking it or dragging it to the Viewer.

2. In the Viewer, open the Motion tab. Open the Crop control by clicking its arrow. You'll then see controls that let you trim all four sides of the clip (Left, Right, Top, Bottom) and feather the edges, which soften the hard edge of a clip into a graded border

fading into the background color or image beneath it. Once cropped, you can also adjust the position of the clip in the Canvas by shifting the center point using the Basic Motion controls (see previous section).

Ⓐ Open Control   Ⓑ Reset to Defaults

Left, Right Top, Bottom   Use the slider or enter a percentage value (0 to 100) to shave away from the true edge of the clip.

Feather   Use the slider or enter a percentage value (0 to 100) to give the border of the clip a softer look. You can only set one feather value for all four sides. Notice that the higher the number you set or the farther you move the slider, the blurrier the edges become.

Make sure you've got the playhead in the Timeline on the clip you are cropping so you can preview your work in the Canvas. You will still have to render the clip to view it in real time in the Canvas (see Chapter 9).

Making Stacked Clips Visible

Remember that if you stack multiple clips in the Timeline and apply certain motion effects to them, you can see multiple clips layered in the same frame. For example, you could crop the left half of one clip away, revealing the left side of the clip that's beneath it in the Timeline. In the Canvas, this gives you a split-screen effect, and you can play these two images side by side (think of the movie cliché where two people on the phone are shown in split-screen). The tutorial shows an example of two clips layered over each other, each cropped in a different way. The top (dominant) clip has been severely cropped on the left and right sides to turn the clip into a vertical strip, and feathered to smooth out the edges. The bottom clip has been cropped significantly from the top and the bottom, creating a horizontal stripe, and also feathered. The effect of having these two clips layered is a crosshatch design made from these two clips, both cropped down to strips. Double-click on these two clips to look at the Crop settings in the Motion tab and try changing the settings to create a different composition between the two clips.

Distorting the Image

Before   After

1. Starting from the Canvas, Browser, or Timeline, open your clip in the Viewer by double-clicking it or dragging it to the Viewer.

2. In the Motion tab, open the Distort control by clicking its arrow.

Distorting an image allows you to change the coordinates of all four corners of the clip to create a new and distorted image. This effect allows you to pull and stretch the image into any kind of four-sided shape, altering the image to fit your new parameters. You can also use the Aspect Ratio control to squeeze the image horizontally or vertically.

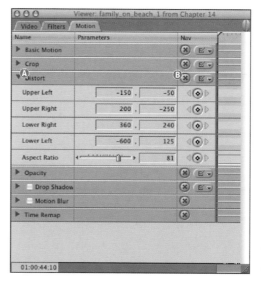

Ⓐ Open Control

Ⓑ Reset to Defaults

Upper Left, Upper Right, Lower Right, Lower Left   Enter X and Y coordinates (–10,000 to 10,000) for each of the clip's four corners. This will pull (negative numbers) or stretch (positive numbers) the corner to this new coordinate. Remember, the origin of the X,Y coordinates (0,0) is at the center of the Canvas or as defined by the center set by Basic Motion (see *Changing Size and Orientation* in this chapter).

Aspect Ratio   Use the slider or enter a value (–10,000 to 10,000) to squeeze the image either horizontally or vertically, creating a squashed image. To squeeze the image horizontally, drag the slider to the right or type in a value greater than 0. To squeeze the image vertically, drag the slider to the left or type in a value that is less than 0 (down to –10,000). The 0 setting ratio will be your default ratio as set in Final Cut Pro (for NTSC DV, this is 4:3; for PAL it is 5:4).

Once you have distorted your image to look the way you want, you can render the clip and watch it in the Canvas (see Chapter 9).

Why Distort the Image?

Image distortion is again something that will be used for many different reasons and situations. You may want to create a dream sequence. The footage looks okay, but you want to add a dimension of skewed perspective to make the dream sequence more unreal. By changing the corners and distorting the image so that the footage no longer follows normal rules of perspective, you can create the feeling of a dream-like world. This effect can also be interesting for experimental purposes, and especially when used with other effects to isolate a single object in the image and distort it in a particular way. As with many of Final Cut's effects, be wary of using them gratuitously. Distort can also look really amateurish if not done with purpose.

Adding a Drop Shadow

Before   After

The drop shadow can create an illusion of three dimensions in your video and can be used to separate a clip or titles from the images behind them by making them pop out. Drop shadows simulate a light shining from an angle onto the clip, casting a shadow on whatever is underneath.

A drop shadow basically duplicates an image or text, placing an exact copy underneath the original, but at a slight offset so that it can be seen from behind the clip, and with the color changed, and a slight blur added.

Drop shadows are often used with a text clip. After you have generated your text clip, you can open the clip's Motion tab and add a drop shadow. This creates a shadow of the actual letters and places it behind your text. Adding a drop shadow is often helpful when text is a little unreadable on a colored background because it makes the words more legible and stand out. Drop shadows can also be used on files brought in from Adobe Photoshop and clips that have been shrunk down by the Scale tool in the Motion tab.

Keep in mind that if a clip fills the whole screen, you won't see any drop shadow, as you must be able to see the edge of a clip for a drop shadow to show up underneath.

1. From the Canvas, Browser, or Timeline, open your clip in the Viewer by double-clicking it or dragging it. This clip could be video, a slug, text, or an Adobe Photoshop file; any kind of clip can have a drop shadow.

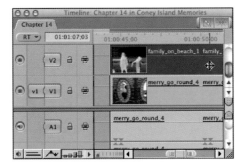

2. In the clip's Motion tab, open the Drop Shadow control by clicking its arrow. You will need to check the box by the Drop Shadow title to turn on a drop shadow for the clip.

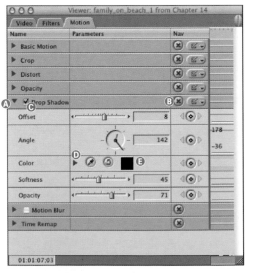

A Open Control

B Reset to Defaults

C Shadow On/Off

D Color Select

E Current Color

Offset This allows you to choose how far from the original clip's position the shadow will be placed. If you have an offset of 1 or 2, the shadow will appear as just a slim edge behind the clip. If you have a larger offset, the shadow will appear to be farther away from the actual clip, and you'll see more of it. Type in an offset and watch how the shadow placement changes. Make sure the playhead in the Timeline is over the clip you are adding a shadow to so you can watch the results in the Canvas.

Angle Use the slider or enter a value for the angle (–720 to 720) for the angle of the simulated "light source" that is casting the shadow. If you are using keyframes to animate the drop shadow, you can type in degrees above 360 to create up to eight spins around the dial. The Angle dial's red hand tells you how many rotations the clip has currently undergone.

Color Click the color swatch to select a color, or use the eyedropper to sample a color from the Canvas. Using color in a drop shadow is another good way to make text more legible. In addition, this allows you change a shadow into a glow (see the sidebar *Creating a Drop Glow*).

Softness Use the slider or enter a percentage value (0 to 100) to control how blurred the edges of the drop shadow are. This is the same concept as feathering.

Opacity Use the slider or enter a percentage value (0 to 100) to set how much of the underlying clip(s) you see through the drop shadow itself. Use this effect to make the shadow look like a real shadow by letting some of the underlying image through (low value), or make the shadow darker and more opaque (high value) so that the clip above really pops out in three dimensions.

3. Once you have the shadow just right, render the clip and watch it in the Canvas (see Chapter 9).

Changing the Speed of the Clip

You may want to create a slow motion effect or speed up your shot for fast action or to get a time-lapse effect. To change a clip's speed, highlight the clip and select Modify > Speed (⌘+J). This will bring up the Speed window. Type in the percentage change you want to make to the clip. For example, typing in **50** would make the clip play twice as slow (and twice as long). Typing in **200** would make the clip play twice as fast (and half as long). You can also type in a new duration and the clip will speed up or slow down to fit that time value. You can also click the Reverse button to make the clip play backwards. Very slow motion can appear a little weird in Final Cut Pro and when printed to video, as the software replicates existing frames to slow down the show, and this can sometimes look jerky. You can fix this somewhat by selecting Frame Blending, which creates new frames based on a blend of the frames before and after. See the section on Time Remapping for a more complicated approach to changing the speed of your clip with keyframes in Chapter 15.

Creating a Drop Glow

Although the effect is called a "drop shadow," the fact that you can change its color to anything you want means that you can also create a glow effect behind the image or text as if there were lights behind it. Simply select a light color and change the offset to 0. Of course, this technique will look better with a darker image or darkly colored text. Just be careful to match this effect to your content—it could look cool for a science fiction film but might look weird with a more dramatic narrative.

Using Motion Blur

Before   After

Motion Blur adds a soft blurring between frames, similar to the effect many DV cameras can add while you are shooting. It's an effect that creates a less stark, more dreamy feel in the footage, and will only apply to things in motion—like a person walking or a camera pan.

From the Canvas, Browser, or Timeline, open your clip in the Viewer by double-clicking it or dragging it.

Click on the clip's Motion Tab in the Viewer.

Scroll down, open the Motion Blur effect, and check the box. Adjust the number of frames to blur together (% Blur) and the smoothness of the blur (Samples). Adjust the Samples value if you are using footage that has been slowed down to blur out the stuttering effect caused by video slow motion.

After adjusting the motion blur, render the clip to view the final results (see Chapter 9).

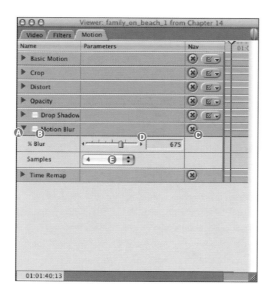

Ⓐ Open Control

Ⓑ Turn Motion Blur On/Off

Ⓒ Reset to Defaults

Ⓓ % to Blur

Ⓔ Sampled Frames

% Blur   Use the slider or enter a percentage value (0 to 10,000) for the number of frames to blur together. Entering 100% blurs across two frames and 10,000% blurs across 10 frames.

Samples   Chose a value for how often frames should be sampled for blurring. The higher the number, the smoother the blur will appear. Lower values will look jittery.

Boxes, Feature Film

Five years ago, if someone came to you with a feature film shot on a production budget of $300, you would have laughed. Nowadays, with the invention of Mini-DV and inexpensive editing tools like Final Cut Pro, a $300 movie is enough to land you a distribution deal.

Boxes—a no-budget feature film shot on DV and cut on Final Cut Pro—is such a story. Rene Besson, the director, camera operator, and editor of the film, explains how they got away with such a low budget shoot in Los Angeles. "We basically refused to spend money. We fed the actors, we bought DV stock, and we paid for haircuts. All of the other office locations are practical office spaces that we had access to. We shot at our apartments, actors' apartments, GoodFellas restaurant, and The Continental." The film was shot primarily on a one-chip Sony TRV8 Mini-DV camera with a wide-angle conversion lens mounted on a Steadicam JR.

A unique and sometimes bleak vision of the variety of boxes that dominate our everyday lives, the film displays, through its unusual approach, the restraints that define and at times immobilize our lives. "I had always toyed with the idea of making a stream-of-consciousness type film: a completely honest picture. One where no matter what you hear in the mind of your main character, you could relate to it."

As the main character Wren, played by Jimmy Vollman, wanders in and out of the boxes that he inhabits—be they his cubicle space, his car, his apartment, his sex life, or his obsessions—we begin to experience the walls that constrain our own lives in peculiar, unconscious ways. "We all live our lives on autopilot so much that we can't even see

coyote arm films and
mondrado filmworks
p r e s e n t s

a film by rene besson
written and produced by
james anthony portolese

boxes
you're in one

jimmy vollman
greta hill
robert berson
paula nikolaidis

music by kool aid (steve enos)
visual effects by bad apple
production designer amanda willa
∞ - producer steve knute lemme

written and produced by
james anthony portolese
directed, photographed, and
edited by rene besson

is this your life?

www.humanboxes.com

Photography courtesy of Coyote Arm Films and Mondrado Filmworks.

that our choices are getting narrower as we get older." By making the film, Besson was able to reflect "on the common things that each day steal our youth and enthusiasm away from us. By creating the film we committed ourselves to living outside the boxes that restrict us."

As an editor, Besson feels he had the perfect grounding to direct, as well as shoot the film. "Anyone who wants to direct should completely understand editing. You have to judge all the elements attained during the production process. If you understand how it is all going to come together, you can make sure you have all the footage you need to manifest your vision. In the case of *Boxes*, I knew how to take advantage of an idea I had that day on the set and get the coverage that I needed to make it work later in the edit."

Color manipulation took a high priority in the post-production process. And Final Cut Pro proved itself to be the perfect tool for *Boxes*. Besson says he "used the color-correction tools in Final Cut Pro because when I applied a filter it would render one frame to the TV monitor, which is invaluable because you get to see it the way it will be when it's done." After all the cuts had been composed, *Boxes* took one week to fully render.

Besson's favorite trick with Final Cut Pro is to "duplicate a piece of media on the Timeline, and then place the duplicate above the original in a second layer. By reducing the opacity of the top layer by about 50%, you will get a nice pop in color density. Also, if you de-interlace the top layer's even lines and the lower layer's odd lines, you will get a nice field blend with very little loss of image resolution."

Boxes, Feature Film

As with many independent films, neither Besson nor producer James Portolese had particular plans for distribution. They simply wanted to make a truthful portrait of our everyday lives. After they showed the film to a contact at Next Wave Films, *Boxes* found its way to the Independent Film Channel, and was purchased as part of its series *DV Theater*, before it even hit the festival track. "We got very lucky. We cast the film in February, shot it in March, cut it in April, had a premiere screening in May, and sold it to IFC in June."

Boxes can be seen in repeat segments of the Independent Film Channel's *DV Theater* series. With the success of *Boxes*, Rene Besson has gone on to work as the Post Production Supervisor on *Manic*, starring Don Cheadle. It is the first digital film financed by IFC through Next Wave Films, and appeared on the festival circuit before being released in the summer of 2002. It was also edited on Final Cut Pro.

15 Making Temporal Changes with Keyframes

So far we have looked at ways of making only static alterations to film clips. That is, the applied change stays consistent over the duration of the clip. However, film is about motion and change. Keyframes are a simple but powerful tool in Final Cut Pro that allow you to gradually alter the values of virtually all effects or motions of a clip over time. They can be used with almost any filter or other setting that affects the way your footage looks or sounds. Keyframes also can be used to lower and raise the volume of a clip's audio as it plays, a process described in Chapter 6, or slowly change the tint of clip from red to blue, or have a clip slowly shrink in the monitor as the footage plays, or...well, you name it. In Final Cut Pro 4, any change that takes place over time is implemented with keyframes. Think of using keyframes as working with your footage not only in the spatial realm, but in the temporal realm as well.

Overview

"'Clearly,' the Time Traveler proceeded, 'any real body must have extension in four directions: it must have Length, Breadth, Thickness, and—Duration. But through a natural infirmity of the flesh, we incline to overlook this fact. There are really four dimensions, three which we call the three planes of Space, and a fourth, Time. There is, however, a tendency to draw an unreal distinction between the former three dimensions and the latter, because it happens that our consciousness moves intermittently in one direction along the latter from the beginning to the end of our lives.'"

H. G. Wells
The Time Machine

If you're familiar with animation software such as 3ds max, Maya, Director, or Flash, you know what a powerful tool keyframes can be. Keyframes in Final Cut Pro are critical points you designate in a sequence to tell the program where a given change or shift takes place for a particular attribute of a specific clip. When you add an effect to a clip in Final Cut Pro, there are attributes you can set to define the exact nature of the effect. When you do so, this effect applies to the entire clip. As the clip plays, the effect does not change settings—it stays constant. However, with Final Cut Pro keyframes, you can designate different effect settings on different frames within one single clip. The clip's effect will then change based on the settings you designated in the keyframes. For instance, with keyframes you could have a clip play in slow motion, then set a keyframe to slow the clip to freeze on a frame, then apply another keyframe to bring the clip back to slow motion, then another keyframe to bring the speed back to normal.

For example, you may have a clip begin to change its size at one point in the Timeline and then reach a new size at another point. Historically, the concept derives from traditional cel animation, where lead artists drew the "key" frames showing the character's initial position and then final position. Other artists would then draw the frames in between to create a fluid motion. In Final Cut Pro 4, you can use keyframes to control the application—over time—of the effects and motion discussed in earlier chapters, such as filters like Brightness And Contrast or the controls in the Motion tab.

Most attributes associated with a particular clip—either built-in as with sound and motion controls or added as with effects—need not be simply on/off toggles. Instead, values are applied in a variety of ways to direct how the control or effect affects the clip. In addition, controls and effects have a keyframe control panel to the right of the normal set of controls that allows you to change an attribute's values while the clip is playing. This control panel consists of a keyframe button to lay down a keyframe, two arrows that transport you to the previous or next keyframe, and a mini-Timeline that shows you where in time various keyframes have been laid. Typically you will work with keyframes in the Viewer, but you can also see keyframes within the Timeline if you have the Clip Keyframe option on.

Motion paths, which create movement of a clip itself within the Canvas, are also achieved through keyframing. When using the Motion tab in the Viewer, you can adjust the size, orientation, and position of a clip. Using keyframes, you can then adjust the size and position at different points within the clip, causing the clip to float by, to shrink or enlarge, or spin on its axis.

The use of keyframes is vast, so this chapter will teach you the concepts behind keyframing that you can then apply to any effect. We'll focus on the effects most commonly keyframed, such as shifting image filters, creating motion, and varying the speed of the clip over time.

Chapter 15: Adding Motion

Open the Final Cut Pro project file labeled Coney Island Memories. After it loads in Final Cut Pro, double-click the Chapter 15 sequence in the Browser and it will open in the Timeline.

In this chapter you will learn how to change positions, effects, filters, and speed over time. We have set up five clip sets to use with the sections in this chapter. The first clip in a set is for you to follow along using the Lessons, while the second shows one possible outcome to let you know the direction we are leading you in. If you want to see exactly how we set up the clip, double-click it in the Timeline to open it in the Browser, and then open the Filters or Motion tab to see the settings.

Remember that, like effects, motion paths have to be rendered before they will show up in the Canvas.

Using Keyframes with Effects

All of the filters we showed you in Chapters 11, 12, and 13 can be changed over time with keyframes. In fact, most filters in the Effects tab of the Browser can be manipulated with keyframes. In this section, we'll use the Invert filter as an example of how to use keyframes to create an image effect that changes over time. This example will take a clip and slowly transform it into a negative

image of itself. This effect is often used in science-fiction films to show an electronic surge or radioactive blast.

1. Select the clip you want to work with and open it in the Viewer by double-clicking it in the Browser, Timeline, or Canvas. You can also drag the clip into the Viewer. Remember, if you select a clip from the Timeline or Canvas, changes will only affect that one clip. However, if you select a clip from the Browser, changes will be in place every time you add this clip to the Timeline from now on.

2. Add the Invert filter, located in the Video Filter **>** Channel folder of the Browser's Effects tab (see *Adding a Filter* in Chapter 11 for more details).

3. Open the Filters tab in the Viewer to find the Invert filter listed. To the right of the filter controls you will see the keyframe controls and a mini-Timeline that represents the clip from In to Out point. If you don't see it, you may need to enlarge the Viewer window horizontally or use the scroll bars to properly view this part of the interface.

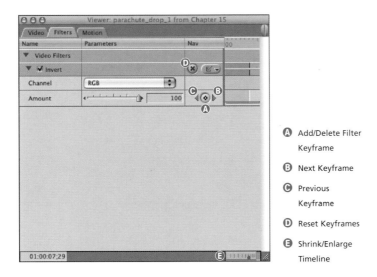

A Add/Delete Filter
   Keyframe

B Next Keyframe

C Previous
   Keyframe

D Reset Keyframes

E Shrink/Enlarge
   Timeline

Add/Delete Keyframe   Clicking this button adds a new keyframe to the current frame or deletes one currently set in that frame. When the playhead is resting on an Invert keyframe, the diamond lights up green; otherwise, it is empty.

Previous Keyframe   Moves the playhead to the previous keyframe. If there is no keyframe before the currently selected frame, this will be grayed out.

Next Keyframe   Moves the playhead to the next keyframe. If there is no keyframe after the currently selected frame, this is grayed out.

Reset   Deletes all keyframes in the clip and resets values to defaults.

Shrink/Enlarge Timeline   As with the Timeline window, moving the slider to the left enlarges the relative Timeline size and to right reduces the size. This does *not* have any effect on values in the Timeline but is used to make it easier to zoom in and out to view parts of the keyframe timeline for more accurate editing.

You can use the scroll bars under the Timeline to scroll forward and backward. This mini-Timeline has its own playhead and zoom bar and shows you graphically where the keyframes are in the clip.

Creating a Custom Layout for Keyframes

If you are working extensively using keyframes, you may want to maximize the width of the Viewer window and then save this as a custom layout. To save the current palette and windows layout as a custom layout, hold down the Option key and choose Window > Arrange > and then either Custom Layout 1 or Custom Layout 2. Then, the next time you choose one of these menu options (without holding the Option key) or use the keyboard shortcut keys (Shift+U and Option+U), the palettes will revert to these locations and sizes. You can also save and restore different keyboard layouts. If a station has multiple editors, each editor can import and restore his or her own customized layout.

4. Place the keyframe timeline's playhead on the first frame of the clip. Click the Add/Delete Keyframe button on the Invert filter to add a keyframe at the beginning of the clip. The Add/Delete Keyframe button will become green, showing that the playhead is resting on a keyframe.

Make sure the Amount slider is set to 0. This effectively turns the filter off at this point in the clip.

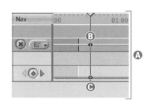

Ⓐ **Filter Timeline**

Ⓑ **Keyframe in Filter:** Indicates a keyframe in this filter for one or more attributes.

Ⓒ **Keyframe for Attribute:** Used to control the attribute (in this case Amount) for the filter at this point in the Timeline.

5. Now move the playhead to the last frame of the clip in the keyframe graphic's mini-Timeline and place the playhead there. Place a second keyframe here by clicking the Ins/Del Keyframe button.

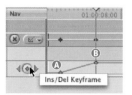

Ⓐ First Keyframe (0%)

Ⓑ Second Keyframe (100%)

6. Type in a new value in the Amount field, up to 100, or drag the green line with the mouse to 100. This will make the image into a complete negative of the original. If you click the Pre-

vious Keyframe to go back to the first one, the setting changes to 0. When you click Next Keyframe, it moves the playhead to the end of the clip and the setting changes to 100.

Of course different filters have different attributes, which will have different values, but the concept of setting keyframes will be the same for all of them: lay down two or more keyframes, change the value of one keyframe, and Final Cut Pro 4 will automatically calculate the values between the previous and/or next keyframe value, filling the intervening space to create a gradual transition between them. In this example we have only set two keyframes, but you can set as many as you want for as many attributes as you want for as many different effects as you want. However, the more complex your effects become, the longer your rendering time will be. Remember that if you make any changes to a keyframe, the whole clip will have to be rerendered (see *Rendering Transitions and Other Effects* in Chapter 9).

TIP
Smoothing the In-betweens

Depending on the attribute having keyframes added to it, Final Cut Pro will either use a linear (straight line) path between two keyframes or a curved path. With a linear change, the amount of change stays consistent from keyframe point to point. With a curved path, the amount of change will increase or decrease as the clip progresses.

To control this, each keyframe can either be a corner point (for linear paths) or a smooth point to allow for a curve between it and the other keyframes. To change a keyframe point from linear to smooth or back, control-click on the keyframe point, and select either Smooth or Corner from the menu.

If you change a keyframe point to be smooth, a Bezier curve handlebar (see the section *Editing and Smoothing a Motion Path* later in this chapter) will appear on that point, allowing you to change the amount of curvature between that keyframe and surrounding keyframes by moving it around.

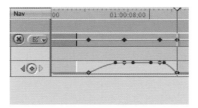

Using Keyframes with Motion Controls

For this exercise, let's take a look at a common effect where we will be slowly increasing the size of the image to mimic the zoom of a relatively still image. Think of the classic TV documentary style of slowly zooming in or out from a still photograph while someone talks in voice-over. Keyframes will allow you to create these kinds of zoom effects along with the motion controls.

The Motion Control tab in the Viewer lets you change the size, shape, and orientation of any clip. These controls can be affected over time with keyframes allowing you to change, the size (scale), angle (rotation), position (center and anchor point), shape (crop and distort), transparency (opacity), drop shadow, and Time Remapping.

TIP

Why Motion Blur Doesn't Use Keyframes

Motion blur is immune to the effects of keyframing because it relies on the motion in the clip to determine the amount of blurring. If you want to change the amount of motion blur in the clip, you can couple it with Time Remapping, which allows you to increase the speed of the clip (see *Setting Variable Speeds in a Clip* later in this chapter).

1.   In the Timeline, open the clip you want to create a zoom effect for in the Viewer. Make sure the playhead is at the beginning of the clip.

2.   In the Viewer's Motion tab, find the Scale value. The default value is 100, which means the image is at 100% of its normal size.

3.   Click the keyframe button beside the Scale value to create a keyframe. You can also create a keyframe by setting your cursor to the Pen tool ✒ (p) and clicking on the Scale Timeline in the Viewer.

4.   Now place the playhead about halfway through the clip

5.   Set another keyframe by clicking on the Scale keyframe button or clicking on the Timeline with the Pen tool.

6.   Use the slider or enter a new Scale value using the motion controls to the left to be used at this point in the clip. In this example, we want to zoom in, so we'll type in a greater value than 100: 200. The image will now blow up to 200% so that parts of the image will now fall outside of the Canvas. Final Cut Pro will automatically go back and resize each frame between the two keyframes to create a gradual change in the clip's size from 100 to 200%.

Most motion effects will require you render them to view the final version in the Canvas unless you are using Real-Time. When you watch the clip, it will now zoom in over time. The distance between the two keyframes determines the speed at which it zooms.

You can add as many keyframes as you want using the steps detailed above to have the image zoom up or down as desired. Remember: values above 100 will be larger while values below 100 will shrink the image.

But these effects are not limited to still images—they can be applied to any clip including video clips and titles. You could also use keyframes with motion controls to make a title grow on the screen or make a video image quickly shrink to a small window.

Using Keyframes to Create Motion Paths

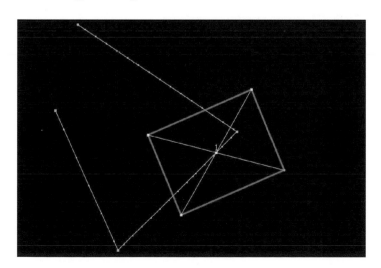

Another way to use keyframes is to create actual motion within your clip or graphics—so that they move across the Canvas or spin around in an implied third dimension. To do this, you use keyframes with the Viewer's Motion tab or apply them to filters such as those in the Perspective folder of the Browser's Effects tab. However, rather than using the Viewer's Timeline and typing in numbers, you will be learning how to manipulate your images directly in the Canvas itself, allowing for more creative expression.

Chapter 14 introduced size, position, and disortion controls as static effects and noted that their real power would become apparent when keyframing was added. Keyframing to create motion effects can create complicated movements that can animate a title sequence or used to fashion more experimental visuals. But be careful: sloppy use of motion paths can easily become an unfortunate lesson about viewer tolerance. In this exercise, we'll add keyframed motion effects to make a clip move across the frame while it is spinning and changing size.

Because adding movement is most effectively done visually, we'll use a method that involves adding keyframes directly in the Canvas rather than in the Viewer. This way, you can drag the image into the Canvas and drop it where you want to, automatically creating new keyframes to mark these movements. Doing this creates what is called a "motion path" by visually dragging and dropping with the mouse. We'll start by resizing the clip so that it is smaller than the actual frame so it has room to really move about.

Choosing Speed with Moving Clips

Moving clips are often best used with a slow motion, to create a subtle movement of a "window" image instead of images zipping around the screen, which can look silly.

1. Open the clip you want to create a motion path for in the Viewer.

2. In the Viewer's Motion tab (see Chapter 14 for more details), change the Scale to a value less than 100. In this example we will use 40. This will shrink the image to fill less than half the frame.

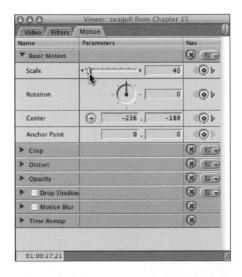

3. Place the playhead in the Timeline at the beginning of the clip. You will see the first frame of the clip in the Canvas, shrunk down to 40%.

4. In the Canvas, open the View popup menu and select the Wireframe option. Wireframe mode represents all clips in the Canvas as simple boxes, each with an X through it. This allows you to drag the clips around without having to worry about the time it takes to redraw the images as they move. Alternatively, you can choose Image+Wireframe to have the wireframe superimposed over the images. This might be an easier way to work when you need to see the image for specific movements that might be affected by the composition.

5. Drag the clip to the exact location in the Canvas where you want it to start moving. We set the position of the image so that it sits in the top-left corner of Canvas, all the better to see the motion.

6. Now you need to add a keyframe to designate this as the starting point. The Canvas has an Add Keyframe button at the bottom-right. Control-click this button and select Center to set a keyframe at this point for the image's initial position.

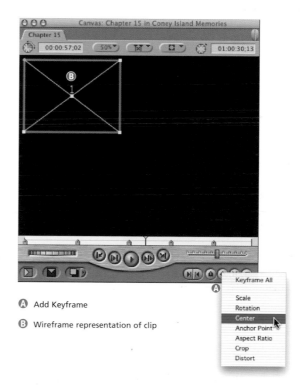

Ⓐ Add Keyframe

Ⓑ Wireframe representation of clip

7. Move the playhead in the Canvas or Timeline to the frame where you want the motion to finish. The clip will still appear in the same place, but you can now move it anywhere within the Canvas area by clicking in the box representing the clip (the Wireframe) and dragging it to the end position you want it to move to. A keyframe will automatically be placed in this frame. (You can see this by checking the Timeline in the Viewer, once you have turned on Show Keyframe Overlays for the sequence, in Edit **>** Preferences **>** Timeline.) For example, you can move it to the bottom-right corner of the frame, causing the clip to move diagonally across the Canvas. A dotted line will appear, tracing the path from beginning to end.

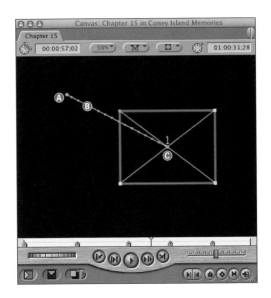

Ⓐ First Keyframe

Ⓑ Movement Path

Ⓒ Second Keyframe

8. You can now keep moving the playhead forward, and dragging and dropping the clip, each time automatically adding a new keyframe and giving new direction and movement to the clip.

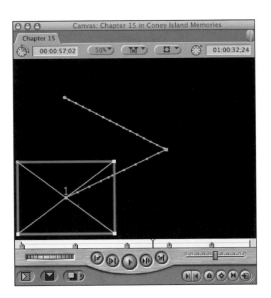

In addition to moving the object, you can also change any of the clip's other motion attributes in the Viewer's Motion tab. For example, you can have the clip grow or shrink, rotate it, crop it, feather its edges, change its opacity, distort the image, add a drop shadow, and so on. To rotate the clip in the Canvas, click on any of the edges of the Wireframe and drag around the center. To change the size, click any of the four corners of the Wireframe and drag outward or inward. You can also control-click the Timeline's keyframe area and choose what motion or effect you want to keyframe in the Timeline.

Most motion effects will require you to either render them to view the final version in the Canvas

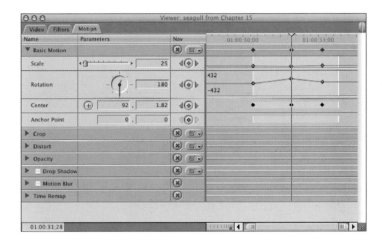

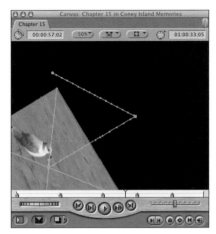

Editing and Smoothing a Motion Path

Once you've "drawn" your motion path in the Canvas, unless you are just that good, you will probably need to edit it to refine the motion. By default, the path between keyframes, be it a motion path or a change in a filter's effect, is a straight line. This, as we know, is the shortest distance between two points, but it's not always the most interesting, and it may not give you the desired effect.

Smoothing a path between keyframes allows you to change a motion path consisting of straight-line segments, like the one you created in the previous exercise, into a smoothly curving motion path like that shown here.

You manipulate motion paths using the Selection tool ▶ (a) and then do one of the following:

- **To adjust the position of a keyframe** (and thus the position the clip moves to), click and drag a green keyframe to the new position.
- **To delete a keyframe,** Option+click a green keyframe. The tool will automatically turn into the Delete Point Tool 🖋- .
- **To add a new keyframe,** click at any point along the motion line except on another keyframe. The tool will automatically change to the Pen tool 🖋 and create a curved path called a Bezier curve to the keyframe, which you can drag to change the shape of the curve.
- **To change a keyframe from being curved to being a corner** (or vice versa), ⌘+click the green keyframe. The tool will automatically turn into the Smooth Pen Tool 🖋 and switch the keyframe type.
- **To adjust the shape of a curved path,** click the Bezier Curve Handlebar and drag. You will notice that the shape of the curve changes as you drag. You can drag around the keyframe to change the orientation of the curve toward or away from the keyframe to change the depth of the curve.
- **To adjust the speed at which the clip moves along the curved path,** click and drag the Speed Control on either side of the keyframe and move it toward or away from the keyframe. Moving toward the keyframe will speed the clip as it moves toward the keyframe and slow it as it moves away.

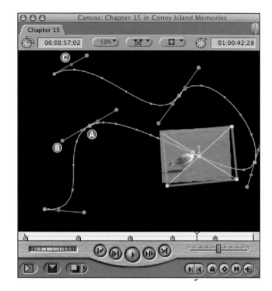

Ⓐ Bezier Curve Point (Keyframe)

Ⓑ Bezier Curve Handlebar

Ⓒ Speed Control

Why is it called a Bezier curve?

This process of creating curved lines on the computer screen was named after Pierre Bezier, who developed it in the 1970s for CAD. See the web site www.moshplant.com/direct-or/bezier/ for more detailed info on the mathematics behind the Bezier curve.

Ideas in Motion

To create a more involved sequence, you can add other clips that are moving at the same time by stacking the clips in different tracks in the Timeline and giving them all separate motion paths. By using these effects in combination, you can have a number of images moving in and out, fashioning a collage of animated imagery.

Be experimental in the effects you mix:

- By adding feathered edges to your clips, you make them appear to float in the frame for a ghostly effect.

- By changing the offset of a drop shadow as a graphic or clip moves around the frame, you create the illusion of a fixed light source.

- By putting a background slug or image behind your other moving clips, you give them a backdrop to move on that's more interesting than the default solid black background.

- By using perspective effects such as Curl and Basic 3D, which are especially geared for use with keyframes.

The only limitation is in your imagination for creating special effect sequences, so the more you experiment with different moving compositions, the more likely you'll discover something unique.

④ Setting Variable Speeds in a Clip

In Chapter 8, we showed you how to quickly change the speed of your video—to slow it down, speed it up, or even play it backward. But that is not enough. What if you want the clip to play at *different* speeds or even slow down and speed up while playing? A new feature in Final Cut Pro 4 called Time Remapping allows you to do just that.

If you have seen the film *The Matrix*, then you are already familiar how this can be used to great effect with sudden changes from slow motion to fast motion and back again to highlight action scenes. This technique is ubiquitous now in everything from Hollywood feature films to car commercials (think of ads where a car is moving in extreme slow motion and then suddenly takes off in a flash). Apple must have heard Final Cut Pro editors calling for a tool to quickly create these effects, and the Time Remap tool was developed.

The basic premise of Time Remapping relies on keyframes, which we've discussed in depth earlier in this chapter. Using the Time Remap tool, you designate a "source frame" that will mark the starting point for your speed change. You can then shift the speeds of the clips around that source frame either up or down. As with all things in Final Cut Pro, there are at least two ways to work with Time Remapping. One of the methods involves using the new Time Remap tool directly in the Timeline. However, the most accurate method involves using that mysterious panel at the bottom of the Motions tab in the Viewer mentioned briefly in Chapter 14, the aptly named Time Remap.

The Pitfalls of Fast Motions

Speeding action up can often look a little silly—think Benny Hill. If you need to imply fast, possibly even superhuman motion, try using Time Remapping to speed up the clip and apply motion blur to soften the edges, giving a less comical look to fast action.

To create a clip with variable speeds using motion controls, follow these steps:

1. Open the clip you want to set variable speeds for in the Viewer.

2. Click the motion Tab and open the Time Remap panel.

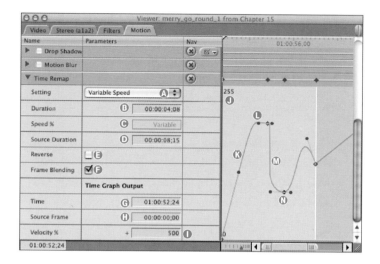

Ⓘ Displays the rate of change in speed for the frame being displayed. Positive values indicate that the clip is playing forward with higher values indicating that the clip is more quickly increasing speed. Negative values indicate that the clip is playing backward with lower values indicating a faster decrease in speed. This value cannot be directly changed.

Ⓙ The Time Graph shows a visual representation of the speed of the clip as it is played.

Ⓚ Upward slanting parts of the curve indicate that the clip playing forward. The steeper the curve, the faster the speed is increasing.

Ⓛ Flat areas indicate where the clip is playing very slowly or stopped.

Ⓜ Downward slanting parts of the curve indicate that the clip is playing backward. The steeper the decline the faster the clip is playing backward.

Ⓝ Keyframes can be added to the Time Graph as either corner or curved Bezier points to control the velocity.

Ⓐ Choose whether to use a constant speed throughout the entire clip (although this can be faster or slower than the true time) or variable speeds throughout the clip.

Ⓑ Displays the current duration of the clip. You can enter a new duration for the clip with larger values causing the clip to slow down and lower values speeding the clip up.

Ⓒ When using constant speed, displays how much faster (values below 100%) or slower (values above 100%) the clip is playing. You can enter speed percentage values (0.1 to 100,000) directly into this field to control the clip speed.

Ⓓ Total duration of the clip (including any trim). This field cannot be changed.

Ⓔ Check to reverse the direction of the clip. This will literally reverse the order of the frames in the clip.

Ⓕ Check to create a smoother transition between frames. This will make the speed change less jerky but also produce a slightly ghost-like effect.

Ⓖ Displays the timecode for the currently selected frame (the current frame under the playhead) in the total sequence. This value cannot be directly changed here.

Ⓗ Displays the timecode for the currently selected frame (the current frame under the playhead) in the clip that is referred to as the *Source Frame*. This value cannot be directly changed here.

3. To set variable rates of speed in a single clip, choose Variable Rate from the drop-down and then do one or more of the following in the Time Graph:

- **To add a new keyframe,** click at any point along the motion line except on another keyframe. The tool will automatically change to the Pen tool 🖋 and create a Bezier curve in the keyframe, which you can click and drag to change the shape of the curve.

- **To adjust the position of a keyframe** (and thus the position the clip moves to), click and drag a blue keyframe to the desired position. Moving a keyframe up from the previous keyframe will cause the clip to play forward. Moving a keyframe down from the previous keyframe will cause the clip to play backward. Moving a keyframe further to the right from the previous keyframe will slow down the clip.

- **To delete a keyframe,** Option+click a blue keyframe. The tool will automatically turn into the Delete Point Tool 🖋- .

- **To change a keyframe from being curved to being a corner** (or vice versa), ⌘+click a blue keyframe. The tool will automatically turn into the Smooth Pen Tool 🖋⌃ and switch the keyframe type.

- **To adjust the shape of a curved path**, click the Bezier Curve Handlebar and drag. You will notice that the shape of the curve changes as you drag. You can drag around the keyframe to change the orientation of the curve toward or away from the keyframe to change the depth of the curve.

Once you have the variable rates set as desired, you can view the results in the Canvas if your computer can support Real-Time Effects, or you can use the QuickView (Tools **>** QuickView) or render the effect (see Chapter 9). This panel can also be used to control the consistent speed of the clip using controls similar to those described in Chapter 8.

Alternate Steps: Setting Variable Speed in the Timeline

Although editing variable speed in the Viewer allows for great accuracy, a more direct way to edit speed is directly in the Timeline.

1. Choose the Time Remap tool from the Tool Palette ⟨⊚⟩ (sss).

2. Turn on the Clip Keyframes toggle located at the bottom left of the Timeline (Option+T) so that you can make adjustments to keyframes directly in the Timeline.

3. In the Timeline, move the playhead to the frame in the clip you want the speed of the clip to shift. Typically, you'll want to find a clip with action in it that you want to have slow down or speed up as an accent.

4. To change the clip speed to the left and right of the source frame, do one of the following:

- Click on this frame and drag the cursor to the left or right. The clip will now be divided into two speeds. If you drag to the left, the left side will be slowed down and the right side will be sped up. A popup will appear letting you know what percentage you are speeding up and slowing down the sections. If you drag to the right, the left side of the clip will be sped up and the right side will be slowed down. You can make your variable speed adjustments snap to increments of 10% by holding down the Shift key while you drag with the Time Remap tool.

- Option+click on this frame and drag the cursor to the left or right. This will move the source frame back or forth in the clip. When you release the mouse, the source frame will be moved to that location in the Timeline and the footage on either side of it will be squeezed and stretched accordingly. Think of this as pinching a point in the clip, pulling it to a different location with the clip acting like a piece of elastic. The clip will now be divided into two speeds, with the shift at the new location of the source frame. If you drag to the left, the left side will be slowed down and the right side will be sped up. If you drag to the right, the left side of the clip will be sped up and the right side will be slowed down. A window will appear letting you know what percentage you are speeding up and slowing down the sections.

Notice how the Clip Keyframe track gives you a visual representation of the variable speed changes and presents lines that designate faster or slower footage.

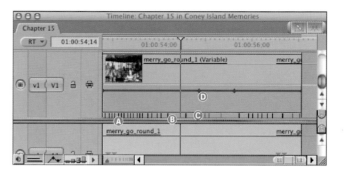

Ⓐ Faster footage has lines close together; slower footage has lines farther apart.

Ⓑ Black lines indicate that the clip is playing forward.

Ⓒ Red lines indicate that the clip is playing backward.

Ⓓ Keyframes appear in the Clip Keyframe line. Click and drag to adjust these positions to compress or stretch time between surrounding keyframes.

Ⓐ Clip Keyframe toggle

Ⓑ Displays data about the speed changes

Let go of the mouse and the variable speed change will go into effect. Time Remapping is a Real-Time effect, so you can preview it instantly without rendering if your system is fast enough. Otherwise, use the QuickView window or render to see how the speed has changed. Repeat Steps 3 and 4 for as many different points that you want to have shifts in the speed of the clip. Each point will be a keyframe in the Timeline.

You may also want to keep the Time Remap panel open in the Viewer. As you make changes in the Timeline, they will be reflected in the Viewer.

Part Four:
Finishing Touches

You have the rough cut of your film with the basic edits and effects. Now you are ready for the finishing touches to create your final cut. To do this, you will need to first tweak your audio and then add the opening and closing titles. In the next few chapters, we will look at ways to edit audio to get the best sound possible and then look at adding a variety of different titles, both simple and complex. The final chapter in this section brings all of the pieces presented in Chapters 6-17 to give you a quick guide overview for putting your film together.

16 Fine-Tuning Your Audio

In the last few chapters we've focused on the video side of the project, but crafting your audio is no less important. In this chapter, we'll look at how audio works in Final Cut Pro. You'll learn how to use it with your video image to create seamless transitions, split edits between sound and image, get rid of pops or unwanted segments such as pauses and "ums," and bring music in from a CD or other source (such as an MP3 or WAV file). In addition, we'll look at adding voice-overs directly to your footage using your computer's microphone and finish by examining the advanced features prvided in Final Cut Pro 4's new audio mixing feature.

Overview

Most of your work with audio will be in the Viewer. In this window you can open up the Audio tab to view and change your audio for a particular clip. Final Cut Pro displays audio signals visually as a waveform, a graphic representation of the sound waves' peaks and valleys. The waveform will show you where the loudest parts of your audio are—the highest peaks—as well as the quietest, represented by the lowest crests. Remember that—especially in the case of interviews and other synchronized speech—sound and video are implicitly linked, and you should use one to help make editing decisions about the other. For example, often you will find that you want to start a video several frames (half a second or so)

before a speaker begins to talk. Find the beginning of their speech in the waveform (which will be the first peak caused by the speech) and set your In point a few frames before the base of the peak. This will ensure that the speech and the video do not begin abruptly at the cut.

With music or other non-synchronized sounds, frame-specific synch between image and sound is less critical than with speech, but it is no less crucial to pay attention to how the sound and visuals interact with each other. There is no exact science for creating a rhythmic cutting style between music and video; it is a skill that you develop through careful practice, study, and a certain amount of intuition. That's where the "art" comes into the picture. Often it is a matter of trial and error. You should never be afraid to experiment, as this is where some of your best work may come from. (Always remember that you have an Undo option if things go seriously wrong.) Watch music videos and even commercials to see how music and cutting often work together. One word of advice is not to always cut on the beat of the music. This makes for obvious

What's That Word Mean?

A few of the most important terms you're likely to encounter in any discussion of digital audio follow:

Decibels (dB) A measurement of audio levels. It is based on a logarithmic scale that relates to loudness as perceived by the human ear. One unit of dB is roughly the smallest change in volume that can be picked up by the human ear.

Gain A number that determines how much the audio is amplified. A negative value makes the audio quieter, while a positive value makes the audio louder. Too much gain can distort the audio.

Spread The value that determines how the audio signal is "spread" over the left and right stereo tracks. A value of –1 means the signal goes completely to the left speaker, a value of 1 means that the signal goes completely to the right speaker. Mono audio is set at a 0 spread, which sends the audio equally to both tracks. If you are working with stereo clips, typically the left channel has its Spread set to –1 while the right channel is set to 1.

Waveform A graphic depiction of sound, which illustrates the frequency of the audio. High peaks represent louder sounds; low peaks, softer sounds.

edits that will actually dilute the impact of the music and the image. It's much more interesting to mix it up, occasionally cutting on the beat, but also cutting off beat, and mixing longer shots with a sudden burst of short cuts.

The waveform representation is found in the Viewer's Audio tab when a clip is open in it. If audio and video clips are linked (see *Linking Audio and Video Clips* in Chapter 7), the Viewer will contain both an audio and video tab if you open either audio or video portion of the clip. If an audio clip is not linked, the Viewer will simply show the Audio tab without any video. This is often the case when you have brought in a separate piece of audio, such as a track from a CD. If the audio is a stereo pair, they will appear together in the same tab, and effects will be applied to them concurrently.

The goal of this chapter is to help you lay in, cut, and mix your audio so that it sounds full and smooth. Audio edits that are not mixed properly can completely disrupt the viewer's attention and detract from the piece. At the same time, a well-done audio transition can make a visual cut work in a way that wasn't possible without the audio.

You will also want to consider where and on what sort of equipment your video will be played. If you're editing for broadcast or professional video, the audio standards are much higher than, say, if you were outputting for home video or the web, where you can probably ignore complex stereo mixing.

Chapter 16: Fun with Audio

Open the Final Cut Pro project file labeled Coney Island Memories. After it loads in Final Cut Pro, double-click the Chapter 16 sequence in the Browser and it will open in the Timeline.

In this chapter you will be primarily dealing with the Audio tab in the Viewer. There are seven pairs of clips in the Timeline for you to work with, one for each exercise in the chapter. The first version is for you to experiment with, and the second shows how the results might look and sound. Remember that you can use the markers in the Timeline to find the clips for each lesson. You can see a list of all of the markers in a sequence by control-clicking the ruler part of the Timeline.

Adjusting Audio Levels and Spread

 To look into the "guts" of the audio of a clip, you'll need to open it up in the Viewer and bring up the Audio tab. In here, you'll see the waveform monitor as well as controls to change the spread and level of the audio. In this exercise, we'll look at the Audio tab and learn how to adjust the audio levels of your clip.

You'll want to test your audio levels when you put them in your sequence by playing them and monitoring the Audio Meter (select Window > Audio Meter or press Option+4 if the Audio Meter is not already open). You'll want to make sure the levels peak (reach their highest point) somewhere between −3 and −12dB. If the meter is ever filled completely, with the red part of the levels holding at the top of the meter, your audio levels are set too high and you'll need to lower them. Audio levels that are set too high and peak above −3dB are likely to distort.

It's also a good idea to have your audio linked as a stereo pair when doing audio correction. If the tracks are not linked, you will have to work on each track individually, which is an unnecessary pain unless the stereo pair has different audio on the left and right tracks. (See *Working with Stereo Pairs in Clips* in Chapter 7 for more details.)

Audio Scrubbing

When you drag your playhead over an area of the Timeline, Canvas, or Viewer that has audio, you can hear the audio "scrubbing"—that is you'll hear whatever audio is under the playhead as you move it back and forth at the speed you move the playhead. This is often helpful to quickly locate a particular piece of audio. However, sometimes this may be a distraction, so Final Cut Pro gives you the option of toggling this on and off.

Select View > Audio Scrubbing. A check mark will tell you if audio scrubbing is on or off. You can also type Shift+S to toggle between on and off modes.

1. Open the clip in the Viewer by double-clicking it in either the Canvas, Timeline, or Viewer, and select the Audio tab. If you click on a video clip that is linked to an audio clip, both tabs will be available in the Viewer.

2. The Audio tab is a control panel where you can play the clip, set In and Out points, and adjust the audio levels.

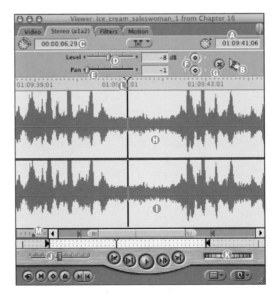

Ⓐ Current Timecode

Ⓑ Drag Handle

Ⓒ Clip Duration

Ⓓ Level Control Slider

Ⓔ Spread/Pan Slider

Ⓕ Keyframe Buttons

Ⓖ Reset Button

Ⓗ Waveform: Right Channel

Ⓘ Waveform: Left Channel

Ⓙ Shuttle

Ⓚ Jog Controls

Ⓛ Playhead

Ⓜ Zoom Control

Current Timecode   Shows the timecode position of the play-head in the Viewer's Audio tab. Type a value in this field to move the playhead to that position or use the + or − keys followed by a number to advance or retreat the playhead a specific number of frames. This window can display two types of time-code: source (original timecode from the source tape) or clip (the timecode from Final Cut's sequence). You can ⌘+click this window to change which one is being viewed.

Drag Handle   Click here and drag the clip into the Browser, Timeline, or Canvas.

Clip Duration   Shows the total duration of the clip between the In and Out points.

Level Control Slider   Drag this slider or enter a numeric value to increase or decrease the sound level (volume) of your clip. This value is in dBs (decibels) and will be in the range of +12 to −60dB.

Spread/Pan Slider   If your clip is a stereo pair (see *Working with Stereo Pairs in Clips* in Chapter 7), this control is labeled Spread, and determines how much stereo separation there will be, by controlling which speaker each channel is sent to. The values range from −1 to +1. At a −1 setting (the default), the left and right channels are fully separated; each one heard only in the corresponding speaker. As the value approaches 0, the channels combine in the speakers. A value of exactly 0 will mix the left and right channel together in both speakers, for monaural sound. As the value approaches +1, the channels begin to reverse speakers until the left channel is in the right speaker and the right channel is in the left speaker. If the clip is not a stereo pair, this control is labeled Pan and works as a balance control, letting you send the single channel to only the left or right

speaker, or both. This effect can create a more three-dimensional sound, adding a sense of space or location to sound coming from different speakers.

Keyframe Buttons   Sets a keyframe at the current location of the playhead for either Level or Spread/Pan. This allows you to vary the levels of the volume or Spread/Pan as the clip plays. See *Using Keyframes with Audio* later in this chapter.

Reset Button   Deletes all keyframes and resets the Level and Spread/Pan of the clip to default levels.

Waveform Display   Lets you see a visual representation of the audio clip in a waveform pattern. This area works as a mini-Timeline just for the audio, where you can use the transport controls to move backward and forward through the clip. Like the Timeline, it has a playhead that determines where in the clip you are playing. You can also use the Magnifying Glass tool in the Tool Palette to zoom in on a specific part of the audio for very specific work, like setting an In or Out point at an exact frame. There is also a Sound Level line that you can drag with the mouse up and down to change the level rather than typing in a new level above. This is also the field where you can graphically change keyframes (see Chapter 15).

Shuttle/Transport/Jog Controls   The same controls found in the Viewer video tab (see *Understanding the Viewer* in Chapter 2), used to move through the footage, this time pertaining to the audio of the clip opened in the Viewer.

Ruler   A representation of the entire audio clip, its In and Out points, and the playhead location. You can use the ruler to see where you are in the clip, but you should use the Waveform Display for your real work, since you can zoom in and out and see the waveform graphic.

Zoom Control   By dragging the marker in the zoom control, you can zoom in and out of the Waveform Display, to get a larger picture of the clip or to go in for detailed work. You can also press ⌘ with the plus (+) or minus (–) key to zoom in and out, centered on the playhead's position. You can also use the zoom dial (M) to keep your playhead in the window.

In addition to these controls, you still have the usual Viewer controls such as Mark Frame, Set In, and Set Out at your command, which now apply to the audio clip. See *The Viewer* in Chapter 2 for a review of these functions.

Adjusting the volume is one of the most common tasks when working with audio. With your clip's Audio tab open in the Viewer, play the audio clip and watch the Audio Meter. If the clip's levels are peaking too high in the meter, you'll want to lower the levels. Typically you don't want sound going higher than –3dB.

Most captured or imported clips will start out with a dB level of 0. The actual volume that this nominal level refers to is determined by how the sound was recorded and the level at which it was captured. When the audio is peaking too high in the Audio Meter or if you need to lower the volume so that another clip can be heard, you'll first want to make a guess as to what new dB level you should set. Play back your adjusted clip and assess whether that's a good level or still needs to be adjusted. Keep doing this until you've got an appropriate level.

Now that you've changed the level, play the audio back and check the Audio Meter levels to make sure it is peaking at an acceptable level. Between –12 and –3dB is good for full volume, but of course if you want the audio to be quieter, or serve as background sound to another, you'll want to set it to peak lower.

Ⓐ –3dB

Ⓑ –12dB

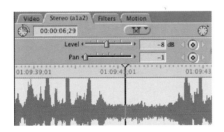

Drag the Level slider to the left or right to change the level, or enter a new dB value directly in the field (remember that you must enter a value between +12dB and –60dB), or simply drag the sound level line in the waveform up or down as shown in the figure.

Changing Audio Settings in the Timeline

You can also change the settings in the Timeline to display the waveform in the audio clip itself, but this can take awhile to load every time you move in the Timeline, so we don't recommend it unless you need to see all the waveforms at a glance. Remember you can always view the waveform in the clip's Audio tab in the Viewer. The command to toggle the waveform display in audio clips on and off is ⌘+Option+W.

Using Keyframes with Audio

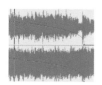
In Chapter 15 we discussed the use of keyframes to make visual changes to a clip over time. Often during the course of a clip it is useful to raise or lower the audio volume (level) over time for a variety of reasons. For this example, we'll apply keyframes to the audio levels of a clip to learn how to change the levels over time as the clip plays. The basic concepts of adding keyframes presented in this section hold true for video keyframes as well.

Select the clip you want to work with and open it in the Viewer by double-clicking it in the Browser, Timeline, or Canvas, or by dragging it to the Viewer. Make sure you have picked either an audio clip or a video clip with an audio clip linked to it.

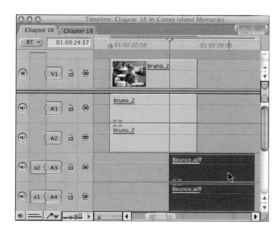

Open the Audio tab. To the right of the Levels slider are the keyframe controls. Make sure the level and spread are set to the value you want initially. The changes you will make in the next few steps will be derivations from these values at different points in the clip. For more details, see the sidebar *What Are the Transport Buttons For?*

Ⓐ Add/Delete Level Keyframe

Ⓑ Add/Delete Spread Keyframe

Ⓒ Reset Level and Spread Keyframes

Using the scrub bar, place the playhead on the first frame you want to adjust the sound levels for. This will mark the beginning of the change. To lay down a keyframe, press the Add/Delete

Keyframe button. A rougher way to add keyframes is to Option+click on the Levels overlay (you must click on the actual line itself) in the waveform display at the frame where you want to add the keyframe. This turns the cursor into a pen tool (which you can also select from the Tool Palette) that places new keyframes. Remember that you can zoom into the waveform display, using either the Magnifying Glass or the Zoom control at the bottom left, to isolate the exact frame you want.

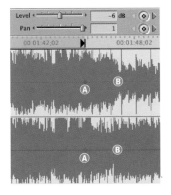

Ⓐ Level Keyframe Marker

Ⓑ Levels Overlay

You will need to add at least two keyframes in order to make changes to the levels, but you can add as many keyframes as you want at any time during the editing process. Once a keyframe is set, it works as an anchor point, which you can drag up or down to change the level at that frame.

4. With the playhead on a keyframe (the Add/Delete Keyframe button will be green), drag the keyframe up or down to change the level at that point in the clip. This will affect the level of

every other frame before and after it until the next keyframe, which is its own anchor point.

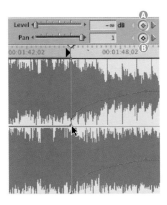

Ⓐ Green indicates that a keyframe is present in the currently selected frame. Clicking will delete the current keyframe.

Ⓑ Open indicates that no keyframe is present in the currently selected frame. Clicking will add a keyframe.

The level of all the frames in between the keyframes will gradually slope up or down (depending on how close they are together and their position above or below each other). In other words, if your first keyframe is set to 0dB and your second keyframe, placed four seconds later in time from the first one, is set to −10dB, the audio will take four seconds to dip down to this lower level, dipping at a constant rate.

You can also enter a new value for keyframes directly in the Level field or by using the Level slider.

5. To move back and forth between the keyframes you have set, click the Previous or Next Keyframe arrow. This will move the playhead backward or forward by one keyframe. Notice that the Add/Delete Keyframe button is lit green whenever the playhead is on top of a keyframe.

Although it's done less often, the steps in this section can equally apply to an audio clip's spread. The major difference is that the Spread Overlay appears as a purple line in the Viewer's Timeline.

What Are the Transport Buttons For?

You will see the transport button group anywhere in Final Cut Pro that allows you to add keyframes. It will be next to the keyframe's mini-Timeline, which allows you to control the particular option's attributes over time. The transport controls allow you to quickly move between, add, and delete keyframes from the keyframe Timeline.

Ⓐ Add/Delete Keyframe
Ⓑ Next Keyframe
Ⓒ Previous Keyframe

Clicking this button adds a new keyframe to the current frame or deletes one currently set in that frame. When the playhead is resting on a keyframe, the diamond lights up green. This means you can adjust the keyframe for the attribute, and it will change that frame to reflect this new value. If the button is not lit up, the playhead is not on a keyframe and you cannot make a change, but clicking the button will add a keyframe.

Previous Keyframe Moves the playhead to the previous keyframe in the Timeline. If no keyframe has been set, this button will be grayed out.

Next Keyframe Moves the playhead to the next keyframe in the Timeline. If no keyframe has been set, this button will be grayed out.

Reset In addition to these controls, there will be a reset button (a red "X") in the general vicinity of all transport buttons. This deletes all keyframes for that attribute in the clip and resets the values to their defaults.

Using Multiple Keyframes with Levels

The simple exercise you've just tried involves only two keyframes, but you can use as many as you like. You must have at least two keyframes to create a shift in the levels, though.

Use three keyframes to create a short drop or rise in the levels and then return to the original level, creating a triangular pattern in the level overlay.

Use four keyframes to completely cut off a moment of audio before returning to normal levels. This creates a "canyon-like" dip in the audio levels. This is where you may want to insert "sound tone" recorded on set to cover up these dips in audio. See the sidebar *Adding Sound Tone*.

Using Split Edit Points

So far, when we've covered the relationship between sound and image, we've often talked about the two as a linked pair. These paired clips move together, and when you make an adjustment to one, Final Cut Pro adjusts the other to match. For example, if you apply a Ripple edit (see *Making Ripple Edits* in Chapter 8) to a video clip that is linked to an audio clip, the audio clip will likewise be trimmed. Having linked clips is indispensable for keeping clips synched together. At times, however, you'll want to separate the audio or video of linked clips in order to use one without the other playing. That is, you'll want to split the edit points of the clip's audio and video tracks.

In this example, we have a clip of a woman serving ice cream to a boy (clip A, the outgoing clip) and a clip of her being interviewed about her job (clip B, the incoming clip). We want to have the audio of her talking (from clip B) begin over the image of her serving ice cream (clip A), so that it is heard out of synch. This will create a voice-over effect that provides a transition into the next clip of her talking.

Locate your two clips in the Timeline. Turn off linking (if the clips are linked) by selecting Sequence > Linked Selections, by pressing Shift+L, or by clicking the Linking toggle switch in the Timeline. You can now drag and manipulate the video and audio of the clip individually.

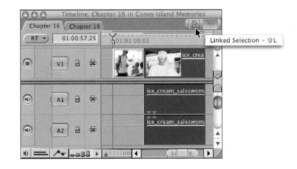

Now play through the clip in the Timeline. Play past the part you will want covered up by the B-roll image of her scooping ice cream and find the point where you want the synch video to cut in. In this example, it would be after the audio of the woman speaking has started, depending on how long you want the image of her scooping ice cream to last. It's a good idea to cut on a frame that does not include too much motion, as motion can cause an awkward, disori-enting cut. When you've found the frame you want to set as your Video In, stop the playhead. You can now either drag the In point of the clip in the Timeline to the playhead, trimming the video footage (you should have snapping on), or you can use the Razor Blade tool to make a cut here and delete the trim at the beginning.

A Audio In

You have now performed a split edit. Your audio extends in front of the video of the clip, and you now must fill that gap in the video track with an image. You can now drag the B-roll clip of the woman scooping ice cream in to fill this gap. First, you will need to erase the audio from this so that it does not replace the interview clip's audio. To do this, make sure linking is still off (see Step 1) and delete the clip's audio by selecting it and pressing

Delete. Now drag the clip to fill the gap in the video track over the interview audio clip so that it snugly meets the interview video clip.

A Linking Toggle

B Gap for B-Roll

Play the two clips. You will first see the woman scooping ice cream and hear the audio from the interview clip. The interview shot will then cut in, synchronized with the audio. You can now make adjustments to this edit like you would any other clip by using the Ripple, Roll, Slide, or Slip trim functions (see Chapter 8). You can also add a transition between the two shots such as a cross-dissolve (see Chapter 10). And don't forget to turn linking back on!

FAQ

How Can I Change a Split Edit Point Quickly?

If you want to change the location of a split edit, you can drag the edits in the Viewer's ruler. The split edits are represented in the ruler by half arrows, the top one for video, the bottom one for audio, and you can click and scrub them back and forth to set different video and audio In or Out points. When you drag an In point, both video and audio In points will move together, keeping the same distance from each other if they are split. Likewise, if you drag an Out point, both audio and video Out points will move together, keeping the same distance apart. If you hold down the Option key while you drag, you can move a video or audio In or Out point separately.

Importing Audio

Final Cut Pro 4 can easily import audio tracks from a data DVD, from a music CD, or from audio files on your hard drive (MP3, WAV, AIFF, or other formats) and create an audio clip in the project folder in your Browser. The method to do this is similar to importing other files, such as a clip, JPEG, or QuickTime (see *Importing Existing Media Files* in Chapter 5).

To import an Audio file from a CD in Final Cut Pro 4, you'll follow the same process for importing any file.

1. Put the CD in your computer's drive. You can use any audio CD that you want, but remember, the songs are probably protected by copyright. You should get permission before using the song.

2. In your Finder, drag the track file(s) from the CD onto your hard drive. You may want to create a special "music," "audio," or "resources" folder for these files. You can also Option+click and drag the CD to the folder to copy the entire CD's contents.

Resources

Some Songs

3. Select File > Import > File and find the tracks on your hard disk that you've copied from the CD. You can also use the File > Import > Folder option to select an entire folder of files folder.

4. Click on the track (or ⌘+click to select multiple tracks) you want to import.

5. The track(s) will appear as audio clips in your project file in the Browser. You should immediately label each clip by clicking its name and typing in a new one. Most clips will be imported with the name of the file from the original source (for audio CDs this will be the track number from the CD).

Clips you've imported can be used like any other clip, and you can link them to video tracks as described in Chapter 6.

Working with Audio Clips Quickly?

Audio clips imported from an audio CD are usually sampled at 44.1kHz instead of the DV standard 48kHz, so you'll need to adjust your Quick-Time Audio Settings in your sequence settings (Sequence > Settings...) to mirror the sample rate. It's not recommended to mix sample rates in the same sequence, so if you are mixing CD audio with other audio, you will need to upsample and transcode your CD audio to play at 48KHz. You can do this by using QuickTime or iTunes to transcode the audio file to an AIFF file. We recommend you convert MP3 files to AIFF files before using them with Final Cut Pro, as MP3s will often play with choppy pops.

The Audio Effects Folder

4 Just as you can use video filters to correct or distort your image, audio clips also have special filters that sweeten or stylize. Most audio effects are used to improve the sound quality, such as removing microphone pops and isolating or removing certain frequencies. New to Final Cut Pro 4 is an "Apple" bin with some other new filters such as Delay and Band Pass. In the Final Cut Pro bin, there are also two special-effects filters, Echo and Reverb, which can be used to make audio sound like it was recorded in a different acoustic space. You can also use these filters to stylize the audio, creating inhuman voices or horror-movie sound effects. As an example, we'll look at the 3 Band Equalizer, a common filter used to adjust the audio to bring out certain frequencies and lower others, which works in the same way as an equalizer on a home stereo. It isolates certain frequencies and lets you amplify or deamplify them.

Note that if a clip is in a stereo pair, any filter you add will be inserted into both channels. In this example, we will practice using the 3 Band Equalizer to bring up her voice over the background sounds.

Add the clip you want to edit by double-clicking it in the Browser, Timeline, or Canvas or dragging it into the Timeline.

Open the Effects tab in the Browser and open the Audio Filters bin. Drag the 3 Band Equalizer into the clip you want to work with. You can also select Effects **>** Audio Filters **>** 3 Band Equalizer from the Final Cut Pro top menu.

3. In the Viewer, open the Audio tab. You should see the filter listed in the Filters tab. If the clips are linked but not a stereo pair, you'll see two lists, one for each channel. The 3 Band Equalizer has the following slider controls.

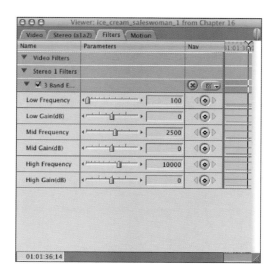

Low Frequency Sets the cutoff point for frequencies to be controlled by the Low Gain setting. Only frequencies below the value you set here will be controlled by Low Gain. Possible values range from 80Hz to 2000Hz. You'll want to set this low enough to isolate the sounds you want to get rid of (an electrical hum or a passing truck, for example) without affecting sounds you want to keep.

Low Gain Sets the signal amplification of the low frequency, ranging from –20 to 20dB.

Mid Frequency Sets which frequency in the mid range you want to isolate. The mid-frequencies range from 400Hz to 8000Hz and overlap with the low and high frequencies. Most sounds are in this range, including most music and human speech.

Mid Gain Sets the amplification of the mid-frequency, ranging from –20 to 20dB.

High Frequency Sets the frequencies in the high range you want to isolate. The high frequencies range from 5000Hz to

Using the 3 Band Equalizer Effectively

Making adjustments to the 3 Band Equalizer takes a lot of practice and requires a good ear. It will also take some experimentation, so try different settings and play them back to familiarize yourself with how changing the gain of different frequencies affects your audio. A good rule of thumb is, if you have excessive background noise such as an air conditioner or rumbling traffic over dialog, cut down the lower frequency and bump up the mid-frequency. Since most human voices are found in the mid-frequency range, this will make the dialog louder and soften the background noise, which usually exists in the lower frequencies.

A good trick is to use multiple 3 Band Equalizers in the same audio clip. This way, you can work with multiple frequencies in the same range. This might be helpful if you have a higher female voice and a deep male voice, both of which are in the mid-frequencies, but still not the same. With some trial and error, you could be able to bump them both up by finding their individual frequencies.

As with any audio filter, the 3 Band Equalizer can be used with keyframes to alter the settings while the clip is playing. See *Using Keyframes with Audio.*

20,000Hz and would be used to isolate sounds like breaking glass, shrieks, or a high-pitched siren.

High Gain   Sets the amplification of the high frequency, ranging from –20 to 20dB.

Keep in mind that most human voices fall in the mid-frequency range, background noise like rumbling traffic in the low-frequency range, and high-pitched noises like squealing brakes in the high-frequency range. The term *gain* refers to the amplification of sounds in the frequency range.

You can adjust these settings by typing in new values or dragging the slider controls. The frequency values range from 10Hz at the lowest to 20,000Hz at the highest.

After adjusting the sound filter, play back the audio. Make sure you've got good speakers or headphones so that you can tell the difference between actual audio problems and your speakers' shortcomings. Usually audio does not need to be rendered, although some more complex filters need to be rendered. (It takes only a few seconds.) You may also need to render audio when there are a lot of clips stacked on top of each other.

Adding Sound Tone

In Chapter 3, we discussed the importance of recording sound tone in every place you shoot a scene so you have "silence" that matches the ambient tone of the space. It is often helpful to use small clips of this audio to smooth over edits or to fill in gaps in the audio seamlessly. To use sound tone effectively, it's a good idea to create a separate lower audio track all its own for sound tone. For example, if you are cutting an interview voice-over and need to add a few seconds of pause between two statements, you will need to fill this pause in with sound tone so that the audio doesn't drop out completely. Open your sound tone clip into the Viewer and set In and Out points so that the clip lasts a little longer than the audio gap. Now drag this clip to the sound tone track and place it to fill this gap. There should be some overlap so that the sound will merge smoothly. You may need to adjust the sound level or add audio transitions to further smooth the sound tone so that it "disappears" into the mix.

Sweetening the Audio with Audio Filters

While we discuss 3 Band Equalizer as our example audio filter, Final Cut Pro offers other audio filters that provide different effects and can help improve problem audio. All of these filters can be found in the Audio Filters bin in the Browser's Effects tab. Some of the more useful audio filters are:

- **Hum Remover:** Removes hums that may appear in your audio from the power source itself. Typically this is at a frequency between 50 and 60Hz.

- **Vocal DeEsser:** Cuts out a hiss-like sound that often occurs when an actor pronounces an "s" into a microphone.

- **Vocal DePopper:** Cuts out the audio pop that often occurs when an actor pronounces a "p" into a microphone.

- **Echo:** Creates an echo effect. This is great for creating dream-like audio or to give a voice a strange, other-worldly feel.

- **Reverb:** Simulates audio recorded in a specific space, such as a small room or a concert hall setting.

Adding a Voice-over

Final Cut Pro 4 lets you add voice-overs directly to your film using your computer microphone. This allows you to record a voice-over in real time as the images play, and have this audio appear directly into your Timeline. To record a voice-over, you'll need a microphone that can input its signal into your computer. This can be a microphone built into your computer, plugged into a mic port, on your DV camera, or set up through a USB audio capture device or a PCI audio card.

You can use this function anywhere, but it is especially helpful if you are editing on the fly—say, editing a segment for quick news broadcast or annotating a clip on a laptop in the field. This way, you don't have to bring the footage back to an audio studio to record and time the voice-over.

Define the target audio track where you want to record (see *Adding and Deleting Tracks in the Timeline* in Chapter 6) and place the playhead at the point in the Timeline where you want the voice-over to begin. You can also set In and Out points in the Timeline to delineate exactly the area you want to record in (see *Setting In and Out Points in the Timeline* in Chapter 6).

Now Select Tool > Voice Over to open up the Voice Over tab in the Tool Bench window.

2. Make sure your microphone is set up correctly to input into the computer. Desktop Macs generally have an external mic plug, while PowerBooks have built-in mics. If the microphone is set up properly, the Voice Over tab will automatically detect it.

A Review: Plays the section of the Timeline that you've delineated as the area in which you want to record voice-over.

B Record/Stop Button: Use this button to start and stop recording the voice-over.

C Discard: Deletes the last audio clip you recorded.

D Status Window: Lets you know the status of recording and shows a visual timeline of how much has been recorded.

E Audio Target Track: Shows which audio track the voice-over will be placed on. This is designated by clicking on the "2" audio setting in the target track area.

F Audio Clip Name: Type a name for the clip.

G Input Window: Set the Source information, the Input information, the audio sample rate, Gain, and an offset. The offset is used because there may be a small delay in the actual real-time recording and the synched time between the laid down audio clip and the sequence. USB typically delays one frame, DV cameras typically delay three frames.

H Headphone Window: Sets the volume for the monitor headphones. If you are not using headphones, you may experience feedback problems while recording.

3. Press the Record button (or Shift+C) in the Voice Over tab. There will be a five-second preroll before recording begins for you to prepare. Speak clearly into the microphone while watching the sequence play and then press the Record button again to stop recording. There will be a two-second post-roll to prevent your audio from clipping.

4. The voice-over audio clip will then appear in your Timeline at the designated point in the designated track. You have built in the post- and preroll that you can trim if you need to do some fine-tuning to the clip, like adding an audio fade.

Watch your sequence with the new audio voice-over included. Adjust the volume, etc., to mix the new audio clip into your sequence. If you don't like the voice-over you recorded, click the Discard button, and then repeat Step 3.

If you recorded your voice-over with a mono microphone, you will probably want to copy the voice-over onto another audio track and then link the two audio clips as stereo pairs, so that the sound will be played in both speakers.

④

TIP

Using the Audio Mixer

New to Final Cut Pro 4 is the Audio Mixer, which lets you view the levels of multiple tracks at once, change their levels, and isolate certain tracks. This feature is especially useful if you are layering dialogue with a musical score. Audio mixing is typically something you will do at the end of the editing process. When you're happy with the picture cut, you can open up the Audio Mixer and make fine adjustments to individual tracks and to the whole sequence to get the levels exactly where you want them.

Choose Tools > Audio Mixer to open the Audio Mixing window.

Ⓐ **View Presets:** Allows you to save different configurations, such as the active channels and channel settings, for quick comparison.

Ⓑ **Active Tracks:** Click to toggle between making a track active or inactive.

Ⓒ **Mute:** Click to mute the track.

Ⓓ **Solo:** Click to mute all but this track.

Ⓔ **Balance:** If a stereo pair, use slider or enter a value (–1 to 1) in field to adjust left/right balance of track.

Ⓕ **Level:** Use slider or enter a value in the field (–12 to –∞, although –144.5 is the highest real number value) to adjust the volume of the audio channel. Stereo pairs will change levels in synch.

Ⓖ **Record Audio Keyframes:** When selected, this automatically creates a keyframe at the position of the playhead when a level or Spread/Pan is changed.

Ⓗ **Master Mute:** Click to mute all audio channels.

Ⓘ **Down Mix:** Mixes down the audio from multiple tracks to one track

Ⓙ **Master Levels:** Use slider or enter a value in the field (–12 to –∞, although –144.5 is the highest real number value) to adjust the relative volume of all audio channel.

This window will give you a list of all the audio tracks you have currently active and provide a separate column for each of these tracks so you can manipulate them separately. When playing through your sequence, you'll see in real time the levels of each audio track.

- To change the level of a specific track, pull down the vertical slider of that track. As with the audio level slider in the Viewer, you can go as high as 12dB and as low as –60dB. This will affect the level of the entire track, keeping the integrity of the individual clip's levels in relative proportion.

- To change the level of the entire sequence, affecting all tracks, drag the slider of the Master volume on the left side. You can drag between 12dB and –96dB. This will collectively change the overall level of all the tracks together.

- When mixing you should use both Final Cut Pro's Audio Meter and your ear to decide how levels are working. We recommend having an exterior speaker system or good headphones to really be able to hear the mix instead of relying on your inadequate internal computer speaker.

- Remember to use keyframes to slowly bring up or bring down levels. Gradual changes can help smooth over diverse audio content and levels.

④

Composing with Soundtrack

Shipping with Final Cut Pro 4 is separate software called Soundtrack that really opens up the world of Final Cut Pro editing to the musician in everyone. While this package is just too big to cover in depth here (it really deserves its own book), Soundtrack is a versatile and extremely user-friendly platform that allows you to create short musical works, beats, and background sounds for your projects. Soundtrack can be used to create a jazzy score for a commercial, an urban beat to play under a documentary interview, or a classical score for a wedding video.

One big asset of Soundtrack is that it comes with hundreds of royalty free loops that you can use to construct your score. These range from hip-hop rhythms to trumpet calls, and you can combine and loop them in any way you want. Soundtrack also has 30 new audio effects, like delay effects, that you can use to create the perfect mode or sound.

Soundtrack is made to work hand-in-hand with Final Cut Pro, and most importantly can save you a lot of time. Instead of having to hire out to an expensive composer, you can now create really professional sounding loops and scores on the same machine that you edit with. When you save a file in Soundtrack, you can immediately import it into Final Cut Pro by choosing File > Import or simply dragging the file into your open Browser.

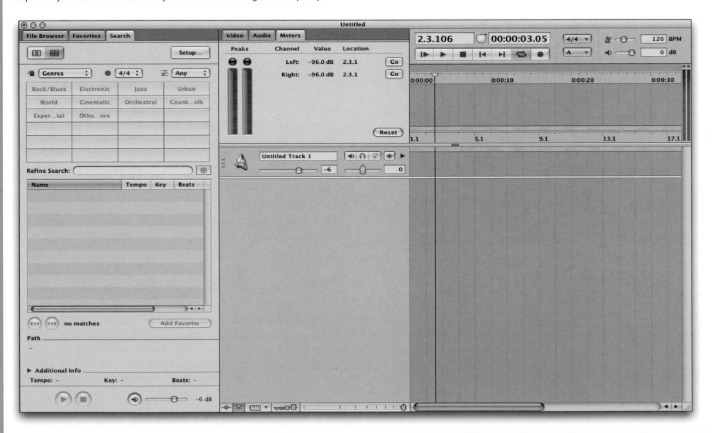

Duality, The Ultimate Screen Test

All filmmakers are inspired by the works of other filmmakers. For some, this inspiration is shown in the style and theme of their work. For others, however, the inspiration is so strong that they feel compelled carry on the actual story. It's amazing what a little inspiration and the right tools can do.

©Copyright 2001 Crew of Two

Dave Macomber and Mark Thomas had no formal background when they produced a popular short film based on the *Star Wars* mythology with special effects that rival the Hollywood epic's own. Originally, they shot a short film titled *Duel* for an actor who wanted to use it as audition material for the role of Anakin in *Star Wars Episode II*. Although the actor didn't get the role, after they finished the film they uploaded it to the Internet for the entire world to see and it became an instant hit with *Star Wars* fans. Despite its success, however, Dave and Mark had felt hurried with the project—which took three weeks from inception to completion—and were not satisfied with the outcome.

So, they decided to start from scratch with, according to Mark, "a really serious effort." They had put the first version together with Radius EditDV, but Mark says, "Because of the complexity of this project, we knew we had to step up from EditDV. Apple had just released Final Cut Pro, so, being diehard Mac fans, the choice was a no-brainer. From the beginning we planned to shoot the movie against blue screen and render our sets digitally." This saved them time by allowing them to construct all of the sets and most of the props using CGI.

The result was *Duality*, the story of a Sith Lord who pits his two apprentices against each other in a light saber duel to the death as a way of choosing between them (we won't ruin the surprise ending).

They shot the entire film on a 30 × 30 film studio cove painted from floor to ceiling in chroma key paint, and used a Canon XL1 as their main camera because it had the ability to shoot in noninterlaced, or "progressive," Frame Movie mode. They then rendered computer-generated backgrounds and animated space ships and robots in Electric Image, adding a few extra touches with Adobe Photoshop. Mark comments, "Many shots were rendered in passes and then comped in Adobe After Effects. We used Commotion Pro for motion tracking and rotoscoping."

When it came time to edit, Mark says that he "likes to put the first rough cut together quickly and then gradually trim and tweak it into shape. I jump around a lot, sometimes fussing with the beginning, then a part near the end, then something in the middle. I feel, rather than think, my way through the edit." In fact, Mark is in the habit of keeping a separate video track in the Timeline just for making test and experimental edits before moving these down into the main track.

Their setup included two dual-processor 500MHz G4s with 1GB of RAM and two internal 40GB 7200RPM IDE hard disks. Mark also splurged and bought a Cinema Display, which, he says, is "perfect for Final Cut Pro's 16:9 window layout setting."

But no matter how much RAM you have or how fast your processor, all editors run into the same frustration: rendering. Mark felt this frustration especially with audio, even if he just nudged a track: "I know that I can mix down audio, but when you do this you lose the ability to easily modify levels and filter settings without going back to an earlier version. I don't like nesting projects because I like to keep things as simple and straightforward as possible."

The final product was then output to QuickTime. "*Duality* was meant for the web, but because we shot the live action on Mini-DV and rendered all of the CGI effects at Mini-DV resolution, it's certainly broadcast quality. The DVD copies we've made look incredible."

To see their film online, check out www.crewoftwo.com.

17 Adding Titles

Most video projects begin and end with a title sequence. It's not only a way of getting across information such as the name of your project or the people involved (the credits), but also a way of introducing your audience to the style and mood of your piece. Whether you prefer white letters on black cards or colorful moving type over images, titles are your chance to create a first important impression for your viewer, so you should spend some time deciding the style and layout.

Overview

> *"Always judge a book by its cover."*
>
> Anonymous

Think of some of the famous title sequences in films and how they set the stage for the action of the movie. Alfred Hitchcock was a master of inventive title sequences. The opening credits for films like *Vertigo* and *Psycho* are just as riveting as the films themselves. On the flip side, Woody Allen has opened all of his films since 1973 with simple white text on black cards underscored by music, but this uncomplicated matter-of-fact approach is very stylish and fits the tone and humor of his movies. Having a lot of fancy gimmicks at your disposal doesn't mean you'll make better title sequences. However, if you use these techniques with skill, you can combine effects to create dazzling displays.

Final Cut Pro gives you a lot of latitude to create your own title cards and sequences. It's often a good idea to complete your project first without the titles, and then add the titles the sequences that fit the feel of the finished piece. If your video is colorful and fast-paced, you may want the titles to reflect this style, so you could use a colorful palette for the titles. Final Cut Pro contains a sophisticated generator for text and titles, including the ability to create title cards, or titles that will be superimposed over moving video.

When you create a title in Final Cut Pro, you actually generate a new, separate clip that you can then place in your Timeline like any normal clip. This clip contains all the information about the title, such as its font, size, and text. A title clip functions in the same way as a video or audio clip; only it is generated entirely within Final Cut Pro. You can trim a title clip using the trim edit techniques such as Ripple or Roll (see Chapter 8) to create a hard transition, or you can add transitions to the title clip to make it dissolve into the rest of the footage. A title is a type of effect like a transition (see Chapter 10) or filter (see Chapters 11 and 12); so when you begin to create a title, you will start in the Effects tab of the Browser. You can also create titles in a separate graphics program if you like. You can easily import picture files from many graphics programs, and Final Cut Pro can work directly with Photoshop files (.psd) to preserve the Photoshop layers in the Timeline allowing you to manipulate each independently.

When you design titles, sometimes keeping things simple is the smartest strategy so that the information isn't overshadowed. Viewers need to be able to read everything on the screen clearly, and they need time to read it, so make sure your titles are on the screen long enough for even a slow reader to catch everything.

Chapter 17: Titles over Images

Open the Final Cut Pro project file labeled Coney Island Memories. After it loads in Final Cut Pro, double-click the Chapter 17 sequence in the Browser and it will open in the Timeline.

In this chapter you will be adding various slugs to the Timeline as well as a non-video clip generated in Photoshop to create titles. Don't worry if you don't have Photoshop. We have already created a file that you can use. There are six sets of clips in this sequence, one for each lesson and an extra for the subsection on creating advanced moving titles. The first clip in a set is for you to practice with, and the second shows what the results might look like.

Adding Static Titles

When you are ready to create a title to use in your sequence, you may want to sketch it out first on paper or have a good mental image in your head. Watch the footage that will come before, after, or under the titles, and try to come up with a creative way to have titles that fit with the visuals.

1. To begin your title, decide on the spot in the Timeline where it will be placed into your sequence. This is where you will place the new title clip after you finish making it. You may have to

clear a spot in the footage if you want the title to appear without video footage under it. You will often want to create a gap at the beginning of the footage that you will drag your title into (see the sidebar *Creating a Gap in the Timeline*).

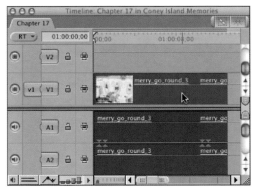

2. Open the Video Generators folder in the Browser's Effects tab. Open the Text folder to see a list of different titling options. Double-click the text effect you want to use, and it will be displayed in the Viewer. For this example, choose Text.

3. In the Viewer you'll see a *generated* clip (a clip created within Final Cut Pro, not captured from an exterior source) ready to be modified for your title. At first, the message "Sample Text" will appear in the title. Notice that the clip in the Viewer has a new tab, located after the Video tab and before the Filters tab, called

Controls. This is where you'll make all your adjustments to the title clip. Click the Controls tab to open it.

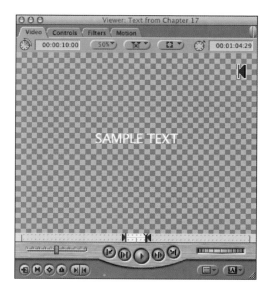

4. The Controls tab allows you to change the text being used in the title sequence. Different effects will have different controls in these areas, but for a simple text title, the controls are:

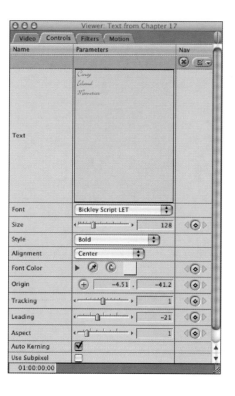

Text Type in your title text, as you want it to look on the screen.

Font Choose the font for the text. In this example, we used a font called Curlz MT, which is preinstalled on most Macs that can run Final Cut Pro. Keep in mind that, unless you render this title clip, if you transfer your project file to another computer that does not have the font you see here, the title will not appear in the font. Instead, it will show up in that computer's default font.

Size Type in the point size or use the slider.

TIP

Creating a Gap in the Timeline

The easiest way to add a title to a sequence, most likely at the very beginning, is to use an Insert Edit. With your playhead poised at the position where you want the title to start in the Timeline, drag the title clip into the Canvas's Edit Overlay window and choose Insert Edit. The sequence will move to allow room for the title, and you can insert it into the sequence (at the designated target track). You can also manually create a space by using one of the many selection tools (see *Using the Tools and the Audio Meter* in Chapter 2) to select the clips you want to move and then dragging them all with the mouse to create a new gap in the Timeline.

Style   Choose styles such as bold, italic, or underline.

Alignment   Choose the type of justification you want.

Font Color   Select the font color. You can double-click the color swatch to open the color wheel window, or you can use the dropper icon to select a color from an image in the Canvas. If you know the HSB code for a specific color, you can enter in the three-number code in the color wheel window.

Origin   Allows you to type in the coordinates of the center of the title. The position 0,0 is the center of the screen. You can type in coordinates or use the crosshair to select the center visually. First select the crosshair and then click within the Canvas (*not* the Viewer) at the point where you want to center the text. Either have the Timeline's playhead on the clip so you can see the placement in the clip, or flip to the Video tab in the Viewer.

Tracking   Lets you control the spacing between letters in the text. Fonts have a default spacing that is generally optimized for reading when printed. Obviously for the screen you may need to play around with this spacing, or you may want to use tracking to create more distinctive titles by spacing the letters out or even animating the spacing over time (see *Using Keyframes to Change the Image* in Chapter 16).

Leading   Lets you control the distance between lines of text. The default for text is single-spaced, but with titles you may want to stylize them by spreading out the lines of text.

Aspect   Controls the height of the letters. 1 is normal. Less than 1 stretches the letters. More than 1 and the letters get squashed.

Auto Kerning   Check this to have Final Cut Pro automatically set the space between letters.

Use Subpixel   Check this for more accurate letter rendering. This can create sharper letters, but slows down rendering.

5. After you have set all of the parameters for your title clip, set the In and Out points in the Viewer as you would any other clip (see Chapter 6 for more details) to create a clip that is as long as you want it. The clip is treated as a still image, so where you set the In and Out points determines only how long the clip plays, not its content. The default for a title clip is defined in the Preferences window (Final Cut Pro **>** User Preferences) under the Still/Freeze Duration box. You can also add other effects to the clip; in this example, we have added a slight drop shadow to help the title pop out from the video beneath.

6. You can either drag the clip from the Viewer into your sequence in the Timeline or drag it to the Edit Overlay window in the Canvas. The clip will appear like any other clip in the Timeline, and will run as long as you set it to. Place the clip where you want

it in the Timeline. Simple Text titles are real-time effects, so you do not have to render the clip to see it play in real time whether your footage was captured in OfflineRT format, but you will need to render it before output. As mentioned above, if you drop the title clip over empty tracks in the Timeline, the background will be black by default (to change the background color, see the section *Creating a Colored Backdrop*). If you drop the title clip over a video image, the text will superimpose over that image and you will want to make sure that the title is legible throughout the entire clip. For example, if the title is white text and you are superimposing it over an image of a cloudy sky, you may not be able to read it. To make it pop out, change the text color or add a drop shadow (see the *Customizing a Title Clip* sidebar). Once again, any title effect you add will have to be rendered before you can view it in real time. Also see the sidebar *Making Sure Your Title Is Title Safe* to avoid cropped titles.

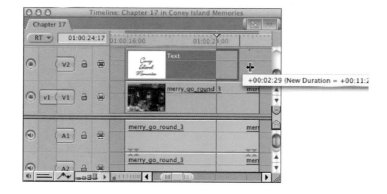

Play it in the Canvas to see how it looks. Once it is perfect, you are ready to render it (see Chapter 9).

Customizing a Title Clip

When creating a title card, you'll want to think about the graphic design and the placement of your elements in the title. To do so, you'll be simultaneously adjusting the size, font, alignment, and origin, among other things, to get the title exactly where you want it to be. A good way to do this easily is to open the title from the Timeline in the Viewer and type your text in the Controls tab. Once your text is entered and you've set a rough duration for the clip, drag it into the Timeline. Now place your playhead in the Timeline over the title clip. You'll get a preview of how your text will look in the Canvas, or you can use Quick-View to preview the changes while still watching the title in motion. With the clip still open in the Viewer, make changes in the Controls tab (you can also use the Motion tab for placement changes). As you make your changes, such as selecting a new origin point or increasing the font size, you'll see those changes reflected immediately in the Canvas or QuickView windows as long as the playhead rests on the clip in the Timeline, so you can quickly decide whether they are working. This is especially helpful if you have laid the text over an image and need to size and shape the text to fit in a specific part of the frame.

Making Sure Your Title Is Title Safe

When you place and size your title graphics, you'll want to make sure that the graphics will be completely visible, with no part cut off on any TV monitor. Because different monitors crop the edges of the image differently, you should use the Title Safe guide to make sure your title graphics will fit the edges of any monitor (the guide is roughly 10 percent smaller than the full frame). You can bring up a Title Safe guide in either the Viewer or the Canvas. Either select View > Title Safe to bring up a wire-frame box, or select Title Safe from the View popup menu in the Viewer or Canvas. All text and graphics in your title should appear within this box.

Adding Moving Titles

Besides static text, you can also add *scrolling* or *crawling* text. You typically see scrolling text in the credits at the end of a Hollywood movie, where the text rolls up the screen vertically. Crawling text moves the text in a line horizontally, like a stock ticker as often seen on news programs. You can also choose a text style called Lower 3rd, a type of title often used in interviews to give someone's name and a brief note about them that appears in the lower third of the screen. Final Cut Pro also provides a Typewriter function, which has each letter of the text appear one at a time, as if being struck by a typewriter head. (Jonathan Demme's *The Silence of the Lambs* used this technique to introduce new locations, and the effect can be seen in many contemporary action films and TV shows like *X-Files*.)

1. After setting a spot in the Timeline for your title, open the Video Generators folder in the Browser's Effects tab. Open the Text folder to see a list of different titling options. Double-click the text effect you want to use (in this example, choose Scrolling Text) and it will be displayed in the Viewer.

2. Click the Controls tab in the Viewer and enter or select appropriate values for the various properties. As noted in *Adding Static Titles*, the properties you can set here depend on the type of title you're creating. Each title format will require slightly different information or may not accept certain kinds of input. For example, a crawling title will not accept a carriage return, because it only creates a single line of text. If you want two lines of crawling text, you need to create two separate crawling text clips and place them on top of each other on two different video tracks. Make sure you space the text differently with the Origin controls so they don't run on top of each other!

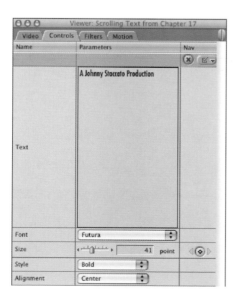

3. After you have set the title parameters, set the duration of the clip using the In and Out points or the duration window in the Viewer. For a scrolling or crawling text clip, the speed is directly determined by the duration (the location of the In and Out points) you have set for the clip. The shorter the duration of the clip, the faster the text will move.

4. Drag the title clip into the section of the Timeline where you want the title to appear, or drag the selected title into the Placement functions in the Canvas. Unlike the simple text title explained in the previous section, all moving titles have to be rendered before they can be played in the Canvas. Render the title clip and view it to see if it plays as you want it to. See the sidebar *Making Sure Your Title Is Title Safe* to avoid cutting off text.

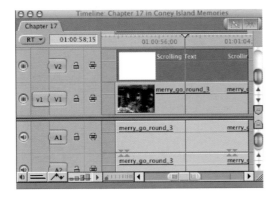

Creating a Colored Backdrop

We've noted that the default background for a title, if there is no clip on a video track under the title clip, is black. While this is fine for some titles, you certainly don't want to be stuck with just one option. One alternative is to create a graphic in a separate graphics program, as discussed in the next section, *Importing a Title Card*. However, you can also generate your own solid-colored backdrops in Final Cut Pro. To do this you need to generate a clip—like a slug, matte, or gradient—that is basically blank to which you can add effects. In this example you'll be adding a tint to the clip and then deciding what color you want.

In the Effects tab in the Browser, open the Video Generators folder and double-click Slug to open a slug in the Viewer.

2. You should now have your blank slug clip in the Viewer. Go back to the Effects tab in the Browser and select Video Filters **>** Image Controls **>** Tint. Drag the Tint icon into the Viewer and drop it on the representation of the slug.

3. Now, when you click on the Filters tab in the Viewer, you will see Tint listed as an effect for the slug. You can click the box on the left of the Tint effect to toggle it on and off.

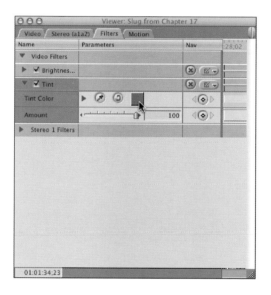

Double-click the color swatch to select the color you want for your background; then click back on the Video tab to bring your now colorful slug into the Viewer.

Often, it's best to use a tint in conjunction with the Brightness and Contrast filter, so drag this filter to the clip and add brightness to create a brighter color. You can also use many other color or opacity effects with your slug. See Chapters 12 and 13 for more details on these effects.

4. Set the duration of your colored slug in the Viewer's Duration control or by setting In and Out points in the Viewer. Then drag the colored slug into an empty video track *under* the title clip where you've typed in your text.

Render the slug and review your work. You can add any of Final Cut Pro's effects to a slug to create many different looks. See Chapters 11 and 12 for details of more advanced effects.

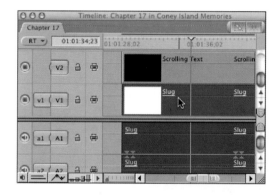

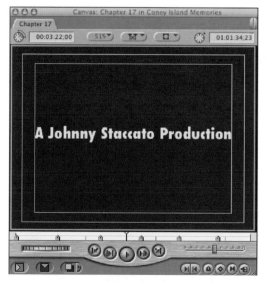

Importing a Title Card

 If you need something more complicated than a title generated within Final Cut Pro, or if you want to create your title in a graphics program, you can import titles and use them within your sequence. These files will often come in the form of JPEGs, but Final Cut Pro recognizes many picture formats. Final Cut Pro can also recognize Adobe Photoshop files, and will preserve the individual layers of a Photoshop file placing each layer on a different video track in the Timeline. If you import a Photoshop file, it will be imported as a sequence rather than a clip, and its multiple layers will be found on the tracks inside this sequence. The sidebar *Creating Your Title Card in Another Program* explains the issue of layering and other considerations for creating titles in Photoshop to be used in Final Cut Pro. Because Final Cut Pro generally has problems with more than about 10 layers, your Photoshop file should have as few layers as the image requires. Also note that while the pixel ratio of DV is 720 × 480, you should not create your title graphics in Photoshop at this ratio. The reason is that there is a difference in the shape of pixels between your computer and video shown on a NTSC monitor. To avoid this problem, create your Photoshop files at a pixel ratio of 720 × 534, perform all your manipulations, rasterize the image with Effects > Video > NTSC Colors, and

then resize to 720 × 480 before saving the graphic. This will prevent the image from appearing squeezed. Photoshop does also offer defaults to create titles, but we've found it's more reliable to create them manually.

In Photoshop or another graphics program, create your title graphic as described in the sidebar *Creating Your Title Card in Another Program*. In our example, we have created a layered Photoshop file and saved it as Coney_title_final2.psd.

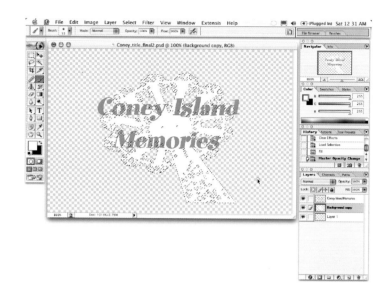

Back in Final Cut Pro, Select File **>** Import **>** File (⌘+I) and then select the file you want to import from the dialog box. If your file doesn't show up, then you probably saved it in a format that Final Cut Pro does not recognize. Try saving the file as a PSD file to retain the layers of the Photoshop files as tracks in Final Cut Pro. To save space you can save as a TIFF (a JPEG will also work) and then import it if you don't want to flatten the image and loose the Photoshop layers.

The picture file will be imported into the currently open project, showing up in the Browser. Double-click the picture file to open it in the Viewer. Remember, if you have imported a layered Photoshop file, Final Cut Pro will treat it as a sequence, not a clip. You can either drag the title sequence directly into your working sequence (see the sidebar *Can I Put One Sequence Inside Another?* in Chapter 8) or open up the sequence separately to work on it.

Once imported, you can double-click the file to open it as its own sequence for editing. Each layer is represented in a separate track and can be individually manipulated by double-clicking it to open in the Viewer. For example, you might want to change the layers' opacity, add a drop shadow, or even animate it using keyframes.

4. Place the imported title clip or layered sequence into your
sequence and position it where you want it. If the size is not quite
right, you can adjust the image to fit exactly on the screen, as you
want it. (See Chapter 15 for a discussion of using keyframes to create complex motion paths for titles or any clip.) You can also add
titles generated in Final Cut Pro if, for example, you are only
importing a graphic that is a background image. Simply place a
text clip (remember, you create a text clip from the Effects tab in
the Browser) on a video track over the video track containing the
graphic, and you'll have your text with the graphic background
together in the same image.

Creating Your Title Card in Another Program

If you are creating titles in a graphics program such as Adobe Photoshop,
you'll need to do a few things to make sure they work properly in Final Cut
Pro. Keep in mind that Photoshop files are usually created to be viewed on a
computer monitor, whereas FCP files are usually created for the NTSC DV
standard.

- First, you will have to make sure you stay within the "title safe
  area" (see the sidebar *Making Sure Your Title Is Title Safe*). This will
  save you from a lot of hassle later when you import your images
  and they don't quite fit or words are too close to the edge of the
  screen.

- It's also crucial to design a title card that has the same aspect ratio as
  the video footage you are creating in Final Cut Pro. (The aspect ratio
  is the width of the screen in relation to its height.) This is a little
  tricky because of the different output destinations of Photoshop and
  FCP files. Computer monitors use square pixels, while NTSC monitors
  use rectangular (or nonsquare) pixels. Thus, in Photoshop you need
  to design for a ratio of 720 × 534 pixels, even though NTSC DV's

native aspect ratio is 720 × 480, to compensate for the difference in
pixel shapes. If you import a file created at 720 × 480 file into Final
Cut Pro and print it to video, the graphic will appear distorted. When
you create your Photoshop file, set the pixel ratio at 720 × 534. Once
your graphic is designed for this ratio, save it as a master file. You'll
now need to resize the image, slightly squashing it, so that it will
seem "normal" in Final Cut Pro. Select Image > Image Size in
Photoshop. Uncheck the Constrain Proportions box and type in the
new ratio of 720 width and 480 height. Click OK and save this as your
Final Cut Pro graphic. The reason for having two Photoshop files is
that if you need to make changes later, you can go back to the original master file set at 720 × 534.

- You will also need to make sure the colors are set for an NTSC monitor, by using the NTSC Colors filter. Select Filters > Video > NTSC
  Colors in Photoshop and apply this effect to your graphic. You will
  need to do this for each individual layer if you are importing a layered graphic.

Advanced Titles

Final Cut Pro 4 has a more advanced titling engine called Title 3D. It is not built into Final Cut Pro, but offers extra effects created by Boris FX (not Apple) that you can install from your Final Cut Pro 4 CD. When you're installing the program for the first time, you have the option of installing the third-party programs Boris Calligraphy and FXScript DVEs by DGM. Check these options on the install. Once installed, Title 3D and Title Crawl will appear in the Video Generators bin and the Video Generators popup menu on the bottom right of the Viewer tab. If you did not install this software initially, just go back to your install CD and run the install program.

These new effects greatly increase your control over the titles you can generate using Final Cut Pro. Whereas the built-in title effect has 12 controls, the Boris FX titles have over 3 dozen controls that allow you to manipulate virtually every aspect of the letterform. You can turn them, stretch them, skew them, pivot them, even tumble them. You can also add up to five different drop shadows to the text at the same time.

This tool can quickly seem overwhelming with all of its options, but play around with it for a bit and you'll be hooked. Still, if all you want is simple text, this may be overkill and you should probably stick with the titles shown earlier in this chapter.

Open the Video Generators folder in the Browser's Effects tab. Under the Text folder you will see the options Title 3D and Title Crawl. Double-click the text effect you want to use, and it will be displayed in the Viewer. For this example, choose Title 3D.

The Title 3D options window will immediately appear. In this new window, you will add your title text and format the text as desired. (See the sidebar *Understanding the Title Options Window* for more details.) Set your text and styles and then click Apply.

In this example, we are adding a drop shadow, a white edge to the letters, and a red-to-black gradient to color the text. We selected a font called Party LET, which you can purchase from MyFonts.com (www.myfonts.com/fonts/letraset/party/party/). If you move your project file to another computer that does not have this font, however, the text will appear in that computer's default font unless the clip has been rendered.

In the Viewer's Control tab, you can manipulate the letters using the Title 3D controls. You have a lot of options here to control the exact placement and appearance of your title text. You can rotate your entire text block or even each individual letter in three-dimensional space. You can lower the text opacity to allow images underneath to show through. You can even set the "distance" at which your text appears to be.

In Chapter 15, we show you how to change all of these attributes over the course of time to allow the text to appear to fade in or out, rotate, or even zoom up, using these same controls with keyframes.

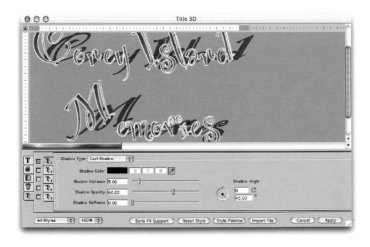

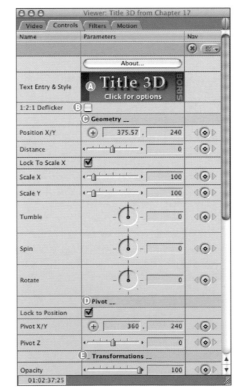

Ⓐ Title 3D Options: Click to reopen the text and style window.

Ⓑ Deflicker: Turn this on to eliminate flicker for output to video.

Ⓒ Geometry Controls: Change the size and orientation of the text block.

Ⓓ Pivot Controls: Change the X, Y, or Z position of the text block on the screen.

Ⓔ Transformations Controls: Set the text block opacity and tracking as well as the skew, scale, tumble, spin, and rotation of each letter.

Once you have the title the way you want it, open the Viewer's Video tab, and drag the title clip onto the Timeline to the point you want the title to appear. In this example, we placed the title clip on the track above the merry-go-round clip so that it will superimpose over top of that image. You can edit the length of the title in the Timeline by dragging its edges to the desired length.

With the title in place, you can view the title in the Canvas. Title 3D is a real-time effect, meaning that you do not have to render it to view in the Canvas if you are using OfflineRT footage. However, you will have to render it before exporting your film.

If you want to edit your title, simply double-click on it in the Timeline, and it will open in the Viewer.

Advanced Moving Titles

In addition to the Title 3D video generator, there is the Title Crawl generator, also by Boris FX. It offers all of the same text tools as the Title 3D mentioned above, but does not give such exact control over the placement of the text. Instead, Title Crawl allows you to animate the titles, either moving horizontally (crawl) or vertically (roll). In addition, it allows you to play around with the edges of the titles to either clip them and/or blend them into the background.

Open the Video Generators folder in the Browser's Effects tab. Under the Text folder you will see the options Title 3D and Title Crawl. Double-click the text effect you want to use, and it will be displayed in the Viewer. For this example, choose Title Crawl.

A new generated clip will be opened in the Viewer for you to manipulate. However, the Title Crawl options window will immediately appear over top. In this window, you will add your title text and format the text as desired. See the sidebar *Understanding the Title Options Window* for more details. Set your text and styles and then click Apply.

In this example, we selected a font called BlairMdITC (which is also available from MyFonts.com) and set it to a nice big 96 pixels. If you move your project file to another computer that does not have this font, however, the text will appear in that computer's default font unless the clip has been rendered.

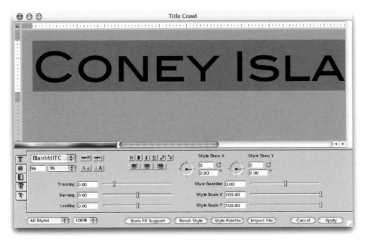

In the Viewer's Control tab, you can set the animation style for the title. Leaving the style at none will produce a static title. There are several simple but interesting effects that you can add to the motion, including cropping the edges so that the title starts further in from the edges of the screen and blending so that the edges of the title fade into the background.

In Chapter 10 we showed you how to change all of these attributes over the duration of the clip to allow the text to appear to fade in or out, have the blended edges move, or make the position change on the screen, using these same controls with keyframes.

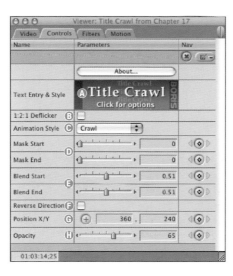

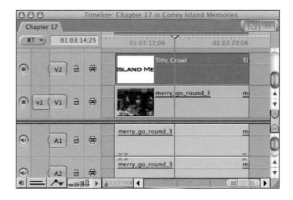

Ⓐ Title Options: Click this to reopen the Title Options window.

Ⓑ Deflicker: Turn this on for output to video to eliminate flicker.

Ⓒ Animation Style: Select between None, Crawl (horizontal), and Roll (vertical).

Ⓓ Mask Start/End: Clips the beginning or end of the title.

Ⓔ Blend Start/End: Fades the beginning or end of the title into the background.

Ⓕ Reverse Direction: Crawl moves left to right. Roll moves up to down.

Ⓖ Position: Sets the X, Y coordinates for the center of the text block.

Ⓗ Opacity: Sets the translucency of the text, allowing images from underneath to show through.

Once you have the title they way you want it, open the Viewer's Video tab, and then drag the title clip onto the Timeline to the point you want the title to appear. In this example, we placed the title clip on the track above the merry-go-round clip so that it will superimpose over the top of that image. You can edit the length of the title in the Timeline by dragging its edges to the desired length.

5. With the title in place, you can view the title in the Canvas. Title Crawl is *not* a real-time effect, so you have to render it to view in the Canvas, or you can use the QuickView window to preview the title while you are still making changes. If you want to edit your title, simply double-click on it in the Timeline, and it will open in the Viewer.

Understanding the Title Options Window

Both the Title 3D and Title Crawl video generator effects use the same window to input title text and set the text's attributes. This window has a lot of controls, but once you start using them, you will notice that most of these controls are similar to those found in a word processor.

(A) Text Area: Type your title text in here. To apply a style, you must select the text you want to affect.

(B) Tab: Set tabs in the ruler.

(C) Font Styles: Set standard font attributes such as bold, italics, justification, tracking, kerning, and leading and some not so standard attributes such as skew.

(D) Paragraph Styles: Set margins and whether or not the text wraps.

(E) Fill: Set the fill color for letters to a solid color or a multicolor gradient.

(F) Letter Edge Styles: Set the appearance of the letters' edges.

(G) Shadow Styles: Set a variety of different shadow styles for the text.

Adding Title Text

1. To create your title text, begin by typing the text into the Title Text area. You can copy and paste text from other sources and use tabs to position and align text as needed.

   For the following steps, make sure to have the text that you want to change highlighted in the text area.

2. Next, select the font, size, and other text attributes you need. You may need a fairly large font size to ensure that the text is legible on the screen. You can select any font that is available on your computer, but remember that if you move this project file to another computer that does not have this font, the text will use that computer's default font.

3. Click the Paragraph Styles Tab. Set margins, whether or not you want the title to wrap, and the width of the page if wrapping.

4. Click on the Fill tab. You can turn the fill on and off. If it's off, the text uses a default gray color. You can set the color of the selected text or set a multicolor gradient.

5. Click the Edge Style tab. You can set up to five different independent edge styles for your text using the five different tabs. Click the box in to the left of these tabs to turn a particular edge effect on or off.

6. Click the Shadow Styles tab. Choose between drop, solid, and cast shadow styles to set up five different independent shadows using the five shadow tabs. To turn a shadow on or off, use the check box next to that tab.

7. When you are finished setting your text and styles, click the Apply button in the bottom right corner, and the changes will be applied to your title.

Creating Animated Titles with Live Type

Although Final Cut Pro offers all of the tools you may ever need for creating simple titles for your project, eventually you may exhaust the limits of the built-in functionality. Shipping with Final Cut Pro 4 is a separate application called Live Type, which provides advanced titling functionality. Live Type not only includes 8GB of ready to use professional effects (some subtle, some cheesy), but also allows you to create sophisticated animated titles using its own Timeline for precise timing. This can allow you to turn your titles into a mini-movie themselves. In fact, because Live Type allows you to insert video footage for use in title, you can blur the line between text and image, integrating them together.

Live Type gives you control over virtually every aspect of your titles, which are accessed through the Inspector palette. These controls include:

- Text: Including exacting typographic controls.
- Style: A variety of common styles that can be applied to the text including shadows, glows, outlines, and extrusions.
- Effects: Allows you to layer different visual effects into a single title.
- Timing: Allows you exacting control of the speed at which not only the title, but effects used within the title are played.
- Attributes: Gives you precise control over each letter (glyph) as well as the background (matte) in the title.

As with SoundTrack, Live Type was designed to work hand-in-glove with Final Cut Pro and is provided as a way to save you time and money by bringing the often expensive task of creating titles in house. However, unlike SoundTrack, you cannot directly import a Live Type file into Final Cut Pro. Instead, first render the file in Live Type (File > Render (Option+⌘+R), which will allow you to save your title as a QuickTime movie that you can import

into Final Cut Pro (see *Importing Existing Media Files* in Chapter 5) and use like any other media clip.

Although Live Type is installed when you install Final Cut Pro 4, and you will be able to view and preview effects, you will need to install the Live Type data from the provided DVDs that came with Final Cut Pro 4 before you render the titles. If for some reason you did not load all 8 GB of effects files (say you have an older PowerBook G4 with a 20MB hard drive that is already bursting at the seams), Live Type will prompt you while rendering as to whether you want to install the needed files from the DVDs or to use a proxy effect. Generally, you will want to install the effects at this point, unless you are just creating a rough cut, in which case the proxy may be all you need for now.

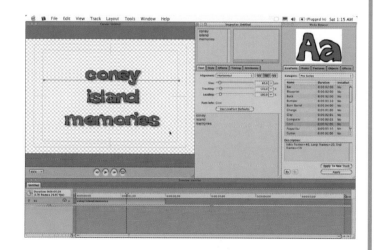

18
Putting It All Together

The story so far: we have shown you the basic techniques you need to put your film together—all of the skills you'll be using on a daily basis. You should now know how to capture footage, edit, trim, add effects, and manipulate your footage in a variety of ways. But these are just the pieces. In this chapter we discuss the nature of editing using Final Cut Pro as a tool, dealing with concepts that go back to the invention of cinema and are the backbone of any project whether it is narrative, documentary, commercial, instructional, dramatic, or even experimental.

Overview

> *"Editing...can transform chance into destiny."*
>
> Jean-Luc Godard

As viewers, we watch a film and experience the total effect of the story: direction, acting, camera work, lighting, sound, and music. All of these parts come together to create a whole that tells a story, makes a point, conveys an idea, or creates a mood. Editing is the process that composes the total effect of the film, taking the many parts and turning them into a completed whole. The way in which shots are placed together creates meaning just as surely as the words spoken by actors, the music, and the cinematography. The juxtaposition of shots allows the editor control over the message, the sense of space and time, and the perspective the audience experiences.

In this chapter we will show you how to take the skills you have developed in the previous chapters and apply them to the creation of a short documentary about Coney Island in Brooklyn, New York. We have provided the clips and a finished version of the movie. You can apply this quick methodology to any project, though.

Before we begin with the nuts and bolts of putting the movie together, it is vital to address the philosophy behind editing. These tips are not specific to Final Cut Pro, but cover a general theory of editing and how editing creates time, space, and mood.

The Juxtaposition of Shots

Editing can be approached in many ways, but there are four primary methods for editing two shots together:

- Editing for temporal relationships, to emphasize the passage of time
- Editing with match cuts, to play off a visual similarity between two shots
- Editing for spatial relationships, to establish physical location or emphasize movement
- Editing for rhythm, to create a temporal pulse or match the beat of a musical piece

These four concepts define the basic relationships that can be drawn between two or more shots.

Editing Based on Temporal Relationships

When one shot cuts to another, the viewer instinctively looks to see what the new image tells them and how it relates to the previous image. By editing shots together to create a sense of time passing, you move the story or scene along. As an editor, when you receive the raw footage for a scene that you will cut together, you have a lot of control over how long that scene will last; both in actual screen time and the time that appears to pass in the world of the film. Imagine a scene where a woman walks out of her house and down the street to a bus stop. This action in real life may take eight minutes, but most likely you don't want to spend eight minutes of screen time showing the whole thing. To shorten the action so that we know she has performed these actions, an editor may choose a few short shots to cut together to suggest this action. We may see her open the door, followed by a quick shot of her feet walking down the street, followed by her waiting at the bus stop. This sequence of three shots might only take up fifteen seconds of screen time, but the viewer knows that these actions took longer than the time they were displayed. By cutting, an editor can create a sense of the progression of time, by presenting shots in a specific order.

The classic Hollywood editing style is to order all shots in strict chronological order. We have shots A, B, C, D, and E, cut together one after the other, and each shot takes us further forward in time. Occasionally, this structure will be broken by a flashback (or more rarely a flash-forward), where we are shown a sequence that occurs at a different time outside the chronology of the main narrative. In *Casablanca*, the film's narrative progresses forward through the story of Rick's Café during World War II, with one break, where we flashback to the first meeting of Rick (Humphrey Bogart) and Ilse (Ingrid Bergman) in Paris years earlier. This sequence becomes its own forward chronology of shots, set at a different time than the main story. We are signaled that we are going into a flashback through the dialogue, as well as through a dissolve transition, which at the time was a relatively fresh way of signaling a transition, even though it's now become a cliché. Some directors, like Wong Kar Wai (*Chungking Express, In the Mood for Love*), intentionally choose not to signal flashbacks or changes in time, and jump between different times with simple straight cuts. This technique questions the linear nature of time, and the need to single out temporal shifts.

Following the innovations of filmmakers like Jean-Luc Godard (who pioneered editing styles that fragmented temporal and spatial relations, often with political and philosophical motivations), recent independent American movies such as Quentin Tarantino's *Pulp Fiction* and Christopher Nolan's *Memento* have played around with the order of time through editing to heighten the thrill of the narrative. *Pulp Fiction* jumps back and forth in time to show what happens to a number of interconnected characters over a certain period so that by the end, all of the pieces have been filled in— just out of order. *Memento* literally edits its story backwards, with the chronologically last scene playing first, until the final scene of the film, which is chronologically first. This structure is used to reflect the main character's own chronic memory problem and give the audience a similar sense of not knowing what has happened before. Here, nonchronological editing reflects a psychological logic, as is often the case in the films of David Lynch, who edits his films with a logic based more on dreams and skewed subjectivity than on an empirical notion of space and chronological time.

Your choice of how to present time depends on the effect you want to achieve and should be based on the content and theme of your project. You should make sure that you're not just playing around with chronology because you can, or you run the risk of simply coming across as gimmicky. However, if the subject matter and style of your piece makes you think about time differently, try editing outside of the chronological box.

Editing with Match Cuts

Another effective way to transition between shots or scenes is to use a visual link between the last frame of the outgoing shot and the first frame of the incoming shot. A prime example of this is in *2001: A Space Odyssey*, which uses the shot of a bone tossed in the air being transformed, through the power of editing, into a spaceship. This is a form of *match cut*, with the shape and orientation of the bone matching the shape and orientation of the space ship.

Match cuts can also take the form of a cut between two shots that are related by color, shape, line, or even movement. David Lean's *Lawrence of Arabia* features a striking edit between Peter O'Toole blowing out a burning orange flame at the tip of a match immediately followed by a long shot of a glowing orange desert landscape. This cut follows the color (and even implied hot temperature) of the tiny match to a massive desert. These kinds of cuts are aesthetically pleasing and can join shots together that might otherwise seem awkward.

Match cuts don't have to be between two static shots that are similar in composition or color. They can also match two movements that share direction or speed. For example, the end of Hitchcock's *North by Northwest* features Cary Grant pulling Eva Marie Saint up onto a ridge above Mount Rushmore after a dramatic chase scene. As he pulls her up, the film cuts to him performing the same action; only this time he's pulling her into the pullout bed of a train car. This type of match cut can obviously be used for humor

to make the move between the two scenes more interesting. In the case of *North by Northwest*, the match cut lets Hitchcock get away with the abrupt switch from an intense dramatic scene to comic/romantic scene and does away with the need to show in tedious detail what happens between the chase scene on the mountain and the obligatory happy ending in the train car.

Match cuts can be fun or thought-provoking, but they can also seem forced and they can be overly used. Remember, they call attention to the cut itself, so you should use them sparingly for greater effect.

Editing for Spatial Relationships

Einstein proved that time and space are not inseparable, and when editing, how you treat space will also affect the portrayal of time. The most common cinematic shorthand for establishing space—"start wide, get closer"—can be seen in just about every television sitcom after a commercial break. The scene starts with an "establishing shot" of the exterior of a house or street. *The Cosby Show, Seinfeld, The Drew Carey Show*—they all start with this kind of shot, which not only tells us which character's house we are entering, but often also reminds us which city we are in. Then we cut to a wide shot of the actual space where the scene takes place, such as the interior of an apartment. Here we can see the entire room, all the characters and where they are standing, as well as the doors, couches, walls, etc. As the characters interact and move, we cut to closer and closer shots, often ending up with intercut shots of individual characters. Think of it as a spatial zoom in, with cuts.

This is the standard form of spatial cutting because it gives the audience everything it needs to know. It quickly sets the stage, letting the viewer know where everyone in the scene is and how they are spatially related to each other from the beginning. Obviously, this is only one method of establishing space through editing, but it is so common, that it's important to see how and why it functions the way it does.

Often, a film will employ the reverse tactic, showing a few details and close-ups before revealing the whole space, pulling back rather than zooming in. Martin Scorsese does this in *Raging Bull*, where we see a quick montage of close-ups, like the handle of a coffee cup, that give us a more intimate, expressive feeling before revealing more. How space is revealed can strongly affect the emotional reaction of the audience, and how they experience the rest of the scene. Carl Dreyer's *The Passion of Joan of Arc* is shot almost entirely in close-ups of faces, so spatial relations between characters and their environment are more dislocated. This effect creates a sense of dislocation appropriate for the Joan of Arc story.

Editing for Rhythm

Editing based on rhythm is an increasingly popular editing form, especially with the dawn of nonlinear editing, which allows for shorter shots, more rapid-fire editing, and quickly trimmed edits.

What used to be almost completely in the realm of commercials, trailers, and music videos has now become a dominant style in feature films. This is partly because the technology makes fast, beat-driven editing easier, but also because more and more Hollywood directors cut their teeth on editing by making commercials and music videos (such as *The Rock's* Michael Bay, *Being John Malkovich's* Spike Jonze, and *Fight Club's* David Fincher). Many movies now have sequences that are edited by rhythm, meaning either they are cut to the beat of soundtrack music, or they create their own visual beat through the pacing of the editing of shots. Bob Fosse's film version of the musical *Cabaret* contains many sequences that are cut together to create a rhythmic pulse, imbuing a more visceral effect on the audience, in the same way that a live musical performance might.

One of the most famous and effective rhythmically edited sequences in cinema history is the shower scene of Hitchcock's *Psycho*, which features a series of several dozen rapid cuts, creating a disjointed rhythm that jerks with the squealing Bernard Hermann score and sends a disturbing chill through the audience.

Chapter 18: The Finished Product

Open the Final Cut Pro project file labeled Coney Island Memories. After it loads in Final Cut Pro, double-click the Chapter 18 sequence in the Browser and it will open in the Timeline.

In this chapter you will be combining the skills of the last 17 chapters to see how to put a finished work together. We have set up a completed film using multiple video and audio tracks, transitions, filters, motion, keyframes, audio-fades, and everything else we have talked about. However, there is no "correct" final edited version. We encourage you to play around with this sequence. Try adding your own edits. Adjust clip lengths, change the in and out music, or add different filters and effects. The possibilities are endless even in this short film.

If you get to a point where you do not like what you have done, you can always create a new sequence and start from scratch.

Every clip in the tutorial video for this chapter can be opened up, changed, moved around, and effects added. Since you've got a saved version on the DVD, feel free to pick through the cut. Look at the way the transitions function, the way the track hierarchy works, how the filters affect the shots. Try rearranging, adding new clips, or changing the B-roll. This is a space for experimentation, so try out anything you can think of.

Laying Down the Edits

Every film has unique characteristics, and thus its own process for creation. Whether you are making a commercial for a carpet company or a four-hour historical epic, all films start (after the footage is captured anyway) by sorting through the footage and laying down the clips in the Timeline. You can use any tools outside of Final Cut Pro to help you get organized and make initial structural decisions. Note cards can be an invaluable way of planning out a structure on paper first. You may be provided storyboards from the director to work from. And, as always, watching other films to see what has come before can give you inspiration.

For the tutorial, we followed a common documentary structure that mixes interviews with "B-roll" (imagery used to cut away from the main interview footage). This format is common in documentaries and news features. To select the clips to be used as A-roll, we looked for interviews where people shared an experience or memory about Coney Island and ordered them in a way that built the clips into a whole.

When creating a sequence that involves speaking interviews, it's often best to edit together the "story" narrative first by cutting together only the interview clips. Then you can add other imagery and effects. For *Coney Island Memories*, we previewed each interview clip in the Viewer. We reviewed the clips carefully and marked them to indicate particularly appropriate bits. We decided which ones were appropriate for a video on Coney Island memories, and which ones told a particularly interesting story. We also used markers (see *Using Markers with Log and Capture* in Chapter 4) to note which parts of the clip would be of most use, and added rough In and Out points to begin trimming the footage. (See *Editing Clips into the Timeline* in Chapter 6).

Ⓐ Add Marker

Ⓑ Set In Point

Ⓒ Set Out Point

Ⓓ Audio/Video In

Ⓔ Audio Out

Ⓕ Video Out

Next, bring the clips into the Timeline. Watch the clips closely and slowly rearrange them in different orders. In our film, after a lot of switching shot order, we arrived at a sequence of the interview shots that cut back and forth between a number of people, each shot adding a new story or impression of Coney Island. (See Chapter 6 for detailed steps on adding and moving your footage in the Timeline.)

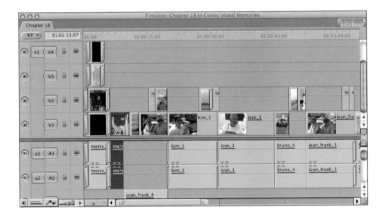

Once you've established the basic clip order, it is time to refine the trim or your clips. At first, when you pull down your clips, you may have already set In and Out points, but you usually want to fine-tune them in the sequence. After you have ordered each clip one after the other, a lot of trimming is necessary. Using the concepts discussed in Chapter 8, you need to trim the clips to remove pauses, extra words, unwanted sounds, and distracting camera movements. The clips will then cut from one to the other in a quick, snappy way, with no distracting video movement or audio noise. In our film, Ripple, Roll, Slip, and Slide edits were all used to fix these trims (see Chapter 8). Make no mistake, this takes a lot of time. You have to watch each In and Out between clips carefully, to find the exact fraction of a second where one clip should end and the next begin.

Ⓐ Out Point

Ⓑ In Point

Ⓒ Trim

Once you have your basic edits in place, you can add transitions to see how they will affect the flow of your video.

Adding the B-Roll

Once the "bed" of the video has been created (see previous section), it is time to add the B-roll. B-roll is any footage that cuts away from the main footage (the A-roll) to show other imagery. For example, when an anchorwoman is talking about a bank robbery, the image might cut away from her to video of the exterior shots of the bank or police on the scene, while her voice continues under the image. B-roll is useful to keep the audience interested and to allow for dynamic cutting when one person is talking. Generally, the B-roll will be placed onto a second (or even third or fourth) track in the Timeline.

In our film, we selected the B-roll of Coney Island based on what the interviewees were discussing. We then layered in and timed the supporting clips to help emphasize the points being made. Cutting a B-roll clip into the Timeline follows the same procedures as adding any other clip:

1. Bring an edited clip into the Timeline and place it roughly where you want it. For B-roll, it's best to create a second track so that you can lay it over the A-roll on the first track without deleting or disrupting the flow of the A-roll footage. See Chapter 6 for details on adding a blank track to the Timeline.

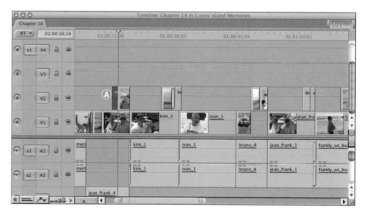

Ⓐ B-Roll: Placed on second video track.

2. Fine-tune the In and Out points of the B-roll shots either directly in the Timeline or by opening the clip in the Viewer. It's important to listen as well as watch to make sure the B-roll comes in at a moment that isn't awkward. For example, if you cut in a B-roll image only after a person speaks one or two words, it will feel as if they were cut off. Listen to the rhythm of speech and find a good moment in the cadence of speech to cut away (think musically!) and

also watch the camera work. You'll want to avoid cutting on quick movements like fast pans or zooms. Chapter 8 shows you how to use the various edit tools for adjusting the In and Out points.

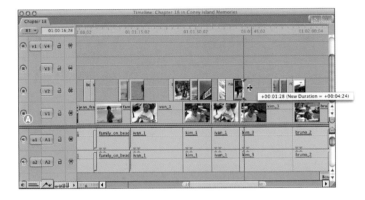

Ⓐ Show/Hide Track: Green indicates that the track is visible.

As we added B-roll on the second video track, the result was short montages of images that made rhythmic cuts over the interviews (see *Editing for Rhythm* earlier in this chapter). Remember that when you use B-roll, you're covering up the person who is

speaking, so it's best when they appear for the first time in the video not to cover them up with B-roll, because the viewer doesn't know who is talking yet. Of course, this isn't a hard rule, and if, for example, the B-roll features the person who is talking under the image, you can get away with starting with B-roll before cutting to the video of the person actually speaking.

What Is Continuity?

Continuity is the process by which a film keeps things such as lighting, movement, or object placement consistent between shots. You have certainly noticed in sloppily edited films that as a scene cuts back and forth, someone's cigarette gets longer and shorter, or a wine glass suddenly is full after being empty in the previous shot. Since many takes and angles of the same scene are taken, and these shots are taken over a period of time, it is often a difficult task for an editor to make sure that everything in the final version doesn't disrupt continuity. (The initial job belongs to a person on set whose task is to watch for continuity breaks. But things can slip by.) Breaks in continuity can occur when props are moved to different places, the lighting in a shot changes between takes (especially a problem when shooting outdoors), there are make-up inconsistencies, or anything else that could possibly be changed, moved, or altered between takes.

Adding Transitions

After you've created a rough cut of the film and added B-roll footage, you can add transitions between shots and audio. Adding transitions is a subjective judgment, of course, and as discussed in Chapter 10, many editors use transitions sparingly if at all. For our example video, we decided to add a few, such as one connecting the opening sequence to the opening B-roll imagery so as to create a bridge into the piece. We also used transitions to make a montage of B-roll play more smoothly over the dialogue.

Also, the final shot, that of the man with his children at Nathan's Hot Dogs, ends with a fade to black, signaling the end of the piece and keeping the video from halting abruptly. See Chapter 10 for more on adding transitions and fades to black.

Select the cut you want to add a transition to from the Timeline. Again, for most edits you will probably want to use a straight cut, where the clips simply go one to the next without any fanfare. However, you may decide that a straight cut is too abrupt for some cuts or that the imagery in the incoming and outgoing clips would be enhanced by a cross dissolve or other transition between the two. This will be especially true where the scene is changing or you want to indicate the passage of time.

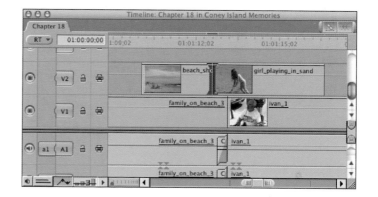

2. Select the transition you want to add from the Browser's Effect tab and drag it to the edit point or select Effects **>** Video **>** Dissolve **>** Cross Dissolve with the edit point highlighted. Remember, you can also control-click the edit itself in the Timeline to bring up a popup window that lets you add the default transition. The cross-dissolve is the most common (and also least cheesy) transitional effect.

3. If you want to make finer changes, adjust the transition in the Transition Editor. You can also lengthen or shorten the transition by dragging the edges of the transition in the Timeline.

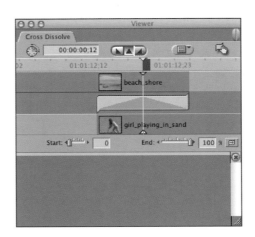

Adding Titles, Effects, and Filters

Adding effects is always one of the last things you should do as it's often easiest to place all your cuts, fine-tune the trim, and have everything lined up the way you want it before you start monkeying with effects. You can use the G4 real time effects feature and the QuickView tab (in the Tool Bench or accessible in the Tools pull down menu) to easily preview your effects before rendering.

 For our tutorial, we used a layered Photoshop file to create the opening title, and then applied a few effects to tint certain B-roll shots. Finally, in the closing "The End" shot, we used motion paths to animate several clips.

Create the title in a graphic editing program and then import it into Final Cut Pro (⌘+I). The title at the beginning of the sample film was imported from Photoshop, and it retains the layers from the Photoshop file (see Chapter 17 for details on importing images from Photoshop). This way, each layer comes in as a separate clip that you can manipulate independently in Final Cut Pro. A keyframed motion path creates a slow movement over the imagery, and we used a Luma Key filter (see Chapter 13 to create the dreamy double exposure of the merry-go-round. To get the double image, we placed the same clip on different tracks, one on top of the other, and slipped the top clip with the Slip edit tool so that the two clips didn't contain exactly the same media. When the Luma Key was added to the top clip, it created a strange double-image look that makes an interesting backdrop for the titles.

In the Browser, double-click on a clip you want to examine to open it in the Viewer; then open the clip's Filters tab.

Ⓐ Add/Delete Keyframe

Ⓑ Turn Filter On/Off

Ⓒ Reset Filter to Default Values

Look to see what filters we used and what their settings are. Try adjusting the settings to see how your changes affect the clip. For this video, we used a host of effects to create a more stylized feeling, using some of the effects to give the video an old, nostalgic glow. In one shot of the boardwalk, we used a tint and edge-feathering to create an image that hints at the look of early 20th century film.

To create this effect, we feathered each of the edges of the clip using the Crop tool in the Motion tab (see Chapter 14) and tinted the image using the Tint filter (see Chapter 11). We converted other shots to black and white with the Desaturate tool (see Chapter 11). The closing montage of clips used a host of effects, such as scale (in the Motion Control tab) and keyframed motion paths (see Chapter 15). This ending graphic uses a lot of different effects together to create a single, moving, graphics-intensive frame. Go to the Timeline to explore this section, and open up the clips and examine their settings. Studying these settings will give you a better idea of how we altered these effects and used them together to create the effect of the whole.

Open the Motion tab in the Viewer and see if any Motion Effects (such as scale or cropping) were used. If keyframes were used, look at the keyframe paths to see how they were set to create motion in the clip. Make changes to these settings and see how they affect the motion or dimensions of the clip. Remember, the Undo function is your friend. Use the ⌘+Z Undo shortcut key to quickly go back step by step to undo changes you make.

Once we had added and rendered the effects, we then mixed the audio so that the voices in the interview, then music, and background sounds were all kept at levels that were not too loud or soft, and so that the voices were always audible. Notice that sometimes keyframes were used to control volume (for example, at the moment when the first interview is heard) and that audio transitions are used at other times. We needed to use a number of audio transitions between clips that had vastly different audio levels. For example, the old man sitting down is in front of traffic, so the background levels on his audio were higher. To adjust for this, we lowered the overall audio level on his clips and added a cross-fade transition to smooth out the change in audio levels.

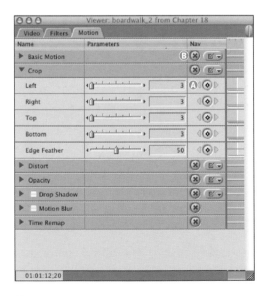

A Add/Delete Keyframe

B Reset Motion Attributes to Default Values

Adding the Musical Score

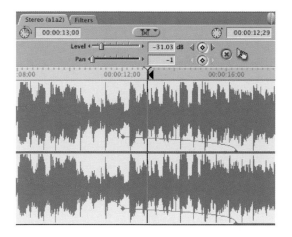

The music you choose to accompany your work is a crucial part of the message you are going to convey. Often, along with the initial images presented, the music at the opening will be the first impression the viewer (listener) has of your piece. If the music is light and energetic, the viewer immediately expects to see images that reflect this tone, and if it is dark and ominous, the viewer has entirely different expectations. In our movie, we chose a song called, appropriately enough, "Bounce," which uses

a Beatlesque guitar intro that sets a jolly carefree tone that worked well with the material. In addition, the song provided a nice guitar solo that we used to transition from the final interview into the final clip. You may also want to use the new Soundtrack software that ships with Final Cut Pro 4 to create your own musical score.

If your audio file is not already in your Browser, choose File > Import > File (⌘+I). This can be direct from a CD, DVD, or your hard drive (see Chapter 16). For our tutorial example, we imported the file Bounce and placed it in the Resources folder.

Final Cut Pro can import a variety of audio formats including QuickTime, MP3, and even files directly from an audio CD. However, using compressed formats like MP3 with "uncompressed" formats will cause trouble in integrating it into your video.

After the music file has been imported, it will appear as a clip (with a speaker icon) in your project file in the Browser and can be manipulated like any other clip. Double-click on the clip to open it in the Viewer.

3   In the Viewer, set In and Out points for the music in the opening piece. You will probably have to go back and forth through the audio and video several times to find the exact spot to begin and/or end the music. You can also put different parts of the music under the video to see how it plays with the image, and then use the ⌘+Z Undo shortcut to take it away if it doesn't work.

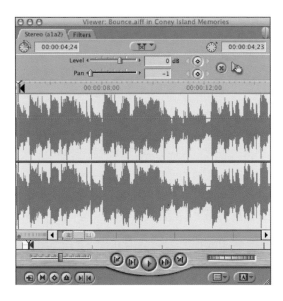

After you identify the portion of the music you want to use, lay the audio file under the beginning of the movie. You will probably need to create a new audio track under your other audio tracks (see *Adding Blank Tracks in the Timeline* in Chapter 6).

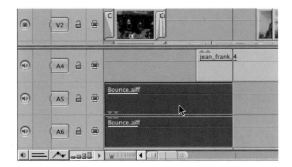

5   Fade the music down into the first interview clip, using keyframes (see *Using Keyframes with Audio* in Chapter 16). You'll need to play back the segment and listen to how the new levels sound. Watch the Audio Meter to make sure the levels are not peaking.

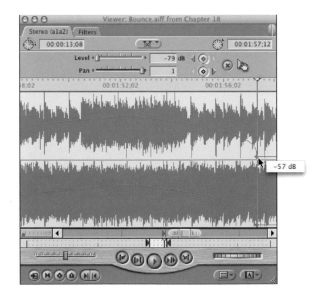

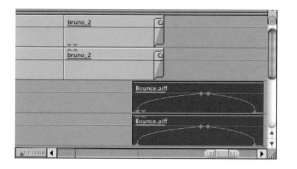

6.   To create the exit music, we wanted to use a guitar solo from the center of the song. So, to move that section of the audio track to the end of the sequence, we used the Razor Blade tool to cut out that part of the song and then placed that newly defined clip over the end of the sequence, bridging the final scene and the exiting title. Finally we faded up the music, paying careful attention not to drown out the final interviewee's comments with the music.

Saving the Finished Product

After you have finished your film, you will want to export it as a Final Cut Pro movie or a QuickTime file (both file formats can be read by QuickTime). Exporting creates a single media file that contains the entire sequence with all filters, keyframes, effects, etc., in the finished sequence without the need of rendering. Exporting a sequence as a movie can be very helpful because it creates a single media file that you can use as clip in any other Final Cut Pro sequence.

You can also take the file and back it up onto an external hard drive for archival purposes. If you've made a video that you want to show at festivals or sell to a distributor, see the Resources appendix on the book's web page (www.sybex.com) for a discussion of getting your video seen by an audience outside of your friends. (See Chapters 20 and 21 for discussions of printing to video and web compression.)

Open the sequence you want to export in the Timeline. If you don't want to export the whole sequence, you can set In and Out points in the Timeline to define which part to include when exporting.

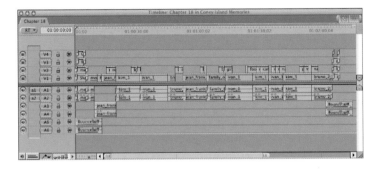

Choose File > Export and choose either Final Cut Pro Movie or QuickTime movie. In our experience, choosing Final Cut Pro Movie yields the best quality, and it's compatible with

QuickTime anyway. Final Cut Pro Movies also base their export settings on the sequence's Timeline settings.

Name the file (use a .mov suffix to keep things clear), designate where to save it to on the hard drive, and click OK. You can choose to export it with different quality settings, so choose the setting you want, but you'll most likely want highest quality (see Chapter 21). Your sequence will be exported into a new single media file and saved on your drive.

Knowing When You Are Finished

First, make sure you've solved any technical problems, such as poorly exposed video, audio jumps between cuts, or awkward video edits. Make sure your audio levels are set correctly throughout the piece, and use keyframes to make any necessary adjustments. If you're not sure about the content, show the piece to friends or someone you trust to judge and comment on your work. Getting a second or third opinion, even by someone who is not an editor, can give you a fresh perspective.

Using an Exported Sequence in Final Cut Pro

Exporting a sequence into a movie erases all cuts and individual clips, squashing everything into one big clip. Not only can you play an exported file in QuickTime, you can also import it (⌘+I) back into Final Cut Pro as a single clip and use that in other sequences. The advantage is you won't need to render anything in the imported clip to see it play in real time, even when you use it in another sequence. Remember, though, that you also can't make any changes to the original cut once it has been made into a movie without changing the original project file and exporting it again.

You can also achieve the same effect by printing the sequence to video and then capturing what you've just printed to video back into Final Cut Pro as a single clip.

Adding a Global Effect to the Finished Product

This technique is particularly useful if you decide to add an effect to an entire sequence; for example, if you want to make the entire video black and white. First export the sequence as a movie (or print it to video and recapture as a single clip). You can then import the movie or clip into a new sequence and apply the across-the-board effect over this new single clip. This will save you a lot of rendering time if you have many other effects within the individual clips of the original sequence.

Gigantic (A Tale of Two Johns), Documentary

"Everybody dies frustrated inside and that is beautiful."

They Might Be Giants

The two Johns of They Might Be Giants (John Flansburgh and John Linnell) started making surreal (and often beautiful) music in 1982. TMBG (as they are often called by fans) has released eight studio albums (including a kids album), numerous videos, and scored a surprise hit and Grammy with "Boss of Me," the theme song to the television show *Malcolm in the Middle*. Their music is at once unique, yet surprisingly familiar, friendly and a little malevolent, childish and amazingly intelligent.

© Copyright 2002 Bonfire Films of America. Photo Credit: Yon Thomas

Capturing such an enigmatic group in a documentary is no small feat, but director A. J. Schnack took on the project because he was "impressed by both their longevity and their true 'do it yourself spirit,' as well as their persistence in continually finding ways to get their music out, whether they were supported by a major label structure or (more often) not."

Gigantic tells the story of They Might Be Giants (who get their name from an obscure movie with George C. Scott playing an escaped mental patient convinced that he is Sherlock Holmes) through performance, animation, videos, and hilarious commentaries from friends and fans.

A. J. and producer Shirley Moyers conducted more than 50 interviews in New York, Los Angeles, San Francisco, and Chicago for the film, and also shot footage in Washington, DC, London, Baltimore, and the Johns' hometown of Lincoln, Massachusetts. "We didn't run into major problems while we were shooting because we had a lot of production experience and most of our setups were pretty contained; plus folks tended to have a lot of love for the band, so lots of people pitched in to be involved with the project."

In fact, TMBG has several fans who were willing to do more than help out behind the camera, including appearances by The Pixies' Frank Black and This American Life's Ira Glass. In addition, A. J. had actors Janeane Garofalo, Michael McKean, Andy Richter, and Harry Shearer recite the band's lyrics for parts of the film. The film also features appearances by Conan O'Brien, Jon Stewart, Joe Franklin, and actor/director Josh Kornbluth.

The documentary is filled with interviews and behind-the-scenes footage, which according to A. J. "required us to be pretty mobile." To stay mobile A. J. and team worked with Sony PD-150 cameras, which he comments are "great because they require very little light." The interviews were shot using China Ball lights on low dimmers and the sound was recorded to DAT via lavaliere microphone and boom simultaneously.

Despite never having worked with Final Cut Pro before, A. J.'s first editor had his own Final Cut Pro setup. After adding a second editor, they began working at Dr. Rawstock in Los Angeles (www.drrawstock.com) using a mixture of internal and external LaCie drives to store everything. "I ended up learning FCP purely from being in the room. I've never taken a class or read a manual, so it's hard for me to say. But I was pleased that I could learn it so fast and that I could figure out stuff on my own."

The film was released theatrically by Cowboy Pictures in over 50 cities with a DVD from Plexifilm to follow. It also appeared in numerous film festivals and won the 2002 Chlotrudis Award for Best Documentary. For more details about the film check out their website www.giganticfilm.com.

Part Five:
After the Editing Is Done

The editing is done and your film is complete, but you won't win any Oscars with it parked on your hard drive. Now you are ready to archive the final product and transfer it to the medium of your choice for distribution. In the final chapters, we'll examine different ways you can output your project from Final Cut Pro, including printing to videotape and compressing your project for the Web. But first, it's important to clean up your project and organize your final media files to free up hard drive space and create an archived version using Final Cut Pro's Media Manager.

19

Managing
Your Media

Even if you have an array of 80GB hard drives, there never seems to be enough space to hold all of the media you will need to create your film. Video seems to abhor a vacuum and will eventually fill every last byte of space you have at your disposal. The Media Manager will help you deal with the space situation. Introduced in Final Cut Pro 2, it has been redesigned in Final Cut Pro 4 with more features and greater reliability. With the Media Manager, you can duplicate media or delete unused media to free up hard disk space. This is great in a crunch when your hard disk is filled up, and you have to capture more media.

Overview

> "It is not through space that I must seek my dignity, but through the management of my thought."
>
> Blaise Pascal

The Media Manager gives you exact control over the media files referenced by the clips in your project. These are the files, housed in your hard disk, that contain the actual audio and video information. The clips in your project merely reference these media files; they are not the same thing. The source material is never actually altered when you edit in Final Cut Pro. The fact that DV editing is nondestructive is what gives you the freedom to experiment, but it also means that footage tends to accumulate until you take steps to manage it.

This chapter shows how you can use the Media Manager to duplicate media files on the hard drive for archiving or use in a new project and also how to remove the parts of a media file that are not currently being used in a sequence to save valuable hard drive space. We'll also look at a feature of Final Cut Pro 4's Media Manager that allows you to change the compression of your media files.

When you launch the Media Manager and instruct it to delete unused files, this Final Cut Pro tool searches through the sequence you've selected and identifies all the media that is used in that sequence. It then searches through all the original source media files on your hard disk that are referenced by the clips in the sequence

and deletes the parts of the media files not being used. The Media Manager may need to split the original source media files into smaller files, keeping the media being used in the sequence and automatically deleting unused portions. One caution: Since this affects the original media, if you are using the footage in another sequence or another project file, this operation will also affect those uses of the clips. You can set buffers, known as *handles*, so that the Media Manager leaves a designated number of seconds before and after the media being used. Then, if you want to make minor edits or trims, you will still have some room to do so.

However, it is important that you not delete any footage until you feel very comfortable with your project and you are sure you will not be making major scene changes. Unlike editing the clips, this *will* change the original media on your hard drive, so make sure that you will not need any of the footage you are getting rid of, and that you still have at least the original source tape to recapture in case of an emergency.

While this is the most common use of the Media Manager, and probably the most helpful, you can also use it to duplicate media onto another disk, which is great when you are archiving a project. The Media Manager will copy the selected sequence and all relevant media files into a new project file to a designated location on your hard disk. You can then burn these files to CD or DVD for offline backup storage. You can also choose whether to have the media clips moved in their entirety or have the Media Manager delete unused portions of the clips and copy only the portions of the footage that made it into the final film.

You may also decide that you need to change the codec (such as DV or OfflineRT) mid-project. For example, you may have captured all your footage at the full-resolution DV codec but then need to make the files smaller to edit on a laptop. You could use the Media Manager to change the codec of the media files to OfflineRT, making the files much smaller and more manageable in the field. Also, when you move media files from one disk to another (or to a different location on the same disk), Final Cut Pro may lose track of the connection between clips in a project and the underlying media files. When that happens, you need to restore the connection before you can work with your clips—a process known as *reconnecting* the media. We'll do that in the last section of this chapter.

The main thrust of this chapter is organization, which is especially crucial for large projects with a lot of footage. When you're finished with a project and need a record or archived copy, it's important to create one without leaving stray files everywhere. If you're going to create an archive of your works, we recommend buying external hard drives (50–60GB at the minimum) and making copies of your projects and media files. Set up a system of organized folders for each project, with subfolders inside for the media clips

and the render files. Use the Media Manager to cut down on unused footage once you are done. Another way to archive a project using minimal hard drive space is to delete all the media files and render files but keep the project file. When you open the file, everything in the project will be offline, but by using batch capture, you can quickly recapture everything from the original source tapes and Final Cut Pro will realign everything to match your edit. (Of course, this is possible only if you still have access to your source tapes, but it's a great space-saving method of archiving.)

Cleaning Up after Yourself

You will be reusing the Chapter 18 sequence with this chapter to practice cleaning up and archiving a project using the built-in Final Cut Pro Media Manager. Open the Final Cut Pro project file labeled Coney Island Memories. After it loads in Final Cut Pro, double-click the Chapter 18 sequence in the Browser and it will open in the Timeline.

Deleting Unused Material

 You've crammed your hard drive with media and at the last minute you need to capture new footage. Unfortunately, there's not enough space on the hard drive for it! What to do? You can use the Media Manager to go through and delete unused parts of the source media files. This frees up much-needed hard drive space and lets you keep working. Keep in mind, though, that it changes the original media on your hard drive and, unless you have the original source material somewhere else, unused portions of the footage will be gone forever. You can choose to clean up a single clip, a selection of clips, an entire sequence of clips, or even a selection of sequences using the Media Manager.

1. Select the clip, clips, sequence, sequences, or project that you want to manage from either the Browser or the Timeline. Whereas selecting a clip from the Timeline to edit in the Viewer affects only that one instance, selecting a clip from the Timeline for

media management will affect all uses of that clip, not only in all sequences, but in any project using that clip.

With the media selected, open the Media Manager window by either selecting File > Media Manager or control-clicking the selected media and selecting Media Manager from the popup window that appears.

In this example, we'll delete unused material from the Chapter 18 project.

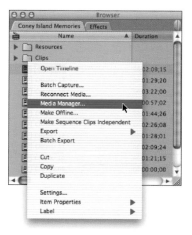

2. In the Media Manager window you will immediately notice the two green bars in the Summary area. The first bar represents the size of the selected media before cleanup, and the second shows the projected size based on the Media settings you will choose in Step 3; it changes as you adjust those settings.

If you are deleting media, as we will be doing here, the second bar should be shorter. Mouse over the bars (which will highlight when you move over them), and you'll see a detailed report of the file size, location, and playing time. In addition, at the top of this area, there is a brief overview of what will be done to the media based on the options selected in this window.

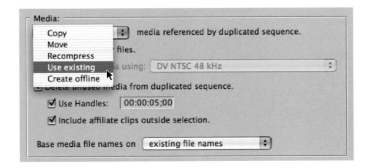

ⓐ Summary: Overview of the current state of the media (original) and what will happen to it based on the Media settings; automatically updated when those settings are changed.

ⓑ Media: Settings for how the selected media should be processed.

ⓒ Project: Options to duplicate selected media and/or create a new project file. This is especially useful for archiving a project.

ⓓ Media Destination: Select a hard-drive location for saving the cleaned-up media.

3. To delete unused media, select Use Existing from the pop-up window in the Media area. This lets Final Cut Pro know that you want to delete media from the existing media files, including the render files. Make sure that Delete Unused Media from Selected Sequence is checked.

Alternatively, if you check the Duplicate Selected Items option and are placing this in a new project, the option will read Delete Unused Media from Duplicated Items.

Click in the box next to Use Handles and specify how much footage (in minutes, seconds, and frames) you want to preserve before and after each clip. This is always a good idea unless you are absolutely certain that your current edits are perfect and that you will never need to adjust them again. We recommend leaving at least 5 to 10 seconds for handles.

4. If you simply want to delete footage from the existing media, uncheck Duplicate Selected Sequence and Place into a New Project. If you want to archive your project, see *Archiving Your Project* later in this chapter.

Because you selected Use Existing, your updated files will automatically be saved in their existing location, so you do not need to select a Media Destination.

The option Base Media File Names On... has two choices in the pop-up menu: Existing Files Names and Clip Names. The name of a clip can be different than the name of the media file it refers to on the hard drive, so here you can delineate which name you want to use as the media files are managed.

Once you are satisfied with your settings, click OK.

5. The Media Manager will first ask you to confirm that you want to modify your media; click Continue. Then it will go through your hard disk and shorten or split up the original media files so that they contain just the media used in the selected sequence (with any handles you've specified). If the Media Manager finds media files that are not used in the selected sequence but are referenced by other clips in other sequences in your project, it will alert you to this by displaying an Additional Items

Found dialog box. If you want to make sure that these clips do not go offline, click Add. Removing unused media can take a while for larger files, so allow some time to do this. You'll be given an estimated time until the operation is done. A fever bar reading "Processing Files" will show you the progress, and you can click Cancel at any time to stop the processing at that point. However, this will not bring back clips that have already been processed, and you may cause some clips to go offline.

Going on the Road with OfflineRT

Final Cut Pro 4's Media Manager has a very handy function: the ability to change the codec (the compression) of your media while you are editing it. Suppose, for example, that you are editing a large project in the editing suite, with media filling up numerous hard drives. Then you need to take your laptop on the road and continue editing the footage. There's no way you can bring all those external hard drives with you, but you can use the Media Manager to change your footage's codec to OfflineRT, making your project and all those media files portable.

To do this, select all the items in your project that you want to recompress, and open the Media Manager by selecting File > Media Manager or control-clicking the selected items and choosing Media Manager. Then choose Recompress from the Media pull-down menu. You can now choose the new codec (in this case, OfflineRT NTSC or PAL) or even create a custom codec. You can use the Duplicate Selected Items/Sequence and Place into a New Project to create a separate project with the OfflineRT clips, so you won't lose your full-resolution DV codec media files.

Archiving Your Project

If you are archiving your video to a different hard drive, burning to CD-ROM, or backing up to removable media such as a tape drive or Iomega Peerless drive, you can use the Media Manager to create a new project file with the sequence and referenced media files all together. It is best to do this after the project is finished and you need to clear your main hard drive for the next project. However, if you are working on an extremely long project, you may also want to perform weekly or even daily backups of your project as a precaution against hard drive failure so that you lose no more than a week or a day of work (believe us, it happens).

Select the sequence or sequences you want to archive in the Browser. To archive an entire project, select the Browser, and then select Edit > Select All (⌘+A).

With the sequence or sequences you want to archive selected, Open the Media Manager window by selecting File > Media Manager or by control-clicking the Sequence icon in the Browser and selecting Media Manager from the popup menu.

In the Media Manager window, select Copy from the Media pull-down menu.

If you want to keep your archive files as small as possible, uncheck the box marked Include Render Files and check Delete Unused Media from Duplicated Sequences. This will remove media only from the duplicated file, not from the original files, allowing you to create a leaner archive.

If you are removing unused media, make sure to add handles to your clips. This adds a specific number of seconds of unused media around the used media, giving you some maneuvering room if you need to tweak your edit. This is highly recommended, and you should leave at least 5 seconds to be safe.

Check the Duplicate Selected Items/Sequence and Place into a New Project box. This creates a totally new project with the managed media.

3. Click the Browse button to choose the location you want this new project to be saved. You can back up to any hard drive or media storage device (such as a Jaz drive) connected to this machine or on its network.

If you are duplicating to an external hard drive, make sure it is hooked up properly and that your computer recognizes it. Remember, this creates a new project file and corresponding media files for the sequence you selected. Final Cut Pro alerts you if there is not enough room in the destination drive.

4. Once you are satisfied with the settings in the Media Manager, click OK to begin archiving.

The media files will be saved into a new folder called "Media" within your destination folder.

If you want to archive to DVD-ROM, you'll need to use the Media Manager to copy the files, and then burn the archive to disc outside of Final Cut Pro with software like Toast.

5. You'll be prompted to enter a name for the new project file, and you can change the destination folder and hard drive. Click Save.

Final Cut Pro alerts you if there is not enough room in the destination folder for this new project. Assuming you've planned correctly and there is enough room, your new project will be created with all the media files in a new folder.

The new project should now open and the clips inside should play correctly, independently from the original project, clips, and sequences. If you did not check Include Render Files, you will have to render everything in the sequence.

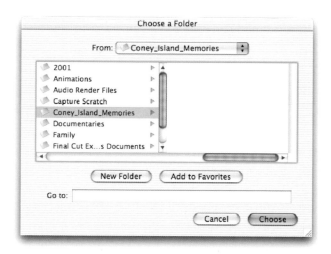

Reconnecting Media

Final Cut Pro always needs to know the location of the media files referenced by your clips in a project. If you move media files between folders or delete them from the disk, the program's reference information about those files will no longer be accurate. When this happens, the clips and the original source material are said to be "disconnected"—the clips in your project file no longer know where their source media files are located. These clips will revert to being offline, a state represented by a red screen reading "Media Offline" in the Viewer or Canvas, by a red slash through the clip in the Browser, and by a white clip in the Timeline. You will need to restore the connection using the Reconnect tool.

For example, when you load the DVD tutorial files for this book into your hard drive, you may have to reconnect the media, since the clips in the Tutorial project file may not be able to find the actual media files. This is because you will have moved them into your hard drive from the DVD.

If a project file has offline media, Final Cut Pro will inform you when you load that project. It will give you the option to immediately try to reconnect them by clicking the Reconnect button. If you instead click the OK button, the clips will remain offline.

You can also manually reconnect clips by highlighting them and then following these instructions.

1. Select the clip(s) you want to reconnect by highlighting them in the Browser or in the Timeline. Remember that offline clips in the Browser will appear with a red slash through them. You

can also select a sequence in the Browser to reconnect all the clips in that sequence. If you don't select anything here, the following steps will do a full reconnect of the open project.

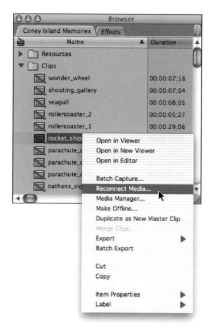

2. Select File > Reconnect Media or control-click the selected clip in the Browser and select Reconnect Media from the pop-up menu.

3. A dialog box will pop up, asking you to select the kind of media you want to reconnect. You can choose Offline, Render, or Online depending on what you have highlighted. Clicking Offline will reconnect all the offline clips to their referenced media. The

Render option will reconnect render files that have become disconnected. (See the sidebar *Where Are Render Files Stored?*) The Online option reconnects a clip to its media file, even if it is already attached. This allows you to change a connection if, for example, a media file becomes corrupted and you need to connect the referencing clip to a new, clean version of the file. Check the Select Files Manually box if you want to find the files yourself and not have Final Cut Pro search for them.

After you have set your options, Click OK.

4. Use the Open dialog box to find the missing media file on your hard drive or any connected drive. You can choose to show only files that match the name of the clip; use this option if you are reconnecting files that were simply moved to a different folder. Final Cut Pro will search the drives for the file and give you the closest match it can find. If this is the correct file, click Select. You can also check Reconnect All Files in Relative Path, which will automatically reconnect all files in the same folder.

This dialog box will continue to reappear until all the media files have been reconnected with their clip referents.

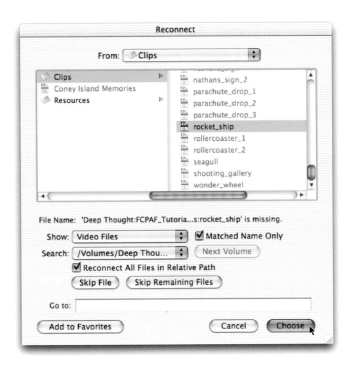

5. When all your clips have been reconnected, the red slash will vanish from the clip icon and you should be able to play your sequence through with all the clips online, and with video and audio information intact. Remember that if your media files have been deleted and do not exist on the hard drive, you cannot reconnect them. You must either bring these media files onto that hard drive from another source or recapture the footage.

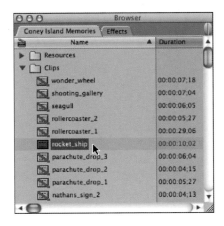

Where Are Render Files Stored?

In Chapter 9 we looked at creating and managing render files, but it is worth reviewing that topic here. When you render a clip, you create a separate file that contains all the information Final Cut Pro has generated so that the clip can play in real time with the rendered properties. For example, if you render a clip with a Desaturate filter on it to make it black and white, a file is saved onto the hard drive that contains the new black-and-white information for the clip. These files are saved in a folder marked Render Files (there's also a folder for audio render files), which Final Cut Pro creates automatically. The location of this folder is based on your Scratch Disk settings.

When you move files around, on, or between hard drives, the render files become disconnected from the clips. To fix this, you'll need to use the Reconnect Media function, check the Render Files box in the Reconnect Options dialog, and follow the instructions for reconnecting clips.

Recapturing OfflineRT Footage to Restore Online Quality

If you've been editing in Final Cut Pro 4 with the OfflineRT feature (see Chapter 5), then eventually you'll need to replace your low-quality footage with the online-quality (high-grade) footage before you output to tape, the web, or DVD. This process is a simple two-part operation.

1. Select your OfflineRT clips in the Browser. You can use the ⌘ key while clicking to select multiple clips, or select the folder containing those clips to select all of them quickly.

2. Press Shift+D to bring up the Make Offline window. You can also select clips and then select Modify > Make Offline.

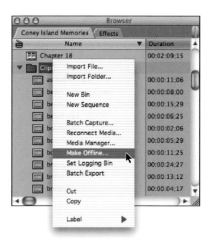

3. A window will ask what you want to do with the existing media these clips are attached to. Select whichever option best suits your needs. If you are low on disk space, it is probably best to delete them from the disk. Click OK.

4. The clip(s) will now appear in the Browser, marked as offline (notice the red slash through each icon). Follow the instructions in Chapter 5's *Batch Capture* section to recapture your clips from the original source material, making sure to change the Capture settings from OfflineRT to an online format.

Once the clips have been recaptured, they will be reinserted into your edited sequences at online quality and you are now ready to output a beautiful, high-resolution version of your project. You should change your sequence settings to reflect the new codec (⌘+O).

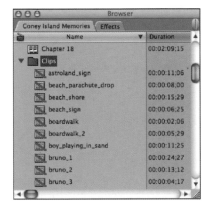

Using the Media Manager to Prepare to Recapture OfflineRT

Although the previous process is the simplest way to recapture your media at high quality, it is often useful to use the Media Manager to set up a copy of your sequences in order to preserve the original OfflineRT version. This simple operation uses the Media Manager to duplicate your sequences in conjunction with the batch capture function, explained in Chapter 5, to create a complete copy of your project with all clips offline. You can then recapture the clips using the original footage to create a final version ready for output. Thus, the original version, with OfflineRT clips, is still available and can be worked on to make changes.

1. Select your OfflineRT media from the Browser, and then open the Media Manager by selecting File > Media Manager. You will be using the Media Manager to duplicate your sequence(s), allowing you to keep a backup of your original edits.

2. In the Media Manager window, select Create Offline from the Media pull-down menu, which will disconnect the clips from the OfflineRT media so that you can recapture the media at high quality.

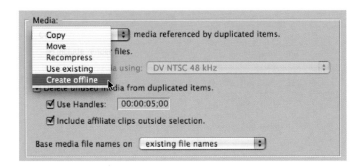

3. Select DV NTSC 48kHz or DV PAL 48kHz from the Set Sequence To menu. This will automatically apply the settings of that codec to the online footage you're about to recapture.

4. To kill two birds with one stone and also delete unused media from your hard disk, click the Delete Unused Media option.

5. Click OK. You'll be asked to name your new (duplicate) project and assign where on the disk you want to save it.

6. Open the new duplicate project. All of the clips will be there, but will be offline. Follow the instructions in Chapter 5's *Batch Capture* section to recapture your clips from the original source material. The Capture Settings should now be set to whatever option you selected in Step 3.

Once the clips have been recaptured, the clips will be reinserted into your edited sequences at online quality and you will be ready to output a beautiful, high-resolution version of your project.

Oxygen Media, TV Innovator

Oxygen Media is a cable network and Internet platform that runs programming and interactive new media that serve the interests of women. Founded in 1998 by Geraldine Laybourne, Marcy Carsey, Tom Werner, Caryn Mandabach, and Oprah Winfrey, the 24-hour cable network features animation, music, talk, health, comedy, movies, and sports. But as anyone knows, launching a successful cable network is a vast undertaking—requiring hefty investment, good programming, savvy marketing, and minimizing production costs.

To help accomplish these goals, Oxygen Media did a bold thing: the new channel invested in the new, non-industry-standard editing software from Apple, Final Cut Pro. Joseph Maidenberg, the director of training at the network, describes why this choice was made.

"We felt that Final Cut Pro could offer us an economic solution to our desire to produce huge amounts of original programming at affordable prices. The DV camera, with its intimacy and access, was a perfect match for Oxygen. DV was a natural companion to Final Cut Pro, which was inexpensive, had no hardware dependencies, and was immediately compatible with DV." Oxygen is also an Apple beta test site for Final Cut Pro.

Oxygen assigns a number of shooter-producers, who make 3–5 minute segments that are then usually rolled into studio shows. Most of this fieldwork is shot with the Sony PD150 mini-DV camera. What's unusual about Oxygen's production process is that many of these shooter-producers also log and make rough cuts of their own pieces before they're passed off. As the director of training, Maidenberg teaches Final Cut Pro classes for shooter-producers, to familiarize them with the editing process. "My position at Oxygen is a unique one, as Oxygen is striving to spread wide the usage of Final Cut Pro in our production process." He further explains this process. "By having a large number of logging/rough-cut stations—mostly iMacs loaded with RAM, a 75GB IBM Deskstar internal drive, external FireWire drives, and Final Cut Pro—shooter-producers have more control over the final look and feel of their pieces. This way, we are able to distribute the labor more efficiently, rather than overburdening our hard-working assistant editors."

For Oxygen's producers and editors, using Final Cut Pro can often be an advantage, as Maidenberg explains. "Considering that a home-based Final Cut Pro system is usually within their financial grasp, they can expand their own operations without taking out a loan for $50,000." Because of this limited production cost, Oxygen can provide more work flexibility for its producers. "A lot of our producers who own their own computers at home use Final Cut Pro there to complete projects."

Combining 14 online Final Cut Pro editing suites with a host of well-equipped iMacs for rough cuts, Oxygen is able to push through its large amount of original programming. Its online suites come super-equipped with top-of-the-line machinery and functionality. "An edit room will usually have between 100GB and 300GB of storage on RAID-based SCSI drives—about half are Medea VideoRaid and half VideoRaid RT—formatted with Atto Dual Channel 80/160 LVD or Adaptec SCSI cards for the G4. Some setups also make use of a JNI fiber card to connect to our 2 terabyte Storage Area Network. Each room comes with a Sony DSR-40 DVCAM/mini-DV deck for DV captures over FireWire, and a Sony BVW-A500 Digital Betacam deck for analog captures over Aurora Igniter with Component I/O and Breakout Box. A few rooms have the Sony BVW-75 Beta-SP instead of Digital Betacam. Each analog deck employs the GeeThree Stealth Serial Port for Timecode control." Regarding his favorite tricks on Final Cut Pro, Maidenberg emphasizes that "one cannot stress how much the well-designed contextual menus (Ctrl+click) make life easier for me as an editor. My favorite trick is to use the Razor Blade tool to cut a clip just before I am about to add some opacity keyframes, so that the entire clip does not need to be rendered." But perhaps Maidenberg's favorite aspect of the program isn't technical at all. "Final Cut Pro is a great program, and part of a great media revolution that, I hope, is putting production tools in the hands of the ordinary person."

Oxygen is available in many areas on cable and is also online at www.oxygen.com.

20 Printing to Video

You've finished the final version of your video. You've added the effects, transitions, and movement. You've mixed the audio and you've gone over the sequences again and again to make sure you've got everything right. You're almost done. After a video has been edited, you want it to be seen, of course. Unless you plan to distribute your video *only* on DVD or via the Internet, you'll want to export your film to videotape—to record the edit made in Final Cut Pro onto a mini-DV tape, a VHS tape, Beta-SP, etc. It can then be broadcast on television or played on a VCR. This chapter will help you put your project on tape so that you can send it out into the world.

Overview

> *"This film is apparently meaningless, but if it has any meaning it is doubtless objectionable."*
>
> British Board of Film Censors

As long as your creation remains on your computer, it will be hard to show off. You need to export it either to videotape or to a digital file so that it can be saved to a CD or DVD, or uploaded to the Internet. In this chapter we will focus on exporting your work to tape; we'll cover compression for other formats in the next chapter.

When you "print" to video, you send the video and audio signal from your computer over a FireWire cable (or through an analog capture card if you are recording directly to analog) to your deck while it is in record mode. In Final Cut Pro, you have two options. The simplest method is to play your sequence in the Timeline with the cables set correctly so that the signal fed into your reference monitor is also feeding into a deck that is set to record. You also can use the more involved Print to Video function, which allows you to create color bars (a standard color and tone reference) and to add a "slate" (a text slug) at the beginning with introductory text.

While the Print to Video option is the obvious choice if you need to add color bars and a slate quickly, many editors have found it easier—and actually more reliable—to just play the sequence in the Timeline and record this signal directly to the tape. Some editors have found that this reduces the chance for dropped frames (meaning as the video records, a frame here and there is

lost, causing the picture to subtly stutter). Either method provides basically the same result—your video is recorded to a videotape that you can play in other decks and dub more copies from.

Of course, you will need to have your hardware and cables correctly put together. If you follow the setup described in Chapter 1 for FireWire, you already have your cables correctly hooked up. If you are using an analog capture card or a media converter, you'll need to switch your video and audio cables so that they input into the analog deck and output from the capture card or media converter. Refer to that chapter to see how to make the connection, for either an analog capture card or a deck connected through FireWire. The only main difference now is that the deck, whether it is analog connected through a capture card or digital connected via FireWire, is now recording from your computer instead of sending to it.

Once you've recorded to video, the video is ready to be seen by other people and sent out for broadcast, home use, festivals, office use—the list is endless. On our Web site (`www.webbedenvironments.com/fcp`) you can find an appendix of useful resources and tips for getting your video seen.

Output to Tape

For this chapter you will again use the Chapter 18 sequence, to practice printing a short film to videotape. You will also need a video deck connected to your computer to record the footage. Open the Final Cut Pro project file labeled Coney Island Memories. After it loads in Final Cut Pro, double-click the Chapter 18 sequence in the Browser and it will open in the Timeline.

Preparing to Record

The easiest way to output your project to video is using a FireWire cable to output directly onto DV tape. In a nutshell, your setup (see Chapter 1) should look like this: FireWire cable connecting the computer to the DV deck or camera. You can also have the FireWire cable hooked up to a media converter box if you are printing to an analog source like VHS. If you are using a capture card, make sure the audio and video cables are connected between the card and the analog deck and are set to input to the analog deck.

Once you've got all of this set up, you're almost ready to go. Before you start, though, let's make sure your settings in Final Cut Pro are correct. As always, first check to make sure that your cable connections are secure and set correctly.

1. Open up the Audio/Video Settings window by selecting Final Cut Pro **>** Audio/Video Settings. Open the A/V Devices tab and review the settings. You will see two pop-up menus in this tab.

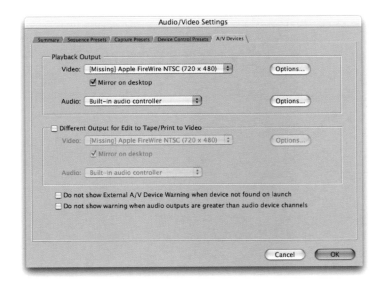

Playback Output Choose the method you want to use to view clips and sequences during any playback, such as a deck with monitor hooked up with a FireWire cable This should already be set to match your system setup (i.e., FireWire or a specific capture card). If your deck is not hooked up correctly, you will see "[Missing] Apple FireWire" in the list. Be sure to turn off the Mirror on Desktop function. Leaving this on will inevitably drop frames during a Print to Video session.

Different Output for Edit to Tape or Print to Video Unless you've got a different setup for printing to video than you did for capturing it, you should keep this option turned off, and the video will be recorded along the same path (FireWire, analog capture card, etc.) as it was captured.

Printing to an Analog Deck

If you are using an analog capture card, you will need to have your audio and video cables going directly from your capture card to the analog deck. You may possibly use a serial cable like the GeeThree serial port or the Griffin Technology Gport if you're running with device control. With this system, you're set to print to your analog deck.

The only change you may need to make is if you're printing to an analog deck from your DV deck or camera rather than directly from a capture card. Most cameras and decks act as simple media converters and can send an analog signal from the deck out—that's how we are able to view the video in the reference monitor while it is recording. If you want to record to a VHS tape, for example, you can simply switch the video and audio outputs from the reference monitor to a VHS VCR. You can use this method with the Sony media converter box, a DV deck, and most DV cameras. You can then hook cords sending the video and audio signals from the VCR to the reference monitor so that you don't lose the picture.

---

2. Click OK to close the Audio/Video Settings window. Play a segment of the sequence in the Timeline and watch it in the Canvas. If your deck is hooked up to a reference monitor via a deck or camera, you will also be able to preview it there. Render your sequence (see Chapter 9) and then watch your footage carefully and make sure that it is the way you want it. It's also a good idea to keep an eye on your video deck's audio monitor and an ear to the speakers to make sure that the sound is coming through clearly.

3. Cue your videotape in its deck. Make sure the tape is at the right spot for recording, usually the beginning of the tape (after the leader). If you're capturing to an analog deck, make sure you've set the proper input settings (Composite, S-Video, etc.) and that the timecode recorder is set properly. Now that your settings and cables are set, you're ready to print to video. You now need to decide whether you want to record your film directly from the Timeline or use the Print to Video option.

Watch Out for Dropped Frames

Whenever you are creating a finished video, you should always have Report Dropped Frames checked in the User Preferences window (select Final Cut Pro > User Preferences or press Option+Q). This will alert you when a frame is dropped while printing, so you can stop the process and start over. Otherwise, if frames are dropped, the quality of your print suffers. It's a good idea to increase your RAM, and even restart the computer before printing to video. You must also make sure you've turned off the Mirror on Desktop function under the External Playback menu in the Audio/Video Settings window's A/V Devices tab.

Recording Directly from the Timeline

Recording directly from the Timeline is the easiest and fastest method for laying down your project to videotape. Some editors prefer this method, as it has been known to reduce the possibility of dropped frames. It involves simply playing the sequence in the Timeline just as if you were watching it while editing, but the video deck is recording it onto tape. It may not be as elegant as Print to Video, but it works.

Place the playhead in the Timeline at the beginning of your sequence (or wherever you want the video to begin recording). Make sure the Video Quality button in the Timeline is set to high.

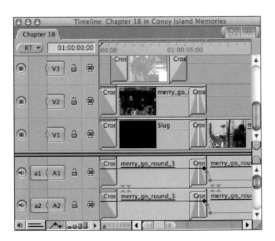

If you want a few seconds of black at the beginning, insert a black slug (from the Video Generators bin in the Browser's Filters tab) at the beginning. You can use an Insert edit to do this. Adding this leader is a good idea since if you start recording with your playhead on an image, you'll get a freeze-frame at the beginning of your tape. You can also just advance all your clips up a few seconds so they don't butt up against the head of the Timeline.

Press the Record button on your video deck. Wait a moment until it engages the tape and begins recording. Most decks will show the timecode on their front display panel, so wait until you see the timecode rolling.

Press the spacebar to begin playing the sequence. If you want to record a specific part of the sequence, set In and Out points in the Timeline to delineate this footage and, instead of pressing the spacebar, select Mark > Play > In To Out (or press Shift+\). This will start the playhead at the In point and stop it at the Out point. Make sure you've turned off looping, by selecting View > Loop Playback, if you don't want the footage to repeat.

5. Note that the last image in your sequence (or the frame at the set Out point) will also end as a freeze-frame, so it's a good idea to put a black slug at the end of your sequence as well, so that the video ends on a black screen.

When the edit has run its course and your sequence has played, let the tape record a little longer, and then press Stop. Rewind the tape and play it through to make sure it recorded properly. It's very important to check the audio and make sure the levels are clear and are not too soft or too loud, causing the audio to peak and distort. You've now got a videotape of your project.

Using Print to Video

The more professional method of making your video is to go through Final Cut Pro's Print to Video process, which gives you more control over the parameters of printing. While this method has been known to drop more frames, this is a rare occurrence as long as you have plenty of memory. Print to Video is better if you need to add elements like color bars and tone, a slate with information, or black handles to the video sequence that will be printed; these will give your video a more professional appearance.

1. Open the sequence you want to print in the Timeline. If you don't want to record the entire sequence, set In and Out points around the part you want to record in the Timeline. Select File **>** Print to Video (Ctrl+M) to open the Print to Video window.

2. The Print to Video window allows you to customize the way your video will be recorded.

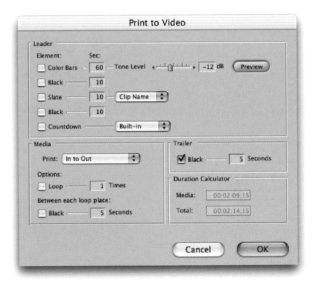

Color Bars   This puts the standard color bars and tone at the beginning of the tape so that anyone else can calibrate their monitor and adjust their sound to match the recording levels on the videotape. It's usually a good idea to put at least 10 seconds, and 60 seconds is the broadcast standard. Generally, you will only want to include color bars for your master copy or if you are outputting for broadcast.

Tone Level   Controls the level of the tone that plays under the color bars. Keep this setting at a standard −12dB unless the person or company you are delivering the tape to tells you differently or your deck requires a different level. As with the color bars, you will only want to include tone level for your master copy or if you are outputting for broadcast.

Black   Puts a slug of black at the beginning, before a slate. It's a good idea to include at least 10 seconds of black here.

Slate   Puts a text slug of information before the video. Either choose to display text you type in yourself in the provided box in this window, or have Final Cut Pro use the clip names, a sequence name, a picture file such as a professionally designed slate, etc. If you're typing in your own slate, it's always a good idea to include the name of the project, the running time of the piece (use the abbreviation TRT for "total running time") and the date of that version of the edit. Make sure you choose a time that allows everything in the slate to be read.

Black   Adds another slug of black after the slate. This is obviously only necessary if you are using a slate.

Countdown   Adds a countdown before the video. This is used for tapes intended for on-air broadcast. If you're not sure you need one, contact the person you are delivering your tape to. Most broadcasters have proprietary countdowns, which can be inserted into FCP. To choose a countdown film file, select File in the Countdown menu, click the folder icon, and then open the file you want to use.

Print   Choose to print an entire sequence or just the part of the sequence between the In and Out points in the Timeline.

Loop   Plays the sequence in a loop. It will play the sequence as many times as you specify or until the tape runs out.

Black Places a designated number of seconds of black between loops.

Trailer Puts a designated number of seconds of black at the end of the sequence. This is highly recommended and you should always include at least 10 seconds of black at the end.

Duration Calculator Shows you the duration of the sequence (Media), as well as the sequence plus all of the other elements such as color bars, countdown, and so on (Total).

After you've set your parameters, click OK. Anything that hasn't been rendered in the sequence will now be rendered, and the sequence will be prepared to print to video.

First the media will be prepared. This is actually a rendering process and may take a few minutes, so Final Cut Pro displays a progress bar to show you how far it has gotten.

After the media is prepared, you will be prompted to start your deck recording and then click OK. This will start printing your sequence to video.

When the printing is done, stop the tape and rewind it to make sure everything recorded properly. Double-check the audio to make sure the levels are good, and not too quiet or loud. You can never be too careful.

What Is a Master Tape?

A *master tape* is a tape containing the final product of the video project. Typically, two master tapes will be made—one that is archived and never touched, and another from which all subsequent dubs are made. A master tape is usually a high-quality tape stock like Beta-SP or D2, although many editors are starting to keep their master tapes on Mini-DV because it's easy to print directly from Final Cut Pro via FireWire without translating to analog.

Which Kind of Tape Should I Use?

You can now deliver this tape to a client, make dubs from it, or pass it around to your friends. It's important to remember that the quality of the tape stock you record on is very important to how your video will look. If you are printing to VHS, your video's going to look very different than the way it looked in the reference monitor on Final Cut Pro. The transition to a low-grade analog tape will make the image muddier. The colors will be handled differently, and the audio will not be as high quality. If you are printing to VHS, you may want to investigate buying high-quality VHS stock from a tape supply store that will give you the best and longest lasting video quality. If you are just doing a test, or making a tape for someone to quickly screen, a cheap tape will do. If you are printing to video and want a nice copy or are making a master tape, never use previously recorded stock, and always buy high-grade tape such as DV or Beta SP. Many master tapes are recorded onto Beta-SP, a high-quality analog stock. More and more, however, editors are printing their final masters on Mini-DV.

21

Outputting Video for CDs, DVDs, and the Web

If you are creating digital video, then in all likelihood you eventually want to distribute your work digitally. There are numerous formats to choose from, including QuickTime, MPEG-2, and MPEG-4. The format you choose is based directly on medium the video is being exported for: Web, DVD, or CD. Exporting creates a single media file that contains the entire sequence with all filters, keyframes, effects, and so forth in the finished sequence without the need for rendering.

In this chapter, we will first explain how to compress your video depending on the medium it is being presented on, and then show you how to create a CD or DVD data disc and how to create a web page.

Overview

> *The play's the thing*
> *Wherein I'll catch the conscience of the king.*
>
> Hamlet from William Shakespeare's *Hamlet*

In the previous chapter we showed you how to output your final work to videotape; however, filmmakers now have a wide variety of media to output their work. Not only can they create files to be recorded on DVD and CD, they can also present their work directly on the web. However, outputting in any of these digital media (rather than analog media as with tape) requires additional processing in order to compress the video for the intended media. Then, once compressed, the video must be either burned to CD or DVD or uploaded for viewing on the web.

Compressing Digital Video

You can use a wide variety of tools to prepare your media files for use on the web, including QuickTime Pro itself. Most of these programs are used to compress files so that they are as small as possible while maintaining the maximum visual quality and allowing for maximum dimensions for presentation. Although you must rely on other software to create a stand-alone DVD, you still need to output your files using Final Cut Pro or in conjunction with Compressor.

Compression uses different *codecs* (short for compression/decompression) to tell the video how to reduce its file size. Simply stated, a codec is a method used by the computer to reduce the file size by reducing the amount of information needed to display the images in your movie and play the audio. The codec then is used by the computer to fill in the missing information during playback. Different codecs have their strengths and weaknesses. Some can drastically compress the file size by using *lossy* techniques that can degrade the fidelity of the movie depending on the amount of compression, while other codecs use *lossless* compression that maintains high fidelity but are less effective for reducing file size.

You have several options as to the file format and codec you use, but the format depends on where you will end up presenting the file:

QuickTime (Video/Audio for Web, CD Data, or DVD Data)   QuickTime is not a codec itself, but a file format that allows you to apply a variety of different codecs to your video, creating what is called a "wrapper" for the video file. In order to play a QuickTime movie, the viewer will need to have QuickTime software installed on their computer. This software is free from Apple for both Mac and Windows and is often preinstalled on computers by the manufacturer.

Although QuickTime movies can not be used directly on DVD video, DVD Studio Pro can read and convert QuickTime files while mastering a DVD so that you do not first have to convert the files to MPEG-2 format.

MPEG-2 (Video/Audio for DVD Video)   MPEG-2 is a codec developed by the Motion Picture Experts Group used for creating small but high-quality digital video. All DVDs use MPEG-2 as their standard compression. If you have DVD Studio Pro installed on the same computer that you are using Final Cut Pro on, then MPEG-2 will show as one of the output options during export. Note: For the examples in this chapter, we will be using the MPEG-2 codec provided with DVD Studio Pro. If you are using DVD Studio Pro 2, you may notice some differences in how the screens look and some of the options.

MPEG-4 (Video/Audio for Web, CD Data, or DVD Data)   MPEG-4 is a codec also developed by the Motion Picture Experts Group for use on the Internet or in wireless devices. MPEG-4 movies can be displayed using QuickTime or other MPEG-4 specific applications.

AIFF (Audio Only for DVD Video)   AIFF (Audio Interchange Format) is a common audio codec used by Macs to maintain high fidelity when only audio (no video) is needed. If you are creating a DVD video, then you will need to output the audio component in AIFF format for use in DVD Studio Pro. Although created by Apple, this codec is also available for Windows machines.

TIFF and JPEG (Still Images)   TIFF (Tagged Image File Format) is a high-quality lossless format used to compress still images, generally for use in printed documents, although these images can be used in a variety of applications, including video. Alternatively, you can export images using the JPEG format (Joint Photographic Experts Group), although this is a lossy compression format that may degrade the image quality.

Output to CD and DVD

Both CDs and DVDs can store information allowing you to record (generally called *burning*) anywhere from 783MB (CDs) to 4.37GB (single-sided DVDs) worth of data that can be transferred between computers equipped with CD and/or DVD drives. This data can be stored either as data (just like saving files to a hard drive) or as part of a stand-alone video disc that cannot only be played back on a properly equipped computer, but also on most standard DVD players.

CD or DVD data   Both CDs and DVDs can be used like hard drives to store raw data files. This data can take any form that you would normally be able to save to your computer's hard drive, including text, programming code, images, video, and audio. The discs can then be used to transfer the data between different computers.

Video CD (VCD) or Super Video CD (SVCD)   A VCD can hold up to 80 minutes on CDs of full-motion video along with quality stereo sound. Although the quality of even the best VCD is about the same as a VHS tape, VCD is usually a bit blurrier. SVCD, on the other hand, has the capacity to hold about 35-60 minutes on a standard CD of high-quality video along with up to two stereo audio tracks and up to four subtitles. The image quality depends how many minutes you choose to store on a CD. Both formats use MPEG-2 to store the video and audio and can be played back on most common stand-alone DVD players as well as computer-based CD and DVD players.

DVD video   In addition to being used for data, DVDs can also be created a stand-alone presentation—referred to as a *DVD video*—that can be played back on most standard DVD players without a computer. Because the process of creating a DVD—generally called *mastering*—can be as involved as actually creating the movie itself, we will not be covering that aspect of DVD creation here, but for suggestions on what software to use, see the sidebar *Should I Use iDVD or DVD Studio Pro 2?* later in this chapter.

Output to the Web

Increasingly, the web is a popular medium for presenting video. Although it still has its drawbacks, the web is the best way to get your work out to the widest audience. Whether you are creating a preview of a larger video, a portfolio of your video work, or an entire movie for viewing online, adding a properly exported Quick-Time or MPEG-4 movie to your web page requires only a few simple lines of code that you can create using a few simple tools:

HTML editor   You will need some way to generate the Hypertext Markup Language (HTML) code used to create your web page. If you are doing a lot of video work with the web, then it will be worth your while to invest in a program such as Adobe GoLive (www.adobe.com) or Macromedia Dreamweaver (www.macromedia .com). These programs provide easy-to-use tools not only for creating web pages without needing to know any code, but also for easily embedding movies into the pages. However, if you are on a more modest budget, all you need to create a web page is a simple text-editing application—such as TextEdit, which comes standard with every Mac—and the code provided in this chapter.

Web server You will need a web address and hard disk space on a computer—called a *server*—that can display your web pages over the Internet. Generally, the server is a computer that you are renting space on through a *hosting service*. If you have, for example, a Mindspring or .Mac account, then you already have some server space. However, even small movies can eat a lot of space, and most hosting services place bandwidth restrictions on the amount of data that can be transferred from your web space for a given month. For most web sites, bandwidth is rarely an issue. However, after you start delivering large video files from your site, you might find that you quickly hit your limit. Before you place your movies online, check with your hosting service to see the exact amount of storage space you have, your available bandwidth, and whether you need to increase your bandwidth to accommodate your videos. If you are looking for a Mac-friendly web hosting service, we recommend MacServe.net (www.macserve.net).

FTP software You will need a file transfer protocol (FTP) program (sometimes called a client) to transfer the web page and video files from your computer to the server. Although Mac OS X has come a long way in its capability to network directly with other computers over the Internet, you will probably still need an FTP program to upload your files for live viewing on the web. Such a program enables you to hook directly into the web server and place files in it that can then be accessed by a web browser. You will, however,

need to get the exact settings indicating how to do this from your hosting company. If you need an FTP client, we recommend Transmit from Panic (www.panic.com/transmit/) or CaptainFTP (captainftp.xdsnet.de).

FAQ

What Is Streaming Video?

Since a movie is a file, one method for playing it back over the Internet is to simply download the entire file to the target computer and then start it playing. However, since video files can be extremely large, this might require that the viewer wait quite a while before anything happens. Another option is to use Fast Start techniques that allow the movie to start playing as soon as enough of it has been downloaded so can start playing and not run out of footage before it finishes downloading. Again, though, this can still require some waiting by the visitor and is impractical for extremely large or live events.

Streaming video, on the other hand, allows you to actually send small packets of video at a time to create a contiguous movie. This works extremely well, especially for broadcasting live events; however, it requires special software on your server. In this chapter we will be looking at how to create non-streaming video using Fast Start techniques. To learn more about streaming QuickTime, visit developer .apple.com/documentation/quicktime/Streaming-date.html.

DVD

Chapter 21: Outputting Your Project for Digital Distribution

Open the Final Cut Pro project file labeled Coney Island Memories. After it loads in Final Cut Pro, double-click the Chapter 18 sequence in the Browser and it will open in the Timeline.

In this chapter you will be reusing the sequence created in Chapter18 to practice exporting versions of the movie from Final Cut Pro 4 for CD, DVD, and the web.

Exporting as a Final Cut QuickTime Movie

Final Cut Pro actually provides multiple methods for exporting your movie in QuickTime format, which you can then use for a variety of purposes including burning to CD or DVD, placing on the web, importing into DVD authoring software for conversion in MPEG-2, or even as a clip in either Final Cut Pro or Final Cut Express.

The first and fastest method you need to learn is how to export to QuickTime as a Final Cut movie. This special QuickTime format is identical to other QuickTime files, but does not substantially compress the movie, so it may have a very high quality and very large file sizes. This process allows you to make a few adjustments to the basic QuickTime settings, but is primarily used with preset settings:

1.   Open the sequence you want to export from the Browser. If you don't want to export the whole sequence, you can set In and Out points in the Timeline to define which part to include when exporting. For this exercise, practice exporting the sequence Chapter 18.

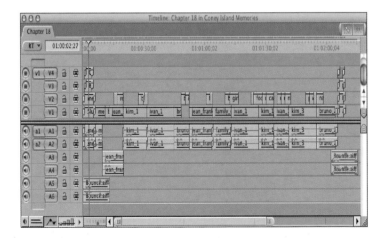

2.   Choose File > Export > QuickTime Movie.

3. In the Save dialog box, type a name for the file (use a .mov extension to keep file types clear) and designate where to save it on the hard disk. In addition, set the following options and then click Save:

Settings   Choose a setting from the drop-down of presets. The setting you choose will depend on your needs and how much you want the movie compressed. For example, if you need digital video output for a NTSC anamorphic, you might choose "DV NTSC 48Khz Anamorphic."

Include   Choose whether to include the audio, video, or both tracks in the exported movie.

Markers   Choose how markers should be treated when saving the movie. For example, you can set up markers to denote DVD chapter breaks if you are exporting to DVD Studio Pro, or you can have Final Cut Pro include all the markers from the sequence into the final movie. This option is very helpful if you'll need to refer to these markers later either in Final Cut Pro or in another

application. For example chapter markers are used in DVD Studio Pro and score markers are used in Soundtrack.

Recompress All Frames   If you are creating a self-contained movie (see below), check to force Final Cut Pro to apply compression to the video even if it has already been compressed previously. Although further decreases the file size, you also run the risk of degrading your movie quality through over-compression.

Make Movie Self-Contained   Check to have the exported movie contain all of the media required for playback. If you leave this option unselected, the file will only point to the original media files on the hard disk, producing a significantly smaller file. Generally, if you are sending the file to another computer, you should select this option to ensure that the movie is not separated from the media used to create it.

If effects have not been rendered, they will be rendered first. Then a progress bar appears, letting you know how much longer it will take to save your movie.

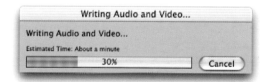

The QuickTime file is saved to your hard disk with an icon that combines the standard Final Cut Pro and QuickTime. You can play this file directly in Final Cut Pro, Final Cut Express, or QuickTime.

Coney_Island_Memories

TIP

Using an Exported Sequence in Final Cut Pro (or Express)

An exported movie is now a media file and can be imported back into Final Cut Pro to create a clip. In fact, both Final Cut Express and Final Cut Pro can exchange files in this manner.

Exporting a sequence into a movie erases all cuts and individual clips, squashing everything into one big clip. Not only can you play an exported file QuickTime file in Final Cut Pro, you can also import it (⌘+I) back into any Final Cut product (Pro or Express) as a single clip and use that in other sequences. The advantage of this is that you won't need to render anything in the imported clip to see it play in real time, even when you use it in another sequence. Remember, though, that you also can't make any changes to the original cut after it has been made into a movie without changing the original project file and exporting it again.

Exporting to Different Movie Formats

In addition to exporting the movie in the QuickTime Final Cut format, you can also export the movie to QuickTime and other video and audio formats using QuickTime conversion. Generally, QuickTime is the most obvious format to export in, especially if you wish to use your files on the web or data discs. Remember, QuickTime is not a format itself, but an "envelope" that can hold many different formats. However, you can also directly export in formats such as AIFF, MPEG-2, MPEG-4, or TIFF using this process if you so desire.

To create a QuickTime version of your sequence, follow these steps:

1. In the Timeline, open the sequence you want to output.

2. Choose File > Export > Using QuickTime Conversion... to open the Save dialog box.

3. In the Save dialog box, choose the general file Format you want to use. For this example, we used the QuickTime Movie format. Then, choose the general settings for the format from the Use drop-down list. These options will change depending on the format you are using.

4. If you need to change the export options for the chosen format, click the Options button to open the Options dialog. The options vary from format to format, and how you set them depends on what you are going to be using the video for. For this exercise, keep the default settings. Later in the chapter we talk about how to set these options for output to web and DVD.

5. Type a name for the new file, locate where you want to save it on the hard disk, and click Save.

After a few seconds or minutes (depending on the size of your movie), the new file is saved to your hard disk and is ready for you to use. The icon used by the file will look very much the same regardless of the format you choose but the format will be named at the bottom of the icon. For QuickTime, it will simply read movie.

Alternative Steps: Exporting for the Web

Although the process for exporting a movie for use on the web is similar to simply outputting it for QuickTime, you will need to make few special considerations. To create a version of your sequence for display on the web, follow these steps:

1. In the Timeline, open the sequence you want to output.

2. Choose File > Export > Using QuickTime Conversion... to open the Save dialog box.

3. In the Save dialog box, choose QuickTime from the Format drop-down list and then one of the preset options from the Use

drop-down list. Which option you choose depends on the Internet speed you expect your audience will be using to view your video and the desired quality of the images you want to deliver:

- Choose **LAN** if the viewer is on an extremely fast connection such as an Ethernet connection or a T1 or T3 line. This will produce the largest images with the best quality.
- Choose one of the **DSL/Cable** settings if the viewer has a fast Internet connection. The lower the level you choose, the more compressed your video will be (and thus the lower quality) in order to cut down on file size.
- Choose **Modem** for the lowest quality but smallest file sizes. You can also choose Modem – Audio only if you do not want to send any video at all, which will substantially reduce the file size.

For this exercise, name the file Coney_Island_Memories.mov in a folder called **movies** with the DSL/Cable – Medium setting. If these options do not appear, make sure that you have QuickTime Pro installed on the computer you are using. This software should have come free with your Final Cut Pro installation disk.

4. At this point, you can click OK to begin saving your video or you can click Options to fine-tune your optimization settings in the Movie Settings dialog box. The default settings for QuickTime work well for most uses, but you might want to tweak these for your specific needs:

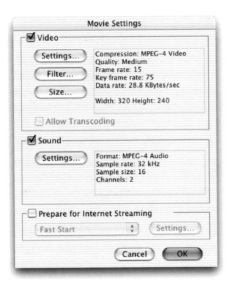

Video Settings   Click this button to access options that set the compression method for the video portion of your work. The default MPEG-4 is best for most uses. You can also save the file directly as an MPEG-4 file, but this loses some of the advantages of QuickTime.

Video Filter   Apply a video filter to the entire sequence while exporting. This option is especially helpful if you are compressing the video and want to add a slight blur to offset the artifacts created by compression.

Video Size   Set the pixel dimensions of the final video output. Generally, if you set this manually, you will want to make

sure to keep the dimensions in proportion. Of course, the larger the physical dimensions, the larger your file size will be. Reducing the video size is often a good way to improve the image quality.

Sound Settings   Click this button to access options that set the compression method for the audio portion of your work. Generally, MPEG-4 for audio will be your best bet.

Prepare for Internet Streaming   Choose from three settings indicating how the video should be treated when played over the Internet. The Fast Start setting enables you to have the video start playing before the entire file is downloaded. The Compressed Header option works faster but requires your audience to be using the newer versions of QuickTime. Hinted Streaming is used if you will be streaming the video; this requires special server software to work.

Now that you have saved your file in the media folder, you will need to add it to a web page (see *Creating a Video Web Page* later in this chapter).

Alternative Steps: Exporting for DVD Video

Although the process for saving your movie for use in a DVD video is similar to exporting it using QuickTime, you will need to consider several special options. To save a file in the MPEG-2 format for DVD video, follow these steps:

1. In the Timeline, open the sequence you want to output and choose File **>** Export **>** QuickTime to open the Save dialog box.

2. In the Save dialog box, choose the MPEG-2 format (there are no general settings in the Use options). It is important to note that the MPEG-2 option will appear only if you have DVD Studio Pro or an MPEG-2 codec loaded on your system.

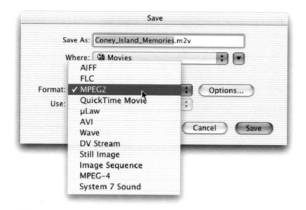

Click the Options button to open the QuickTime MPEG Encoder dialog box. Set the options and click OK. If you see different options, you are using a different version of the MPEG-2 Encoder than the one shipped with DVD Studio Pro version 1. However, this list includes the crucial controls. The QuickTime MPEG options are as follows:

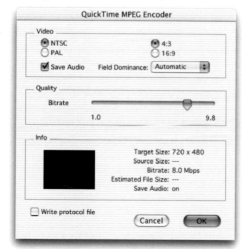

Video Format   Choose between NTSC and PAL video formats. To avoid distortion, choose the format in which you edited your video; this should already be preselected.

Aspect Ratio   Choose an aspect ratio: either 4:3 (television) or 16:9 (cinema). To avoid distortion, choose the ratio that you have used in editing; this should already be preselected.

Save Audio   Select this check box to include the audio as part of the MPEG-2 file. This will increase the file size.

Field Dominance   Choose Automatic (recommended), Upper, or Lower. This needs to be set based on the field dominance used when the video was captured and the equipment being used. Generally, the Automatic option is your safest bet.

Bitrate   Use this slider to set the image quality as a factor of the number of bits used to record each second of video. The higher the value, the better the image quality, but the larger the file size.

Info   This section displays information about the file that will be created, based on the settings, including a thumbnail of the currently selected frame and an estimated file size.

Write Protocol File   Select this check box to create a text file with the information about how the file was created. This can be handy if you are not mastering the DVD yourself and need to provide the person who will do so with details they need to get the best results.

After setting the options and entering a filename (making sure to keep the .m2v extension), click Save. Your computer will churn away, compressing the video and showing a progress bar.

After the file has been created, you are ready to use it with your DVD authoring software to master your DVD.

Alternative Steps: Exporting Still Images

Although, naturally, you are going to want to export your entire video as a "motion picture," at times you might want to export a single still image or sequence of images. For example, if you are making a poster for your movie, you will probably want to export still images in TIFF format. If you need still images on your web site, you'll want to export images as JPEG-formatted files.

To create a single still image or series of still images from your video, follow these steps:

1. In the Viewer, Timeline, or Canvas, place the playhead in the frame you want to export as a single image or simply within the clip to export the clip as a series of still images. For this exercise, choose any frame in the Chapter 18 project file.

2. Choose File > Export > QuickTime.

3. In the Save dialog box, you can choose to export either a single frame or a sequence of frames from the clip:

- Still Image to export only the selected frame.
- Image Sequence to export multiple still images from the selected clip. Final Cut Pro will automatically create each file and number them.

4. Choose one of the Use settings (generally leave this on Default Settings or Previous Settings) and then click the Options button if you need to change the export options—for example, if this is the first time you are exporting images.

5. In the Export Image Sequence Settings dialog box, set the following options and then click OK:

Format Choose a file format for the still image(s). Generally, if the image is for print, use the TIFF format, but if the image is destined for the web, use JPEG.

Frames per Second If you are outputting an Image sequence, enter the number of still images to be created for each second of the clip between its In and Out points. The lower the number, the fewer still images will be produced. For example, if the clip lasts 2 seconds, and you set this value to 3, you will get 6 still images created from the sequence. If you are exporting only a single still image, leave this blank.

Insert Space before Number   Select this check box to use a space between the clip name and its number in the sequence. For example, if you name the clip Carousel, the files will be numbered Carousel 1, Carousel 2, Carousel 3, and so forth.

Options   Click this button to set the compression settings for the file format type you selected. One common setting for all file formats is Depth. Generally, you will want to leave this on Best Depth to produce the highest-quality still images.

6.   Back in the Save dialog, type a name for this still image or to be used as the base title for the series of images and choose where you want to save it.

7.   Click the Save button, and your new file or files are created. These files can be opened in Photoshop, Illustrator, and most other graphic or photo programs, including Final Cut Pro itself.

Using Photoshop to Fix Interlacing in Still Images

You might notice that some exported stills look as if every other line has shifted over. This is due to *interlacing* used with some video formats, but it can be quickly corrected in graphics programs such as Photoshop by using the De-Interlace filter. (Still images from Final Cut Pro are all 72dpi, so you might also want to use Photoshop to change the resolution to 300dpi if your image is going to be printed.) To fix interlacing in a still video image, follow these steps:

1. Open the image in an image-editing program that has the De-Interlace filter. For this example, we used the workhorse of digital editing software, Photoshop.

2. In Photoshop, access the De-Interlace filter (Filter > Video > De-Interlace).

3. In the De-Interlace dialog box, choose whether to eliminate Odd or Even fields and whether the new fields should be created by dupli-

cating fields or through interpolation. Then click OK. The eliminate option will depend on the image, but generally Interpolation produces sharper results.

The image's quality should improve noticeably. If not, or if you want to try different options, choose Edit > Undo (⌘+Z) to undo the filter and then start with Step 2 again.

If you have a batch of images that you need to de-interlace, Photoshop enables you to create that action by using the Actions palette to quickly apply the filter. You can then use the Batch command (File > Automate > Batch) to create a droplet, enabling you to simply drop a folder of images onto an icon to have them all de-interlaced at once.

Using Apple Compressor to Create Smaller Files

Apple released a new tool with Final Cut Pro 4 to help even novice developers get the best results possible from their video footage. The aptly named Compressor allows you to systematically apply compression to a file as well as create multiple versions for different uses. For example, you could create three different compressed versions of a single video for small, medium, and large file sizes to give viewers a choice depending on their Internet connection speed. Compressor can open a wide variety of video formats including QuickTime, MPEG (2 and 4), AIFF, TIFF, and Final Cut (Pro and Express) files.

1. In Final Cut Pro 4, open the sequence you want to compress and choose File > Export > Using Compressor... The Sequence will be automatically transferred to Compressor. If you have already exported your file using Final Cut Pro using one of the methods described in the previous section, you can simply drag that file from your desktop into the Batch window, although you can also use the tried and true File > Import (⌘+I).

2. You should now see your media file listed in Compressor's Batch window. Once your files are in the Batch list, you will need to either apply one of the existing preset compressions or create a

new compression tailored for your needs (see the sidebar *Creating a QuickTime (or Other) Preset in Compressor*).

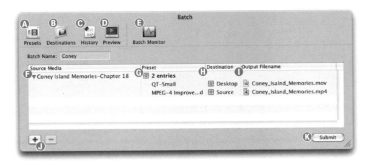

Ⓐ Click to open the Presets dialog to create new compression settings.

Ⓑ Click to specify different areas on your hard drive to output files to.

Ⓒ Click to open a panel showing previous batch compressions.

Ⓓ Click to open a dialog to preview the compression changes.

Ⓔ Click to open the Batch Monitor application used to monitor files during compression. This application opens automatically when you submit the files for compression.

Ⓕ Shows the name of the source file being compressed.

Ⓖ Shows the compression presets being applied to the source file. Click to add another preset. Each preset represents a separate compressed file that will be output.

Ⓗ Shows where each compressed file will be saved. Click to change the destination.

Ⓘ Shows the name of the new compressed file being created. Double-click to change the filename, but make sure to preserve the files extension.

Ⓙ Click + to add a new source file or – to delete the selected source file from the list.

Ⓚ Click to submit all files for batch compression.

3. In the Preset column next to your media file, click the drop-down arrows next to "0 entries" to select a preset to apply. You can also click and drag presets directly from the Presets dialog to the media file to apply them.

A new line will be added under the media file showing the preset type being applied, where the new file will be created (Destination), and the new filename (Output Filename). You can apply as many different compression types as you want to a single media file to create multiple output files for different purposes. For example, you may need the file for a CD, for a DVD, and for the web, and all three would need different compressions applied to them. You can change the Destination and Output Filename to suit your needs by clicking these fields.

Once you have set the presets, click the Submit button and wait. You may be waiting for a while, so sit back, watch some TV, and relax.

The Batch Monitor application will open (and Compressor will close) and show you the progress as it creates each of the output files. This process may take quite a while, so you may want to go get a coffee, watch a movie, or write a novel while you are waiting. In fact, we wrote this entire book while waiting for one particularly large movie to be compressed.

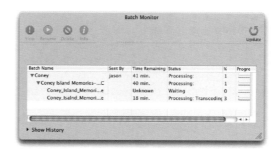

Creating a QuickTime (or Other) Preset in Compressor

Compressor comes with several dozen different MPEG-2 and MPEG-4 compression presets, but you will need to create one if you want to use the .mov format, and you may want to create customized presets for a variety of purposes.

To set up the QuickTime preset:

1. Click the Presets button on the Batch panel.

2. Click the Plus Icon on the Presets panel to add a new preset to the list.

3. Enter the name of the new preset by double-clicking its name in the list and typing the new name.

4. Set the options for the new preset in the Encoder tab, and then choose QuickTime as the encoder.

   • Click the *Settings* button next to Video to set the quality for the video, choose the compression scheme (MPEG-4 will generally give best results) to use from the drop-down at the top of the dialog and click OK.

   • Click the *Settings* button next to Audio to set the quality of the

audio by selecting the compressor type being used, the rate, bit size, and whether the audio will be stereo or mono.

   • Choose whether the preset should be used for streaming, and choose the streaming type to be used. Generally, you will want this set to None, unless you have special streaming software installed on your web server.

5. Click the Filters tab to add visual filters or adjust the brightness and contrast that will be used while the video is being encoded.

6. Click the Geometry tab and set the crop (margins in from the left, right, top, and bottom) and the dimensions (output size) for the final video. This is especially helpful for resizing the video to make it smaller and thus a smaller file size.

7. Click the Actions tab and check whether you want to add an e-mail notification when the video is finished being encoded or to run a particular AppleScript.

You can now close the Presets window and return to the Batch window where the newly created preset will be available to you.

Creating a CD or DVD Data Disc

If you are attempting to transfer large files, such as video files, one of the best ways is to simply burn them to a DVD, using the DVD as a data disc. When most people hear the term *DVD*, they immediately think of media for viewing movies. However, DVDs can hold up to 4.37GB of information, making them the best way to transfer raw video files short of carting around an external hard disk.

To burn data files to a CD or DVD, follow these steps:

1. Insert the DVD-R disc or CD-R disc into your drive.

2. You will be prompted to enter a name for the DVD and choose how to process the disk. Choose "Finder" from the list, which will allow you to use this disk in the Finder before it is formatted.

3. Drag the file or files you want to add to the disc icon from the Finder onto the disc icon. A progress dialog appears, letting you know how long it will take to prepare the files. This might take several minutes depending on the size of the files being transferred, but this will not actually place the data on the disc yet. You can continue to drag files to the disc until you eject it or you control-click and choose Burn Disk.

4. Either control-click and choose Burn Disk or eject the disk to burn the collected data. A dialog will appear asking you whether you want to burn the data or not.

5. Choose Burn. The computer will then begin placing the data on the disc, displaying a progress bar and estimated time remaining. This will take at least as long as it did to prepare the data in Step 2. After burning, you will again have to wait as the computer verifies the data that was burned, which can also take a lot of time. You can click Cancel during this phase if you do not want to wait. This will not affect the disc itself, but you cannot make changes if the data is corrupted, and you run the risk of unknowingly having a corrupted disk.

After the disc is burned, you can take it to any other computer with a DVD or CD drive (even if the drive cannot itself burn CDs or DVDs) and use the files. Of course, Final Cut Pro files will work only on Macs with Final Cut Pro installed, and video files will play only on PCs with QuickTime or compatible software (such as Windows Media Player) installed. If you are transferring Final Cut Pro project files and captured video clips, you might need to reconnect the files after they are loaded into Final Cut Pro.

Which Format Should I Use: DVD-R or DVD+R?

There are several DVD formats that can be used with DVD burners. Until recently, Mac computers only supported DVD-R (that's DVD *dash* R) and were unable to use DVD+R (DVD *plus* R) formatted discs. Both DVD-R and DVD+R are used to record data once. However, with the release of OS 10.3, Macs now support both disc types. However, if you are using a pre-OS 10.3 Mac, then you will want to buy DVD-R discs *only*.

For more details, see the DVD FAQ: `www.dvddemystified.com/dvdfaq.html`.

Should I Use iDVD or DVD Studio Pro 2?

Unlike recording to video (see previous chapter), Final Cut Pro cannot output directly to DVDs. Instead, you have to output your sequence or sequences as DV files (QuickTime or MPEG-2) and then use a separate authoring program to create a DVD that can play on standard DVD players. There are many DVD authoring programs on the market, but the two primarily used on the Mac both come from Apple; which you choose will depend on the kind of projects you are working on and the amount of money you want to spend.

The case for iDVD   iDVD comes free with any Mac equipped with the DVD-burning SuperDrive. It is an easy-to-use program that does not require a huge learning curve to master. Although iDVD is not a professional grade program, it is useful if you simply need to create a rough cut of a DVD video. iDVD provides built-in templates to speed production but does not limit your ability to create your own backdrops or buttons, and, for power users, can even use AppleScripts to better integrate with your workflow.

The case for DVD Studio Pro 2   For production of professional DVDs (such as broadcast, film, and product training) when high-quality output is expected, you will need to invest in DVD Studio Pro 2. In many ways, DVD Studio Pro 2 is an extension of the Final Cut products (Pro and Express) and uses many similar interface elements. After you have mastered Final Cut Pro, moving to DVD Studio Pro should not prove a daunting challenge. DVD Studio Pro 2 also provides a bevy of professional templates, but also enables you to create nonlinear interactive DVDs by using a Timeline similar to Final Cut Pro.

Creating a Video Web Page

In the section *Exporting to Different Movie Formats* earlier in this chapter, we showed you how to export your video for Web distribution. After you have created the QuickTime or MPEG-4 file, your next step is to create an HTML file with the movie file embedded in it and then upload the movie file and HTML file to a web server. These files can then be viewed by anyone with an Internet connection and a Web browser with the QuickTime plug-in.

To create a web page for your video, follow these steps:

1. Open a text-editing program or a specialized web page editing program, create a new file, and add the code:

```
<html>
<head>
    <title>Coney Island Memories</title>
</head>
<body>
    <object width="320" height="256">
        <param name="src" value="movies/Coney_Island_
        Memories.mov">
        <param name="loop" value="true">
        <param name="cache" value="true">
        <param name="autoplay" value="true">
        <param name="controller" value="true">
        <embed type="video/quicktime"
            src="movies/Coney_Island_Memories.mov"
            width="320" height="256"
            loop="true"
            cache="true"
            autoplay="true"
            controller="true">
    </object>
</body>
</html>
```

In this example, we will be showing the movie called ConeyIsland-Memories.mov, which is located in the folder called media. This code looks as though it "embeds" the video file into the web page twice, first using the <embed> tag and then again using the older <object> tag. However, the video will appear only once on the page. The web browser will use whichever of the tags it recognizes first, ignoring the other one. Using redundant tags, though, ensures that any web browser can view your video regardless of which tag it recognizes.

2. To tailor this code to your needs, you will need to change the source (src="movies/LandSeaAir.mov") in both the <embed> and <object> to the folder and file you are using. You can also set other attributes:

- **Width** and **height** define the overall dimensions of the movie player. If you are including a controller for the video, you will need to add an extra 16 pixels to the height. So, for example, a 240 pixel high movie would actually be given a height of 256 pixels. You should also never set the width or height to less than 2 even if the movie is being hidden, as this can lead to unpredictable playback.

- **Loop** can be set to true or false depending on whether you want the movie to repeat after it finishes playing.

- **Cache** can be set to true or false if you want to have the movie stored by the browser's cache for faster replay. True is generally recommended for faster replay.

- **Autoplay** can be set to true to have the movie start playing immediately after loading, or to false to wait for the viewer to click the Play button.

- **Volume** can be set from 0 to 100 for the volume the movie plays at. This can be adjusted by the viewer if the controls are present.

- **Controller** can be set to true to show player controls: volume, play/pause, progress bar. A false value will keep the controller from showing, which prevents the viewer from changing the volume, pausing the video, or jumping around in the video.

You can also add any other standard HTML content you want to this page, including background graphics and text, but we have kept the page simple here.

3. Save your new HTML file in the same folder as the media folder created in the previous exercise. You can name this file anything you want (we called ours index), but do not use any spaces and end the filename with the extension .html.

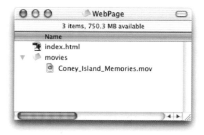

Use your FTP software to upload the HTML file and video file to your web server. Exactly how you do this will depend on the FTP software you are using. With Transmit, you would log onto your web server (by using its FTP address as opposed to its actual web address), navigate to the folder you want to add the files to, and then simply drag the folder containing your web page and video file to the target folder.

You will then need to wait while the files are uploaded. This could take some time, depending on the size of the video file and the speed of your Internet connection.

You can now visit this web page by using a browser to display the movie. You can see this video playing on our web site at www .webbedenvironments.com/fcp/WebPage/index.html

How Are Video Files Displayed on the Web?

Video images are not natively supported by browsers, but rely on plug-ins—separate chunks of code that are used by the browser to tell them how to display different MIME types. MIME (which actually stands for Multipurpose Internet Mail Extensions) is used to define particular media types, which are then associated with a particular plug-in that supports the display of that media type in the web browser. Although this provides great versatility, since different formats can be added without updating the browser, it also means that the browser has to have the plug-in to display particular files.

Although often thought of as a stand-alone application for displaying video, QuickTime can also be used as a plug-in to display video and audio directly in a web browser. Although typically using files with the .mov extension, QuickTime can also play MPEG files, Flash files, and AIFF Files, among many others. The other great thing about the QuickTime plug-in is that it comes preinstalled with most web browsers.

What Other Plug-ins Can I Use to Display Video on the Web?

In this chapter we have only addressed how to create files that can be displayed using the QuickTime plug-in. However, you can use a variety of different formats, each with its own associated MIME types and plug-ins. The most popular alternatives to QuickTime are the Windows Media (www.microsoft.com/windowsmedia) and Real (www.real.com) formats, both of which offer their own strengths and weaknesses for video over the Internet.

Glossary of Terms

A-ROLL
The primary footage in a sequence. Usually contains running narration or dialog and shows the main action (see also *B-roll*).

ALPHA CHANNEL
An invisible layer of data in a *clip* that stores the *opacity* information for a *frame*. Alpha channels are used in many forms of digital imaging and exist in many of the files you can *import* into Final Cut Pro. In DV editing, they are primarily used when *compositing* multiple clips (see Chapter 13).

ANALOG
A format that uses magnetic tape to record audio and video information with a varying wavelength of voltage. Examples include VHS and Beta-SP tapes (see also *digital video*).

ANAMORPHIC
An image's aspect ratio that has the horizontal proportions of 16:9. Anamorphic images are shot with a special lens that squashes the image. Final Cut Pro has a feature that "unsquashes" the image to its undistorted horizontal size.

ASPECT RATIO
The dimension of the *frame* in which the image is presented. The standard for television is roughly a 4:3 aspect ratio. The cinemascope or *anamorphic* ratio is 16:9.

AUDIO METER
A Final Cut Pro tool that displays the *decibel* level of both audio channels while a *clip* is being played. This allows you to make sure the audio is not being distorted during playback (see Chapters 2 and 16).

AUDIO MIXER
A window that lets you mix multiple tracks of audio simultaneously. It also allows you to add universal *keyframes*, and isolate and mute specific audio tracks (see Chapter 16).

B-ROLL
Secondary *footage* used in a *sequence* to cut away from the main footage (the *A-roll*). It typically shows details related to the primary action in a separate image, such as pigeons scattering in the air as two characters walk down a city street (see Chapter 18).

BATCH CAPTURE
The process of *capturing footage* from a source tape that takes in multiple *clips* at once (see Chapter 5).

BATCH CAPTURE LIST
A list that outlines the *clips* and *camera log* information needed for a *batch capture*. This list will generally be a word processing table or spreadsheet file that can be used by FCP to create offline clips ready for capture (see Chapter 4).

BEZIER HANDLES
Controls used to add curves in a *keyframe* path. These controls stick out as "handle bars" perpendicular to the path and can be rotated to change the curve (see Chapter 15).

BIN
A folder in the *Browser* that allows you to organize your *clips*, *sequences*, and other *media* (see Chapter 5).

BROWSER
The window where the *project files*, *bins,* and all your *clips* are stored and organized. The Browser also contains the *Effects* tab, which contains *filters* and *generators* (see Chapter 2).

BUTTON LIST
A bar in the *Timeline* that allows you to add and delete shortcut buttons. Almost every function or tool of Final Cut Pro is available as a shortcut button that can be added to this bar (see Chapter 2).

CAMERA LOG

A list of information about a shoot, including scene and take numbers, aperture settings, and other notes recorded during filming, which can then be used as a *batch list* (see Chapter 3). Some of this information can be imported into Final Cut Pro directly to create the batch list.

CANVAS

The window that shows the *footage* contained in the *Timeline*. The Canvas will show whatever *frame* is under the Timeline's *playhead* (see Chapter 2). The Canvas only plays the Timeline's *clips*, and is not an area for adjusting clips like the *Viewer*. An exterior monitor will play whatever plays in the Canvas window.

CAPTURE

The process of bringing *footage* from a source tape into the computer's hard drive as a *media file* for use in Final Cut Pro (see Chapter 5).

CAPTURE CARD

A card that allows *analog* (and sometimes other forms of DV) footage to be translated into a *digital* format using a specific *codec*, like the Aurora card.

CLIP

A graphic representation of a *media file*, containing video, audio, and/or graphics. Clips are housed in the *Browser*, and are the individual pieces of *footage* that you actually edit together in the *Timeline*. Clips can be manipulated, distorted, and trimmed without affecting the original media file they represent. Clips are used as the building blocks for any video sequence.

CLOSE GAP

Selecting a gap in the *Timeline* and pressing delete will perform a "Close Gap" function, which removes the gap and ripples all the following footage back to fill it (see Chapter 6).

COLOR BARS

A standard graphic of different colored bars used to calibrate monitors correctly. The color bars can be added quickly to a *project* using the dropdown menu in the bottom-right corner of the *Viewer*. This way, others viewing or broadcasting your project can make sure they've calibrated their equipment correctly.

CODEC

Abbreviation for Compression/Decompression Algorithm. A codec transfers video and audio from its uncompressed state to its compressed state and vis versa. *DV* operates as a codec, as do *analog* capture cards such as Aurora (see Chapter 1).

COMPOSITING

The process of overlapping the video information from two or more *clips* (see Chapter 13).

COMPRESSION

Removal of information from a file to reduce its storage requirements (size). Generally, this entails some loss of image and audio quality (see Chapter 21).

CONTEXTUAL MENU

A menu that appears by control-clicking a certain area of the screen (i.e., a clip in the *Browser*). The contextual menu lists a series of options related to the topic clicked on.

CUT

The edit point between two *clips* in the *Timeline* (see Chapter 7). Cuts can either be straight cuts (one clip going directly to the next) or *transitions,* where *effects* such as cross-dissolves are used between the two clips (see Chapter 8).

DECIBEL (DB)

A logarithmic measure of sound intensity (level) in the audio of a *clip*. In Final Cut Pro, the audio level can be viewed using the *Audio Meter* and adjusted by changing the level in the *Viewer's* Audio tab. Generally the audio level for a clip should fall somewhere between –12 and –3dB (see Chapter 16).

DECK

Common name for any piece of equipment that plays and/or records video and audiotape. A deck is used to play back your source tape *footage* when *capturing*, as well as to record a Final Cut Pro *sequence* back to tape when printing to video.

DEVICE CONTROL

The ability to control an exterior *deck* (such as a DV deck or a Beta-SP machine) from Final Cut Pro. The deck itself must support this feature, and it must be connected to the computer via *FireWire* or through a *serial* device control port like a GeeThree serial port (see Chapter 1).

DIGITAL VIDEO (DV)
A video format that stores information in the computer's language of 1s and 0s, allowing the video to be edited nondestructively in computer memory and preventing loss of quality from transfer to transfer (see also *analog*).

DROP FRAME TIMECODE
A type of *timecode* that adjusts itself for *NTSC*'s 29.97 frame rate by dropping a *frame* from its count at regular intervals (see Chapter 2).

DV START/STOP DETECTION
A tool that scans a single clip and places a marker at any point where the camera turned on and off while recording the footage (see Chapter 4).

EDIT POINT
See *Cut*.

EFFECT
The umbrella term for *filters*, *motion*, *transitions*, *generators*, and anything that manipulates a clip beyond basic cutting (see Chapters 11, 12, 13, 14, and 15). In Final Cut Pro, all effects are located in the *Browser's* Effects tab.

FINE CUT
A version of your edit that is near the final version, with exact edits, mixed sound, etc.

FIREWIRE
A type of cable connection between computers and *DV decks* or cameras (and even external hard drives) that allows for extremely rapid transfer of digital information. Developed by Apple as its implementation of the *IEEE 1394a* standard. The equivalent Sony implementation is known as *i.LINK* (see Chapter 1).

FOOTAGE
See *Media*.

FRAME
One still image that, played within a series of other frames, creates the illusion of movement in video.

FRAMES PER SECOND (FPS)
The number of *frames* shown in a second of *footage*. The more frames shown per second, the more seamless the illusion of continuous motion. The *NTSC* (North American) standard runs at 29.97 fps while PAL (used in much of Europe and elsewhere) and SECAM (used in France and parts of Africa) uses 25 fps.

GAIN
In audio, the degree to which a signal is amplified, controlling the loudness of the sound. In video, the level of the whites.

GAMMA CORRECTION
In Final Cut Pro, an *effect* that alters the midtones of an image, leaving the deep blacks and bright whites alone. Technically, the term refers to adjustments to a video signal to compensate for properties of a cathode ray tube. The Final Cut Pro effect controls the way this adjustment is applied to a *clip*.

GENERATOR
An *effect* that creates a new *clip* inside Final Cut Pro that has not been *captured* from a video or audio source. These kinds of clips include *slugs* and *titles* (see Chapter 9).

IEEE 1394
A standard defining a type of connection between computers and *DV decks* or cameras (and even external hard drives) that allows for very rapid transfer of digital information. Apple Computer's implementation is known as *FireWire* and is compatible with most peripherals. Sony's version, known as *i.LINK,* comes on all Sony DV cameras (see Chapter 1).

IMPORT
The process of bringing in a file into Final Cut Pro, such as a media *clip*, a Photoshop file, or a track from a CD (see Chapter 5).

IN POINT
A point that *trims* a *media file* so that it begins at that designated *frame* (see also *Out point*). The *Timeline* will not show *footage* before the In point during playback, but the *media* is still there on the hard drive and the In point can be changed at any time during the editing process to reveal more or less of the media (see Chapter 6).

INSERT EDIT

A type of edit that pushes all *clips* after it forward to accommodate the incoming clip (see Chapter 6). See also *Overwrite edit, Ripple edit, Roll edit, Slide edit, Slip edit.*

I.LINK

Sony's implementation of the *IEEE 1394* standard, which is implemented by Apple as *FireWire*.

JUMP CUT

A *cut* that pieces together two *clips* of the same scene shot from a similar angle, typically less than 30 degrees difference (see Chapter 18).

KEYING

The process of making video information transparent so that another *clip* can be seen through it from a clip lower in the *Timeline* (see Chapter 13).

KEYFRAME

A marker that allows *effects* or motion attributes to be changed over time in a *clip* (see Chapter 15).

LIFT

The process of removing a clip from the *Timeline* while leaving a gap in its place (see Chapter 6).

LOG AND CAPTURE

The two-stage process by which you create source *footage* ready for Final Cut Pro to work with. Logging provides the essential information the program will need about the *clip* so it can take it from a source tape, and capturing brings the *media files* from the source into the computer's hard drive and associates each file with its log information (see Chapters 4 and 5).

LOG BIN

The designated *bin* where offline logged *clips* will be created and await *capture* (see Chapter 4).

LUMA KEY

A process that changes a clip's *opacity* based on the brightness or darkness of the pixels (see Chapter 13). See also *keying*.

MARKERS

A way of designated and labeling certain *frames* in a *clip* (see Chapter 4).

MATCH CUT

A *cut* whose incoming and outgoing *clips* share a similar composition, graphic element, or movement (see Chapter 18).

MEDIA

1. The audio and video content of a *clip*. Used interchangeably with *footage*.
2. A physical storage device used to record data, such as CD, DVD, hard drive, film, or video.
3. General term for information delivery methods.

MEDIA FILE

The actual file on your hard disk of the captured *footage* whose representation in the form of *clips* is being edited in Final Cut Pro. The media file is unaffected by changes made to the clips (see Chapter 5).

MINI-DV TAPE

A tape used for recording audio and video information with a *digital video* camera. Mini-DV tapes record this information digitally and can transfer this information directly into a hard drive through *FireWire*.

MOTION PATH

A line or group of interconnected lines that show the path of a moving element in the *Canvas*. Motion paths are created by using *keyframes* to mark the movements (see Chapter 15).

NESTED SEQUENCE

A *sequence* that has been placed inside another sequence (see Chapter 6).

NON-DROP FRAME TIMECODE

A type of *timecode* that never drops a *frame* because it runs on a frame rate that uses whole numbers, such as NTSC that runs at 30fps or the *PAL* system's 25 frames per second rate (see Chapter 2). See also *drop frame timecode*.

NTSC
The North American standard for video resolution and sample rate. It runs at 29.97 frames per second and with DV, has a resolution of 720 × 480 pixels (see also *PAL*).

OPACITY
The transparency of a *clip* as defined by the properties of its *alpha channel*.

OUT POINT
A point that trims a *clip* so that it ends at that designated *frame* (see also *In point*). All media after the Out point in a clip is ignored during playback, but the Out point can be changed during the editing process to reveal more or less of the media (see Chapter 6).

OVERWRITE EDIT
A type of edit that places the incoming *clip* over any *footage* in its way on the target track in the *Timeline* (see Chapter 6). See also *Insert edit, Ripple edit, Roll edit, Slide edit, Slip edit.*

PAL
The video standard used in much of Europe and much of the rest of the world. It runs at 25 frames per second (see also *NTSC*) and for DV has a 720 × 540 pixel ratio.

PLAYHEAD
In either the *Canvas* or the *Viewer*, a vertical bar in the *Timeline* that designates which *frame* you are watching in a *clip*. You can drag the playhead to *scrub* quickly through a clip. The playhead also appears in the Mini-Timeline of the Canvas and Viewer.

PRINT TO VIDEO
The process of recording a sequence from Final Cut Pro to a digital videotape, such as a *Mini-DV tape*, or to an *analog deck* (see Chapter 20).

PROJECT FILE
The file on your hard drive that stores information about how your *clips* and *sequences* are organized in the *Browser* and how they are edited in the *Timeline*. It also contains information on *effects* and *rendering*. No media is actually contained in this file.

RENDER
The process of preparing an effected clip for real-time viewing. Performed internally by Final Cut Pro, it consists of actually calculating the *effect* and applying it frame-by-frame to the image. This creates a special render file in which the information describing the image has been modified. Editing the clip after the effect has been rendered will probably require that the effect be rerendered (see Chapter 9).

RIPPLE EDIT
A type of edit that trims or extends the duration of one *clip*, and moves the surrounding clips to accommodate the new time (see Chapter 8). See also *Insert edit, Overwrite edit, Roll edit, Slide edit, Slip edit.*

ROLL EDIT
A type of edit that changes the edit point between two *clips* without affecting their placement in the *Timeline*, thus keeping their combined length the same (see Chapter 8). See also *Insert edit, Overwrite edit, Ripple edit, Slide edit, Slip edit.*

ROUGH CUT
An edited sequence that contains your *clips* in a general order, possibly with simple *effects* and *transitions*. This cut is used to establish whether the edit is good enough to spend time fine-tuning to create a *fine cut* (see Chapter 6).

SCRATCH DISK
The hard drive or drive partition where audio, video, and render files will be stored during editing. This can be your startup disk or any other hard drive mounted to your machine (see Chapter 2).

SCRUB
The action of moving back and forth through a *clip* or a sequence by dragging the mouse back and forth over a Scrub bar.

SEQUENCE
A string of *clips*, containing audio, video, and graphic clips that have been edited together. A sequence appears as a line item in the *Browser*, and as tabs in the *Timeline* and *Canvas*. Only one sequence tab can be viewed at a time in the Timeline or Canvas; however, you can have *nested sequences.*

SLIDE EDIT
A type of edit that changes the placement of a *clip* in the *Timeline* but does not affect the duration or *In* and *Out points* (see Chapter 8). See also *Insert edit, Overwrite edit, Ripple edit, Roll edit, Slip edit.*

SLIP EDIT
A type of edit that changes the In and Out points of a *clip* without changing duration or placement (see Chapter 8). See also *Insert edit, Overwrite edit, Ripple edit, Roll edit, Slip edit.*

SLUG
A video *clip* that has no properties of its own until *effects* or filters are added to it. The default slug is black (see Chapter 17). See also *generator.*

SPLIT EDIT
An edit in which a *clip's* audio and video do not start at the same time (see Chapter 16).

STEREO PAIR
Two audio *clips* that are linked so that one plays from the left speaker and the other from the right speaker (see Chapter 7).

SUBCLIP
A clip created in Final Cut Pro from a part of a whole captured clip. The subclip operates as its own clip, but is still referencing media from the original source clip (see Chapter 8).

THREE-POINT EDITING
A concept used by Final Cut Pro that requires only three points to be designated for an *edit* to occur (see Chapter 6).

TIME REMAPPING
Adjusting the motion speed of a clip at a certain frame within the clip, creating a sudden speed up or slow down of the action (see Chapter 8).

TIMECODE
A coding system that designates each *frame* of video or audio with a number that incrementally increases with each frame. The format is 00:00:00:00 where the last two zeros represent frames, the next two zeros represent seconds, the next two zeros represent minutes, and the first two zeros represent hours.

TIMELINE
The Final Cut Pro window where you view and make edits to a *sequence* of *clips* represented graphically, their length corresponding to the duration of the clip (see Chapter 2).

TITLE SAFE AREA
The area of the video *frame* that will be visible on any TV monitor; titles placed within this area will not be cut off. Final Cut Pro provides a Title Safe guide that you can bring up in the *Viewer* of the *Canvas* window (see Chapter 17).

TRANSITION
Any type of change between two *clips* that incorporates both images during the transition rather than being a straight *cut* in which one clip abruptly ends and the next begins. The most common transition is the cross-dissolve, in which the two clips seamlessly blend over the whole screen until the new clip replaces the old (see Chapter 8).

TRIM
The process of adding or subtracting *frames* from a *clip's* edge (see Chapter 8).

VIEWER
The Final Cut Pro window used to work with an individual *clip*— viewing the clip, inserting *In* and *Out points*, adding filters or other *effects*, adjusting the audio, or changing its motion (see Chapter 2).

WHITE BALANCE
The balance of colors in an image relating to what is perceived as true white. Improper white balance is a common problem with DV footage and the Color Corrector filter can fix this problem (see Chapter 11).

Index

Note to the reader: Throughout this index **boldfaced** page numbers indicate primary discussions of a topic. *Italicized* page numbers indicate illustrations.

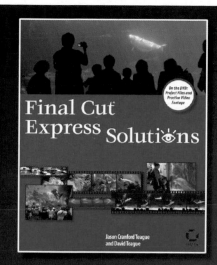
 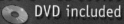

About the Authors

Jason Cranford Teague has been working in digital media design since 1994. Over the years, his clients have included Bank of America, Coca-Cola, Virgin, CNN, Kodak, Siemens, The European Space Agency, and WebMD. A graduate of Rensselaer Polytechnic Institute where he spent a very cold year getting his M.S. in Technical Communication, Jason is regularly asked to speak at conferences about design for Web, print, and video. An internationally recognized writer and columnist, Jason is the author of numerous books and articles including the best selling *DHTML and CSS for the World Wide Web*, *Final Cut Express Solutions*, *SVG for Web Designers, and Photoshop CS at Your Fingertips.* In addition, he has written for the Apple Developers Connection, Adobe, *Macworld* Magazine, and ClNet as well as appearing on TechTV's "The Screen Savers." Jason runs Bright Eye Media (www.brighteyemedia.com), which specializes in web sites for education and entertainment.

David Teague works as a writer, filmmaker, film curator, and teacher. His film work includes numerous award-winning documentaries, independent features, and short films. He has shot and edited music films for artists such as David Bowie, Laurie Anderson, and the Kronos Quartet. In addition to this book, he co-authored *Final Cut Express Solutions* with his brother Jason. David teaches film editing at DCTV in New York City and also runs Flicker, a bimonthly film festival of new short Super-8 and 16mm films. (www.flickernyc.com). He lives in Brooklyn, New York.

Web Sites for This Book

In addition to the DVD, we have set up a web site to provide additional materials for the book, including a streaming version of the film on the DVD, alternate edits of the movie, updates for the book, and answers to frequently asked questions that we receive. You can find the site at www.webbedenvironments.com/fcp.

If you want to reach us with questions about the book, Final Cut Pro, digital video editing, or if you want to share projects you created using what you learned in this book, feel free to write us at fcp@webbedenvironments.com.

You can also find information about the book and provide us with feedback about it at www.sybex.com.